Lecture Notes in Computer Science   5894

Commenced Publication in 1973
Founding and Former Series Editors:
Gerhard Goos, Juris Hartmanis, and Jan van Leeuwen

T0223376

Rudesindo Núñez-Queija
Jacques Resing (Eds.)

Network Control and Optimization

Third Euro-NF Conference, NET-COOP 2009
Eindhoven, The Netherlands, November 23-25, 2009
Proceedings

 Springer

Volume Editors

Rudesindo Núñez-Queija
Centrum Wiskunde & Informatica (CWI)
P.O. Box 94079, 1090 GB Amsterdam, The Netherlands
E-mail: sindo@cwi.nl
and
University of Amsterdam
Department of Quantitative Economics
Operations Research
Roetersstraat 11, 1018 WB Amsterdam, The Netherlands

Jacques Resing
Eindhoven University of Technology
Department of Mathematics and Computer Science
P.O. Box 513, 5600 MB Eindhoven, The Netherlands
E-mail: j.a.c.resing@tue.nl

Library of Congress Control Number: 2009938723

CR Subject Classification (1998): C.2, C.4, D.2.8, H.3.4, K.6.2

LNCS Sublibrary: SL 5 – Computer Communication Networks
and Telecommunications

ISSN 0302-9743

ISBN 978-3-642-10405-3 Springer Berlin Heidelberg New York

springer.com

© Springer-Verlag Berlin Heidelberg 2009

Typesetting: Camera-ready by author, data conversion by Scientific Publishing Services, Chennai, India
Printed on acid-free paper   SPIN: 12796199   06/3180   5 4 3 2 1 0

Preface

We are proud to present the proceedings of NET-COOP 2009, the international conference on network control and optimization, co-organized by EURANDOM/Eindhoven University of Technology and CWI. This year's conference at EURANDOM, held November 23–25, was the third in line after previous editions in Avignon (2007) and Paris (2008). NET-COOP 2009 was organized in conjunction with the Euro-NF workshop on "New Trends in Modeling, Quantitative Methods, and Measurements." While organized within the framework of Euro-NF, NET-COOP enjoys great interest beyond Euro-NF, as is attested by the geographic origins of the papers in these proceedings.

The NET-COOP conference focuses on performance analysis, control and optimization of communication networks, including wired networks, wireless networks, peer to peer networks and delay tolerant networks. In each of these domains network operators and service providers face the challenging task to efficiently provide service at their customer's standards in a highly dynamic environment. Internet traffic continues to grow tremendously in terms of volume as well as diversity. This development is fueled by the increasing availability of high-bandwidth access (both wired and wireless) to end users, opening new ground for evolving and newly emerging wide-band applications. The increase in network complexity, as well as the plurality of parties involved in network operation, calls for efficient distributed control. New models and techniques for the control and optimization of networks are needed to address the challenge of allocating communication resources efficiently and fairly, while accounting for non-cooperative behavior. The papers presented at NET-COOP 2009 addressed these issues, covering a wide range of methodologies, including queueing and congestion theory, control theory, game theory, scheduling theory and simulation.

The 25 presented papers were grouped into 8 sessions on the subjects "battery control," "cooperation and competition," "distributed control," "performance analysis methods," "queueing analysis" (two sessions) and "wireless communications" (two sessions). A subset of 18 papers is included here. The remaining presentations (all upon invitation) concerned papers either in preparation or published elsewhere.

We gladly take the opportunity to thank all those who contributed to the strong collection of papers included. Of course, we are thankful to all authors who submitted their papers for presentation at the conference and publication in these proceedings. All papers were reviewed by three or four members of the Technical Program Committee. A special word of appreciation goes to all TPC members – listed below – for their hard work, as well as to their co-workers who helped them in this task. Their reviews were of enormous help in the paper selection, and of great use to the authors in preparing the camera-ready versions of their papers.

The smooth organization of the conference was due to Sem Borst, Onno Boxma (General Chairs) and Lucienne Coolen (Local Arrangements). Ivo Adan, Rob van der Mei and Bert Zwart put together a top-notch invited-speaker's program. We further wish to thank the conference's invited speakers: Eitan Altman, Rami Atar, Hans van den Berg, Costas Courcoubetis, Mor Harchol-Balter, Philippe Robert, Devavrat Shah and Damon Wischik. We also gratefully acknowledge the financial support of Euro-NF, the Prof. J.W. Cohen foundation and EURANDOM.

We hope that you, like us, find these proceedings a valuable contribution to research in the scope of NET-COOP.

November 2009   Sindo Núñez Queija
                                                        Jacques Resing

Organization

General Chairs

Sem Borst   Eindhoven University of Technology and Alcatel-Lucent
                            Bell Labs
Onno Boxma   EURANDOM and Eindhoven University of Technology

Local Arrangements

Lucienne Coolen   EURANDOM and Eindhoven University of Technology

Steering Committee

Eitan Altman   INRIA and University of Avignon
Tijani Chahed   GET
Sergey Foss   Heriot Watt University
Peter Glynn   Stanford University
Mikael Johansson   KTH
Daniel Kofman   GET
Laurent Massoulié   Thomson
Alexandre Proutière   Microsoft Research
Jorma Virtamo   Helsinki University of Technology

Invited Speakers Committee

Ivo Adan   Eindhoven University of Technology and University of
                            Amsterdam
Rob van der Mei   CWI and VU University Amsterdam
Bert Zwart   CWI and VU University Amsterdam

Technical Program Chairs

Rudesindo Núñez-Queija   CWI and University of Amsterdam
Jacques Resing   Eindhoven University of Technology

Technical Program Committee

P. Antoniadis	Université de Paris 6, France
K. Avrachenkov	INRIA Sophia Antipolis, France
U. Ayesta	CNRS-LAAS, France and BCAM, Spain
T. Basar	University of Illinois, USA
M. Baykal-Gursoy	Rutgers University, USA
N. Bean	University of Adelaide, Australia
R. Bekker	VU Amsterdam, The Netherlands
T. Bonald	Orange-FT, France
V. Borkar	TIFR, India
R. Boucherie	University of Twente, The Netherlands
C. Courcoubetis	AUEB, Greece
G. De Veciana	University of Texas, USA
A. Ephremides	University of Maryland, USA
B. Gaujal	INRIA Grenoble, France
M. Haviv	Hebrew University Jerusalem, Israel
N. Hegde	Orange-FT, France
M. Johansson	KTH, Sweden
M. Jonckheere	Eindhoven University of Technology, The Netherlands
H. Kameda	University of Tsukuba, Japan
P. Key	Microsoft Research, UK
J. van Leeuwaarden	Eindhoven University of Technology, The Netherlands
M. Lelarge	INRIA-ENS, France
L. Leskela	Helsinki University of Technology, Finland
S. Low	Caltech, USA
M. Mandjes	University of Amsterdam, The Netherlands
R. Mazumdar	University of Waterloo, Canada
J. Niño-Mora	University Carlos III Madrid, Spain
I. Norros	VTT, Finland
A. Pacheco	IST Lisbon, Portugal
B. Prabhu	CNRS-LAAS, France
A. Proutière	Microsoft Research, UK
U. Rieder	University of Ulm, Germany
N. Shimkin	Technion, Israel
N. Stier	Columbia University, USA
D. Towsley	University of Massachusetts, USA
B. Van Houdt	University of Antwerp, Belgium
M. Vojnovic	Microsoft Research, UK
A. Wierman	Caltech, USA
S. Wittevrongel	Ghent University, Belgium

Table of Contents

Wireless II

Distributed Control

Cooperation and Competition

Stability Properties of Networks with Interacting TCP Flows

Carl Graham[1], Philippe Robert[2], and Maaike Verloop[3],[*]

[1] UMR 7641 CNRS — École Polytechnique, Route de Saclay, 91128 Palaiseau, France
`carl@cmapx.polytechnique.fr`
[2] INRIA Paris — Rocquencourt, Domaine de Voluceau, 78153 Le Chesnay, France
`Philippe.Robert@inria.fr`
`http://www-rocq.inria.fr/~robert`
[3] CWI, P.O. Box 94079, 1090 GB Amsterdam, The Netherlands
`I.M.Verloop@cwi.nl`
`http://www.cwi.nl/~maaike`

Abstract. The asymptotic behavior of a Markovian model describing the interaction of several classes of permanent connections in a network is analyzed. For this model, each of the connections has a self-adaptive behavior in that its transmission rate along its route depends on the level of congestion of the nodes on its route. In this situation Graham and Robert [6] has shown that the invariant distributions are in a one-to-one correspondence with the solutions of a fixed point equation in a finite dimensional space. The purpose of this paper is to investigate the problem of uniqueness of the equilibrium of these networks, i.e., the uniqueness of the solutions of the associated fixed point equation. Uniqueness results of such solutions are proved for different topologies: rings, trees and a linear network and with various configurations for routes through nodes.

1 Introduction

Data transmission in the Internet network can be described as a self-adaptive system to the different congestion events that regularly occur at its numerous nodes. A connection, a TCP flow, in this network adapts its throughput according to the congestion it encounters on its path: Packets are sent as long as no loss is detected and throughput grows linearly during that time. On the contrary when a loss occurs, the throughput is sharply reduced by a multiplicative factor. This scheme is known as an Additive Increase and Multiplicative Decrease algorithm (AIMD).

Globally, the TCP protocol can be seen as a bandwidth allocation algorithm on the Internet. From a mathematical modelling perspective, the description is somewhat more difficult. While the representation of the evolution of the throughput of a single TCP flow has been the object of various rigorous works,

---

[*] Part of this work was done during a 3-month visit of Maaike Verloop at INRIA Paris — Rocquencourt with financial support of the European Network of Excellence EURO-NF.

R. Núñez-Queija and J. Resing (Eds.): NET-COOP 2009, LNCS 5894, pp. 1–15, 2009.

there are few rigorous studies for modelling the evolution of a large set of TCP connections in a quite large network.

A possible mathematical formulation which has been used is via an optimization problem: given K classes of connections, when there are x_k connections of class $k \in \{1, \ldots, K\}$, their total throughput achieved is given by λ_k so that the vector (λ_k) is a solution of the following optimization problem

$$\max_{\lambda \in \Lambda} \sum_{k=1}^{K} x_k U_k(\lambda_k / x_k),$$

where Λ is the set of admissible throughputs which takes into account the capacity constraints of the network. The functions (U_k) are defined as *utility* functions, and various expressions have been proposed for them. See Kelly *et al.* [8], Massoulié [10] and Massoulié and Roberts [11]. With this representation, the TCP protocol is seen as an adaptive algorithm maximizing some criterion at the level of the network.

A different point of view has been proposed in Graham and Robert [6]. It starts on the local dynamics of the AIMD algorithm used by TCP and, through a scaling procedure, the global behavior of the network can then be described rigorously. It is assumed that there are K classes of *permanent* connections going through different nodes and with different characteristics. The loss rate of a connection using a given route is described as a function of the congestions at the nodes along its path. The congestion at node j, u_j, is defined as the (possibly weighted) sum of the throughputs of *all* the connections that use node j. The interaction of the connections in the network is therefore expressed via the loss rates.

It has been shown in Graham and Robert [6] that under a mean-field scaling, the evolution of a class k connection, $1 \leq k \leq K$, can be asymptotically described as the unique solution of an unusual stochastic differential equation. Furthermore, it has also been proved that the equilibrium distribution of the throughputs of the different classes of connections is in a one to one correspondence with the solution of a fixed point equation $(\mathcal{E})$ of dimension J (the number of nodes).

Under "reasonable" conditions, there should be only one solution of $(\mathcal{E})$ and consequently a unique stable equilibrium of the network. Otherwise this would imply that the state of the network could oscillate between several stable states. Although this is mentioned here and there in the literature, this has not been firmly established in the context of an IP network. It has been shown that multistability may occur in loss networks, see Gibbens *et al.* [5] and Marbukh [9] or in the context of a wireless network with admission control, see Antunes *et al.* [1]. Raghunathan and Kumar [13] presents experiments that suggest that a phenomenon of bi-stability may occur in a context similar to the one considered in this paper but for wireless networks.

It turns out that it is not easy to check in practice whether the fixed point equation $(\mathcal{E})$ has a unique solution or not. The purpose of this paper is to investigate in detail this question for several topologies. The paper is organized as follows. Section 2 reviews the main definitions and results used in the paper. In addition, a simple criterion for the existence of a fixed-point solution is given. Section 3 presents a uniqueness result for a tree topology under the assumptions that all connections use the root. Section 4 considers a linear network. Section 5 studies several scenarios for ring topologies and a uniqueness result is proved for connections going through one, two, or all the nodes. Two main approaches are used to prove uniqueness: monotonicity properties of the network and contraction arguments.

A general conjecture that we make is that when the loss rates are increasing with respect to the level of congestion, this implies the uniqueness of the equilibrium in a general network.

2   A Stochastic Fluid Picture

In this section, a somewhat simplified version of the stochastic model of interacting TCP flows of Graham and Robert [6] is presented.

The Case of a Single Connection

Ott *et al.* [12] presents a fluid model of a single connection. Via scalings with respect to the loss rate, Dumas *et al.* [3] proves various limit theorems for the resulting processes. The limiting picture of Dumas *et al.* [3] for the evolution of the throughput of a single long connection is as follows.

If the instantaneous throughput at time t of the connection is $W(t)$, this process has the Markov property and its infinitesimal generator is given by

$$\Omega(f)(x) = af'(x) + \beta x(f(rx) - f(x)) \tag{1}$$

for f a C^1-function from $\mathbb{R}_+$ to $\mathbb{R}$.

The Markov process $(W(t))$ increases linearly at rate a. The constant a is related to the distance between the source and the destination. It increases inversely proportional to the round trip time RTT: typically $a = C_0/(C_1 + RTT)$, for some constants C_0 and C_1.

Given $W(t) = x$, the process $(W(t))$ jumps from x to rx (r is usually $1/2$) at rate βx. The expression βx represents the loss rate of the connection. Of course, the quantities a, β and r depend on the parameters of the connection.

The density of the invariant distribution of this Markov process is given in the following proposition. It has been analyzed in Ott *et al.* [12] at the fluid level and by Dumas *et al.* [3], see also Guillemin *et al.* [7]. The transient behavior has been investigated in Chafai *et al.* [2].

Proposition 1. *The function*

$$H_{r,\rho}(w) = \frac{\sqrt{2\rho/\pi}}{\prod_{n=0}^{+\infty}(1 - r^{2n+1})} \sum_{n=0}^{+\infty} \frac{r^{-2n}}{\prod_{k=1}^{n}(1 - r^{-2k})} e^{-\rho r^{-2n} w^2/2}, \quad w \geq 0, \tag{2}$$

with $\rho = a/\beta$, is the density of the invariant distribution of the Markov process $(W(t))$ whose infinitesimal generator is given by Equation (1). Furthermore, its expected value is given by

$$\int_0^{+\infty} w H_{r,\rho}(w)\, dw = \sqrt{\frac{2\rho}{\pi}} \prod_{n=1}^{+\infty} \frac{1 - r^{2n}}{1 - r^{2n-1}}. \tag{3}$$

A Representation of Interacting Connections in a Network

The network has $J \geq 1$ nodes and accommodates $K \geq 1$ classes of permanent connections. For $1 \leq k \leq K$, the number of class k connections is $N_k \geq 1$, and one sets

$$N = (N_1, \ldots, N_K) \quad \text{and} \quad |N| = N_1 + \cdots + N_K.$$

An *allocation matrix* $A = (A_{jk}, 1 \leq j \leq J, 1 \leq k \leq K)$ with positive coefficients describes the use of nodes by the connections. In particular the route of a class k connection goes through node j only if $A_{jk} > 0$. In practice, the class of a connection is determined by the sequence set of nodes it is using.

If $w_{n,k} \geq 0$ is the throughput of the nth class k connection, $1 \leq n \leq N_k$, the quantity $A_{jk} w_{n,k}$ is the weighted throughput at node j of this connection. A simple example would be to take $A_{jk} = 1$ or 0 depending on whether a class k connection uses node j or not. The total weighted throughput u_j of node j by the various connections is given by

$$u_j = \sum_{k=1}^{K} \sum_{n=1}^{N_k} A_{jk} w_{n,k}.$$

The quantity u_j represents the level of utilization/congestion of node j. In particular, the loss rate of a connection going through node j will depend on this variable.

For $1 \leq k \leq K$, the corresponding parameters a, r, and β of Equation (1) for a class k connection are given by non-negative numbers a_k and r_k, and a function $\beta_k : \mathbb{R}_+^J \to \mathbb{R}_+$, so that when the resource vector of the network is $u = (u_j, 1 \leq j \leq J)$ and if the state of a class k connection is w_k:

- Its state increases linearly at rate a_k. For example $a_k = C_{0,k}/(C_{1,k} + R_k)$ where R_k is the round trip time between the source and the destination of a class k connection.
- A loss for this connection occurs at rate $w_k \beta_k(u)$ and in this case its state jumps from w_k to $r_k w_k$. The function β_k depends only on the utilization of all nodes used by class k connections. In particular, if a class k connection goes through the nodes $j_1, j_2, \ldots, j_{l_k}$, one has

$$\beta_k(u) = \beta_k(u_{j_1}, u_{j_2}, \ldots, u_{j_{l_k}}).$$

A more specific (and natural) choice for β_k would be

$$\beta_k(u) = \delta_k + \varphi_{j_1}(u_{j_1}) + \varphi_{j_2}(u_{j_2}) + \cdots + \varphi_{j_{l_k}}(u_{j_{l_k}}), \tag{4}$$

where $\varphi_{j_\ell}(x)$ is the loss rate at node j_ℓ when its congestion level is $x \geq 0$, and δ_k is the loss rate in a non-congested network. Another example is when the loss rate β_k depends only on the sum of the utilizations of the nodes used by class k, i.e.,

$$\beta_k(u) = \beta_k \left(\sum_{l=1}^{l_k} u_{j_l} \right). \tag{5}$$

Asymptotic Behavior of Typical Connections

If $(W_{n,k}(t))$ denotes the throughput of the nth class k connection, $1 \leq n \leq N_k$, then the vector

$$(W(t)) = ([(W_{n,k}(t)), 1 \leq k \leq K, 1 \leq n \leq N_k], t \geq 0)$$

has the Markov property. As it stands, this Markov process is quite difficult to analyze. For this reason, a mean field scaling is used to get a more quantitative representation of the interaction of the flows. More specifically, it is assumed that the total number of connections $|N|$ goes to infinity and that the total number of class k connections is of the order $p_k|N|$, where $p_1 + \cdots + p_K = 1$.

For each $1 \leq k \leq K$, one takes a class k connection at random, let n_k be its index, $1 \leq n_k \leq N_k$. The process $(W_{n_k,k}(t))$ represents the throughput of a "typical" class k connection. It is shown in Graham and Robert [6] that, as $|N|$ goes to infinity and under mild assumptions, the process $[(W_{n_k,k}(t)), 1 \leq k \leq K]$ converges in distribution to $(\overline{W}(t)) = [(\overline{W}_k(t)), 1 \leq k \leq K]$, where the processes $(\overline{W}_k(t))$, for $1 \leq k \leq K$, are independent and, for $1 \leq k \leq K$, the process $(\overline{W}_k(t))$ is the solution of the following stochastic differential equation,

$$d\overline{W}_k(t) = a_k\,dt - (1-r_k)\overline{W}_k(t-) \int \mathbb{1}_{\{0 \leq z \leq \overline{W}_k(t-)\beta_k(u_{\overline{W}}(t))\}} \mathcal{N}_k(dz,dt), \tag{6}$$

with $u_{\overline{W}}(t) = (u_{\overline{W},j}(t), 1 \leq j \leq J)$ and, for $1 \leq j \leq J$,

$$u_{\overline{W},j}(t) = \sum_{k=1}^{K} A_{jk}p_k\mathbb{E}(\overline{W}_k(t)),$$

where $(\mathcal{N}_k, 1 \leq k \leq K)$ are i.i.d. Poisson point processes on $\mathbb{R}_+^2$ with Lebesgue characteristic measure.

Because of the role of the deterministic function $(u_{\overline{W}(t)})$ in these equations, the Markov property holds for this process but it is not *time-homogeneous*. The analogue of the infinitesimal generator $\overline{\Omega}_{k,t}$ is given by

$$\overline{\Omega}_{k,t}(f)(x) = a_k f'(x) + x\beta_k(u_{\overline{W}}(t))(f(r_k x) - f(r_k)).$$

The homogeneity holds when the function $(u_{\overline{W}}(t))$ is equal to a constant u^*, which will be the case at equilibrium. In this case a class k connection behaves like a single isolated connection with parameters $a = a_k$ and $\beta = \beta_k(u^*)$.

The Fixed Point Equations

The following theorem, Theorem 6.1 of Graham and Robert [6], gives a characterization of the invariant distributions for the process $(\overline{W}(t))$.

Theorem 1. *The invariant distributions for solutions $(\overline{W}(t))$ of Equation (6) are in one-to-one correspondence with the solutions $u \in \mathbb{R}_+^J$ of the fixed point equation*

$$u_j = \sum_{k=1}^{K} A_{jk}\phi_k(u), \quad 1 \leq j \leq J, \tag{7}$$

where

$$\phi_k(u) = p_k\sqrt{\frac{2}{\pi}}\left(\prod_{n=1}^{+\infty} \frac{1 - r_k^{2n}}{1 - r_k^{2n-1}}\right)\sqrt{\frac{a_k}{\beta_k(u)}}. \tag{8}$$

If u^* is such a solution, the corresponding invariant distribution has the density $w \to \prod_{k=1}^{K} H_{r_k, \rho_k}(w_k)$ on $\mathbb{R}_+^K$, where $\rho_k = a_k/\beta_k(u^*)$ and $H_{r,\rho}$ is defined in Proposition 1.

The above theorem shows that if the fixed point equation (7) has several solutions, then the limiting process $(\overline{W}(t))$ has several invariant distributions. Similarly, if equation (7) has no solution then, in particular, $(\overline{W}(t))$ cannot converge to an equilibrium. These possibilities have been suggested in the Internet literature through simulations, like the cyclic behavior of some nodes in the case of congestion. See Floyd and Kohler [4] for example.

Under mild and natural assumptions, such as the loss rate being non-decreasing with respect to the utilization in the nodes, we show that for some specific topologies there exists a unique fixed point. We believe that such a uniqueness result will hold, in fact, for any network in general (under suitable regularity properties on the functions β_k, $k = 1, \ldots, K$). Before proceeding to the examples, we first present an existence result that holds for a general network.

2.1   An Existence Result

In this section the existence of a solution to the fixed-point equation (7) is proved for a quite general framework.

If u is a solution of Equation (7) and $z_k = \phi_k(u)$, $1 \leq k \leq K$, then the vector $z = (z_k)$ satisfies the relation $u = Az$, i.e., $u_j = A_{j1}z_1 + A_{j2}z_2 + \cdots + A_{jK}z_K$, $1 \leq j \leq J$, and as well

$$z = \Phi(z) \stackrel{\text{def.}}{=} (\phi_k(Az), 1 \leq k \leq K). \tag{9}$$

The proposition below gives a simple criterion for the existence of a fixed point.

Proposition 2. *If the functions $u \to \beta_k(u)$, $1 \leq k \leq K$, are continuous and non-decreasing, and if there exists a vector $z^{(0)} \in \mathbb{R}_+^K$ such that the relations*

$$z^{(0)} \leq \Phi(z^{(0)}), z^{(0)} \leq \Phi(\Phi(z^{(0)})), \text{ and } \Phi(z^{(0)}) < \infty,$$

hold coordinate by coordinate, then there exists at least one solution for the fixed point Equation (9) *and therefore also for Equation* (7).

Proof. Define the sequence $z^{(n)} = \Phi(z^{(n-1)})$, $n = 1, 2, \ldots$. From $z^{(0)} \leq \Phi(z^{(0)})$ and $z^{(0)} \leq \Phi(\Phi(z^{(0)}))$, it follows that $z^{(0)} \leq z^{(1)}$ and $z^{(0)} \leq z^{(2)}$. Since the function Φ is non-increasing, one gets that the relation

$$z^{(0)} \leq z^{(2)} \leq \ldots \leq z^{(2n)} \leq \ldots \leq z^{(2n+1)} \leq \ldots \leq z^{(3)} \leq z^{(1)}$$

holds. Hence, there are $z_*, z^* \in \mathbb{R}_+^K$ such that

$$\lim_{n \to \infty} z^{(2n)} = z_* \text{ and } \lim_{n \to \infty} z^{(2n-1)} = z^*,$$

with $z_* \leq z^*$. Since $z^{(2n)} = \Phi(z^{(2n-1)})$ and $z^{(2n+1)} = \Phi(z^{(2n)})$, by continuity we also have that $z^* = \Phi(z_*)$ and $z_* = \Phi(z^*)$.

Define the set $D = \{z : z_* \leq z \leq z^*\}$. Note that $z^* \leq z^{(1)} = \Phi(z^{(0)}) < \infty$, hence D is bounded. In addition, for $z \in D$,

$$z_* = \Phi(z^*) \leq \Phi(z) \leq \Phi(z_*) = z^*,$$

since the function Φ is non-increasing. One can therefore apply the Brouwer fixed point theorem to Φ restricted to the compact convex set D, and conclude that D contains at least one fixed point of the function Φ. The proposition is proved.

The conditions of Proposition 2 trivially hold when β_k is continuous and non-decreasing, and $\beta_k(0) > 0$ for all $k = 1, \ldots, K$, since then $0 \leq \Phi(0)$, $0 \leq \Phi(\Phi(0))$ and $\Phi(0) < \infty$. In particular, when the function β_k is given by (4), $\delta_k > 0$ is a sufficient condition for the existence of a fixed point.

3 Tree Topologies

We consider a finite tree network. A connection starts in the root and then follows the tree structure until it leaves the network at some node. The set of routes is therefore indexed by the set of nodes, i.e., a connection following route $G \in \mathcal{T}$ starts in the root and leaves the tree in node G.

The tree can be classically represented as a subset $\mathcal{T}$ of $\cup_{n \geq 0} \mathbb{N}^n$ with the constraint that if $G = (g_1, \ldots, g_p) \in \mathcal{T}$, then, for $1 \leq \ell \leq p$, the element $H = (g_1, \ldots, g_\ell)$ is a node of the tree as well. In addition, node H is the g_ℓth child of generation (level) ℓ and the ancestor of G for this generation. One writes $H \subseteq G$ in this situation and $H \vdash G$ when $\ell = p - 1$, i.e., when G is a daughter of H. The quantity $u_{[H,G]}$ denotes the vector $(u_P, P : H \subseteq P \subseteq G)$. The root of the tree is denoted by $\emptyset$. Assume that $A_{HG} = 1$ if route G is such that $H \subseteq G$, and 0 otherwise. Equation (7) writes in this case,

$$u_H = \sum_{G \in \mathcal{T}, H \subseteq G} \phi_G(u_{[\emptyset,G]}), \quad H \in \mathcal{T},$$

8   C. Graham, P. Robert, and M. Verloop

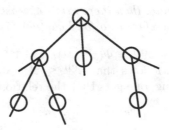

Fig. 1. Tree with connections starting at root node

which is equivalent to the recursive equations

$$u_H = \phi_H(u_{[\emptyset,H]}) + \sum_{G \in \mathcal{T}, H \vdash G} u_G, \quad H \in \mathcal{T}. \tag{10}$$

Proposition 3. *If the functions $\beta_H, H \in \mathcal{T}$, are continuous and non-decreasing, then there exists a unique solution for the fixed point equation (7).*

Proof. Let H be a maximal element on $\mathcal{T}$ for the relation $\subseteq$, i.e., H is a leaf, and denote by $P(H)$ the parent of node H. Equation (10) then writes

$$u_H = \phi_H(u_{[\emptyset,P(H)]}, u_H). \tag{11}$$

The function ϕ_H being non-increasing and continuous, for a fixed vector $u_{[\emptyset,P(H)]}$, there exists a unique solution $u_H = F_H(u_{[\emptyset,P(H)]}) \geq 0$ to the above equation. Furthermore, the function $u_{[\emptyset,P(H)]} \to F_H(u_{[\emptyset,P(H)]})$ is continuous and non-increasing. For such an H, for $H' = P(H)$, Relation (10) can then be written as

$$u_{H'} = \phi_{H'}(u_{[\emptyset,P(H')]}, u_{H'}) + \sum_{G \in \mathcal{T}, H' \vdash G} F_G(u_{[\emptyset,P(H')]}, u_{H'}).$$

Since $\phi_{H'}$ and F_G, with G a leaf, are non-increasing and continuous, there exists a unique solution $u_{H'} = F_{H'}(u_{[\emptyset,P(H')]}) \geq 0$ and the function

$$u_{[\emptyset,P(H')]} \to F_{H'}(u_{[\emptyset,P(H')]}),$$

is continuous and non-increasing. By induction (by decreasing level of nodes), one obtains that a family of continuous, non-increasing functions $F_G, G \in \mathcal{T}$, $G \neq \emptyset$, exists, such that, for a fixed vector $u_{[\emptyset,P(G)]}$, $u_G = F_G(u_{[\emptyset,P(G)]})$ is the unique solution of

$$u_G = \phi_G(u_{[\emptyset,P(G)]}, u_G) + \sum_{G' \in \mathcal{T}, G \vdash G'} F_{G'}(u_{[\emptyset,P(G)]}, u_G).$$

Equation (10) at the root then writes

$$u_\emptyset = \phi_\emptyset(u_\emptyset) + \sum_{G \in \mathcal{T}, \emptyset \vdash G} F_G(u_\emptyset),$$

and this equation has a unique solution $\bar{u}_\emptyset$. Now, one defines recursively (by increasing level of nodes)

$$\bar{u}_G = F_G(\bar{u}_{[\emptyset, P(G)]}), \quad G \in \mathcal{T}.$$

Then clearly $(\bar{u}_G, G \in \mathcal{T})$ satisfies Relation (10) and is the unique solution.

4 Linear Topologies

In this section we consider a linear network with J nodes and $K = J + 1$ classes of connections. Class j connections, $1 \le j \le J$, use node j only, while class 0 connections use all J nodes. Assume $A_{jk} = 1$ if class k uses node j, and 0 otherwise. Equation (7) is in this case

$$u_j = \phi_0(u) + \phi_j(u_j), \ 1 \le j \le J, \tag{12}$$

with $u = (u_1, \ldots, u_J)$.

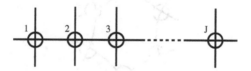

Fig. 2. A linear network with J nodes and $K = J + 1$ classes of connections

Proposition 4. *If the functions, $\beta_k, 0 \le k \le J$, are continuous and non-decreasing, then there exists a unique solution for the fixed point equation (7).*

Proof. Let $\bar{\phi}_j(x) = x - \phi_j(x)$, $x \in \mathbb{R}$, which is continuous and non-decreasing. Hence, (12) can be rewritten as

$$u_j = \bar{\phi}_j^{-1}(\phi_0(u)) = \bar{\phi}_j^{-1}\left(\frac{\alpha_0}{\sqrt{\beta_0(u)}}\right), \ 1 \le j \le J, \tag{13}$$

for some constant α_0, see Equation (8). In addition, define the function $\psi_j(x) = \bar{\phi}_j^{-1}(\alpha_0/\sqrt{x})$, $x \in \mathbb{R}$, which is continuous and non-increasing. From (13) we obtain the relation

$$\beta_0(u) = \beta_0\left(\psi_1(\beta_0(u)), \ldots, \psi_J(\beta_0(u))\right).$$

Since β_0 is non-decreasing and ψ_j is non-increasing, the fixed point equation $\beta = \beta_0(\psi_1(\beta), \ldots, \psi_J(\beta))$ has a unique solution $\beta^* \ge 0$. Hence, the Relation (13) has a unique fixed point, which is given by $u_j^* = \bar{\phi}_j^{-1}(\alpha_0/\sqrt{\beta^*})$.

5   Ring Topologies

In this section, the topology of the network is based on a ring. Several situations are considered for the paths of the connections.

Routes with Two Consecutive Nodes

It is assumed that there are J nodes and $K = J$ classes of connections and class $j \in \{1, \ldots, J\}$ uses two nodes: node j and $j+1$. Assume $A_{jk} = 1$ if class k uses node j, and 0 otherwise. Equation (7) is in this case

$$u_j = \phi_{j-1}(u_{j-1}, u_j) + \phi_j(u_j, u_{j+1}), \ j = 1, \ldots, J. \tag{14}$$

For $y_j = \phi_j(u_j, u_{j+1})$, the above equation can be rewritten as follows

$$y_j = \phi_j(y_{j-1} + y_j, y_j + y_{j+1}), \ j = 1, \ldots, J. \tag{15}$$

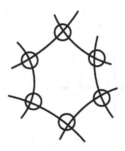

Fig. 3. Routes with two consecutive nodes

Proposition 5. *If the functions β_k, $1 \leq k \leq K$, satisfy the assumptions of Proposition 2, then there exists a unique solution for the fixed point equation (7).*

Proof. From Proposition 2 we have that Equation (15) has at least one fixed point solution. Let $x = (x_j : j = 1, 2, \ldots, J)$ and $y = (y_j : j = 1, 2, \ldots, J)$ both be fixed points.

If the relation $y_j < x_j$ holds for all $j = 1, \ldots, J$, then the inequality

$$\phi_j(y_j + y_{j-1}, y_{j+1} + y_j) = y_j < x_j = \phi_j(x_j + x_{j-1}, x_{j+1} + x_j),$$

and the fact that the function ϕ_j is non-increasing, give directly a contradiction.

Consequently, possibly up to an exchange of x and y, one can assume that there exists $m \in \{1, \ldots, J\}$ such that $y_m \leq x_m$ and $y_{m+1} \geq x_{m+1}$. Define $c_j = x_j - y_j$ and $d_j = y_j - x_j$. Hence, $c_m \geq 0$ and $d_{m+1} \geq 0$. Without loss of generality, it can be assumed that the classes are ordered such that $d_{m-1} \leq d_{m+1}$. Since the function ϕ_m is non-increasing, and

$$\phi_m(y_m + y_{m-1}, y_m + y_{m+1}) = y_m \leq x_m = \phi_m(x_m + x_{m-1}, x_m + x_{m+1}),$$

we have that either

$$y_m + y_{m-1} \geq x_m + x_{m-1} \text{ and/or } y_m + y_{m+1} \geq x_m + x_{m+1},$$

i.e., $d_{m-1} \geq c_m$ and/or $d_{m+1} \geq c_m$. Because $d_{m-1} \leq d_{m+1}$, then, necessarily, $d_{m+1} \geq c_m \geq 0$. Hence

$$\phi_{m+1}(y_{m+1} + y_m, y_{m+1} + y_{m+2}) = y_{m+1}$$
$$\geq x_{m+1} = \phi_{m+1}(x_{m+1} + x_m, x_{m+1} + x_{m+2}).$$

Since ϕ_{m+1} is non-increasing, one has $y_{m+1} + y_{m+2} \leq x_{m+1} + x_{m+2}$ and consequently $d_{m+1} \leq c_{m+2}$.

From $0 \leq c_m \leq d_{m+1} \leq c_{m+2}$, we obtain $x_{m+2} \geq y_{m+2}$, which, using the same steps as before, implies $c_{m+2} \leq d_{m+3}$. In particular, by induction it can be concluded that

$$c_j \leq d_{j+1} \leq c_{j+2} \leq d_{j+3}, \text{ for all } j = 1, \ldots, J,$$

where the indices $j+1, j+2$, and $j+3$ are considered as modulo J. This implies that $c_j = d_j = c$, for all $j = 1, \ldots, L$, and hence $x_j = y_j$ for $j = 1, \ldots, J$. We can conclude that the fixed point is unique.

The rest of this part will be devoted to a contraction argument that can be used to get a unique solution to the fixed point equation.

Proposition 6. *If the functions* β_k, $1 \leq k \leq K$, *are Lipschitz, continuous differentiable, and non-decreasing, then there exists a unique solution for the fixed point equation* (7).

Proof. The proof consists in showing that (15) has a unique solution. By the Implicit function theorem, there exists a unique $x_j(y_{j-1}, y_{j+1})$ such that,

$$x_j(y_{j-1}, y_{j+1}) = \phi_j(y_{j-1} + x_j(y_{j-1}, y_{j+1}), x_j(y_{j-1}, y_{j+1}) + y_{j+1}), \qquad (16)$$

and this function $(y_{j-1}, y_{j+1}) \rightarrow x_j(y_{j-1}, y_{j+1})$ is positive and continuous differentiable. Taking the partial derivative to y_{j-1} on both sides of this identity, one gets that

$$\frac{\partial x_j(y_{j-1}, y_{j+1})}{\partial y_{j-1}} = \frac{\partial \phi_j(s_1, s_2)}{\partial s_1}\bigg|_{s=s(y)} \times \left(1 + \frac{\partial x_j(y_{j-1}, y_{j+1})}{\partial y_{j-1}}\right)$$
$$+ \frac{\partial \phi_j(s_1, s_2)}{\partial s_2}\bigg|_{s=s(y)} \times \frac{\partial x_j(y_{j-1}, y_{j+1})}{\partial y_{j-1}},$$

with $s(y) = (y_{j-1} + x_j(y_{j-1}, y_{j+1}), x_j(y_{j-1}, y_{j+1}) + y_{j+1})$. Hence,

$$\frac{\partial x_j(y_{j-1}, y_{j+1})}{\partial y_{j-1}} = \left[\frac{\partial \phi_j(s_1, s_2)}{\partial s_1} \bigg/ \left(1 - \frac{\partial \phi_j(s_1, s_2)}{\partial s_1} - \frac{\partial \phi_j(s_1, s_2)}{\partial s_2}\right)\right]\bigg|_{s=s(y)} \leq 0.$$

A similar expression holds for $\partial x_j(y_{j-1}, y_{j+1})/\partial y_{j+1} \leq 0$, and one can conclude that

$$\left| \frac{\partial x_j(y_{j-1}, y_{j+1})}{\partial y_{j-1}} \right| + \left| \frac{\partial x_j(y_{j-1}, y_{j+1})}{\partial y_{j+1}} \right| \tag{17}$$

$$= -\left[\left(\frac{\partial \phi_j(s_1, s_2)}{\partial s_1} + \frac{\partial \phi_j(s_1, s_2)}{\partial s_2} \right) / \left(1 - \frac{\partial \phi_j(s_1, s_2)}{\partial s_1} - \frac{\partial \phi_j(s_1, s_2)}{\partial s_2} \right) \right]\Bigg|_{s=s(y)}.$$

If $x_j(0, y_{j+1}) = 0$, then by Relation (16), one gets that, for some constant α_j, see Equation (8),

$$0 = \phi_j(0, y_{j+1}) = \alpha_j / \sqrt{\beta_j(0, y_{j+1})},$$

which holds only if $y_{j+1} = \infty$. Hence, $x_j(0, y_{j+1}) > 0$. Since $x_j(y_{j-1}, y_{j+1})$ is continuous and positive, and $x_j(0, y_{j+1}) > 0$, one obtains that there exists an $M_j^- > 0$ such that $y_{j-1} + x_j(y_{j-1}, y_{j+1}) > M_j^-$ for all $y_{j-1}, y_{j+1} \geq 0$. Similarly, there exists an $M_j^+ > 0$ such that $x_j(y_{j-1}, y_{j+1}) + y_{j+1} > M_j^+$. This gives the following upper bound,

$$-\frac{\partial \phi_j(s_1, s_2)}{\partial s_i}\Bigg|_{s=s(y)} = \frac{\alpha_j}{2} \frac{\partial \beta_j(s_1, s_2)}{\partial s_i}\Bigg|_{s=s(y)} \beta_j(s(y))^{-3/2}$$

$$\leq \frac{\alpha_j}{2} \frac{L}{(\beta_j(M_j^-, M_j^+))^{3/2}},$$

where we used that β_j is non-decreasing, Lipschitz continuous (with constant L) and differentiable. From Equation (17)) one now obtains that there exists a constant $0 < C < 1$ such that

$$\left| \frac{\partial x_j(y_{j-1}, y_{j+1})}{\partial y_{j-1}} \right| + \left| \frac{\partial x_j(y_{j-1}, y_{j+1})}{\partial y_{j+1}} \right| < C.$$

Hence, the mapping $T : \mathbb{R}_+^J \to \mathbb{R}_+^J$ with $T(y) = (x_j(y_{j-1}, y_{j+1}))$ for $j = 1, \ldots, J)$ is a contraction, and has a unique fixed point (y_j^*), i.e., Equation (15) has a unique solution.

Routes with One Node or Two Consecutive Nodes

Consider now a ring with J nodes and $K = 2J$ classes. Class j uses two nodes: nodes j and $j+1$, $j = 1, \ldots, J$. Class $0j$ uses one node: node j, $j = 1, \ldots, J$. We assume that $A_{jk} = 1$ if and only if class k uses node j, and zero otherwise.

We focus on functions β_k that satisfy (5). Equation (7) is in this context

$$u_j = \phi_{0j}(u_j) + \phi_{j-1}(u_{j-1} + u_j) + \phi_j(u_j + u_{j+1}), \quad 1 \leq j \leq J.$$

For $y_j = \phi_j(u_j + u_{j+1})$ and $y_{0j} = \phi_{0j}(u_j)$, $j = 1 \ldots, J$, the above equation can be rewritten as follows, for $j = 1, \ldots, J$,

$$\begin{cases} y_j = \phi_j(y_{j-1} + 2y_j + y_{j+1} + y_{0j} + y_{0j+1}), \\ y_{0j} = \phi_{0j}(y_{0j} + y_{j-1} + y_j). \end{cases} \tag{18}$$

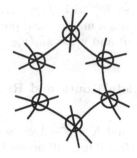

Fig. 4. Routes with one node or two consecutive nodes

Proposition 7. *If the functions β_k and β_{0k} for $1 \leq k \leq J$, are Lipschitz, continuously differentiable, non-decreasing, and satisfy (5), then there exists a unique solution for the fixed point equation (7).*

Proof. By the Implicit function theorem, for each j, there exists a unique $x_{0j}(t)$ satisfying the relation $x_{0j}(t) = \phi_{0j}(x_{0j}(t)+t)$, and this function is non-increasing and continuous differentiable. One now has to solve the equation

$$y_j = \phi_j(y_{j-1} + 2y_j + y_{j+1} + x_{0j}(y_{j-1} + y_j) + x_{0,j+1}(y_j + y_{j+1})). \qquad (19)$$

From the fact that $-1 \leq x'_{0j}(t) \leq 0$, it can be easily checked that the right-hand side of Equation (19) is non-increasing in y_j. Hence, there exists a unique $x_j(y_{j-1}, y_{j+1})$ such that $y_j = x_j(y_{j-1}, y_{j+1})$ satisfies Equation (19), and this function $(y_{j-1}, y_{j+1}) \to x_j(y_{j-1}, y_{j+1})$ is positive and continuous differentiable (by the Implicit function theorem). In particular, $x_j(y_{j-1}, y_{j+1}) = \phi_j(f_j(y))$, for all $j = 1, \ldots, J$, with

$$f_j(y) = y_{j-1} + 2x_j(y_{j-1}, y_{j+1}) + y_{j+1}$$
$$+ x_{0j}(y_{j-1} + x_j(y_{j-1}, y_{j+1})) + x_{0,j+1}(x_j(y_{j-1}, y_{j+1}) + y_{j+1}).$$

From this one can derive that

$$\frac{\partial x_j(y_{j-1}, y_{j+1})}{\partial y_{j-1}} = \phi'_j(f_j(y)) \left[1 + x'_{0j}(y_{j-1} + x_j(y_{j-1}, y_{j+1}))\right]/$$

$$\left[1 - \phi'_j(f_j(y))(2 + x'_{0j}(y_{j-1} + x_j(y_{j-1}, y_{j+1}))\right.$$

$$\left. + x'_{0,j+1}(x_j(y_{j-1}, y_{j+1}) + y_{j+1}))\right] \leq 0,$$

and a similar expression holds for $\partial x_j(y_{j-1}, y_{j+1})/\partial y_{j+1} \leq 0$. As in the proof of Proposition 6, an upper bound on $-\phi'_j(f_j(y))$ can be obtained. This implies that there exists a constant $0 < C < 1$ such that

$$\left|\frac{\partial x_j(y_{j-1}, y_{j+1})}{\partial y_{j-1}}\right| + \left|\frac{\partial x_j(y_{j-1}, y_{j+1})}{\partial y_{j+1}}\right| < C, \quad j = 1, \ldots, J.$$

Hence, the mapping $T : \mathbb{R}_+^J \to \mathbb{R}_+^J$ with $T(y_1, \ldots, y_J) = (x_j(y_{j-1}, y_{j+1}), j = 1, \ldots, J)$ is a contraction, and has a unique fixed point (y_j^*). One concludes that there exists a unique solution y_j^* and $y_{0j}^* = x_{0j}(y_{j-1}^* + y_j^*)$, $j = 1, \ldots, J$, of (18).

A Network with a Complete Route and Routes with Two Consecutive Nodes

Consider a ring with J nodes and $K = J + 1$ classes. Class $1 \le j \le J$ uses two nodes: node j and $j + 1$ and class 0 uses all nodes $1, \ldots, J$.

Fig. 5. A network with a complete route and routes with two consecutive nodes

We focus on functions β_k that satisfy (5). Equation (7) is in this context

$$u_j = \phi_0 (u_1 + \cdots + u_J) + \phi_{j-1}(u_{j-1} + u_j) + \phi_j(u_j + u_{j+1}).$$

For $y_j = \phi_j(u_j + u_{j+1})$ and $y_0 = \phi_0(u_1 + u_2 + \cdots + u_J)$, the above equation can be rewritten as follows

$$\begin{cases} y_j & = \phi_j(y_{j-1} + 2y_j + y_{j+1} + 2y_0), \quad j = 1, \ldots, J, \\ y_0 & = \phi_0(Jy_0 + 2\sum_{j=1}^J y_j). \end{cases} \tag{20}$$

Proposition 8. *If the functions β_k, $0 \le k \le J$ are of the form (5) and satisfy the assumptions of Proposition 2, then there exists a unique solution for the fixed point equation (7).*

Proof. From Proposition 2 we have that Equation (20) has at least one fixed point solution. Let $x = (x_j : j = 0, 1, \ldots, J)$ and $y = (y_j : j = 0, 1, \ldots, J)$ both be fixed points.

If the relation $y_j < x_j$ holds for all $j = 1, \ldots, J$, then

$$\phi_j(2y_j + y_{j-1} + y_{j+1} + 2y_0) = y_j < x_j = \phi_j(2x_j + x_{j-1} + x_{j+1} + 2x_0).$$

Since the function ϕ_j is non-increasing, one gets that

$$2y_j + y_{j-1} + y_{j+1} + 2y_0 > 2x_j + x_{j-1} + x_{j+1} + 2x_0.$$

Summing over all $j = 1, \ldots, J$, we obtain

$$4(y_1 + \cdots + y_J) + 2Jy_0 > 4(x_1 + \cdots + x_J) + 2Jx_0,$$

which implies that $x_0 < y_0$. However, ϕ_0 is non-increasing, so that

$$y_0 = \phi_0 \left(2(y_1 + \cdots + y_J) + Jy_0\right) \leq \phi_0 \left(2(x_1 + \cdots + x_J) + Jx_0\right) = x_0.$$

Hence, we obtain a contradiction.

We can conclude that there is an $m \in \{1, \ldots, J\}$ such that $y_m \leq x_m$ and $y_{m+1} \geq x_{m+1}$. To show that $x = y$, one proceeds along similar lines as in the proof of Proposition 6.

References

1. Antunes, N., Fricker, C., Robert, P., Tibi, D.: Stochastic networks with multiple stable points. Annals of Probability 36(1), 255–278 (2008)
2. Chafai, D., Malrieu, F., Paroux, K.: On the long time behavior of the TCP window size process (2009) (preprint), http://arxiv.org/abs/0811.2180
3. Dumas, V., Guillemin, F., Robert, P.: A Markovian analysis of Additive-Increase Multiplicative-Decrease (AIMD) algorithms. Advances in Applied Probability 34(1), 85–111 (2002)
4. Sally, F., Kohler, E.: Internet research needs better models. SIGCOMM Comput. Commun. Rev. 33(1), 29–34 (2003)
5. Gibbens, R.J., Hunt, P.J., Kelly, F.P.: Bistability in communication networks. In: Disorder in physical systems, pp. 113–127. Oxford Sci. Publ., Oxford Univ. Press, New York (1990)
6. Graham, C., Robert, P.: Interacting multi-class transmissions in large stochastic networks. Annals of Applied Probability (to appear, 2009)
7. Guillemin, F., Robert, P., Zwart, B.: AIMD algorithms and exponential functionals. Annals of Applied Probability 14(1), 90–117 (2004)
8. Kelly, F.P., Maulloo, A.K., Tan, D.K.H.: Rate control in communication networks: shadow prices, proportional fairness and stability. Journal of the Operational Research Society 49, 237–252 (1998)
9. Marbukh, V.: Loss circuit switched communication network: performance analysis and dynamic routing. Queueing Systems: Theory and Applications 13(1-3), 111–141 (1993)
10. Massoulié, L.: Structural properties of proportional fairness: Stability and insensitivity. Annals of Applied Probability 17(3), 809–839 (2007)
11. Massoulié, L., Roberts, J.: Bandwidth sharing: Objectives and algorithms. In: INFOCOM 1999 Eighteenth Annual Joint Conference of the IEEE Computer and Communications Societies, pp. 1395–1403 (1999)
12. Ott, T.J., Kemperman, J.H.B., Mathis, M.: The stationary behavior of ideal TCP congestion avoidance (August 1996) (unpublished manuscript)
13. Raghunathan, V., Kumar, P.R.: A counterexample in congestion control of wireless networks. Performance Evaluation 64(5), 399–418 (2007)

Quantile Sensitivity Estimation

Bernd Heidergott and Warren Volk-Makarewicz

Department of Econometrics and Operations Research, De Boelelaan 1105,
Amsterdam 1081 HV, The Netherlands

Abstract. Quantiles are important performance characteristics that
have been adopted in many areas for measuring the quality of service. Recently, sensitivity analysis of quantiles has attracted quite some attention.
Sensitivity analysis of quantiles is particularly challenging as quantiles
cannot be expressed as the expected value of some sample performance
function, and it is therefore not evident how standard gradient estimation
methods can be applied. In this paper we present a straightforward quantile sensitivity estimator based on measure-valued differentiation (MVD).
We compare our new estimator with the known infinitesimal perturbation analysis (IPA) estimator and discuss implementation issues. Numerical examples will illustrate our results.

1 Introduction

The α-quantile of a random variable Y is the smallest number u that satisfies
$\mathbb{P}(Y \geq u) \leq \alpha$. Quantiles are also known as *value at risk* (VaR) and are widely
used as measures of quality in the service industry. Unfortunately, the α-quantile
can only be obtained in closed form in special cases and one usually has to resort
to simulation (resp. statistical estimation) for evaluating a quantile. In this paper
we assume that Y can be influenced through some control parameter θ and we
provide estimators for the sensitivity of the α-quantile with respect to θ.

This research is motivated by the following. In communication systems, a
service contract with a provider usually guarantees that the α-quantile of the
sojourn time of a typical job through the systems does not exceed a specified
value η. Suppose that θ is the capacity of a server in a communication link.
Then the sensitivities of the α-quantile of the sojourn time of a job provide
a measure for the influence of θ on the service quality. This information is of
particular interest to the provider as the sensitivity information allows pricing of
the service. To see this note that from the provider's point of view the standard
performance should be optimal subject to the service requirement expressed in
the quantile. Under suitable conditions, the performance optimization problem
can be solved in an iterative way by the Lagrange multiplier method [15] yielding
the shadow price of the service quality restriction and thus providing information
on the economic impact of θ on the overall profit.

While quantiles provide natural quality (resp. risk) measures, there is an ongoing discussion in the literature on the applicability of these measures. In particular, VaR is under much criticism as the VaR measure does not, in general,

R. Núñez-Queija and J. Resing (Eds.): NET-COOP 2009, LNCS 5894, pp. 16–29, 2009.
© Springer-Verlag Berlin Heidelberg 2009

satisfy the requirement that the risk measure should exceed the mean loss, or the requirement that the risk measure should be subadditive. As a result of this lack of coherence, investment decisions based on VaR may introduce the wrong incentives, leading to counterproductive behavior.

Often, only very little information on the loss variable Y is available, and quantiles are measured by means of non-parametric statistic methods. On the other hand, there are many fields of interest where sufficient knowledge is available to build parametric models for Y. For the research presented in this paper, we assume that Y depends on some control parameter θ and that a model for Y is available. This is a typical situation in communication systems, where Y may represent the sojourn in some queueing network.

The paper is organized as follows. Section 2 recapitulates the basic results known for quantile estimators. The sensitivity estimation problem is discussed in Section 3. Simulation based methods for derivative estimation are presented in Section 4 and our new estimator will be established. A detailed discussion of the sensitivity estimators and numerical results will be presented in Section 5 and Section 6. We conclude the paper by identifying topics of further research.

2   Estimating Quantiles

Bahadur, [2], provides a quantile estimator for i.i.d. data, and shows that the estimator is strongly consistent and has an asymptotic normal distribution; and for a thorough review of quantile estimation for i.i.d. data we refer to [19]. An extension to dependent data is given in [18].

In the following we briefly describe the standard estimation procedure for VaR. Let X be a random variable and h some measurable mapping. Given a sample $Z = X_1, \ldots, X_n$ of n i.i.d copies of X, denote the order statistic of $h(X_1), \ldots, h(X_n)$ by $h(X_{(1)}), \ldots, h(X_{(n)})$. Note that $X_{(k)}$ is not the order statistic of $X_1, \ldots, X_n$. For simplicity, assume that X is a continuous random variable, then

$$h(X_{(1)}) < h(X_{(2)}) < \cdots < h(X_{(n)}) \quad \text{w.p. } 1 \tag{1}$$

Let q_α denote the α-VaR of $Y = h(X)$. The natural estimator for q_α, given the data set for Z, reads

$$q_{n,\alpha}(Z) = h(X_{(\lceil n\,\alpha \rceil)}) \tag{2}$$

where $\lceil r \rceil$ denotes the ceiling function yielding the smallest integer larger than or equal to r. A basic result from order statistics shows that $q_{n,\alpha}$ converges to q_α as n tends to infinity with probability one.

3   Quantile Sensitivity

The general problem of sensitivity estimation has been studied extensively in the simulation literature (see, for instance, [4], for a recent review). Simulation methods for estimating sensitivities of quantiles fall into two broad categories: methods that involve resimulation and those that do not. The first category, based on finite-difference (FD) approximations, is easy to understand and implement. Let θ denote the parameter of interest and let $C(\theta)$ denote the cost function given by an expected value. Specifically, in case of quantile estimation, $C(\theta)$ is the expected value of an appropriate order statistic. The so called forward-FD-method for the first-order sensitivity is to approximate the sensitivity by $(C(\theta + \Delta) - C(\theta))/\Delta$, where Δ denotes the size of the perturbation. A variant that is more accurate but also more costly than the forward-FD-method is $(C(\theta + \Delta/2) - C(\theta - \Delta/2))/\Delta$. Note that resimulation is required because $C(\theta + \Delta), C(\theta - \Delta)$ and $C(\theta)$ have to be established by simulation. The key problem of the finite-difference approximation is the tradeoff between the bias and variance of the estimator (e.g., [3]). If Δ is too large, the estimate would be biased because of the nonlinearity of $C(\theta)$, whereas small values of Δ lead to significant variance. When $C(\theta)$ is differentiable, FD approximations should be expected to converge to the true value with Δ small enough. However, this is not the case numerically for simulation methods. In fact, if Δ is too small, the variation between $C(\theta)$ and $C(\theta \pm \Delta)$ makes the FD estimate unstable. Although using common random numbers in resimulation can reduce the estimation error, the above observations remain valid even if variance reduction techniques or stratified sampling are employed, see [14] and [21].

Methods in the second category produce unbiased estimates but are more elaborate. Popular direct methods include *infinitesimal perturbation analysis* (IPA), the score function or *likelihood ratio* (LR) method and *measure-valued differentiation* (MVD). IPA differentiates each simulated outcome with respect to the parameters of interest (e.g., [5]). For LR (e.g., [6]) and MVD (e.g., [16]), on the other hand, one differentiates the probability density function respectively the probability measure rather than the simulated outcome. The domain of applicability of LR is a subset of that of MVD. Moreover, MVD generally enjoys smaller variances than LR. The domains of applicability of IPA and MVD, do not contain each other. When IPA and MVD both apply, IPA is generally simpler to implement and computationally more efficient, whereas MVD enjoys smaller variances. Recently it has been shown for problems that are relevant in applications that MVD may outperform IPA also in terms of computational efficiency, see [9] and [10]. In addition, different from IPA, MVD does not require the mapping h to be differentiable.

4   Methodological Discussion

4.1   The Sample Path Approach

IPA is based on sample path derivatives. To illustrate the IPA approach, assume that X_θ is differentiable with respect to θ with probability one. Provided that interchanging differentiation and taking expectation is justified, the IPA estimate is based upon the following

$$\frac{d}{d\theta}\mathbb{E}[h(X_\theta)] = \mathbb{E}\left[\frac{d}{d\theta}h(X_\theta)\right] = \mathbb{E}\left[h'(X_\theta)\frac{d}{d\theta}X_\theta\right], \qquad (3)$$

where h' denotes the derivative of $h(x)$ with respect to x. Note that IPA requires h to be differentiable. More specifically, the key condition for (3) to hold is that there exists a mapping l and a random variable X such that for all admissible θ_1, θ_2 it holds that $|h(X_{\theta_1}) - h(X_{\theta_2})| \leq l(X)|\theta_1 - \theta_2|$, with $\mathbb{E}[l(X)] < \infty$. An example of an IPA estimate will be presented in Section 5.1.

The IPA approach to sensitivity analysis of quantiles is best explained for the case where θ is scaling parameter. The fact that θ is a scaling parameter implies that $X_\theta = \theta X_1$ with probability one. Provided that h is monotone increasing and differentiable, only the numerical values of the order statistic $h(X_{\theta,(1)}), \ldots, h(X_{\theta,(n)})$ are effected by θ but not the order itself. In other words, the index of the random variable constituting the quantile estimator is independent of θ. For example, if $k = \lceil n\alpha \rceil$ for some value of θ, then

$$\frac{d}{d\theta} q_{n,\alpha} = \frac{1}{\theta} X_{\theta,k} h'(X_{\theta,k}) \quad \text{w.p. 1 and} \quad \frac{d}{d\theta} \mathbb{E}[q_{n,\alpha}] = \mathbb{E}\left[\frac{1}{\theta} X_{\theta,k} h'(X_{\theta,k}) \right] \quad (4)$$

The following result has been established in [12], and [13].

Theorem 1. *Suppose that*

(i) there exists a mapping l and a random variable X such that for all $\theta_1, \theta_2 \in \Theta$ it holds that $|h(X_{\theta_1}) - h(X_{\theta_2})| \leq l(X)|\theta_1 - \theta_2|$, with $\mathbb{E}[l(X)] < \infty$,
(ii) q_α is differentiable,
(iii) $\mathbb{P}(h(X_\theta) = q_\alpha) = 0$ for all $\theta \in \Theta$,
(iv) the sample path estimator satisfies

$$\sup_n \mathbb{E}\left[\left(\frac{d}{d\theta} q_{n,\alpha} \right)^2 \right] < \infty,$$

then

$$\lim_{n \to \infty} \mathbb{E}\left[\frac{d}{d\theta} q_{n,\alpha} \right] = \frac{d}{d\theta} q_\alpha.$$

The simplicity of the IPA approach comes at the price of the following two main restrictions:

(i) the mapping h has to be (at least) differentiable w.p. 1 and Lipschitz continuous (see the first condition in Theorem 1), and
(ii) the random variable X_θ has to have a continuous density $f(\theta, x)$ that is continuous with respect to both arguments.

Let $\{Z_k : 1 \leq k \leq m\}$ be a sample of m i.i.d. copies of $Z = (X_1, \ldots, X_n)$, and recall the definition of $q_{n,\alpha}(Z)$ in (2). Then under appropriate conditions, it holds that

$$\lim_{m,n \to \infty} \frac{1}{m} \sum_{k=1}^{m} \frac{d}{d\theta} q_{n,\alpha}(Z_k) = \frac{d}{d\theta} q_\alpha$$

with probability one, [12] and [13] for details.

4.2   The Distributional Approach

For the distributional approach we assume that μ_θ is a probability measure on $\mathbb{R}$ having density $f(\theta, x)$, for $x \in \mathbb{R}$, and X is a random variable distributed according to μ_θ. Suppose that for h it holds that

$$\frac{d}{d\theta}\mathbb{E}_\theta[h(X)] = \frac{d}{d\theta}\int h(x)f(\theta,x)\,dx = \int h(x)\frac{\partial f}{\partial \theta}(\theta,x)\,dx \qquad (5)$$

where we assume that f is continuous and its derivative $\partial f(\theta, x)/\partial\theta$ exists for all x. At this point one can use the SF method for estimating the derivative by defining

$$\psi_\theta(x) := \frac{1}{f(\theta,x)}\frac{\partial f}{\partial\theta}(\theta,x) \qquad (6)$$

Then the score-function (likelihood ratio) $\psi_\theta(x)$ is defined almost everywhere and, according to (5), satisfies

$$\frac{d}{d\theta}\mathbb{E}_\theta[h(X)] = \mathbb{E}[\psi_\theta(X)h(X)]. \qquad (7)$$

While simple and elegant, the above formula suffers in applications from the fact that the score-function $\psi_\theta(x)$ introduces considerable additional variance. Fortunately, there is an alternative way of dealing with (5). Denoting $\mu_\theta'(dx) = \partial f(\theta, x)/\partial\theta\,dx$, i.e, the signed measure with density $\partial f(\theta, x)/\partial\theta$, one obtains

$$\frac{\partial}{\partial\theta}\mathbb{E}_\theta[h(X)] = \frac{\partial}{\partial\theta}\int h(x)f(\theta,x)\,dx = \int h(x)\mu_\theta'(dx). \qquad (8)$$

The signed measure μ_θ' is called the *weak derivative* of μ_θ. Note that equation (8) is an implicit definition of the measure μ_θ'. By a standard result from measure theory, μ_θ' is uniquely defined if (8) holds for any continuous and bounded h. Specifically, let $\mathcal{D}$ denote a set of cost functions, containing the continuous and bounded ones, such that (8) holds for all $h \in \mathcal{D}$, then μ_θ is called $\mathcal{D}$-differentiable. The $\mathcal{D}$-derivative is unique and in general can be written as the re-scaled difference of two probability measures, making (8) suitable for Monte Carlo simulation. This is known as the *weak derivative* or the *measure-valued differentiation* (MVD) technique and it also leads to unbiased gradient estimation; see [16], [8], or [10]. Indeed, if $\mu_\theta' = c_\theta(\mu_\theta^+ - \mu_\theta^-)$, with $\mu_\theta^\pm$ probability measures and c_θ a constant, then we have

$$\frac{d}{d\theta}\mathbb{E}_\theta[h(X)] = c_\theta\mathbb{E}_\theta[h(X^+) - h(X^-)] \qquad (9)$$

where $X^\pm$ are random variables distributed according to $\mu_\theta^\pm$ respectively, not necessarily independent. In applications, it is desirable to generate X^+ and X^- such that they are correlated. This allows for reducing the variance of the derivative estimator $h(X^+) - h(X^-)$. This can be achieved for many distributions that are of importance in applications, see [10]. An example of an MVD estimate will be presented in Section 5.1.

To apply MVD to sensitivity estimation for quantiles, assume that μ_θ is weakly differentiable such that $\mu_\theta' = c_\theta(\mu_\theta^+ - \mu_\theta^-)$. Let $Z^{+,j} = X_1^{+,j}, \ldots, X_n^{+,j}$ a sample of n independent random variables where all except the jth element are i.i.d copies of X and the jth element is distributed according to μ_θ^+. In the same vein, let $Z^{-,j} = X_1^{-,j}, \ldots, X_n^{-,j}$ a sample of n independent random variables where all except the jth element are i.i.d copies of X and the jth element is distributed according to μ_θ^-. Below we will show that under some mild regularity conditions it holds that

$$\frac{d}{d\theta}\mathbb{E}_\theta[q_{n,\alpha}(Z)] = c_\theta \mathbb{E}_\theta\left[\sum_{j=1}^{n}\left(q_{n,\alpha}(Z^{+,j}) - q_{n,\alpha}(Z^{-,j})\right)\right]. \qquad (10)$$

In words, the derivative of the expected value of the quantile estimator is given by the difference between the standard quantile estimator applied to the data set with one element replaced by the positive part of the weak derivative and one element replaced by the negative part of the weak derivative. Comparing to IPA we note that

(i) MVD requires no restriction of the class of distributions (except weak differentiability of course). This is different from IPA where discrete distributions are ruled out.

(ii) Neither differentiability nor Lipschitz continuity of h are required.

In the following we will give the precise statement on the validity of (10). In order to do, we will introduce some notation and methodology. Let $\Theta \subset \mathbb{R}$ be an open set, and let μ_θ be a probability measure on some measurable space $(S, \mathcal{F})$. In particular, assume that S is metrizable and that $\mathcal{F}$ denotes the Borel-field on S. Let $\mathbb{R}$ be equipped with the usual topology and let it be equipped with the corresponding Borel-field. We denote by $\mathcal{B}$ the set of real-valued and Borel-measurable mappings on S. Denote by $L^1(\mu_\theta, \Theta)$ the set of measurable mappings g such that $\int |g(x)|\mu_\theta(dx) < \infty$ for any $\theta \in \Theta$. For $h \in L^1(\mu_\theta, \Theta)$, with $h \geq 0$, denote the set of mappings g that are, up to a multiplicative constant, bounded by $\max(1, h)$ by $\mathcal{D}_h$, i.e. , $g \in \mathcal{D}_h$ if g is measurable and there exits a finite constant c such that $|g(x)| \leq c\max(h(x), 1)$ for all x. Note that the continuous and bounded mappings are a subset of $\mathcal{D}_h$.

Theorem 2. *Let $h \in L^1(\mu_\theta, \Theta)$. If μ_θ is $\mathcal{D}_h$-differentiable at θ, then it holds that*

$$\frac{d}{d\theta}\mathbb{E}_\theta[q_{n,\alpha}(Z)] = c_\theta \mathbb{E}_\theta\left[\sum_{j=1}^{n}\left(q_{n,\alpha}(Z^{+,j}) - q_{n,\alpha}(Z^{-,j})\right)\right]$$

Proof. Note that
$$q_{n,\alpha}(Z) = f(X_\theta(1), \ldots, X_\theta(n)),$$
where f is some measurable mapping. Moreover it holds that

$$|q_{n,\alpha}(Z)| \leq \prod_{i=1}^{n}\max(1, |h(X_\theta(i)|). \qquad (11)$$

We have assumed that μ_θ is $\mathcal{D}_h$ differentiable. Since $\mathcal{D}_h$ is the set of measurable mappings bounded, up to a multiplicative constant, by the measurable mapping $\max(1, h)$, $\mathcal{D}_h$ is a Banach space when equipped with the $\max(1, h)$-norm defined by

$$\|g\|_{\max(1,h)} = \sup_{x \in S} \frac{|g(x)|}{\max(1, h(x))}.$$

By (11) it holds that the $\prod_{i=1}^n \max(1, h)$-norm of f is finite. Hence, the product rule of weak differentiability applies, see [8], which yields the desired result. $\quad\square$

Theorem 2 establishes an unbiased MVD estimator for the quantile estimator for fixed sample size n. Under appropriate smoothness conditions, this result implies that

$$\frac{d}{d\theta} q_\alpha = \lim_{n \to \infty} c_\theta \mathbb{E}_\theta \left[\sum_{j=1}^n \left(q_{n,\alpha}(Z^{+,j}) - q_{n,\alpha}(Z^{-,j}) \right) \right].$$

A proof of the above limit results is postponed to the full length version of the paper.

5   A Comparison of the Quantile Estimators for the Exponential Distribution

In this section, we will compare the IPA and the MVD quantile sensitivity estimator for the case of exponential distribution. We will compare the variance and the bias of the estimators. Moreover, we will illustrate how the numerical performance of the MVD estimator can be enhanced by applying a conditioning technique.

5.1   Derivative Estimation for the Exponential Distribution

Let X_θ denote an exponentially distributed random variable with mean θ and note that X_θ can be sampled as follows. For U uniformly distributed on $[0, 1]$ and independent of everything else, X_θ can be sampled from

$$X_\theta = -\theta \ln(1 - U). \tag{12}$$

Taking derivatives yields

$$\frac{d}{d\theta} X_\theta = -\ln(1 - U) = \frac{1}{\theta} X_\theta \tag{13}$$

and it holds that

$$\frac{d}{d\theta} \mathbb{E}[X_\theta] = \mathbb{E}\left[\frac{1}{\theta} X_\theta \right]. \tag{14}$$

Hence, X_θ/θ is an unbiased estimator for $d\mathbb{E}[X_\theta]/d\theta$. It is noticeably the IPA estimator.

Let $f(\theta, x) = \exp(-x/\theta)/\theta$ denote the density of X_θ. Note that $f(\theta, x)$ is differentiable with respect to θ and it holds that

$$\frac{\partial}{\partial \theta} f(\theta, x) = \frac{1}{\theta^2}(x-1)e^{-\frac{x}{\theta}} = \frac{1}{\theta}\left(\frac{x}{\theta}e^{-\frac{x}{\theta}} - \frac{1}{\theta}e^{-\frac{x}{\theta}}\right).$$

Noting that

$$\hat{f}(\theta, x) = \frac{x}{\theta}e^{-\frac{x}{\theta}}$$

is the density of the distribution of the sum of two independent exponential random variables with mean θ, known as Erlang distribution, the derivative expression becomes

$$\frac{d}{d\theta}\int g(x)f(\theta, x)\,dx = \int g(x)\frac{\partial}{\partial \theta}f(\theta, x)\,dx$$
$$= \frac{1}{\theta}\left(\int g(x)\hat{f}(\theta, x)\,dx - \int g(x)f(\theta, x)\,dx\right), \quad (15)$$

for any $g \in \mathcal{D}_{\exp(\eta x)}$, for some $\eta > 0$. Recall that $\mathcal{D}_{\exp(\eta x)}$ denotes the set of measurable mappings bounded by $\max(1, \exp(\eta x))$ up to a multiplicative constant, which implies that all finite polynomials are in $\mathcal{D}_{\exp(\eta x)}$.

Letting Y_θ be an exponential random variable with mean θ and independent of X_θ, the sum $Y_\theta + X_\theta$ is Erlang distributed and the MVD estimator in (15) reads in random variable language

$$\frac{d}{d\theta}\mathbb{E}[g(X_\theta)] = \frac{1}{\theta}\mathbb{E}[g(X_\theta + Y_\theta) - g(X_\theta)], \quad (16)$$

for $g \in \mathcal{D}_{\exp(\eta x)}$; see (9).

In the following section, we will discuss the IPA and MVD quantile sensitivity estimator of the exponential distribution.

5.2   Quantile Sensitivity Estimation for the Exponential Distribution

Suppose we are interested in estimating the sensitivity of the α-quantile of the exponential distribution with respect to the mean. We assume that $Z_\theta = X_{\theta,1}, \ldots, X_{\theta,n}$ is a sample of n i.i.d. exponentially distributed random variables with mean θ. The basic estimator for the α-quantile of the exponential distribution is then given by

$$q_{n,\alpha}(Z_\theta) = X_{\theta,\lceil n\alpha \rceil}.$$

By (12) the index of the element of Z that yields the $\lceil n\alpha \rceil$-largest element is independent of θ, more specifically it holds that

$$q_{n,\alpha}(Z_\theta) = \theta X_{1,\lceil n\alpha \rceil}. \quad (17)$$

Denote the α-quantile of the exponential distribution with mean θ by $q_{\alpha,\theta}$. Since equality (17) holds for all n, it holds that

$$\theta q_{\alpha,1} = q_{\alpha,\theta}.$$

Taking derivatives yields

$$\frac{d}{d\theta} q_{\alpha,\theta} = q_{\alpha,1} = \frac{1}{\theta} q_{\alpha,\theta}.$$

For the above reasons the IPA estimator in essence estimates the α-quantile of the exponential distribution with mean one and then re-scales the estimator by $1/\theta$ for estimating the sensitivities.

For the MVD estimator we use the estimator forward in Theorem 2. For the construction of the estimator we use the representation in (16). This representation has the advantage that the negative part of the weak derivative and nominal sample coincide. The MVD estimator thus becomes

$$\frac{d}{d\theta} \mathbb{E}_\theta [q_{n,\alpha}(Z_\theta)] = \frac{1}{\theta} \mathbb{E}_\theta \left[\sum_{j=1}^n \left(q_{n,\alpha}(Z_\theta^{+,j}) - q_{n,\alpha}(Z_\theta) \right) \right]. \tag{18}$$

To better understand the statistical behavior of the MVD estimator, note that $q_{n,\alpha}(Z_\theta^{+,j}) - q_{n,\alpha}(Z_\theta)$ only is non-zero if re-sampling the j-element of Z_θ effects $q_{n,\alpha}(Z_\theta)$. More specifically, let $X_{\theta,k} = q_{n,\alpha}(Z_\theta)$, i.e., $\lceil n\alpha \rceil = k$, then $q_{n,\alpha}(Z_\theta^{+,j}) - q_{n,\alpha}(Z_\theta) \neq 0$ in the following cases

- if $j \neq k(= \lceil n\alpha \rceil)$

$$X_{\theta,j}^{+,j} < X_{\theta,k} < X_{\theta,j}$$

  or

$$X_{\theta,j} < X_{\theta,k} < X_{\theta,j}^{+,j}$$

- if $j = \lceil n\alpha \rceil$

$$X_{\theta,\lceil n\alpha \rceil+1} < X_{\theta,j}^{+,j}$$

  or

$$X_{\theta,\lceil n\alpha \rceil-1} > X_{\theta,j}^{+,j}.$$

Above, in the first case, the value of the non-zero contribution is in $[X_{\theta,k-1} - X_{\theta,k}, 0)$ since if $X_{\theta,j}^{+,j} < X_{\theta,k-1}$, the $\lceil \alpha N \rceil^{th}$ order statistic of the perturbed sample is $X_{\theta,k-1}$. Analogously, the value of the non-zero contribution in the second case is in $(0, X_{\theta,k+1} - X_{\theta,k}]$. For the instance where $j = k$, a non-zero contribution always occurs with a range of $X_{\theta,j}^{+,j} - X_{\theta,j} \in [X_{\theta,k-1} - X_{\theta,j}, X_{\theta,k+1} - X_{\theta,j}]$. This version of the estimator ensures that $X_{\theta,j}^{+,j}$ is generated such that the contribution of the jth perturbation in MVD estimator, $X_{\theta,j}^{+,j} - X_{\theta,j}$, has always a value in the interior of the range that is dependent on the values of $X_{\theta,j}$ and $X_{\theta,k}$ Following the representation in (16) we will sample a conditional Erlang distribution so that, by conditioning on the above cases, the contribution of the sample is non-zero.

In the experiments presented in this section, we compare the IPA estimator of $X_{\theta,k}$ to the above MVD estimator, with $X_{\theta,k}$ being exponentially distributed above with parameter $\theta = 1$. This is achieved by progressively simulating random variables until $|X_{\theta,k} - q_\alpha| < \epsilon$, where the maximal bias is limited to a prescribed tolerance ϵ. Here, $q_\alpha = -\theta \log(1 - \alpha)$. After obtaining our collection of random variables, we calculate the sensitivity of the quantile using both approaches. We repeat the experiment a total of $N = 1000$ times. To compare the efficiency of the estimators, we determine their bias compared to the derivative of the quantile function (w.r.t θ), and construct an empirical cdf plot for both derivative estimators. We also compare the variance, and in addition the work-normalized variance (WNV). The work-normalized variance balances the computational effort and variance of the estimator, and is given by the product of the variance and the expected work per run balancing computational effort and estimator variance, see [7].

For the experiments, a sample of n observations $(X_{\theta,j})_{j=1}^n$ is split into sub-samples. Each sub-sample will be used to evaluate one realization of the order statistic. Using m as the size of each sub-sample and k is the number of sub-samples, such that $n = k \cdot m$. Following [12], we let k and m depend on n through a parameter δ as follows: $m = n^{1/3+\delta}$ and $k = n^{2/3-\delta}$. For our experiments, we choose a sample size n such that the tolerance (within ϵ) is first met. For given δ, k and m determined and then rounded up to the nearest integer. For our experiments, we choose $\delta = 2/7, 1/2, 1, 5/4$, and thereby incrementally increasing k and decreasing m. Table 1 displays the relationship between k and m for the above values of δ. The bias and the WNV of the MVD and IPA estimator for each choice of δ is then compared. For both parts, the tolerance level $\epsilon = 10^{-2}$. Below, we present the results. Tables 2 and 3 contain the results for the first part of the experiment.

We depict the situation for $\alpha = 0.9$ in Figure 1 in more detail, see the Appendix.

Compared to the MVD estimators, it is easily observed that the IPA estimator for the quantile has less bias, lower variance, and is computationally quicker to compute (the WNV of IPA is by a factor of 10^3 smaller than that of MVD). Here, the performance function is $h(X) = X$ and the IPA derivative estimator is the appropriate order statistic divided by its parameter. Here, this is a test to see how well the MVD estimator does compared to a situation where the IPA estimator performs efficiently.

The MVD estimator degrades in performance in regions were the value of the density function is low (i.e., the tails of the density functions which have unbounded support) or when the length of the sub-sample increases. This inference

Table 1. The relationship between m and k for the chosen values of δ

δ	Relationship between m and k
2/7	$m = k^{3/4}$
1/2	$m = k$
1	$m = k^2$
5/4	$m = k^3$

Table 2. Statistics for bias, variance and WNV of the MVD and IPA derivative estimators for $q_{0.50}$

	$\alpha = 0.50$							
	$\delta = 2/7$		$\delta = 1/2$		$\delta = 1$		$\delta = 5/4$	
	MVD	IPA	MVD	IPA	MVD	IPA	MVD	IPA
$q_{0.5}$ bias	0.8098	0.0182	0.7789	0.0125	0.7124	0.0078	0.6858	0.0068
$q_{0.9}$ bias	1.0638	0.0458	0.9961	0.0391	0.9655	0.0180	0.9925	0.0150
Variance	0.0082	0.0007	0.0148	0.0008	0.0417	0.0008	0.0884	0.0008
$\text{WNV}_{\text{MVD}}/\text{WNV}_{\text{IPA}}$	2.157×10^3		3.682×10^3		2.460×10^4		9.596×10^4	

Table 3. Statistics for bias, variance and WNV of the MVD and IPA derivative estimators for $q_{0.90}$

	$\alpha = 0.90$ (WNV = Work-Normalised Variance)							
	$\delta = 2/7$		$\delta = 1/2$		$\delta = 1$		$\delta = 5/4$	
	MVD	IPA	MVD	IPA	MVD	IPA	MVD	IPA
$q_{0.5}$ bias	6.8699	0.0526	6.4828	0.0328	6.1284	0.0102	5.9773	0.0075
$q_{0.9}$ bias	8.241	0.1678	7.7807	0.1064	7.4070	0.0367	7.8179	0.0195
Variance	0.3127	0.0058	0.6064	0.0075	1.9369	0.0068	3.3603	0.0082
$\text{WNV}_{\text{MVD}}/\text{WNV}_{\text{IPA}}$	1.031×10^4		1.569×10^4		1.256×10^5		3.449×10^5	

is due to the density being low, there is greater variability between successive order statistics leading to more varied estimates when sampling from a gamma distribution conditioned in the interval. Also, the convergence in a Weak Law of Large Number sense of the order statistic to quantile is mitigated by the increased number of random variables that need to be computed.

The generation of the versions of the perturbed random variables for the MVD estimator allows for schemes different from the ones discussed above. A search for generating schemes that reduce variance of the MVD estimator is topic of further research.

6   A Queueing Network Example

In this section, we will apply the quantile estimator to a more elaborate example where the true quantile is not known. We consider the following model. Jobs arrive to a communication link according to a Poisson λ arrival stream. If an arriving job finds upon arrival to the link a free slot at the first server, the job is admitted, otherwise the job is lost. The link consists of two servers in a row. Each of the servers has a capacity of two jobs and the service rate, denoted by μ_1 and μ_2, is assigned to the jobs present at the server in processor sharing manner. After completing service at server one, a job moves to server two as soon as there is a free place available. After finishing service at server two, a job leaves the link. We assume that the service rate at the second server is adjustable, that is, we take

Table 4. The quantiles of the mean sojourn time and the time to completion of the first 100 jobs through the communication link

Parameter Vector $(\lambda, \mu_1, \mu_2 = \theta)$	Mean Sojourn Time				Time to completion			
	$\alpha = 0.05$	$\alpha = 0.50$	$\alpha = 0.90$	$\alpha = 0.95$				
(1,1,0.5)	1.8304	2.0996	2.4266	2.4643	102.60	129.24	155.12	161.09
(1,1,0.8)	2.3626	2.5497	3.0288	3.1209	112.34	130.67	157.09	161.98
(1,1,1)	2.7475	3.2145	3.6904	3.8295	116.63	133.12	158.50	169.54
(1,1,1.25)	3.2338	3.9791	4.5741	4.6711	126.79	141.86	169.39	177.09
(1,1,2)	5.5107	6.7760	7.7473	8.0574	155.42	179.54	217.73	222.45

Table 5. The MVD estimate of the quantiles of the mean sojourn time of the first 100 jobs through the communication link

Quantiles of the MVD estimate of the mean sojourn time			
Parameter Vector $(\lambda, \mu_1, \mu_2 = \theta)$	Quantile Level		
	$\alpha = 0.05$	$\alpha = 0.50$	$\alpha = 0.90$	$\alpha = 0.95$
(1,1,0.5)	-5.8937	-5.3175	-3.9152	-3.8733
(1,1,0.8)	-8.4507	-6.1609	-5.1037	-4.6799
(1,1,1)	-10.1471	-6.9473	-5.9813	-5.8086
(1,1,1.25)	-12.9254	-8.3908	-6.3991	-6.0342
(1,1,2)	-22.9155	-10.4173	-6.3395	-4.6150

$\mu_2 = \theta$ as our design parameter. In the following we will apply the MVD estimate to determine the derivative of the α-quantile of the mean sojourn time of the first $n = 100$ jobs that pass the link respect to θ for $\alpha = 0.05, 0.50, 0.90, 0.95$. We assume that the system is initially empty. For this problem, IPA fails to apply as the sample path is discontinuous with respect to θ.

In the following we discuss the MVD estimator. The average sojourn time is weakly $\mathcal{D}_{\exp(\eta x)}$ differentiable for $\eta > 0$, see [10], and the MVD estimator put forward in Section 4.2 applies. A detailed proof of unbiasedness of the MVD estimator is postponed to the full length version of the paper.

Below we provide the quantiles for the mean sojourn time and the time to completion for chosen sets of parameters based on 100 replications. We see these results in Tables 4 and 5. To determine the bias, we claim that the true value of the sensitivity for a given set of parameters is the mean of 5000 experiments of the average sojourn time.

As the mean service for buffer two, θ, increases, the MVD estimate for the α-level quantile of the mean sojourn time also increases, as $\gamma(2, 1/\theta)$ has twice the mean as the exponential distribution with the same scale parameter. Hence, on average it will take longer for server 2 to serve the jobs relative to the unperturbed system and thus a longer sojourn time. The values of the quantiles are also more spread due to the fact that the density function has greater variance for larger values of θ.

7   Conclusion

We established a new quantile sensitivity estimator based on measure-valued differentiation. We compared the new estimator with the known IPA estimator. In general, the MVD-estimator applies under less restrictive conditions than the IPA estimator, and we presented a simple queueing example where the MVD estimator applies but the IPA estimator fails. On the other hand, for special cases, the IPA estimator outperforms the MVD estimator as we have illustrated with the case of the exponential distribution where the parameter of interest is a scaling parameter of the distribution. Numerical examples suggest that the performance of the MVD estimator could be improved by combining the estimator with importance sampling. This is topic of further research.

References

1. Avramidis, Wilson: Correlation-induction techniques for estimating quantiles in simulation experiments. Operations Research 46, 574–591 (1998)
2. Bahadur: A note on quantiles in large samples. Ann. Math.Statist. 37, 577–580 (1966)
3. Fox, Glynn: Replication schemes for limiting expectations. Probability in the Engineering and Informational Sciences 3, 299–318 (1989)
4. Fu: Gradient estimation. In: Henderson, Nelson (eds.) Handbooks in Operations Research and Management Science: Simulation, pp. 575–612. Elsevier, Amsterdam (2006)
5. Glasserman: Gradient Estimation via Perturbation Analysis. Kluwer Academic Publishers, Norwell (1991)
6. Glynn: Likelihood ratio gradient estimation for stochastic systems. Comm. ACM 33, 75–84 (1990)
7. Glynn, Whitt: The asymptotic efficiency of simulation estimators. Operations Research 40, 505–520 (1992)
8. Heidergott, Leahu: Weak differentiability of product measures. Mathematics of Operations Research (to appear)
9. Heidergott, Vázquez-Abad, Farenhorst-Yuan: A perturbation analysis approach to phantom estimators for waiting times in the G/G/1 queue. Discrete Event Dynamic Systems (in press)
10. Heidergott, Vázquez-Abad, Pflug, Farenhorst-Yuan: Gradient estimation for discrete-event systems by measure-valued differentiation. Transactions on Modeling and Computer Simulation (accepted January 2009)
11. Heyde, Kou: On the controversy over tail weight of distributions. Operations Research Letters 32, 399–408 (2004)
12. Hong: Estimating quantile sensitivities. Operations Research 57, 118–130 (2009)
13. Hong, Liu: Simulating sensitivities of conditional value at risk. Management Science 55, 281–293 (2009)
14. Jäckel: Monte Carlo Methods in Finance. Wiley, United Kingdom (2002)
15. Kushner, Yin: Stochastic Approximation and Recursive Algorithms and Applications. Springer, Heidelberg (2003)
16. Pflug: Optimization of Stochastic Models. Kluwer Academic Publishers, Norwell (1996)

17. Pflug: Some remarks on the value-at-risk and the conditional value-at-risk. In: Uryasev, S. (ed.) Probabilistic Constrained Optimization Methodology and Applications, pp. 272–281. Kluwer, Dordrecht (2000)
18. Sen: On the Bahadur representation of sample quantiles for sequences of phi-mixing random variables. J. Multivariate Anal. 2, 77–95 (1972)
19. Serfling: Approximation Theorems of Mathematical Statistics. Wiley, New York (1980)
20. Trindade, Uryasev, Shapiro, Zrazhevsky: Financial prediction with constrained tail risk. J. Banking Finance 31, 3524–3538 (2007)
21. Zazanis, Suri: Convergence rates of finite-difference sensitivities estimates for stochastic systems. Operations Research 41, 694–703 (1993)

Appendix

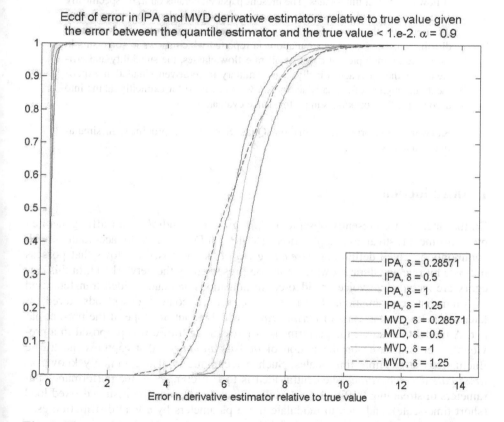

Fig. 1. The empirical cdf of the bias of the derivative estimates for both the MVD and IPA estimators, with $\alpha = 0.90$ and $\delta = 2/7, 1/2, 1, 5/4$

Performance Evaluation of Multi-rate Streaming Traffic by Quasi-Stationary Modelling

Philippe Olivier

France Telecom, Orange Labs
CORE/TPN Laboratory, 38-40 rue du Général Leclerc
92794 Issy-les-Moulineaux Cedex 9, France
phil.olivier@orange-ftgroup.com

Abstract. A Quasi-Stationary approach to evaluate streaming traffic performance was recently proposed, which combines in a simple way the traffic variations
at flow and packet time-scales. The present paper elaborates on it, by specifically
focusing on the multi-class/multi-rate aspects of the model. A first original contribution is the theoretical description of flow peak rates in terms of a continuous
distribution. Then, a set of simulations is reported which shows in some simple
cases, e.g., a multiplex of constant bit rate flow classes, the suitability and efficiency of the approach. Finally, a preliminary trace-driven simulation experiment, although not fully satisfactory, shows some need for explicitly taking into
account the flow peak rates in performance evaluation.

Keywords: Performance evaluation, Quasi-Stationary approximation, simulation, streaming traffic.

1 Introduction

On the Internet, we presently observe a rapid growth of audio/video traffic generated
by real-time or streaming applications (VoIP, VoD, TV,...). In accordance with
commonly accepted definitions, *streaming traffic* is composed of flows that possess
intrinsic bit rate and duration which must be preserved by the network [1]. In this category are included all voice or video communications and audio/video transfers used
for immediate consumption. Note that video, or other content, downloads stored for
later use belong to the class of *elastic traffic* which is out of scope of the present paper. A model to evaluate the performance of streaming traffic was proposed in a previous paper [2], based on the notion of *quasi-stationarity*, that captures the traffic
fluctuations at multiple time-scales. Such a technique is also commonly known as
time-scale decomposition. The central idea is to first compute some performance parameters of streaming traffic using a packet-level model under an assumed fixed load
(short time-scale), and then to modulate these parameters by a load distribution estimated through a flow-level traffic model (long time-scale).

Recent related works have mainly used the Quasi-Stationary (QS) approach for
performance evaluation of integrated streaming and elastic traffics in IP [1][6] or
wireless networks [4][14]. The QS approximation in those cases benefits from the different time-scales which characterize the respective dynamics of streaming and elastic

R. Núñez-Queija and J. Resing (Eds.): NET-COOP 2009, LNCS 5894, pp. 30–44, 2009.
© Springer-Verlag Berlin Heidelberg 2009

flows. For instance, Web-browsing flow-level dynamics occur at a much shorter time-scale than those of voice or video calls. In the present paper, differing from these works although applying the same idea, the QS approximation makes use of the different time-scales of flow-level and packet-level dynamics in IP traffic. Moreover, the focus is on streaming traffic only. A similar approach was followed, with more restricted scope, to evaluate cell loss of Variable Bit Rate (VBR) video traffic in ATM networks [7] or to dimension VoIP-dedicated network links [10].

The theoretical basis for QS modelling was presented in detail in [2]. The present paper further investigates the approach, putting special emphasis on the peak rate properties of flows within the traffic aggregate. The first aim is to provide deeper insight in the multi-class handling aspect of the model, specifically in the way the global performance parameters may be evaluated via weighted sums of the parameters conditioned on local load. We then extend the discrete description of multi-class traffic to a continuous description involving a spectrum of flow internal bit rates, mainly in order to handle traffic aggregates with not well-known traffic composition.

The second main objective is to provide simulation results in order to support the approach. A first set of experiments, very simple and involving a multiplex of multi-class, multi-rate, Constant Bit Rate (CBR) flows, is designed to validate the assumptions themselves of the QS model. Another experiment is presented, maybe more ambitious but rather in a preliminary state. Its purpose is to use trace-driven simulations in order to check the continuous state approach previously described, and to apply the QS model on a very general traffic mix.

The rest of the paper is organized as follows. The theoretical framework and general principles of QS modelling are recalled in Section 2. The definition of performance indicators for streaming traffic is provided in Section 3, both at the flow and packet levels. In Section 4, the principles and results of simulations are presented. Section 5 summarizes the main contributions and concludes the paper.

2 Theoretical Model

2.1 General Principles

The QS assumption allows analyzing the superposition of long-term rate fluctuations of traffic due to the dynamics of flow transfers and short-term variations at packet level. A succession of stationary states is assumed, each with a constant rate, or a constant number of flows, within which packet-level traffic can be viewed as a local stochastic process in equilibrium and independent from each flow state to another [6].

Let $R(t)$ denote the long-term, time-varying, bit rate of the overall aggregated traffic offered to a link of capacity C (bits/s). The process $R(t)$ is assumed stationary (in the long term) and to follow some statistical distribution of density $P(R)$. For a given bit rate R, $Q(R)$ will denote a generic probabilistic packet-level performance indicator only conditioned on the total bit rate: packet loss probability, mean waiting delay, or extreme delay probability (jitter). The QS principle uses the theorem of total probabilities to obtain the overall performance indicator Q by unconditioning $Q(R)$ over all possible states (we purposely keep the probability state measure written as it is in (1), instead of $P(R).dR$, for reasons which will appear later):

$$Q = \int_R Q(R) \cdot d(\Pr \{\text{state} = R\}) . \tag{1}$$

2.2 Multi-class Discrete Description

We focus here on a multi-class, multi-rate, traffic process and thus adopt a discrete formulation. Traffic on the considered link is a multiplex of J classes of flows, each of them evolving according to a total bit rate R_j. The system is characterized by a very general state vector $n = (n_j)$ of the number of flows of class j, $j=1,J$, distributed according to some stationary state probabilities $\pi(n)$. The total bit rate is $R(n) = \sum_{j=1,J} R_j(n)$ at each state, and its distribution is named $\Pi(R)$ (note the distinct notation from the density $P(R)$ in the continuous state case).

Class-based performance. Consider as above some (packet-level) probabilistic performance parameter $Q_j(n)$, depending on state n. The performance, for instance the mean packet delay, refers to the mean delay experienced by the whole set of class-j packets, and not the mean delay seen by an outside observer. Hence we must deal with stationary state probabilities, which we denote by $\pi_j(n)$, measured from an arbitrary, random, element of class j. Thus, the overall performance Q_j for class-j packets writes, as a discrete instance of the general Quasi-Stationary formulation (1):

$$Q_j = \sum_n \pi_j(n) Q_j(n) . \tag{2}$$

The index j in (2) will be omitted when the performance is to be evaluated for all packets of the traffic aggregate. Suppose now that flow classes have constant bit rates $R_j(n)$ at each state n. The class-based state probabilities $\pi_j(n)$ are then proportional to both the class rates $R_j(n)$ and the outside observer state probabilities $\pi(n)$, as can be rigorously established by the following reasoning. Under the "natural" assumption that flow rate processes are ergodic, the state probabilities can be calculated as asymptotic time averages. Thus, (i) consider a long observation time, (ii) compute the cumulative time duration and number of class-j bits associated to a given state n, and then (iii) let the observation time tend to infinity so as to estimate the state probabilities $\pi(n)$ and $\pi_j(n)$ as time ratio and bit ratio limits, respectively. This provides the sought relationship between the two kinds of state probabilities:

$$\pi_j(n) = \frac{R_j(n)}{E[R_j]} . \pi(n) , \quad n = (n_j), _{j=1,J} .$$

Then we get the overall performance: $Q_j = \dfrac{1}{E[R_j]} \sum_n R_j(n) \pi(n) Q_j(n) . \tag{3}$

Similarly, we get the overall performance for the whole traffic aggregate:

$$Q = \frac{1}{E[R]} \sum_R R \Pi(R) Q(R) . \tag{4}$$

Consider now two simple cases of application of (3): that of a class whose bit rate is independent of system state n and that of classes composed of CBR flows.

Class j whose rate R_j is independent of state n. We thus have $R_j(n) = E[R_j]$ and the state probabilities as viewed from class-j packets are equal to the stationary flow state probabilities. In this case, the overall performance indicator Q_j is given like in (2), but with $\pi_j(n) = \pi(n)$ as if we did not care about class-based state probabilities. This is the situation, for instance, when we study VoIP performance in a multimedia traffic aggregate within which the weight of voice traffic can be considered negligible.

J classes composed of CBR flows. Individual flow bit rates are r_j, $j=1,J$, and the total bit rate is $R = \sum_{j=1,J} n_j r_j$. The flow process evolves according to the stationary state probabilities $\pi(n) = \pi(n_1,...,n_J)$ over all feasible states n, i.e., those states which fulfil the requirement $n \cdot r = \sum_{j=1,J} n_j r_j \leq C$ when Admission Control (AC) is applied (if not, no limit is set on the flow state space). In the case where flows arrive according to independent Poisson processes, the state probabilities simply write as:

$$\pi(n) = \pi(0) \prod_{j=1,J} \frac{A_j^{n_j}}{n_j!}, \quad (n \cdot r \leq C), \tag{5}$$

where A_j is the traffic offered by class-j flows. The probability $\pi(0)$ is obtained, as usually, from the normalization condition that all feasible state probabilities sum to 1.

Note that, for present purposes, we do not need to compute all state probabilities; only those of the total bit rate are required. When all rate parameters, C and $(r_j)_{j=1,J}$, can be assumed integers, we conveniently use the Kaufman-Roberts (K-R) recursion formula [9][13] to compute the state probabilities $\Pi(R)$ of the ordered total bit rates:

$$\Pi(R) = \frac{1}{R} \sum_{j=1,J} A_j r_j \Pi(R - r_j). \tag{6}$$

When there is no AC, which will be the case in the rest of the study, we show that the overall performance (3) for one given class j can be transformed into a rate-shifted version of the overall performance with uniform weighting. The local equilibrium equation $n_j \pi(n) = A_j \pi(n - e_j)$ holds for each state n and each class j in this case (e_j is the unit vector in the jth direction of the flow state vector n). The desired expression is deduced, following a derivation similar to that of the K-R recursion formula:

$$Q_j = \sum_R \Pi(R) Q_j(R + r_j). \tag{7}$$

From (4) and (7), we may guess that possible performance discrepancies between two classes of traffic, or between one class and the whole traffic, should be weak in most cases unless the bit rates r_j are not too low compared to the link capacity C. This will be checked later, in Section 4.2.

Let us now derive a useful relation between total rate statistics and those of flow constant rate, which holds when all numbers of class-j flows are independent and

Poisson distributed. According to the independence assumption, the variance of total bit rate is:

$$\text{Var}[R] = \sum_{j=1,J} \text{Var}[n_j r_j] = \sum_{j=1,J} \text{Var}[n_j] r_j^2 . \tag{8}$$

A *bit-wise* weight of class j is defined as $\alpha_j = \text{E}[R_j]/\text{E}[R]$, which can be seen as the probability that any random element of information, bit, byte (or packet if packet length is constant), pertains to class j. We then define a bit-wise probability distribution function f of flow peak rate r using δ, the Dirac function at r_j location:

$$f(r) = \sum_{j=1,J} \alpha_j \delta(r - r_j) .$$

The mean value of this distribution is: $\text{E}[r] = \sum_{j=1,J} \alpha_j r_j = \dfrac{1}{\text{E}[R]} \sum_{j=1,J} \text{E}[n_j] r_j^2$.

Combining the last equation with (8) and recalling that $\text{Var}[n_j] = \text{E}[n_j]$, since all numbers of class-j flows are Poisson distributed, we get the very simple result that the dispersion of total bit rate, DSP$[R]$, equals the bit-wise mean value of flow bit rates:

$$\text{DSP}[R] = \frac{\text{Var}[R]}{\text{E}[R]} = \text{E}[r] . \tag{9}$$

2.3 Multi-rate Continuous Description

Return to the general framework in terms of a continuous description of bit rates. First, in order to cover all preceding weights necessary to compute the overall performance, we call $G(R)$ the general form of the weighting function. In other words, $d(\Pr\{\text{state} = R\}) = G(R)P(R)dR$ is the state probability density measured in the packet space. Thus, omitting for simplicity the possible index j when the performance is to be evaluated for class-j packets, the overall performance indicator in the general case can be written as:

$$Q = \int_R Q(R) G(R) P(R) dR . \tag{10}$$

In [2], the importance of the weighting function $G(R)$ was illustrated with the example of fluid packet loss. To summarize, if the packet loss at total rate R is $P_L(R) = (R - C)^+$ / R, where $(X)^+$ denotes max$(X, 0)$, then with, and *only with*, the weighting function $G(R) = R/\text{E}[R]$ as in (4), the overall packet loss probability becomes:

$$P_L = \frac{1}{\text{E}[R]} \int_R (R - C)^+ P(R) dR = \frac{\text{E}[(R - C)^+]}{\text{E}[R]} . \tag{11}$$

Adopt now a continuous rate description, not only for the total bit rate, but also for the flow peak rates, in order to generalize the statistical relation (9) derived in the case of discrete multi-class traffic. We let the number of classes in the discrete model tend to infinity so as to handle infinitesimal classes, each of them composed of constant rate flows. The purpose is to handle aggregates of VBR flows when the traffic composition and rate fluctuations are not well known, and to get in such cases a representation model which nevertheless allows QS modelling. In particular, we will take into account the possible occurrence of high flow peak rates within the traffic mix.

Assume a continuous spectrum of peak rates r in the interval $[r_{min}; r_{max}]$ obviously included in $[0; C]$ where C is the link bit rate. Define as $dn(r)$ the (stochastic) infinitesimal number of flows with rate r at a given random time. In analogy with the discrete case above, each of this process is supposed to be Poisson and independent to the other ones. Of course, these are strong assumptions, but they are quite unavoidable in order to proceed with the analysis. The following relations may be written:

- The instantaneous total bit rate is: $R = \int_r r\, dn(r)$.

- The probability mass of peak rate on $[r; r + dr]$, the equivalent of class weight α_j, is:

$$f(r)dr = \frac{r}{E[R]} . E[dn(r)].$$

$f(r)$ is thus the probability density function of peak rate, as measured from traffic elements, bytes or bits. Assuming the variance property of superposed independent processes still holds in the asymptotic continuous case, we get:

$$\text{Var}[R] = \int_r \text{Var}[r\, dn(r)] = \int_r r^2\, \text{Var}[dn(r)].$$

Then, $\text{Var}[R] = \int_r r^2\, E[dn(r)] = \int_r E[R]\, r\, f(r)dr$, recalling the Poisson assumption on $dn(r)$, and finally: $\text{Var}[R] = E[R].E[r]$. Therefore, (9) still holds in the continuous rate description. This is an important relationship which tells us that the statistical dispersion of the *flow-level bit rate* equals the mean *packet-level peak rate*. It is particularly useful for Gaussian modelling of the total bit rate: the rate distribution is entirely specified by its mean (the average rate observed during a busy-hour time interval) and its variance. The latter is obtained, via the dispersion (9), from the mean peak rate which in turn may be estimated by rather simple analysis of the packet arrival process within flows, according to an adequate definition of flows, see Section 4.3.

3 Key Performance Indicators

3.1 Flow-Level Performance

In the case of a single class of flows with constant bit rate, such as voice calls or video streams with constant bit rate coding, the state probabilities $\pi(n)$ of the number of flows in progress follow well-known distributions [5], as long as the total traffic process results from the superposition of independent individual demands, arriving at exponentially distributed intervals: a Poisson, Binomial, Erlang or Engset distribution, according to whether the source population is of finite or infinite size, and whether an AC procedure is in action or not.

At the flow level, the blocking probability is the adequate performance indicator when AC is deployed. It is given by the Erlang-B or the Engset formula [5] in the case of infinite or finite-size population, respectively. In the multi-rate flow model, a per-class blocking probability may be defined as $P_B(j) = \sum_{n \cdot r \leq C < n \cdot r + r_j} \pi(n)$.

Alternatively, when there is no AC, the adequate flow-level performance indicator is the probability of link congestion. Link congestion states lead to very poor traffic performance where, in particular, the link buffer is almost permanently saturated. Consistently with previous considerations on the weighting function $G(R)$, we provide more specific definitions of the congestion probability, compared to the simple probability (from an outside observer) that total rate is greater than link capacity. In the continuous and discrete state descriptions, the definitions write as (12) and (13). Note that, with Poisson flows, a practical simplification also holds for expression (13) which only requires the computation of total rate probability distribution, as in (7).

$$P_C \equiv \int_C^\infty G(R) P(R) dR \,, \tag{12}$$

$$P_{C,j} \equiv \frac{1}{E[R_j]} \sum_{R(n) \geq C} R_j(n) \pi(n) \,. \tag{13}$$

3.2 Packet-Level Performance

The Key Performance Indicators (KPIs) that are generally considered to qualify the QoS of streaming services are the packet loss probability, mean packet delay and jitter, the variation of delay. Jitter will be defined here as some quantile, say 99%, of the packet delay distribution, among various possible definitions mentioned in [8]. The subject of KPI targets for voice and video communications will not be addressed here, since they are generally formulated End-to-End. Dealing with one network resource only (one IP link), we rather consider a much smaller part of the parameter budget, e.g. an order of magnitude of 1 ms or 10 ms for packet delay.

Infinite buffer length. We first consider the delay created by an infinite buffer. (There is no loss in this case.) A convenient tool here is the probability that packet waiting time exceeds a specified target, obtained through the complementary cumulative distribution function (ccdf) of packet waiting time. Fixed-length clients queuing systems are considered in the following, so that waiting times x may be measured in packet units. The ccdf of packet waiting time is named as: $Q(x) \equiv \Pr\{X > x\}$. Note that we omit in all what follows, like in (10), any possible index j denoting class-j performance evaluation. This does not change the reasoning and results as long as class-j local performance only depends on the total bit rate at any given state, which is one permanent assumption in the presented QS approach.

In [2], specific models have been developed for VoIP traffic in isolation and for the general case of multiservice streaming traffic. We now give for the latter the salient features of packet delay performance computation. The central point is to approximate the packet delay ccdf by that of an upper-bound M/D/1 queue: for any given load $\rho = R / C$, we apply the principle of negligible jitter conjectured in [3], according to which the waiting delay of streaming packets is always less than that provided by an M/D/1/FIFO queue fed by Maximum Time Unit (MTU) packets, 1500 Bytes in general, at same load.

We then apply the general QS formulation given by (10) where $Q(R,x)$, replacing $Q(R)$, denotes the ccdf of packet waiting time conditioned on the current bit rate R. When $R \geq C$, the load is greater than 1, the queue is unstable and no stationary regime occurs (there may be some exceptions in the critical regime where $R = C$). Thus, the probability of exceeding any finite target x is always equal to 1. This provides a trivial upper bound to the waiting time ccdf in overload. Equation (10) may then be re-formulated in the following form, with a bounded integration interval:

$$Q(x) \leq Q_{\sup}(x) = 1 + \int_0^C (Q(R,x) - 1) G(R) P(R) dR . \tag{14}$$

The upper bound $Q_{\sup}(x)$ converges towards a strictly positive limit when target delay x tends to infinity: when $R < C$, the queue length has a finite stationary regime and the ccdf $Q(R,x)$ tends to 0. We deduce:

$$Q_{\sup}(x) \xrightarrow[x \to \infty]{} \int_C^\infty G(R) P(R) dR . \tag{15}$$

The limit is exactly the above-defined link congestion probability P_C (12). This gives prominent importance to this parameter, as representative of extreme delay probability. It will thus be included in the considered KPIs in the simulation results section below. Besides, (15) shows that the (upper-bound) waiting time distribution has an atom in $+\infty$; as a consequence, all its moments are infinite, particularly the mean and variance. This drawback is alleviated by considering a finite buffer.

Finite buffer length. We consider a queue with maximum size $K + 1$ packets (K waiting positions and 1 service position). For any given load R / C, the queue in this case admits a stationary regime. Packet loss $P_K(R)$ at each load can be computed as the result of an M/D/1/K queue [5]. Then, letting the total bit rate R vary, the overall packet loss probability P_K is obtained by formula (10). Regarding the packet delay distribution $Q_K(x)$ conditioned on packet acceptance, the general form of QS equation (10) has to be re-written, taking into account the loss probabilities P_K and $P_K(R)$:

$$Q_K(x) = \frac{1}{1 - P_K} \int_R Q_K(R,x)(1 - P_K(R)) G(R) P(R) dR . \tag{16}$$

We approximate the packet waiting time by K when the load exceeds 1, since in such situations the buffer is almost permanently saturated. This at least is a conservative upper bound. Hence, when $R > C$, $Q_K(R,x) = 1$ for all $x < K$. When the load is less than 1, we approximate the ccdf of packet waiting time by the truncation at K of the corresponding ccdf with an infinite buffer. The waiting time of any random packet in a GI/G/1/K queue is always less than in the corresponding GI/G/1 queue, conditionally to its acceptation (see [2] for detailed explanations). We thus get:

$$Q_K(x) \leq \frac{Q(x) - P_K}{1 - P_K}, \quad 0 \leq x < K. \tag{17}$$

The main practical interest of this upper-bound lies in the fact that waiting time distributions are much more difficult to obtain for finite queues than for infinite queues (see the M/D/1 example). Once $Q(x)$ is computed, so is $Q_K(x)$ for any buffer size, provided the packet loss (not so prominent indeed, in most cases) is also known.

4 Simulations

The QS assumption requires that the two time-scales of flows and packets are well separated. A rough estimate of the flow to packet time-scale ratio is the mean number of packets per flow. We verified in [2] and in further experiments that the latter should be set to buffer length at the minimum, in order to reach stationarity at packet level within each flow state. For streaming services (VoIP, VoD, TV), flow length is high enough in most cases. For signalling traffic or highly interactive transfers (Web, gaming, etc.), it is less probable that this requirement is fulfilled. Hence QS models appear well adapted to packet-level performance evaluation of streaming traffic.

4.1 Single Class Traffic

We performed simple event-driven simulations, using the MATLAB® software, to generate flows and packets without any protocol environment since we deal with open-loop traffic. In each experiment, flow length is exponentially distributed with a mean value greater than buffer size, so as to fulfil the above requirement. Moreover, simulation times were long enough, more than 5 million packets were generated, to ensure statistical validity of both flow and packet-related distributions.

We first aim at assessing the effectiveness of the QS approach for a single class of traffic. A finite FIFO queue is fed by Poisson streams of CBR flows composed of regularly spaced fixed length packets, i.e., typical of VoIP calls. The buffer size is equal to the link capacity, defined as the link speed to flow bit rate ratio.

Fig. 1 provides the obtained KPIs, congestion probability, packet loss, mean packet delay and jitter as defined in §3.2, for a range of loads between 0.6 and 1 on a 10 Mbps link fed by 100 Kbps voice calls. Thus link capacity is 100, a low value which provides a kind of worst case. Clearly, the agreement between model and simulation results is very good, showing in this case the soundness of principles and assumptions of the QS model: (i) conditioning the probabilistic performance parameters on the elementary stationary processes; (ii) ignoring the transient phases linked to the time-scale separation between flow and packet dynamics; and (iii) considering an upper-bound to the packet delay in the finite buffer size case. Moreover, it can be observed that the waiting delay quantile (jitter) is particularly useful for link dimensioning regarding its quasi-binary behaviour with a sharp transition phase, as also noticed in [2].

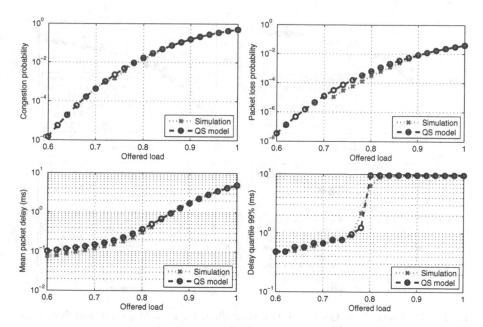

Fig. 1. Comparison of the QS model with simulations for a 10 Mbps link and a single class of traffic composed of VoIP calls at 100 Kbps

4.2 Multi-class Traffic

Consider now a multi-class traffic scenario. The link speed is 10 Mbps and three traffic classes are offered with peak rates 100 Kbps, 1 Mbps and 4 Mbps, representative of VoIP calls, streaming VoD and TV channels, respectively. The link capacity, referring to the lower peak rate, is thus equal to 100. Fig. 2 provides the obtained KPIs for a range of loads between 0 and 1. We notice that with such a small capacity, e.g., typical of an access or a second-grade backhaul link, performance discrepancies between traffic classes can be observed. For higher link speeds, it was checked (not shown to save place) that performance among classes is hardly distinguishable.

On the plots of Fig. 2, the agreement between model and simulations is reasonably good, thus validating the QS assumptions specific to the multi-class analysis: (i) the local performance is independent of classes and is only driven by the total bit rate; and (ii) performance differentiation is provided only by the flow-level state distribution. However, regarding the latter, the difference is not that important. This justifies the modelling approach taken in the following section, where the traffic aggregate is considered as a whole without considering separate discrete classes.

4.3 Trace-Driven Simulation

The purpose of the trace-driven experiment is to check the validity of our "continuous spectrum of bit rates" approach. We seek to apply the QS model assuming a Gaussian distribution of the aggregated bit rate, where the mean and variance will be provided by the above analysis applied to the data trace, see Section 2.3 and (9) in particular.

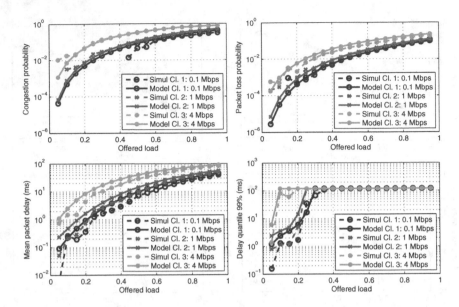

Fig. 2. Comparison of the QS model with simulations for a 10 Mbps link and three traffic classes with peak rates 100 Kbps, 1 Mbps and 4 Mbps, respectively

Data trace analysis. The data trace we used was collected on one site of the France Telecom IP network [11]. The trace of nearly 2 hours was obtained in September 2005 on a backbone link connecting a Point of Presence (POP) in Paris to an overseas POP located in La Reunion Island, actually serving ADSL subscribers in majority. The downstream traffic alone was captured on two link interfaces at 155 Mbps on which traffic load is equally shared. The results shown below concern one of these links only. The main reasons to study this particular data set are: (i) due to scarcity of resource for this type of link, the traffic load is rather high, about 0.7, in nominal conditions, which is not common in backbone networks; (ii) a wide range of flow peak rates are observed, as pointed out soon, which makes sense in the present study.

The Gaussian approximation for long-term bit rate fluctuations is well accepted concerning backbone links with a high level of traffic aggregation, see [15] and references therein. However, the crucial problem remains of estimating the variance of the Gaussian distribution, which is critically linked to the chosen integration time. This is typically illustrated in Fig. 3 where the variance of total bit rate is plotted in logarithmic scale versus the integration time, on a range $[10^{-4}$ s; 10 s], from a sub-sample of our data set. A linear fit is provided, together with a comparison with an ideal Poisson process for which the decreasing rate is -1. Here, due to correlations at the packet level induced by flow-level fluctuations, the variance decreasing rate is lower. Such a variance-time plot is a classical tool used in packet network traffic analyses which aim at identifying self-similar, or more generally scale-based, phenomena [12].

Without any further knowledge on traffic composition, the choice of integration time should be arbitrary, and so the performance parameters eventually derived from the QS model. The peak rate analysis developed in Section 2.3 will provide a convenient way to solve the problem.

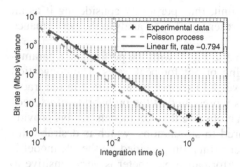
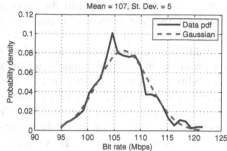

Fig. 3. Variance-time plot of the total bit rate from trace – Mean total bit rate = 107 Mbps

Fig. 4. Distribution of the total bit rate sampled and averaged at 0.1 s scale

We first select a reasonable, and somewhat arbitrary, integration time of 0.1 s and then compute the distribution of total bit rate. The distribution is well fitted by a Gaussian law, see Fig. 4, and its statistical dispersion is about 0.23 Mbps. This will be (abusively) referred to as the "No Peak Rate" (No PR) scenario in the following.

Then, we estimate the distribution of flow internal peak rates. A flow is defined at the user level, which was found to be most suitable for traffic analysis [11], in particular due to the fact that, with such a definition, flows tend to arrive according to Poisson processes (contrary to, e.g., micro-flows defined at the UDP or TCP connection level [12]). A flow is thus defined as a set of packets with the same IP *destination address* since, on a backbone link, there is no more explicit user identifier at our disposal, and since we consider the downstream link only.

Within each flow, instantaneous peak rates are estimated packet-to-packet, and then gathered among all identified flows in order to compute the overall distribution of peak rates. The ccdf is plotted in Fig. 5, which reveals that about 3% of packets are transmitted at nearly the link speed and almost 10% at a peak rate greater than 10 Mbps. Note that an almost identical distribution was obtained on the companion link.

These very high rate bursts most probably are created by the queuing process at the router output; nevertheless, they suggest the presence of bursts, of which peak rates may be higher than link speed, at the router ingress. A more detailed investigation on the characteristics and possible origins of such high peak rates is out of scope of the paper. We only focus on the proper way to take them into account in the evaluation of traffic performance. From the distribution in Fig. 5, we obtain a mean peak rate of 16 Mbps when bit-weighting is applied, as required in the model; this value will provide the dispersion of the flow-level bit rate in the "Peak Rate" (PR) scenario of the QS model, according to (9).

Simulation experiment. All the packets of the traffic sample are used to feed a single server FIFO queue with different values of service speed, ranging from 100 to 160 Mbps. Recall the mean carried traffic is 107 Mbps and the actual link capacity is 155 Mbps, so there is no point in increasing the simulated link speed any further. The buffer size is set to a quite low value, 1 ms, in order to be roughly compatible with the expected lengths of high peak rate bursts within flows. It is essential to keep in mind that the stream of time-stamped packets in each case, i.e., for each simulated link speed, is offered unchanged to the service unit, thus purposely considering it as an open-loop, or exogenous, traffic since the present goal is to analyse the performance of unresponsive traffic.

Simulation results are compared in Fig. 6 and Fig. 7 with the performance parameters provided by both QS models, accounting or not for peak rates. The congestion probability is not plotted since this flow-level KPI cannot be measured in the trace-driven simulation; besides, in Fig. 7, jitter is represented as the probability of exceeding an extreme packet delay, here 0.5 ms. We observe that QS models always provide upper-bound estimates of the KPIs, compared to simulations, which is desirable for the sake of conservativeness. However, overestimation provided by the PR model is too high, especially for packet loss. This performance parameter is very sensitive to buffer size indeed, at least in simulations. Packet delay is less sensitive to buffer size, as can be inferred from (17), and is rather well predicted by the PR model at very high loads (link capacity less than 110 Mbps, say), contrary to the No PR model which excessively overestimates simulation results in this area. The latter seems to be due to the fact that, with the QS model not accounting for peak rates, the spread of the flow-level rate distribution is quite low (variance = 0.23 Mbps x mean) so that, in overload scenarios, the probability of link congestion is very close to 1 and then the buffer is almost permanently saturated.

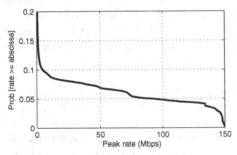

Fig. 5. Cumulative distribution of internal flow peak rates from a trace sub-sample

Fig. 6. Comparison of packet loss as provided by the trace-driven simulation and the QS model accounting or not for peak rates

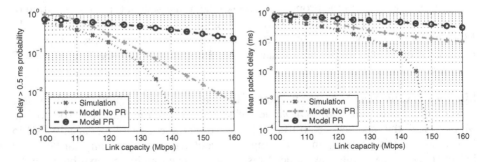

Fig. 7. Comparison of jitter and mean packet delay as provided by the trace-driven simulation and the QS model accounting or not for peak rates

These are somewhat preliminary results and we must admit they are not completely convincing. We might say they are nevertheless encouraging in the sense that the need to take flow peak rates into account, one way or another, is clearly shown, even if a fully satisfactory way of handling it is still to be found.

5 Conclusion

In this paper, further investigation of the QS modelling approach was performed for performance evaluation of streaming traffic. The main achievements are:

- New insight was provided with respect to multi-class handling, particularly in the distinction between different packet weighting functions to consider when evaluating the overall performance parameters.
- Flow peak rates are parameters of fundamental importance since they govern the traffic fluctuations at flow level; their impact on expected performance was characterized within a continuous spectrum description of bit rate variations.
- Simulation experiments were designed to validate the QS approach. The accordance between theory and simulation was excellent for a single class of CBR flows, and quite good for a multi-rate traffic multiplex.

These observations and results tell us that the QS model is a suitable and efficient approach to analyze the performance of streaming traffic, which is by essence unresponsive and made of long enough flows compared to buffer size, and then to dimension network links accordingly. Further work should essentially consist in consolidating the trace-driven simulation approach, in order to compare with real traffic performance, since the preliminary attempt shown here was not fully satisfactory. At least it showed the need for some way of taking flow peak rates into account.

Acknowledgments. The author is grateful to S. Oueslati and T. Bonald, from Orange Labs, for many fruitful discussions; he also greatly acknowledges the comments and suggestions from reviewers which helped to improve the paper in several respects.

References

1. Benameur, N., Ben Fredj, S., Delcoigne, F., Oueslati-Boulahia, S., Roberts, J.W.: Integrated admission control for streaming and elastic traffic. In: Smirnov, M., Crowcroft, J., Roberts, J., Boavida, F. (eds.) QofIS 2001. LNCS, vol. 2156, pp. 69–81. Springer, Heidelberg (2001)
2. Bonald, T., Olivier, P.: Quasi-Stationary models for performance analysis of real-time traffic. In: Proc. of the 18th ITC Specialist Seminar on Quality of Experience, Karlskrona, Sweden, pp. 135–144 (2008)
3. Bonald, T., Proutière, A., Roberts, J.W.: Statistical performance guarantees for streaming flows using Expedited Forwarding. In: Proc. of IEEE INFOCOM 2001 (2001)
4. Borst, S., Hegde, N.: Integration of Streaming and Elastic Traffic in Wireless Networks. In: Proc. of IEEE INFOCOM 2007, pp. 1884–1892 (2007)
5. Cooper, R.: Introduction to Queueing Theory, 2nd edn. Elsevier, North Holland, Amsterdam (1981)

6. Delcoigne, F., Proutière, A., Régnié, G.: Modeling integration of streaming and data traffic. Performance Evaluation 55(3-4), 185–209 (2004)
7. Frater, M.R., Rose, O.: Cell loss analysis of broadband switching systems carrying variable bit rate video traffic. Telecommunication Systems 4(1), 318–338 (1995)
8. ITU-T, Recommendation Y.1540: Internet protocol data communication service - IP packet transfer and availability performance parameters (2002)
9. Kaufman, J.S.: Blocking in a shared resource environment. IEEE Trans. Comm. 29, 1474–1481 (1981)
10. Lindberg, P.: Some dimensioning models for IP telephony. In: Proc. of Networks 1998, Sorrento, Italy, pp. 457–462 (1998)
11. Olivier, P.: Internet data flow characterization and bandwidth sharing modelling. In: Proc. of ITC' 20, Ottawa, Canada, pp. 986–997 (2007)
12. Paxson, V., Floyd, S.: Wide-area traffic: the failure of Poisson modelling. IEEE/ACM Trans. Networking 3(3), 226–244 (1995)
13. Roberts, J.W.: A service system with heterogeneous user requirement. In: Pujolle, G. (ed.) Performance of Data Communications Systems and Their Applications, pp. 423–431. North-Holland, Amsterdam (1981)
14. Tan, H.-P., Nuñez-Queija, R., Gabor, A.F., Boxma, O.J.: Admission control for differentiated services in future generation CDMA networks. Performance Evaluation 66, 488–504 (2009)
15. van den Berg, H., Mandjes, M., van de Meent, R., Pras, A., Roijers, F., Venemans, P.: QoS-aware bandwidth provisioning of IP links. Computer Networks 50, 631–647 (2006)

On Opportunistic Cooperation for Improving the Stability Region with Multipacket Reception*

Beiyu Rong and Anthony Ephremides

Department of Electrical and Computer Engineering
University of Maryland, College Park, MD 20742, USA
{byrong,etony}@umd.edu

Abstract. We investigate the composite effects of multipacket reception (MPR) and relaying capability in affecting the stability region of a wireless network. With a general MPR channel, a trade-off arises as to whether to activate the relay simultaneously with the source so that both transmissions might be successful, or to let the relay remain silent to overhear the source's transmission and then activate the cooperation. As such, we consider a two-user multiple-access system where the user with a better user-destination channel may act as the relay for the other. An opportunistic cooperation scheme through scheduling the relay's transmission is proposed. Then the optimal scheduling probability for maximizing the stability region is characterized, and the corresponding stability region is derived. We show that the stability region of the opportunistic scheme may be convex under certain channel conditions, and may strictly outer-bound the stability region of the conventional cooperation scheme.

Keywords: Cooperative relaying, multipacket reception, opportunistic scheduling, stability region, queueing theory.

1 Introduction

Cooperative relaying has been widely acknowledged as an important tool to provide spatial diversity and enhance communication rates in wireless networks. Users can overhear the transmission from other users due to the wireless multicast advantage of the medium, and hence, have the capability to relay messages for each other. This relaying idea was first exploited at the physical layer, wherein performance metrics, such as Shannon capacity, are studied using information-theoretical formulations [1, 2, 3]; later, several works investigate such relaying capability at the medium access control (MAC) layer in conjunction with bursty traffic arrivals, and performance gains in terms of stable throughput have been obtained [4, 5, 6, 7]. In some of these works, cognitive cooperation has received attention, in which the cognitive relay senses idle time slots to transmit [4, 5].

* This work was supported by the MURI grant W911NF-08-1-0238.

R. Núñez-Queija and J. Resing (Eds.): NET-COOP 2009, LNCS 5894, pp. 45–59, 2009.
© Springer-Verlag Berlin Heidelberg 2009

Allowing the relay to transmit only when the other user is idle, is motivated by the objective of avoiding interference among multiple simultaneous transmissions which may result in unsuccessful reception of any transmitted packet. However, such destructive interference assumption does not accurately capture the behavior of wireless channels; in wireless environments, a packet might survive the interference caused by concurrent transmissions, if the received Signal-to-Interference-Noise Ratio (SINR) exceeds the threshold required for correct decoding. Furthermore, if the receiver is equipped with a multiuser detector, it may decode packets successfully from more than one transmitter at a time. The multipacket reception (MPR) model has been studied extensively without user cooperation, focusing on the stability issue and on transmission rates [8,9,10,11]. In the cognitive cooperation system where the relay has some chance to capture the other user's transmitted packet and then help to relay that packet, there is a trade-off between the scheduling of simultaneous transmissions with reduced success probability against single transmission.

Based on these considerations, this paper proposes an *opportunistic* scheduling strategy [12,13] at the relay node while taking into account multipacket reception capability. By observing the other user's queue state, the relay is scheduled to transmit with probability p if the other user is transmitting. The relay node is also a user of the network with its own source information to transmit, and it acts as the relay for the user which has a relatively weak user-destination channel. We are interested in characterizing the optimal scheduling probability that maximizes the stability region of the network. The stability region is defined as the set of all arrival rate vectors such that there exists scheduling probability $p \in [0, 1]$ under which all queues remain bounded. The reader is referred to [14] for a precise technical definition of queueing stability. We show that by optimally choosing the scheduling probability, which in general is a function of the arrival rate, the stability region can be a convex polyhedral region for certain channels; this strictly contains the stability region of the conflict-free scheduling which is bounded by a straight line.

When transmission at the relay is allowed concurrently with transmission from the source, the nodes access the channel via a *partial* random access fashion. The stability analysis regarding random access is known to be very difficult even for the simple collision channel model; due to this difficulty, we consider only the two-user case, for which the closed form of the stability region is obtained explicitly. We should remark here that although the motivating reason for cooperation is not discussed, the fact that all users can simultaneously increase their stable throughput rates when cooperation is used can serve as a motivation for cooperation. Together with opportunistic scheduling, the stability region is further improved over the non-cooperative case under certain channel conditions.

2   System Model

The slotted multiple access channel we consider throughout this paper is shown in Fig. 1. It consists of two source users s_1 and s_2, and a common destination node

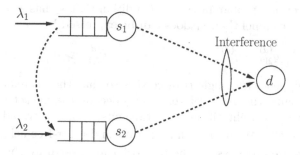

Fig. 1. The slotted two-user multiple access system we study in this paper. User s_2 acts as the relay for s_1. With an MPR channel model, s_2 is scheduled to transmit opportunistically.

d. Packets of fixed length arrive to the source node s_i independently according to a Bernoulli process with rate λ_i (packets per slot) in each time slot, $i \in \{1, 2\}$. The transmission of one packet takes the duration of exactly one time slot, and the packets to be transmitted are stored in the buffer of the source nodes, which are assumed to be of infinite size. The MPR channel model is similar to that specified in [10,11]; given that the set $\mathcal{M}$ of source users transmit, the probability that node n decodes the packet from the source m (for $m \in \mathcal{M}$) is denoted by:

$$q_{m|\mathcal{M}}^{(n)} = \mathbf{P} \,[\text{packet from } m \text{ is received at node } n | \text{users in set } \mathcal{M} \text{ transmit}] \quad (1)$$

This MPR model captures the effects of fading, attenuation and interference at the physical layer. If a packet is not successfully decoded, the receiver simply drops the packet. In the two-user cooperative multiple access channel, the source users are ordered in such a way that s_2 has a better channel to the destination than s_1 does. Thus, s_2 serves to relay s_1's packets if these packets are not decoded by the destination but decoded by s_2 successfully. In such settings, there are five reception probabilities associated with this network, specifically,

$$q_{1|1}^{(d)} = \mathbf{P} \,[\text{packet from } s_1 \text{ is received at } d | \text{ only } s_1 \text{ transmits}]$$

$$q_{2|2}^{(d)} = \mathbf{P} \,[\text{packet from } s_2 \text{ is received at } d | \text{ only } s_2 \text{ transmits}]$$

$$q_{1|1}^{(2)} = \mathbf{P} \,[\text{packet from } s_1 \text{ is received at } s_2 | \text{ only } s_1 \text{ transmits}]$$

$$q_{1|1,2}^{(d)} = \mathbf{P} \,[\text{packet from } s_1 \text{ is received at } d | \text{ both } s_1 \text{ and } s_2 \text{ transmit}]$$

$$q_{2|1,2}^{(d)} = \mathbf{P} \,[\text{packet from } s_2 \text{ is received at } d | \text{ both } s_1 \text{ and } s_2 \text{ transmit}] \quad (2)$$

Because of the interference caused by concurrent transmissions, the probability that a packet transmitted by s_i is decoded by d given that only s_i transmits is larger than the corresponding probability given that both s_1 and s_2 transmit, that is,

$$q_{1|1}^{(d)} > q_{1|1,2}^{(d)} \qquad\qquad q_{2|2}^{(d)} > q_{2|1,2}^{(d)} \qquad (3)$$

With these reception probabilities, the condition that s_2 has a relatively better user-destination channel than s_1 does can be expressed by

$$q_{2|2}^{(d)} > q_{1|1}^{(d)} \qquad\qquad q_{2|1,2}^{(d)} > q_{1|1,2}^{(d)} \qquad\qquad (4)$$

Nodes are equipped with single transceivers so that they cannot transmit and receive at the same time. Therefore, s_2 can decode the packet transmitted by s_1 with positive probability if only s_1 transmits, as is illustrated by the reception probability $q_{1|1}^{(2)}$. We also assume instant and error-free acknowledgements (ACKs), which are broadcast to the network over a separate channel with negligible bandwidth. With all these settings, the relaying process of the network is as follows: when s_1 transmits a packet and s_2 remains silent, if the destination d decodes the packet successfully, it sends back an ACK and the packet exits the network; otherwise, if d doesn't decode the packet but s_2 decodes the packet, s_2 sends back an ACK and queues the packet for retransmission, while s_1 drops that packet upon receiving the ACK from s_2; if neither s_2 nor d decodes the packet, the packet remains at s_1's queue for retransmission later on.

Denote by Q_i^t the length of the queue at s_i in slot t. Then the evolution for Q_i^t has the following form

$$Q_i^{t+1} = [Q_i^t - Y_i^t]^+ + X_i^t \qquad\qquad (5)$$

where X_i^t denotes the number of arrivals in slot t to the queue at s_i, Y_i^t denotes the number of departures from s_i, and $[x]^+$ represents $\max(0, x)$. The queue at s_i is stable if

$$\lim_{t\to\infty} \mathbf{P}\left[Q_i^t < x\right] = F(x) \quad\text{and}\quad \lim_{x\to\infty} F(x) = 1 \qquad\qquad (6)$$

The system is stable if and only if all queues are stable. Under our model, the vector of queue lengths (Q_1^t, Q_2^t) forms an irreducible, aperiodic Markov chain, and system stability is equivalent to the positive recurrence of the Markov chain. When opportunistic scheduling at s_2 is carried out, the queues at s_1 and s_2 interact in a complicated manner which makes the stability analysis difficult to track; we adopt the stochastic dominance approach introduced in [15] to decouple the queues and derive the stability region. For each single queue, a primary tool we use to determine queueing stability is Loynes' Theorem [14], which states that if the arrival and service processes of a queue are strictly stationary and ergodic, the queue is stable if and only if the average total arrival rate is strictly less than the average service rate.

3   Cooperation Schemes and Stability Analysis

To obtain a baseline for the evaluation of the performance of the cooperative system with/without opportunistic scheduling, the stability region of the multiple access system without cooperation is derived first. The two source users access the channel via conflict-free scheduling, and the system is stable if the proportion of time the system is busy is less than 1. Denote by ρ_i the proportion of time source user s_i ($i \in \{1,2\}$) is transmitting; the system is stable if

$$\rho_1 + \rho_2 < 1 \tag{7}$$

where ρ_i is the utilization factor of s_i, given by $\rho_i = \lambda_i/\mu_i$, where λ_i is the average arrival rate to s_i, and μ_i is the average service rate seen by s_i. Without cooperation, each user delivers its packets to the destination by itself, and the successful delivery probability is $q_{i|i}^{(d)}$ as the two users never transmit together. Therefore, the stability region of the non-cooperation scheme (NC) is given by

$$\Re_{\text{NC}} = \left\{ (\lambda_1, \lambda_2) : \frac{\lambda_1}{q_{1|1}^{(d)}} + \frac{\lambda_2}{q_{2|2}^{(d)}} < 1 \right\} \tag{8}$$

In the following part of this section, we carry out the stability analysis with respect to two cooperative communication schemes:

1. Conventional cooperation (CC)
2. Cooperation with opportunistic scheduling based on queue state (C-OPP)

The detailed description of each of the cooperation schemes is provided in the corresponding subsection, and the closed form of the resulting stability region is derived explicitly. In the cooperation scheme C-OPP, the optimal scheduling probability for maximizing the stability region is characterized. It should be noted here that when s_2 transmits a packet, it randomly picks up a packet from its queue, either its own packet or a packet relayed from s_1; we will show that the stability region is the same for both situations.

3.1 CC Scheme

In the conventional cooperation scheme, s_2 accesses the channel only when it senses an idle time slot of s_1 (we assume perfect sensing); s_1 transmits a packet whenever it is backlogged, and if the packet is decoded by either s_2 or the destination d, the packet will be dropped from s_1. Hence, the average service rate seen by s_1 is $\mu_1 = 1 - (1 - q_{1|1}^{(d)})(1 - q_{1|1}^{(2)})$; and by Loynes' Theorem, the stability condition for the queue at s_1 is

$$\lambda_1 < \mu_1 = q_{1|1}^{(2)} + q_{1|1}^{(d)} - q_{1|1}^{(2)} q_{1|1}^{(d)} \tag{9}$$

To determine the stability condition of the queue at s_2, we first need to calculate the average arrival rate to s_2 from s_1. In each time slot, a packet will be relayed to s_2 from s_1 if both of the following two events occur: (1) s_1 is backlogged, which happens with probability λ_1/μ_1, (2) the transmitted packet is decoded by s_2 but not decoded by the destination d. So the average arrival rate to s_2 from s_1 is

$$\lambda_{1 \to 2} = \mathbf{P}\left[Q_1 \neq 0\right] q_{1|1}^{(2)} (1 - q_{1|1}^{(d)}) = \frac{q_{1|1}^{(2)} (1 - q_{1|1}^{(d)})}{q_{1|1}^{(2)} + q_{1|1}^{(d)} - q_{1|1}^{(2)} q_{1|1}^{(d)}} \lambda_1 \tag{10}$$

A packet at s_2 will be dropped from s_2's queue if and only if s_1 is empty, and the packet transmitted from s_2 is successfully decoded by the destination d, so the service rate received by s_2 is

$$\mu_2 = \mathbf{P}\left[Q_1 = 0\right] q_{2|2}^{(d)} = \left(1 - \frac{\lambda_1}{q_{1|1}^{(2)} + q_{1|1}^{(d)} - q_{1|1}^{(2)} q_{1|1}^{(d)}}\right) q_{2|2}^{(d)} \tag{11}$$

And the stability condition for the queue at s_2 is $\lambda_2 + \lambda_{1 \to 2} < \mu_2$, which yields

$$\frac{\left(q_{1|1}^{(2)} + q_{2|2}^{(d)} - q_{1|1}^{(2)} q_{1|1}^{(d)}\right) \lambda_1}{q_{2|2}^{(d)} \left(q_{1|1}^{(2)} + q_{1|1}^{(d)} - q_{1|1}^{(2)} q_{1|1}^{(d)}\right)} + \frac{\lambda_2}{q_{2|2}^{(d)}} < 1 \tag{12}$$

The network is stable if both source queues are stable. Therefore, the stability region is characterized by the intersection of the two stability conditions given by Eq. (9) and Eq. (12). From these two stability conditions, it can be easily verified that the stability of s_2 dominates that of s_1, so the stability region of the CC scheme is given by

$$\Re_{CC} = \left\{ (\lambda_1, \lambda_2) : \frac{\left(q_{1|1}^{(2)} + q_{2|2}^{(d)} - q_{1|1}^{(2)} q_{1|1}^{(d)}\right) \lambda_1}{q_{2|2}^{(d)} \left(q_{1|1}^{(2)} + q_{1|1}^{(d)} - q_{1|1}^{(2)} q_{1|1}^{(d)}\right)} + \frac{\lambda_2}{q_{2|2}^{(d)}} < 1 \right\} \tag{13}$$

Due to the conflict-free scheduling which decouples the two queues, the stability region of the conventional cooperation scheme is bounded by a straight line; this region yet strictly contains the non-cooperative stability region given in Eq. (8), that is, $\Re_{CC} \supset \Re_{NC}$. This is because, since both $\Re_{CC}$ and $\Re_{NC}$ are bounded by straight lines, we need only to compare the intersections of these lines with the axes. The intersection points for the CC scheme can be easily calculated to be

$$\lambda_1^*(CC) = \frac{q_{2|2}^{(d)} \left(q_{1|1}^{(2)} + q_{1|1}^{(d)} - q_{1|1}^{(2)} q_{1|1}^{(d)}\right)}{q_{1|1}^{(2)} + q_{2|2}^{(d)} - q_{1|1}^{(2)} q_{1|1}^{(d)}}, \qquad \lambda_2^*(CC) = q_{2|2}^{(d)} \tag{14}$$

and the corresponding values for the NC scheme are

$$\lambda_1^*(NC) = q_{1|1}^{(d)}, \qquad\qquad \lambda_2^*(NC) = q_{2|2}^{(d)} \tag{15}$$

So $\lambda_2^*(CC) = \lambda_2^*(NC)$; and since $q_{2|2}^{(d)} > q_{1|1}^{(d)}$, it can be easily seen that $\lambda_1^*(CC) > \lambda_1^*(NC)$. Hence, $\Re_{CC}$ strictly contains $\Re_{NC}$.

3.2   C-OPP Scheme

In contrast to the conventional cooperation scheme where s_2 only transmits during the idle time slot of s_1, under the C-OPP scheme, s_2 observes the queue length Q_1 at s_1, and is scheduled opportunistically: if $Q_1 = 0$, s_2 will transmit with probability 1 if it's backlogged; otherwise, if $Q_1 \neq 0$ and hence s_1 transmits, s_2 is scheduled to transmit with probability p if it has packets. In the latter case, if s_2 is scheduled to transmit together with s_1, the two transmissions will cause interference to each other; and since s_2 cannot receive and transmit at the same time, the relay-assistance of s_2 is sacrificed for taking advantage of the multipacket reception capability, under which both transmissions can reach the destination successfully with probability $q_{1|1,2}^{(d)}q_{2|1,2}^{(d)}$, strictly greater than zero.

With such opportunistic scheduling, the two queues interact in such a way that the service process of each queue depends on whether the other queue is empty or not; in addition, the arrival process to s_2 from s_1 depends on the departure process from s_1. A useful tool to bypass this thorny problem is the stochastic dominance approach [15]; by utilizing this dominance approach and the constrained optimization technique, a complete description of the stability region of the C-OPP scheme is given in the following theorem.

Theorem 1. *By optimizing over all possible scheduling probability $p \in [0,1]$ at s_2, the stability region of the C-OPP scheme $(\Re_{C\text{-}OPP})$ for the MPR channel model is defined as follows:*

1. if

$$\eta = q_{1|1}^{(2)}(1 - q_{1|1}^{(d)})q_{1|1,2}^{(d)} + (q_{1|1}^{(2)} + q_{1|1}^{(d)} - q_{1|1}^{(2)}q_{1|1}^{(d)})q_{2|1,2}^{(d)}$$
$$- (q_{1|1}^{(2)} + q_{1|1}^{(d)} - q_{1|1}^{(2)}q_{1|1}^{(d)} - q_{1|1,2}^{(d)})q_{2|2}^{(d)} > 0, \qquad (16)$$

the achievable stability region (by optimizing the scheduling probability p) is given by $\Re_{C\text{-}OPP} = \Re_1 \bigcup \Re_2$, where

$$\Re_1 = \left\{ (\lambda_1, \lambda_2) : \frac{(q_{2|2}^{(d)} - q_{2|1,2}^{(d)})\lambda_1}{q_{2|2}^{(d)}q_{1|1,2}^{(d)}} + \frac{\lambda_2}{q_{2|2}^{(d)}} < 1, \quad for\ 0 \leq \lambda_1 \leq q_{1|1,2}^{(d)} \right\} \quad (17)$$

$$\Re_2 = \left\{ (\lambda_1, \lambda_2) : \frac{q_{1|1}^{(2)}(1 - q_{1|1}^{(d)}) + q_{2|1,2}^{(d)}}{q_{1|1}^{(2)} + q_{1|1}^{(d)} - q_{1|1}^{(2)}q_{1|1}^{(d)} - q_{1|1,2}^{(d)}}\lambda_1 + \lambda_2 \right.$$
$$\left. < \frac{q_{1|1}^{(2)}(1 - q_{1|1}^{(d)})(q_{1|1,2}^{(d)} + q_{2|1,2}^{(d)}) + q_{1|1}^{(d)}q_{2|1,2}^{(d)}}{q_{1|1}^{(2)} + q_{1|1}^{(d)} - q_{1|1}^{(2)}q_{1|1}^{(d)} - q_{1|1,2}^{(d)}}, \quad for\ \lambda_1 > q_{1|1,2}^{(d)} \right\} \quad (18)$$

In the rate region defined by $\lambda_1 \leq q_{1|1,2}^{(d)}$, the boundary of the subregion $\Re_1$ is achieved by setting the optimal scheduling probability to be $p^* = 1$; and in the rate region defined by $\lambda_1 > q_{1|1,2}^{(d)}$, the optimal p^* which achieves the boundary of $\Re_2$ is given by $p^* = \frac{q_{1|1}^{(2)} + q_{1|1}^{(d)} - q_{1|1}^{(2)}q_{1|1}^{(d)} - \lambda_1}{q_{1|1}^{(2)} + q_{1|1}^{(d)} - q_{1|1}^{(2)}q_{1|1}^{(d)} - q_{1|1,2}^{(d)}}$.

2. otherwise, that is, if

$$\eta = q_{1|1}^{(2)}(1 - q_{1|1}^{(d)})q_{1|1,2}^{(d)} + (q_{1|1}^{(2)} + q_{1|1}^{(d)} - q_{1|1}^{(2)}q_{1|1}^{(d)})q_{2|1,2}^{(d)}$$
$$- (q_{1|1}^{(2)} + q_{1|1}^{(d)} - q_{1|1}^{(2)}q_{1|1}^{(d)} - q_{1|1,2}^{(d)})q_{2|2}^{(d)} \leq 0, \qquad (19)$$

the optimal scheduling probability is given by $p^* = 0$, which means that s_2 only transmits during the idle time slot of s_1, hence the C-OPP scheme reduces to the CC scheme, and the stability region is known to be given by Eq. (13), which is,

$$\Re_{C\text{-}OPP} = \left\{ (\lambda_1, \lambda_2) : \frac{\left(q_{1|1}^{(2)} + q_{2|2}^{(d)} - q_{1|1}^{(2)}q_{1|1}^{(d)}\right)\lambda_1}{q_{2|2}^{(d)}\left(q_{1|1}^{(2)} + q_{1|1}^{(d)} - q_{1|1}^{(2)}q_{1|1}^{(d)}\right)} + \frac{\lambda_2}{q_{2|2}^{(d)}} < 1 \right\} \quad (20)$$

Proof. The key part of the dominance approach is as follows: first, construct an appropriate dominant system in which one queue can be decoupled from the other, which makes the stability analysis tractable: then, prove that the dominant system and the original system behave in the same way at the boundary of the stability region. We construct the dominant system $\mathcal{S}'$ which dominates the original system $\mathcal{S}$ in the following fashion:

1. If $Q_1 = 0$ and $Q_2 = 0$, s_2 transmits a dummy packet with probability 1;
2. If $Q_1 \neq 0$ and $Q_2 = 0$, s_2 transmits a dummy packet with probability p.

All the other assumptions, channel models, arrival and reception processes remain unaltered in the dominant system. Since the transmission of dummy packets will not contribute to the throughput but cause interference to the concurrent transmission from the other source, it is true that each queue will have a successful departure in $\mathcal{S}$ whenever it has one in $\mathcal{S}'$. Therefore, the queue lengths of the dominant system can no longer be smaller than the corresponding queue lengths of the original system; and the stability of the dominant system implies the stability of the original system.

In the dominant system $\mathcal{S}'$, the service process of the queue at s_1 depends on whether s_2 transmits or not: (a) if s_2 transmits together with s_1 (which happens with probability p), the service rate seen by s_1 is $q_{1|1,2}^{(d)}$; (b) if s_2 remains silent when s_1 transmits, s_1 receives the service rate of $q_{1|1}^{(2)} + q_{1|1}^{(d)} - q_{1|1}^{(2)}q_{1|1}^{(d)}$, because the packet is dropped from s_1 when either s_2 or the destination d decodes the packet. Hence, the average service rate of s_1 is

$$\mu_1 = (1-p)(q_{1|1}^{(2)} + q_{1|1}^{(d)} - q_{1|1}^{(2)}q_{1|1}^{(d)}) + pq_{1|1,2}^{(d)} \quad (21)$$

And the queue at s_1 is stable if and only if:

$$\lambda_1 < \mu_1 = (1-p)(q_{1|1}^{(2)} + q_{1|1}^{(d)} - q_{1|1}^{(2)}q_{1|1}^{(d)}) + pq_{1|1,2}^{(d)} \quad (22)$$

The analysis of the queue at s_2 will be a bit more complicated. First we analyze the total arrival process to s_2. The total arrival process consists of two parts: 1) the external Bernoulli arrivals with rate λ_2; and 2) the arrivals from s_1, with the rate $\lambda_{1 \to 2}$ to be calculated. There is an arrival to s_2 from s_1 if the following events happen together: (1) s_1 is non-empty and transmits, which has probability λ_1/μ_1 as s_1's queue is a discrete-time M/M/1 queue[1], (2) s_2 remains silent, which happens with probability $1 - p$, (3) the packet transmitted by s_1 is decoded by s_2 but not decoded by d, which occurs with probability $q_{1|1}^{(2)}(1 - q_{1|1}^{(d)})$. These three events are independent, and the total arrival rate to s_2 is

$$
\lambda_{s_2} = \lambda_{1 \to 2} + \lambda_2 = \mathbf{P}\left[Q_1 \neq 0\right](1 - p)q_{1|1}^{(2)}(1 - q_{1|1}^{(d)}) + \lambda_2
$$

$$
= \frac{(1 - p)q_{1|1}^{(2)}(1 - q_{1|1}^{(d)})}{(1 - p)(q_{1|1}^{(2)} + q_{1|1}^{(d)} - q_{1|1}^{(2)}q_{1|1}^{(d)}) + pq_{1|1,2}^{(d)}}\lambda_1 + \lambda_2 \qquad (23)
$$

Then we analyze the service rate of s_2. The departure process of s_2 also depends on the queue state at s_1. Specifically, if $Q_1 \neq 0$ and s_1 transmits, s_2 transmits with probability p, and the packet from s_2 is decoded by d with probability $q_{2|1,2}^{(d)}$; otherwise, if $Q_1 = 0$, s_2 transmits with probability 1 and sees a successful delivery probability $q_{2|2}^{(d)}$. So the average service rate of s_2 is:

$$
\mu_{s_2} = \mathbf{P}\left[Q_1 = 0\right]q_{2|2}^{(d)} + \mathbf{P}\left[Q_1 \neq 0\right]pq_{2|1,2}^{(d)}
$$

$$
= (1 - \frac{\lambda_1}{\mu_1})q_{2|2}^{(d)} + \frac{\lambda_1}{\mu_1}pq_{2|1,2}^{(d)} \qquad (24)
$$

where μ_1 is given in Eq. (21). The queue at s_2 is stable if and only if

$$
\lambda_{s_2} < \mu_{s_2} \qquad (25)
$$

with λ_{s_2} and μ_{s_2} as written in Eq. (23) and Eq. (24) respectively.

The network is stable if both queues are stable; after some simple algebra, the stability condition for a fixed scheduling probability p is defined by

$$
\lambda_1 < (1 - p)(q_{1|1}^{(2)} + q_{1|1}^{(d)} - q_{1|1}^{(2)}q_{1|1}^{(d)}) + pq_{1|1,2}^{(d)} \qquad (26)
$$

$$
\frac{\left(q_{1|1}^{(2)}(1 - q_{1|1}^{(d)}) + q_{2|2}^{(d)}\right) - p\left(q_{1|1}^{(2)}(1 - q_{1|1}^{(d)}) + q_{2|1,2}^{(d)}\right)}{(1 - p)\left(q_{1|1}^{(2)} + q_{1|1}^{(d)} - q_{1|1}^{(2)}q_{1|1}^{(d)}\right) + pq_{1|1,2}^{(d)}}\lambda_1 + \lambda_2 < q_{2|2}^{(d)} \qquad (27)
$$

We argue that the boundary of the stability region of the dominant system indeed *coincides* with that of the stability region of the original system: given that $\lambda_1 < (1 - p)(q_{1|1}^{(2)} + q_{1|1}^{(d)} - q_{1|1}^{(2)}q_{1|1}^{(d)}) + pq_{1|1,2}^{(d)}$, if for some λ_2 the queue at s_2 is stable in the dominant system, then the corresponding queue in the original system must be stable; conversely, if for some λ_2 the queue at s_2 is unstable in the dominant system, then this queue never empties, and s_2 always transmits source information when it accesses the channel. In other words, s_2 will not transmit

---

[1] We use the notion of discrete-time M/M/1 queue to describe a queueing system with Bernoulli arrival process and geometrically distributed service times.

dummy packets, and as long as s_2 never empties, the dominant system and the original system behave exactly in the same way. Thus, we can conclude that the original system and the dominant system are indistinguishable at the boundary points, and $\Re_{\text{C-OPP}}$ is indeed the closure of rate pairs (λ_1, λ_2) constrained by Eq. (26) and Eq. (27) as p varies over $[0, 1]$.

To obtain the closure, we utilize the constrained optimization technique similarly as in [10]. We fix λ_1 and maximize λ_2 as p varies over $[0, 1]$. By replacing λ_1 by x and λ_2 by y, the boundary of the stability region given by Eq. (26) and Eq. (27) for a fixed p can be written as:

$$y = q_{2|2}^{(d)} - \frac{\left(q_{1|1}^{(2)}(1 - q_{1|1}^{(d)}) + q_{2|2}^{(d)}\right) - p\left(q_{1|1}^{(2)}(1 - q_{1|1}^{(d)}) + q_{2|1,2}^{(d)}\right)}{(1 - p)\left(q_{1|1}^{(2)} + q_{1|1}^{(d)} - q_{1|1}^{(2)}q_{1|1}^{(d)}\right) + pq_{1|1,2}^{(d)}} x \quad (28)$$

$$\text{for} \quad 0 \leq x \leq (1 - p)(q_{1|1}^{(2)} + q_{1|1}^{(d)} - q_{1|1}^{(2)}q_{1|1}^{(d)}) + pq_{1|1,2}^{(d)} \quad (29)$$

To maximize y in Eq. (28), we differentiate it with respect to p, which gives:

$$\frac{dy}{dp} = \frac{\eta x}{\left((1 - p)(q_{1|1}^{(2)} + q_{1|1}^{(d)} - q_{1|1}^{(2)}q_{1|1}^{(d)}) + pq_{1|1,2}^{(d)}\right)^2} \quad (30)$$

with η as given by Eq. (16) or Eq. (19). The denominator of Eq. (30) is strictly greater than zero; and the numerator excluding x, which is η, can be either positive or negative.

- In the case that $\eta > 0$, the first derivative $\frac{dy}{dp}$ is strictly positive and y is an increasing function of p. Thus, it appears that the optimal value of p^* is 1. But caution is needed here. As seen by Eq. (29), this constraint is valid only for $x \leq (1 - p)(q_{1|1}^{(2)} + q_{1|1}^{(d)} - q_{1|1}^{(2)}q_{1|1}^{(d)}) + pq_{1|1,2}^{(d)}$. Clearly, p^* can take the value 1 if and only if $x \leq q_{1|1,2}^{(d)}$. So in the subregion defined by $0 \leq x \leq q_{1|1,2}^{(d)}$, the optimal probability is $p^* = 1$; substituting $p = 1$ into Eq. (28) gives the boundary of the subregion characterized by $\Re_1$ in Eq. (17). Now consider x for $x > q_{1|1,2}^{(d)}$, since y increases with p, and p satisfies $p \leq \frac{q_{1|1}^{(2)} + q_{1|1}^{(d)} - q_{1|1}^{(2)}q_{1|1}^{(d)} - x}{q_{1|1}^{(2)} + q_{1|1}^{(d)} - q_{1|1}^{(2)}q_{1|1}^{(d)} - q_{1|1,2}^{(d)}}$ according to Eq. (29), the optimal p is given by $p^* = \frac{q_{1|1}^{(2)} + q_{1|1}^{(d)} - q_{1|1}^{(2)}q_{1|1}^{(d)} - x}{q_{1|1}^{(2)} + q_{1|1}^{(d)} - q_{1|1}^{(2)}q_{1|1}^{(d)} - q_{1|1,2}^{(d)}}$. By substituting p^* into Eq. (28), we obtain the boundary of the subregion as characterized by $\Re_2$ in Eq. (18).
- In the case that $\eta \leq 0$, we have $\frac{dy}{dp} \leq 0$ for all $p \in [0, 1]$, and so y is a decreasing function of p in the range of all possible values of x. Hence, the optimal p^* is equal to zero, and the opportunistic cooperation scheme reduces to the conventional cooperation scheme, with the stability region given by Eq. (13) in Section 3.1. ■

A) Comparison between CC and C-OPP: When the condition expressed in Eq. (16) is satisfied, $\Re_{\text{C-OPP}}$, characterized by $\Re_1 \bigcup \Re_2$, becomes a convex polyhedron; this can be easily verified, and the procedure is as follows: both subregions $\Re_1$ and $\Re_2$ are bounded by a straight line, and the intersection point connecting the two straight lines can be calculated to be $(\lambda'_1(\text{C-OPP}), \lambda'_2(\text{C-OPP}))$, where

$$\lambda'_1(\text{C-OPP}) = q^{(d)}_{1|1,2}, \qquad \lambda'_2(\text{C-OPP}) = q^{(d)}_{2|1,2} \tag{31}$$

From Eq. (17), the intersection point of the line which bounds $\Re_1$ with the y-axis is

$$\lambda^*_2(\Re_1) = q^{(d)}_{2|2} \qquad (\text{for } \lambda^*_1(\Re_1) = 0) \tag{32}$$

and from Eq. (18), the intersection point of the line which bounds $\Re_2$ with the x-axis is

$$\lambda^*_1(\Re_2) = \frac{q^{(2)}_{1|1}(1 - q^{(d)}_{1|1})(q^{(d)}_{1|1,2} + q^{(d)}_{2|1,2}) + q^{(d)}_{1|1}q^{(d)}_{2|1,2}}{q^{(2)}_{1|1}(1 - q^{(d)}_{1|1}) + q^{(d)}_{2|1,2}} \qquad (\text{for } \lambda^*_2(\Re_2) = 0) \tag{33}$$

If we form a straight line by connecting these two points, and denote it by L, it turns out that $(\lambda'_1(\text{C-OPP}), \lambda'_2(\text{C-OPP}))$ strictly lies above L. This can be easily checked, as the value of λ_2 at L when $\lambda_1 = \lambda'_1(\text{C-OPP})$ is

$$\lambda'_2(L) = \frac{q^{(d)}_{2|2}q^{(d)}_{2|1,2}(q^{(d)}_{1|1} + q^{(2)}_{1|1}(1 - q^{(d)}_{1|1}) - q^{(d)}_{1|1,2})}{q^{(2)}_{1|1}(1 - q^{(d)}_{1|1})(q^{(d)}_{1|1,2} + q^{(d)}_{2|1,2}) + q^{(d)}_{1|1}q^{(d)}_{2|1,2}} \tag{34}$$

This is strictly less than $\lambda'_2(\text{C-OPP})$ if and only if $\eta > 0$. Therefore, when $\eta > 0$, the stability region $\Re_{\text{C-OPP}}$ is strictly convex.

Then we compare $\Re_{\text{C-OPP}}$ and $\Re_{\text{CC}}$. If we can show that L strictly outer-bounds $\Re_{\text{CC}}$, it suffices to say that $\Re_{\text{C-OPP}}$ strictly outer-bounds $\Re_{\text{CC}}$ since the boundary of $\Re_{\text{C-OPP}}$ strictly lies above L as shown above. Because $\Re_{\text{CC}}$ is bounded by a straight line, to compare L and $\Re_{\text{CC}}$, it is enough to compare the intersection points of these lines with the axes. The two intersection points of L are given by Eq. (32) and Eq. (33); and the corresponding values for $\Re_{\text{CC}}$ are given by Eq. (14). Clearly, $\lambda^*_2(\Re_1) = \lambda^*_2(\text{CC})$, and it can be shown that $\lambda^*_1(\Re_2) > \lambda^*_1(\text{CC})$ if and only if $\eta > 0$. Hence, in this case, we conclude that $\Re_{\text{C-OPP}}$ strictly contains $\Re_{\text{CC}}$, that is, $\Re_{\text{C-OPP}} \supset \Re_{\text{CC}}$.

On the other hand, when the condition in Eq. (19) is satisfied, the MPR channel is not strong enough to support simultaneous transmissions, and the optimal opportunistic scheduling becomes the conflict-free scheduling, which is the CC scheme. So even in the worst case, the C-OPP scheme can do as well as the CC scheme.

B) Effects that affect η: The value of η determines whether the channel supports simultaneous transmissions to some degree so that the opportunistic cooperation scheme can outperform the conventional scheme: if $\eta > 0$, simultaneous transmissions are supported; if $\eta \leq 0$, the opportunistic scheme reduces to the conventional one by scheduling s_1 and s_2 separately. A simple examination of η reveals how it is affected by those reception probabilities defined in Eq. (2):

- The effect of $q_{1|1}^{(d)}$, $q_{2|2}^{(d)}$: we observe that η decreases as $q_{1|1}^{(d)}$ or $q_{2|2}^{(d)}$ increases. A higher value of $q_{1|1}^{(d)}$ means that s_1 is more likely to deliver its packets to the destination without interference from s_2, so it is more preferable to schedule s_2 not to interfere with s_1; likewise, a higher value of $q_{2|2}^{(d)}$ implies a good channel from s_2 to d, and intuitively, we would like to exploit more relaying opportunity by scheduling s_2 to be silent when s_1 transmits, so that s_2 can possibly decode the transmitted packet of s_1 and then relay the packet.
- The effect of $q_{1|1,2}^{(d)}$ and $q_{2|1,2}^{(d)}$: η is an increasing function of both $q_{1|1,2}^{(d)}$ and $q_{2|1,2}^{(d)}$, this is not surprising because the action of simultaneous transmissions is more preferable by a strong MPR channel.
- The effect of $q_{1|1}^{(2)}$: η can be rearranged to be written as $q_{1|1}^{(2)}(1 - q_{1|1}^{(d)})(q_{1|1,2}^{(d)} + q_{2|1,2}^{(d)} - q_{2|2}^{(d)}) + q_{1|1}^{(d)}q_{2|1,2}^{(d)} - q_{1|1}^{(d)}q_{2|2}^{(d)} + q_{1|1,2}^{(d)}q_{2|2}^{(d)}$. Setting $q_{1|1}^{(2)}$ to be zero gives the value of the non-cooperative case with MPR channel. Hence, if $q_{1|1,2}^{(d)} + q_{2|1,2}^{(d)} - q_{2|2}^{(d)}$ is strictly greater than zero (which implies a strong MPR channel), cooperation adds a positive contribution to η which makes it more likely for η to be positive, and, hence, the opportunistic scheduling can take effect to outperform the conventional scheme.

4   Numerical Results

In this section, we compare the stability regions of the two cooperation schemes (CC and C-OPP) and the non-cooperation scheme (NC). Two plots are given to illustrate how different categories of MPR channel affect the C-OPP scheme. In Fig. 2, the reception probabilities are chosen to be $q_{1|1}^{(d)} = 0.3$, $q_{2|2}^{(d)} = 0.7$, $q_{1|1}^{(2)} = 0.4$, $q_{1|1,2}^{(d)} = 0.2$ and $q_{2|1,2}^{(d)} = 0.5$ so that Eq. (16) is satisfied. As we have proved, the C-OPP scheme supports simultaneous transmissions to some degree, and hence, supports a convex stability region which strictly contains the stability region of the CC scheme, which is bounded by a straight line. In the subregion defined by $\lambda_1 \leq q_{1|1,2}^{(d)}$, the optimal scheduling probability p^* is 1; while in the subregion defined by $\lambda_1 > q_{1|1,2}^{(d)}$, the optimal p^* is $\frac{q_{1|1}^{(2)} + q_{1|1}^{(d)} - q_{1|1}^{(2)}q_{1|1}^{(d)} - \lambda_1}{q_{1|1}^{(2)} + q_{1|1}^{(d)} - q_{1|1}^{(2)}q_{1|1}^{(d)} - q_{1|1,2}^{(d)}}$. The convexity of the region also implies that higher sum rates can be achieved.

In Fig. 3 the reception probabilities are chosen to be $q_{1|1}^{(d)} = 0.3$, $q_{2|2}^{(d)} = 0.8$, $q_{1|1}^{(2)} = 0.4$, $q_{1|1,2}^{(d)} = 0.2$ and $q_{2|1,2}^{(d)} = 0.4$ so that the condition in Eq. (19) holds. It is seen that the optimal scheduling strategy sets $p^* = 0$, which reduces the C-OPP scheme to the CC scheme by scheduling s_2 to transmit only when s_1 is empty. So even in the worst case, the C-OPP scheme can perform as well as the CC scheme.

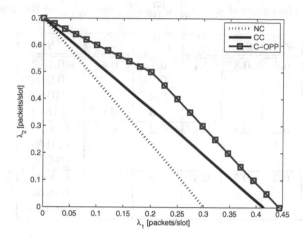

Fig. 2. Comparison of the stability regions under NC, CC, and C-OPP schemes when $\eta > 0$. $\Re_{\text{C-OPP}} \supset \Re_{\text{CC}} \supset \Re_{\text{NC}}$

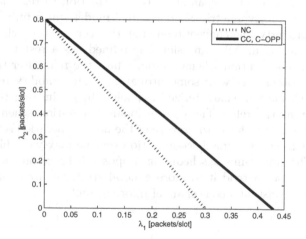

Fig. 3. Comparison of the stability regions under NC, CC, and C-OPP schemes when $\eta \leq 0$. $\Re_{\text{C-OPP}} = \Re_{\text{CC}} \supset \Re_{\text{NC}}$

Under all channel conditions, both cooperation schemes outperform the non-cooperation scheme; so cooperation among users improves the stability region, thus leads to higher stable throughput simultaneously for both users.

In addition, a number of channel reception probability sets are tested to demonstrate their effects on affecting the value of η. The results are listed in Table 1.

Table 1. The effects of $q_{1|1}^{(d)}$, $q_{2|2}^{(d)}$, $q_{1|1}^{(2)}$, $q_{1|1,2}^{(d)}$ and $q_{2|1,2}^{(d)}$ on the value of η

$q_{1|1}^{(d)}$	$q_{2|2}^{(d)}$	$q_{1|1}^{(2)}$	$q_{1|1,2}^{(d)}$	$q_{2|1,2}^{(d)}$	η
0.4	0.8	0.4	0.1	0.4	−0.1520
			0.2	0.4	−0.0480
			0.2	0.5	0.0160
			0.3	0.6	0.1840
0.3	0.8	0.4	0.2	0.5	0.0420
0.4					0.0160
0.5					−0.0100
0.4	0.7	0.4	0.2	0.5	0.0600
	0.8				0.0160
	0.9				−0.0280

5   Conclusion

In a two-user wireless multiple access system, cooperation is performed by en-
abling the user with a better channel to the destination to relay for the other
user. With a general asymmetric MPR channel model which fully exploits the
physical layer property, the conventional cognitive cooperation where the relay
only transmits during an idle time slot was refined. As a result, we proposed
an opportunistic cooperation scheme, under which the relay user transmits together with the other user with some probability. The stability region of this
opportunistic scheme was characterized explicitly by optimizing the transmission probability at the relay. The conventional cooperation scheme results in
higher stable throughput for both users over the non-cooperation scheme, and it
was shown that the opportunistic cooperation scheme may yield higher performance gains. The opportunistic scheduling proposed is based on the queue state
only; it is possible to extend it to more general strategies by exploiting other
factors such as the instantaneous channel information.

References

1. Sendonaris, A., Erkip, E., Aazhang, B.: User Cooperation Diversity-Part I: System
   Description. IEEE Trans. Commun. 51, 1927–1938 (2003)
2. Sendonaris, A., Erkip, E., Aazhang, B.: User Cooperation Diversity-Part II: Implementation Aspects and Performance Analysis. IEEE Trans. Commun. 51, 1939–
   1948 (2003)
3. Laneman, J.N., Tse, D.N.C., Wornell, G.W.: Cooperative Diversity in Wireless Networks: Efficient Protocols and Outage Behavior. IEEE Trans. Inform. Theory 50,
   3062–3080 (2004)
4. Sadek, A.K., Liu, K.J.R., Ephremides, A.: Cognitive Multiple Access via Cooperation: Protocol Design and Performance Analysis. IEEE Trans. Inform. Theory 53,
   3677–3696 (2007)

5. Simeone, O., Bar-Ness, Y., Spagnolini, U.: Stable Throughput of Cognitive Radios With and Without Relaying Capability. IEEE Trans. Commun. 55, 2351–2360 (2007)
6. Rong, B., Ephremides, A.: Protocol-level Cooperation in Wireless Networks: Stable Throughput and Delay Analysis. In: 7th International Symposium on Modeling and Optimization in Mobile, Ad Hoc, and Wireless Networks, Seoul, Korea (2009)
7. Rong, B., Ephremides, A.: Cooperation Above the Physical Layer: the Case of a Simple Network. In: IEEE International Symposium on Information Theory, Seoul, Korea (2009)
8. Ghez, S., Verdú, S., Schwartz, S.: Stability Properties of Slotted ALOHA With Multipacket Reception Capability. IEEE Trans. Autom. Control 33, 640–649 (1988)
9. Ghez, S., Verdú, S., Schwartz, S.: Optimal Decentralized Control in the Random Access Multipacket Channel. IEEE Trans. Autom. Control 34, 1153–1163 (1989)
10. Naware, V., Mergen, G., Tong, L.: Stability and Delay of Finite-user Slotted ALOHA With Multipacket Reception. IEEE Trans. Inform. Theory 51, 2636–2656 (2005)
11. Shrader, B., Ephremides, A.: Random Access Broadcast: Stability and Throughput Analysis. IEEE Trans. Inform. Theory 53, 2915–2921 (2007)
12. Viswanath, P., Tse, D.N.C., Laroia, R.: Opportunistic Beamforming Using Dumb Antennas. IEEE Trans. Inform. Theory 48, 1277–1294 (2002)
13. Borst, S.C.: User-level Performance of Channel-aware Scheduling Algorithms in Wireless Data Networks. IEEE Trans. Networking 13, 636–647 (2005)
14. Loynes, R.: The Stability of a Queue With Non-independent Inter-arrival and Service Times. Proc. Camb. Philos. Soc. 58, 497–520 (1962)
15. Rao, R., Ephremides, A.: On the Stability of Interacting Queues in a Multiple-access System. IEEE Trans. Inform. Theory 34, 918–930 (1988)

A Restless Bandit Marginal Productivity Index for Opportunistic Spectrum Access with Sensing Errors

José Niño-Mora*

Carlos III University of Madrid
Department of Statistics
Av. Universidad 30
28911 Leganés (Madrid), Spain
jnimora@alum.mit.edu
http://alum.mit.edu/www/jnimora

Abstract. This paper introduces a tractable priority-index multichannel sensing policy in a discrete-time model of opportunistic spectrum access for cognitive radio networks, which aims to be close to optimal under a discounted or average throughput minus sensing cost performance objective. The policy dynamically allocates transmission opportunities arising in a collection of asymmetric channels licensed to primary users to a set of secondary unlicensed users. Channel availabilities follow independent binary-state Markov dynamics, and are partially observed via error-prone spectrum sensors. The paper formulates the model as a multiarmed restless bandit problem with real-state projects, and then deploys Whittle's (1988) marginal productivity (MP) index policy. The challenging issues of indexability (existence of the index) and efficient index evaluation are resolved by deploying recent results of the author for real-state restless bandit indexation. Preliminary computational results are reported showing that the MP policy can achieve substantial gains over the myopic and random policies.

Keywords: multichannel opportunistic spectrum access, cognitive radio, partially observed Markov decision processes, restless bandit marginal productivity index, spectrum sensing errors.

1 Introduction

1.1 Background and Motivation

Opportunistic spectrum access (OSA) in cognitive radio networks is an emerging research area motivated by the need to use more efficiently the scarce radio frequency spectrum available. The traditional static spectrum allocation to a set

---

* The author's work has been supported in part by the Spanish Ministry of Science and Innovation project MTM2007–63140 and an I3 faculty endowment grant, and by the Autonomous Community of Madrid grant CCG08–UC3M1ESP–4162.

R. Núñez-Queija and J. Resing (Eds.): NET-COOP 2009, LNCS 5894, pp. 60–74, 2009.

of licensed *primary users* (PUs) results in severe inefficiencies, as measurements indicate that low spectrum utilization levels (often under 30%) are typical.

Such inefficient spectrum usage by PUs stands in stark contrast to a dramatic surge in demand for access to spectrum by unlicensed *secondary users* (SUs), due to emerging technologies such as wireless Internet, sensor networks, radio frequency ID tags, and satellite digital audio broadcasting. OSA seeks to exploit transmission opportunities created by PUs' bursty usage patterns, dynamically granting SUs access to licensed channels when these are perceived to be unused. This has spurred a recent surge of research on design of OSA policies for dynamic spectrum allocation to SUs, which are both computationally tractable and near-optimal relative to given performance objectives. See, e.g., [4].

The design of such policies is complicated by the fact that the identification of transmission opportunities in PUs' channels is error-prone, as SUs are furnished with spectrum sensors that are hindered by two types of error: *false alarms* (an idle channel is sensed to be busy) and *misdetections* (a busy channel is sensed to be idle. Whereas the former give rise to overlooked transmission opportunities, the latter introduce the possibility of *interference* or *collisions* with PUs. In order to allow SUs to opportunistically access their allotted channels, PUs require that such *collision probabilities* be bounded below acceptable levels.

The following issues play a significant role in the design of OSA policies: (i) The error-prone nature of sensors calls for a distinction between *spectrum sensing* (deciding which channels to sense) and *spectrum access* (deciding whether to access a sensed channel given the sensor's outcome) policies; (ii) the need for synchronization between a secondary transmitter and receiver pair across a channel requires use of shared information on channel status, which is furnished by *acknowledgments* (ACKs) of receipt; and (iii) since SUs typically correspond to mobile applications running on expensive battery power, policy design should take into account the cost of sensor usage.

1.2   Prior Work: POMDP and Restless Bandit Models for OSA

The design of optimal transmission policies for a single SU on a single PU channel is addressed in [5] in a discrete-time *partially observed Markov decision process* (POMDP) model under perfect sensing but with transmission errors. An optimal policy is characterized by a *threshold* in the *belief state* (which tracks the probability that the channel is available), above which the SU should transmit. In this and most related work, channel availability dynamics follow the Gilbert–Elliott binary-state Markov model. An extension incorporating spectrum sensing time and sensing errors along with SU's delay and energy costs and throughput rewards is addressed in [4], where structural properties of optimal policies are proved and heuristic control policies are proposed.

A multichannel discrete-time finite-horizon undiscounted POMDP formulation for OSA with sensing errors is introduced in [12]. Given the prohibitive computational cost of finding an optimal policy when the number of channels is large, a suboptimal myopic rule is proposed and tested. Such work is developed in [2], which establishes a key *separation principle* decoupling the design of sensing and access policies. An optimal channel access policy is obtained by maximizing the immediate reward subject to the collision probability constraint.

A promising approach to the design of OSA policies seeks to exploit the special structure of the above POMDP models as *multiarmed restless bandit problems* (MARBPs) with real-state projects. The MARBP concerns the optimal sequential allocation of effort to a collection of projects, modeled as binary-action (active or passive) MDPs. In the classic case where only one project is to be engaged at each time and passive projects do not change state, there is [3] an optimal policy of index type: a *Gittins index* is attached to each project as a function of its state, and then a project of largest index is activated at each time. Yet, the bandit formulation of the OSA problem is not classic, since passive projects (where a "project" is a PU's channel and the active action is to sense the channel) can change state. Still, by ignoring passive dynamics [1] proposes the resulting Gittins index policy in an OSA model with sensing errors.

Although *index policies* are generally suboptimal for the MARBP, Whittle introduced in [11] a heuristic index policy based on an index for restless bandits, which emerges from a Lagrangian relaxation and decomposition approach that also yields a bound on the optimal problem value. The *Whittle index*, which has been extended (cf. [8]) into the more general concept of *marginal productivity* (MP) *index* —after its economic interpretation— raises substantial research challenges as (i) *indexability* (existence of the index) needs to be established for the model at hand; and (ii) the index needs to be efficiently evaluated.

Over the last decade, the author has developed a methodology for resolving such issues on *restless bandit indexation* in the discrete-state case, in work reviewed in [8]. More recently [9] announces extensions to real-state restless bandits, which are the cornerstone of the present paper's approach, and are also deployed in a multitarget tracking model with Kalman filter dynamics in [10].

The potential of real-state MARBP models is being increasingly recognized. OSA with perfect sensing has been addressed by the author in [9] via an MARBP formulation which incorporates latency and energy consumption costs in the performance objective. The analysis yields a closed-form index policy which appears to perform well. Such an approach has been independently investigated in [6] by direct techniques.

1.3 Goals and Contributions

This paper extends such a line of work by investigating an MARBP formulation of OSA across asymmetric channels which incorporates sensing errors, the main goal being to obtain a tractable index policy that performs well based on restless bandit indexation. The paper deploys the methodology for real-state restless bandit indexation announced in [9] to establish indexability and efficiently evaluate the MP index . Further, the paper presents some evidence that the resulting MP index policy outperforms the conventional myopic policy advocated in previous work, in instances with asymmetric channels. Proofs are omitted due to space constraints. They will be included in the journal version of this work, along with extensive computational experiments.

1.4   Organization of the Paper

The remainder of the paper is organized as follows. Section 2 describes the multichannel OSA model and its MARBP formulation. Section 3 discusses the restless bandit indexation methodology for real-state restless bandits introduced in [9] as it applies to the design of index policies for OSA. Section 4 deploys such a methodology in the present model to verify indexability and evaluate the MP index. Section 5 reports the results of a preliminary computational study to assess the tractability of index evaluation and the relative performance of the MP index policy relative to the myopic and random policies.

2   OSA Model and Restless Bandit Formulation

2.1   Multichannel OSA Model

We consider a system consisting of a set of M unlicensed SUs labeled by $m \in \mathsf{M} \triangleq \{1, \dots, M\}$, seeking to communicate with a corresponding set of receivers by dynamically detecting and exploiting transmission opportunities in a network of $N \geq M$ channels licensed to PUs, labeled by $n \in \mathsf{N} \triangleq \{1, \dots, N\}$. The system evolves over time slots $t = 0, 1, \dots$, on which all SUs and PUs are synchronized.

Channel n has a bandwidth of $b^{(n)}$ Mbs per slot, which a SU transmitting through it will fully use, as SUs are assumed to have an infinite supply of data to transmit. The channel's availability status to SUs evolves over time slots as a binary-state (1: available to SUs, i.e., free from its PU; 0: unavailable to SUs, i.e., occupied by its PU) Markov chain $s_t^{(n)}$ with transition probabilities $p^{(n)} = \mathsf{P}\{s_{t+1}^{(n)} = 0 \,|\, s_t^{(n)} = 1\}$ and $q^{(n)} = \mathsf{P}\{s_{t+1}^{(n)} = 1 \,|\, s_t^{(n)} = 0\}$. We assume that the channel has positive autocorrelation $\rho^{(n)} \triangleq 1 - p^{(n)} - q^{(n)} > 0$.

Although the state $s_t^{(n)}$ of each channel n is not directly observable by SUs, it is tracked by its *belief state*, which measures the posterior probability $X_t^{(n)} \in \mathsf{X} \triangleq [0, 1]$ that the channel is available (to SUs) conditional on the history of past observations and actions, and is updated via Bayes' rule. We assume that the current belief-state vector $\boldsymbol{X}_t = \left(X_t^{(n)}\right)$ is known to all SUs at the start of each slot t. SUs can gain information on the state of a channel n by sensing it using embedded homogeneous sensors, which give a *sensor outcome* $o_t^{(n)} \in \{0, 1\}$. The channel's *detection quality* is modeled by the *false alarm* probability that the channel is sensed as unavailable when it is available, $\epsilon^{(n)} \triangleq \mathsf{P}\{o_t^{(n)} = 0 \,|\, s_t^{(n)} = 1\}$, and the *misdetection* probability that the channel is sensed as available when it is unavailable, $\delta^{(n)} \triangleq \mathsf{P}\{o_t^{(n)} = 1 \,|\, s_t^{(n)} = 0\}$. As in [2], we assume that

$$\delta^{(n)} + \epsilon^{(n)} < 1. \tag{1}$$

We further assume that if a SU attempts to transmit through channel n in a slot where the channel is occupied by its PU this will result in a *collision*, with the effect that neither the PU nor the SU transmit any data. Each channel n has a *collision tolerance* level $\zeta^{(n)}$, which is the maximum admissible probability that such a collision takes place.

To avoid collisions between multiple SUs (if $M \geq 2$) vying for the same channel in a slot, we assume that a *central coordinator* dynamically allocates channels to SUs. Thus, at the start of each slot the coordinator selects at most M PU channels. Each such channel, if any, is then allocated to a SU, who will sense it and, based on its sensor's outcome, will decide whether to access the channel. If, say, J channels are so selected, for fairness' sake we assume that the allocation of such channels to SUs is carried out in a uniform random fashion, so each subset of J SUs has the same probability of being selected.

The coordinator's decisions are formulated by *action processes* $a_t^{(n)} \in \{0, 1\}$ for $n \in \mathsf{N}$, where $a_t^{(n)} = 1$ means that channel n is selected to be sensed by a SU at slot t. Such actions are prescribed by a *scheduling policy* $\boldsymbol{\pi}$, to be drawn from the class $\boldsymbol{\Pi}$ of *admissible policies*, which are nonanticipative (being based at each slot on the history of belief states and actions) and satisfy the sample-path constraint that no more than M channels be sensed at each slot,

$$\sum_{n \in \mathsf{N}} a_t^{(n)} \leq M, \quad t = 0, 1, 2, \ldots \tag{2}$$

Once a SU is allocated a channel n and senses it in slot t, it makes an *access decision*, which is randomized by the access probability $y^{(n)}(o)$ given sensor outcome $o \in \{0, 1\}$. The *separation principle* established in [2] decouples channel sensing and access decisions, as it prescribes to choose access probabilities that maximize the SU's probability of accessing the channel after sensing it when it is available, subject to the constraint that the channel's collision probability does not exceed interference tolerance level $\zeta^{(n)}$. Optimal access probabilities $y^{*,(n)}(0)$ and $y^{*,(n)}(1)$ are hence determined by solving the linear program (LP)

$$\begin{aligned}
\kappa^{(n)} = &\max \; \epsilon^{(n)} y^{(n)}(0) + (1 - \epsilon^{(n)}) y^{(n)}(1) \\
&\text{subject to} \\
&(1 - \delta^{(n)}) y^{(n)}(0) + \delta^{(n)} y^{(n)}(1) \leq \zeta^{(n)} \\
&0 \leq y^{(n)}(o) \leq 1, \quad o \in \{0, 1\}.
\end{aligned} \tag{3}$$

which yields

$$y^{*,(n)}(0) = \max\{0, (\zeta^{(n)} - \delta^{(n)})/(1 - \delta^{(n)})\}, \; y^{*,(n)}(1) = \min\{1, \zeta^{(n)}/\delta^{(n)}\}. \tag{4}$$

Synchronization between SU and receiver pairs requires updates on channels' belief states to be based on *acknowledgments* (ACKs) of receipt $K_t^{(n)} \in \{0, 1\}$. After a successful transmission on channel n, the transmitter receives a positive ACK ($K_t^{(n)} = 1$), receiving otherwise a negative ACK ($K_t^{(n)} = 0$).

The dynamics of channel n's belief state under each sensing action are as follows. If the channel's belief state at the beginning of slot t is $X_t^{(n)}$ and the channel is not sensed ($a_t^{(n)} = 0$), then its next belief state will be

$$X_{t+1}^{(n)} = q^{(n)}(1 - X_t^{(n)}) + (1 - p^{(n)}) X_t^{(n)} = q^{(n)} + \rho^{(n)} X_t^{(n)}. \tag{5}$$

On the other hand, if the channel is sensed $(a_t^{(n)} = 1)$ then its next belief state is obtained in a randomized fashion depending on whether or not an ACK is received. If it is $(K_t^{(n)} = 1)$, which happens with probability

$$P\{K_t^{(n)} = 1\} = \kappa^{(n)} X_t^{(n)},$$

where $\kappa^{(n)}$ is the optimal value of LP (3), then the next belief state will be

$$X_{t+1}^{(n)} = 1 - p^{(n)} = q^{(n)} + \rho^{(n)}. \tag{6}$$

Yet, if no ACK is received $(K_t^{(n)} = 0)$, then it is easily seen that

$$X_{t+1}^{(n)} = q^{(n)} + \rho^{(n)} \frac{1 - \kappa^{(n)}}{1 - \kappa^{(n)} X_t^{(n)}} X_t^{(n)}. \tag{7}$$

We assume that a SU successfully transmitting on channel n in a time slot will make full use of the channel's bandwidth, transmitting $b^{(n)}$ Mbs, at the expense of incurring a *sensing cost* $c^{(n)} \geq 0$. Hence, $R^{(n)}(x, a) \triangleq \left(b^{(n)} \kappa^{(n)} x - c^{(n)}\right) a$ is the expected one-slot net reward (throughput minus sensing cost) earned by taking action a on channel n when it occupies belief state x.

2.2 MARBP Formulation

Consider the following dynamic optimization problems: (1) find a discount-optimal policy,

$$\max_{\pi \in \Pi} \mathsf{E}_x^\pi \left[\sum_{t=0}^\infty \sum_{n \in \mathsf{N}} \beta^t R^{(n)}\left(X_t^{(n)}, a_t^{(n)}\right) \right], \tag{8}$$

where $0 < \beta < 1$ is the discount factor, $\boldsymbol{X}_0 = \boldsymbol{x} = (x^{(n)})$ is the initial joint belief state, and $\mathsf{E}_x^\pi[\cdot]$ denotes expectation under policy π conditional on $\boldsymbol{X}_0 = \boldsymbol{x}$; and (2) find an average-optimal policy,

$$\max_{\pi \in \Pi} \liminf_{T \to \infty} \frac{1}{T} \mathsf{E}_x^\pi \left[\sum_{t=0}^T \sum_{n \in \mathsf{N}} R^{(n)}\left(X_t^{(n)}, a_t^{(n)}\right) \right]. \tag{9}$$

Problems (8) and (9) are MARBPs with real-state projects, which are generally intractable. We will seek to design and compute heuristic index policies, which attach an index $\lambda^{(n)}(x^{(n)})$ to each channel n as a function of its belief state $x^{(n)}$, depending on channel parameters $p^{(n)}$, $q^{(n)}$, $\kappa^{(n)}$ and $b^{(n)}$. At time t, the index policy selects at most M channels to sense, using $\lambda^{(n)}(X_t^{(n)})$ as a sensing-priority index for channel n (where a higher index value represents a larger sensing priority), among those channels, if any, for which the index exceeds the sensing cost, i.e., $\lambda^{(n)}(X_t^{(n)}) > c^{(n)}$, breaking ties arbitrarily.

  In the sequel, we shall focus for concreteness on discounted-reward problem (8), although our approach also applies to average-reward problem (9).

3   Restless Bandit Indexation for OSA

3.1   Relaxed Problem, Lagrangian Relaxation, and Decomposition

Along the lines introduced in [11] for the equality-constrained case, we first construct a *relaxation* of (8), relaxing the requirement (2) that policies sense at most M channels at each time by the averaged version that the expected total discounted number of sensed channels does not exceed $M/(1 - \beta)$, i.e.,

$$\mathsf{E}_{\boldsymbol{x}}^{\boldsymbol{\pi}} \left[\sum_{t=0}^{\infty} \sum_{n \in \mathsf{N}} \beta^t a_t^{(n)} \right] \le \frac{M}{1 - \beta}. \tag{10}$$

Denoting by $\boldsymbol{\Pi}^{\mathrm{NA}}$ the class of nonanticipative scheduling policies (which can sense any number of channels at any time), the *relaxed primal problem* is

$$\max \left\{ \mathsf{E}_{\boldsymbol{x}}^{\boldsymbol{\pi}} \left[\sum_{t=0}^{\infty} \sum_{n \in \mathsf{N}} \beta^t R^{(n)} \big(X_t^{(n)}, a^{(n)} \big) \right] : \text{ subject to } (10), \boldsymbol{\pi} \in \bar{\boldsymbol{\Pi}}^{\mathrm{NA}} \right\}. \tag{11}$$

Note that the optimal value $V^{\mathrm{R}}(\boldsymbol{x})$ of (11) gives an *upper bound* on the optimal value $V^*(\boldsymbol{x})$ of (8).

To address (11) we deploy a Lagrangian approach, attaching a multiplier $\lambda \ge 0$ to constraint (10) and then dualizing it. The resulting problem

$$\max_{\boldsymbol{\pi} \in \boldsymbol{\Pi}^{\mathrm{NA}}} \mathsf{E}_{\boldsymbol{x}}^{\boldsymbol{\pi}} \left[\sum_{t=0}^{\infty} \sum_{n \in \mathsf{N}} \beta^t \left\{ R^{(n)} \big(X_t^{(n)}, a_t^{(n)} \big) - \lambda a_t^{(n)} \right\} \right] + \frac{M}{1 - \beta} \lambda \tag{12}$$

is a *Lagrangian relaxation* of (11), whose optimal value $V^{\mathrm{L}}(\boldsymbol{x}; \lambda)$ gives an upper bound on $V^{\mathrm{R}}(\boldsymbol{x})$. The *Lagrangian dual problem* is to find an optimal value $\lambda^*(\boldsymbol{x})$ of λ, i.e., a value giving the best such upper bound, which we denote by $V^{\mathrm{D}}(\boldsymbol{x})$:

$$\min_{\lambda \ge 0} V^{\mathrm{L}}(\boldsymbol{x}; \lambda). \tag{13}$$

Note that (13) is a convex optimization problem, since $V^{\mathrm{L}}(\boldsymbol{x}; \lambda)$ is convex in λ. Although *weak duality* $(V^{\mathrm{R}}(\boldsymbol{x}) \le V^{\mathrm{D}}(\boldsymbol{x}))$ is ensured, satisfaction of *strong duality* $(V^{\mathrm{R}}(\boldsymbol{x}) = V^{\mathrm{D}}(\boldsymbol{x}))$ calls for further investigation.

Lagrangian relaxation (12) *decomposes* into the single-channel subproblems

$$\max_{\pi^{(n)} \in \Pi^{(n)}} \mathsf{E}_{x^{(n)}}^{\pi^{(n)}} \left[\sum_{t=0}^{\infty} \beta^t \left\{ R^{(n)} \big(X_t^{(n)}, a_t^{(n)} \big) - \lambda a_t^{(n)} \right\} \right], \tag{14}$$

where $\Pi^{(n)}$ is the class of nonanticipative sensing policies for channel n *in isolation*. Note that in channel n's subproblem (14) multiplier λ represents an additional sensing cost, to be added to the channel's regular sensing cost $c^{(n)}$.

3.2   Indexability and Whittle's Marginal Productivity Index Policy

Consider now channel n's subproblem (14) treating sensing charge λ as a scalar parameter, which is now allowed to take negative values. The following defines a key structural property of such a parametric restless bandit subproblem, termed *indexability*, which simplifies its solution and hence that of Lagrangian dual (13).

Definition 1. We say that subproblem (14) is *indexable* if there exists an *index* $\lambda^{*,(n)}(x)$ which is a scalar function of the channel's belief state $x \in \mathsf{X}$ such that, for any value of multiplier $\lambda \in \mathbb{R}$, the active action $a_t^{(n)} = 1$ (sensing the channel) is optimal in state $X_t^{(n)} = x$ iff $\lambda^{*,(n)}(x) \geq \lambda$.

The indexability property of restless bandits was introduced by Whittle in [11], and then extended by the author (cf. [8]) leading to the unifying concept of *marginal productivity* (MP) *index* after its economic interpretation: the *Whittle MP index* $\lambda^{*,(n)}(x)$ gives the MP of sensing channel n when it occupies state x.

If each single-channel subproblem (14) were indexable and a tractable procedure were available to evaluate index $\lambda^{*,(n)}(x)$, then this would readily yield a computationally tractable algorithm to solve Lagrangian dual problem (13) —provided the objective of (14) could also be efficiently evaluated— and thus compute the upper bound $V^D(x)$ referred to above. Further, we could then use for multichannel problem (8) the resulting Whittle's MP index policy, based on using $\lambda^{*,(n)}(X_t^{(n)})$ as channel n's sensing-priority index.

3.3   Sufficient Indexability Conditions and MP Index Evaluation

Yet, as noted in [11], indexability needs to be established for the model at hand. For such a purpose, the author introduced in work reviewed in [8] general sufficient indexability conditions for discrete-state restless bandits, based on satisfaction of *partial conservation laws* (PCLs), along with an index algorithm.

The author has recently extended the scope of such conditions to real-state restless bandits in results announced in [9], which are reviewed next. The following discussion focuses on a single-project restless bandit problem modeling the optimal sensing subproblem for a single channel, whose label n is dropped from the ensuing notation. We thus write, e.g., the channel's belief state and action processes as $X_t \in \mathsf{X} \triangleq [0,1]$ and $a_t \in \{0,1\}$, respectively. Note that the channel's state dynamics imply that the state subset $\widetilde{\mathsf{X}} \triangleq [q, p+q]$ is absorbing.

Let us evaluate the performance of an admissible channel sensing policy $\pi \in \Pi$ along two dimensions: the *work measure*

$$g(x, \pi) \triangleq \mathsf{E}_x^\pi \left[\sum_{t=0}^\infty \beta^t a_t \right],$$

giving the expected total discounted number of times the channel is sensed under policy π, starting in belief state $X_0 = x$; and the *reward measure*

$$f(x, \pi) \triangleq \mathsf{E}_x^\pi \left[\sum_{t=0}^\infty \beta^t R(X_t, a_t) \right],$$

giving the corresponding expected total discounted net reward earned.

We can then formulate the channel's optimal sensing subproblem (14) as

$$\max_{\pi \in \Pi} f(x, \pi) - \lambda g(x, \pi). \tag{15}$$

We shall refer to (15) as the channel's λ-*charge subproblem*. Problem (15) is a real-state MDP, whose optimal value function we denote by $V^*(x; \lambda)$.

In order to solve (15) it suffices to consider *deterministic stationary policies*, which are naturally represented by their *active (state) sets*, i.e., the set of belief states where they prescribe the active action (sense the channel). For an active set $S \subseteq \mathsf{X}$ we shall refer to the S-*active policy*.

We shall further focus attention on the subclass of *threshold policies*. For a given *threshold level* $z \in \mathbb{R}$, the z-*threshold policy* senses the channel in state x iff $x > z$, so its active set is $B(z) \triangleq \{x \in \mathsf{X} : x > z\}$. Note that $B(z) = (z, 1]$ for $0 \le z < 1$, $B(z) = \mathsf{X} = [0, 1]$ for $z < 0$, and $B(z) = \emptyset$ for $z \ge 1$. We shall denote by $g(x, z)$ and $f(x, z)$ the corresponding work and reward measures.

In the following we shall use the notation

$$\phi^0(x) \triangleq q + \rho x, \quad \phi^1(x) \triangleq q + \rho \frac{1 - \kappa}{1 - \kappa x} x = \phi^0(x) - \rho \kappa \frac{1 - x}{1 - \kappa x} x. \tag{16}$$

For fixed z, work measure $g(\cdot, z)$ is characterized as the unique solution to

$$g(x, z) = \begin{cases} 1 + \beta \kappa x g(q + \rho, z) + \beta(1 - \kappa x) g(\phi^1(x), z), & x > z \\ \beta g(\phi^0(x), z), & x \le z. \end{cases} \tag{17}$$

Similarly, reward measure $f(\cdot, z)$ is characterized by

$$f(x, z) = \begin{cases} R(x, 1) + \beta \kappa x f(q + \rho, z) + \beta(1 - \kappa x) f(\phi^1(x), z), & x > z \\ R(x, 0) + \beta f(\phi^0(x), z), & x \le z. \end{cases} \tag{18}$$

We shall further use the marginal counterparts of such measures. For a threshold z and action a, denote by $\langle a, z \rangle$ the policy that takes action a in the initial slot and adopts the z-threshold policy thereafter. Define the *marginal work measure*

$$w(x, z) \triangleq g(x, \langle 1, z \rangle) - g(x, \langle 0, z \rangle), \tag{19}$$

and the *marginal reward measure*

$$r(x, z) \triangleq f(x, \langle 1, z \rangle) - f(x, \langle 0, z \rangle). \tag{20}$$

If $w(x, z) \ne 0$, define further the *MP measure*

$$\lambda(x, z) \triangleq \frac{r(x, z)}{w(x, z)}. \tag{21}$$

The following definition extends to the real-state setting a corresponding definition introduced by the author in [7] for discrete-state restless bandits.

Definition 2. We say that subproblem (15) is *PCL-indexable* (with respect to threshold policies) if the following conditions hold:

(i) *positive marginal work*: $w(x, z) > 0$ for $x \in X$ and $z \in \mathbb{R}$; and
(ii) *nondecreasing index*: the following index is monotone nondecreasing in x,

$$\lambda^*(x) \triangleq \lambda(x, x), \quad x \in X. \tag{22}$$

The next result, which extends the scope of a corresponding result in [7] for discrete-state restless bandits to the real-state setting, states the validity of the PCL-based sufficient indexability conditions deployed in this paper. It further shows how to evaluate the Whittle MP index.

Theorem 1. *If subproblem (15) is PCL-indexable, then it is indexable and the index $\lambda^*(x)$ given by (22) is its Whittle MP index.*

4   Indexability Analysis and Index Evaluation

In [9], the sufficient indexability conditions above were announced and deployed in a special case of the present model, which corresponds to perfect sensing (i.e., $\kappa = 1$). In such a case, the evaluation equations (17) and (18) for $g(x, z)$ and $f(x, z)$ can be solved in closed form. This allows a direct verification of such conditions by algebraic means, and yields a closed-form index formula.

Although in the case $\kappa < 1$ of concern herein such evaluation equations become considerably more complex, we are still able to solve them in closed form. This section outlines how to do so, and further shows how to use such solutions to evaluate the index $\lambda^*(x)$.

In the sequel we focus on the case where the channel's sensing cost is $c = 0$.

4.1   Case I: Threshold $z < q$

In the case $z < q$, under the z-threshold policy X_t remains above threshold after first getting above threshold. Further, if $X_0 \leq z$ then $X_1 \geq q > z$. Elementary arguments give that the work measure and the marginal work measure have the following evaluations. For $x \in X$, $g(x, z) = 1/(1 - \beta)$ for $x > z$, and $g(x, z) = \beta/(1 - \beta)$ for $x \leq z$. Hence, $w(x, z) = 1$.

To obtain $f(x, z)$ for such z, we use the following argument. Consider first the case where the initial state x is above threshold $x > z$. Then, as pointed out above, X_t will stay above threshold for all t, under the active dynamics

$$X_{t+1} = \begin{cases} q + \rho, & \text{with probability (w.p.) } \kappa X_t \\ \phi^1(X_t), & \text{w.p. } 1 - \kappa X_t. \end{cases}$$

Now, since $\kappa x(q + \rho) + (1 - \kappa x)\phi^1(x) = \phi^0(x)$, it follows that the expected state at time t, $\mathsf{E}_x^z[X_t]$, is the same as that under the deterministic passive dynamics, $\phi_t^0(x)$, which is recursively generated by $\phi_0^0(x) \triangleq x$ and $\phi_t^0(x) \triangleq \phi^0(\phi_{t-1}^0(x))$.

The solution to such a recursion is

$$\phi_t^0(x) = \phi_\infty^0 - \rho^t(\phi_\infty^0 - x), \quad \text{where } \phi_\infty^0 \triangleq \frac{q}{1-\rho} = \lim_{t \to \infty} \phi_t^0(x).$$

Based on the above we obtain, for $x > z$,

$$f(x,z) = b\kappa \mathsf{E}_x^z\left[\sum_{t=0}^\infty \beta^t X_t\right] = b\kappa \sum_{t=0}^\infty \beta^t \phi_t^0(x) = b\kappa\left[\frac{\phi_\infty^0}{1-\beta} - \frac{\phi_\infty^0 - x}{1-\beta\rho}\right],$$

and, for $x \le z$,

$$f(x,z) = \beta f(\phi^0(x), z) = \beta b\kappa\left[\frac{\phi_\infty^0}{1-\beta} - \frac{\phi_\infty^0 - \phi^0(x)}{1-\beta\rho}\right].$$

From this, it is readily obtained that the marginal reward measure is $r(x,z) = b\kappa x$, and therefore the index $\lambda^*(x)$ in (22) has the evaluation

$$\lambda^*(x) = \frac{r(x,x)}{w(x,x)} = b\kappa x, \quad 0 \le x < q. \tag{23}$$

The following cases below refer to $\phi_t^1(x)$, the tth iterate of function $\phi^1(x)$ in (16), recursively defined by $\phi_0^1(x) = x$ and $\phi_t^1(x) = \phi^1(\phi_{t-1}^1(x))$ for $t \ge 1$. Note that, for any $x \in \mathsf{X}$, $\phi_t^1(x)$ converges as $t \to \infty$ to the limit

$$\phi_\infty^1 \triangleq \frac{1 - \rho + (q+\rho)\kappa - \sqrt{(1 - \rho + (q+\rho)\kappa)^2 - 4\kappa q}}{2\kappa},$$

which is the unique root of $\phi^1(x) = x$ in $[q, q + \rho]$.

It holds that $\phi_\infty^1 \le \phi_\infty^0$ iff κ is close enough to 1, say $\kappa \ge \kappa^*$, which we assume henceforth. This will be the case iff the error probabilities are small enough, so

$$\kappa \triangleq \epsilon \frac{\max\{0, \zeta - \delta\}}{1 - \delta} + (1 - \epsilon) \min\left\{1, \frac{\zeta}{\delta}\right\} \ge \kappa^*.$$

4.2　Case II: Threshold $z \in [q, \phi_\infty^1]$

In this case it is easily seen that, again, once the state X_t gets above the threshold z, it stays so thereafter. Let $t^*(x, z) \triangleq \min\{t \ge 0 : \phi_t^0(x) > z\}$. Then, $g(x, z) = \beta^{t^*(x,z)}/(1-\beta)$, from which the $w(x, z)$ can be evaluated via (19).

Further, arguing along the lines in Section 4.1, we obtain

$$f(x,z) = \begin{cases} b\kappa\left[\dfrac{\phi_\infty^0}{1-\beta} - \dfrac{\phi_\infty^0 - x}{1-\beta\rho}\right], & x > z \\[3ex] \beta^{t^*(x,z)} b\kappa\left[\dfrac{\phi_\infty^0}{1-\beta} - \dfrac{\phi_\infty^0 - \phi_{t^*(x,z)}^0(x)}{1-\beta\rho}\right] & x \le z, \end{cases}$$

from which the $r(x, z)$ can be evaluated via (20).

From this it is readily obtained that the index $\lambda^*(x)$ in (22) has the evaluation

$$\lambda^*(x) = \frac{r(x,x)}{w(x,x)} = b\kappa x, \quad q \leq x \leq \phi_\infty^1. \tag{24}$$

4.3   Case III: Threshold $z \in (\phi_\infty^1, \phi_\infty^0)$

In this case, the process X_t jumps infinitely often above and below threshold. Define the map $\phi(x,z) \triangleq 1_{\{x>z\}}\phi^1(x) + 1_{\{x\leq z\}}\phi^0(x)$, and let $\phi_0(x,z) = x$, $\phi_t(x,z) = \phi(\phi_{t-1}(x,z),z)$ for $t \geq 1$. Then, letting $a_t(x,z) \triangleq 1_{\{\phi_t(x,z)>z\}}$, $(\phi a)_t(x,z) \triangleq \phi_t(x,z)a_t(x,z)$,

$$\tilde{a}(x,z) \triangleq a_0(x,z) + \sum_{t=1}^\infty \beta^t a_t(x,z) \prod_{s=0}^{t-1} \big[1 - \kappa(\phi a)_s(x,z)\big],$$

$$\widetilde{(\phi a)}(x,z) \triangleq (\phi a)_0(x,z) + \sum_{t=1}^\infty \beta^t (\phi a)_t(x,z) \prod_{s=0}^{t-1} \big[1 - \kappa(\phi a)_s(x,z)\big],$$

we obtain the following result via probabilistic arguments.

Proposition 1. *For $x \in \mathsf{X}$ and $z \in (\phi_\infty^1, \phi_\infty^0)$,*

$$g(x,z) = \tilde{a}(x,z) + \beta\kappa\widetilde{(\phi a)}(x,z)\frac{\tilde{a}(q+\rho,z)}{1 - \beta\kappa\widetilde{(\phi a)}(q+\rho,z)},$$

$$f(x,z) = b\kappa\widetilde{(\phi a)}(x,z)\left[1 + \beta\kappa\frac{\widetilde{(\phi a)}(q+\rho,z)}{1 - \beta\kappa\widetilde{(\phi a)}(q+\rho,z)}\right].$$

Using Proposition 1, the marginal work and reward $w(x,z)$ and $r(x,z)$ are readily evaluated via (19)–(20), and hence so is the index $\lambda^*(x)$ in (22) for $\phi_\infty^1 < x < \phi_\infty^0$. In practice, one needs to truncate the above infinite series.

4.4   Case IV: Threshold $z \in [\phi_\infty^0, q + \rho]$

In this case, it is easily seen that the process X_t, starting at x, hits set $[0, z]$ after a finite number of time slots, remaining there afterwards. Therefore,

$$g(x,z) = f(x,z) = 0, \quad x \leq z.$$

For $x > z$, let $m^*(x,z) \triangleq \{t \geq 1: \phi_t^1(x) \leq z\}$. We have the following result.

Proposition 2. *For $x > z$ and $z \in [\phi_\infty^0, q+\rho]$, $g(x,z)$ and $f(x,z)$ are evaluated as in Proposition 1. In this case, the infinite series to evaluate $(\phi a)_t(x,z)$ and $\widetilde{(\phi a)}(x,z)$ reduce to finite sums with $m^*(x,z) - 1$ terms.*

Using Proposition 2, the marginal work and reward $w(x,z)$ and $r(x,z)$ are evaluated via (19)–(20), and hence so is index $\lambda^*(x)$ in (22) for $\phi_\infty^0 \leq x \leq q + \rho$.

4.5   Case V: Threshold $z > q + \rho$

In this case it is readily seen that $g(x, z) = 1_{\{x > z\}}$, and hence $w(x, z) = 1$. Further, $f(x, z) = b\kappa x 1_{\{x > z\}}$, and hence $r(x, z) = b\kappa x$. Therefore,

$$\lambda^*(x) = \frac{r(x, x)}{w(x, x)} = b\kappa x, \quad q + \rho \leq x \leq 1. \tag{25}$$

4.6   Verification of PCL-Indexability and Index Evaluation

Based on the results in Sections 4.1–4.5 we obtain the following result.

Proposition 3. *The single-channel OSA problem is PCL-indexable with respect to threshold policies under the β-discounted criterion, for $0 \leq \beta < 1$. Therefore, it is indexable, and the index $\lambda^*(x)$ calculated above is its Whittle's MP index.*

We can also extend the result of Proposition 3 to the average criterion. Thus, denoting by $\lambda^*_\beta(x)$ the MP index for discount factor β, it holds that $\lambda^*_\beta(x)$ increases monotonically to a finite limiting index $\lambda^*(x)$ as $\beta \nearrow 1$.

5   Computational Experiments

5.1   Index Evaluation

The author has implemented a MATLAB script for index evaluation using the results in Sect. 4. The index was then computed for an OSA channel instance with parameters $p = 0.2$, $q = 0.1$, $\rho = 1 - p - q = 0.7$, $b = 1$, $\delta = 0.03$, $\epsilon = 0.08$ and $\zeta = 0.05$, for which $\kappa = 0.9216$. The infinite series in case III (cf. Section 4.3 were approximately evaluated by truncating them to $T = 10^4$ terms, although it appears that much smaller values of T suffice to obtain enough accuracy. The discount factor β varied over the range $\beta = 0.1, 0.2, \ldots, 0.9, 0.9999999$, where the latter β value is meant to approximate the limiting index as $\beta \nearrow 1$. For each β, the index $\lambda^*(x)$ was evaluated on a grid of x values of $\mathsf{X} = [0, 1]$ of width 10^{-3}.

Fig. 1 shows the results. As required by the PCL-indexability conditions, in each case the index $\lambda^*(x)$ was monotone nondecreasing (in fact, strictly increasing) in x. Note that the index $\lambda^*(x)$ is continuous in x, being also piecewise differentiable. Further, for fixed x the index $\lambda^*(x)$ is increasing in β, converging as $\beta \nearrow 1$ to a limiting index that can be used for average-criterion problem (9). For each x, the time to compute $\lambda^*(x)$ was negligible.

5.2   Benchmarking the MP Index Policy

The author has performed a small-scale preliminary simulation study to assess the relative performance of the MP index policy against alternative simpler policies: the myopic index policy, based on index $\lambda^{\mathrm{MY}}(x) = b\kappa x$, and the random selection policy, which picks a channel to sense at random (with equal probability

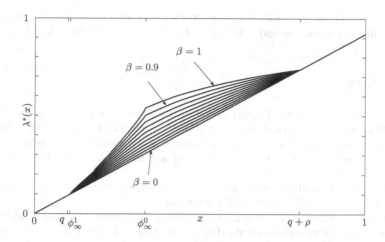

Fig. 1. The Whittle MP index for different discount factors β

Table 1. Benchmarking results

N	random	myopic	MP	upper bound
2	0.984 ± 0.004	1.476 ± 0.007	1.623 ± 0.008	1.738
3	1.150 ± 0.003	2.128 ± 0.005	2.291 ± 0.006	2.527
4	1.054 ± 0.002	2.113 ± 0.005	2.311 ± 0.006	2.527

for each channel). Further, the upper bound based on the Lagrangian relaxation discussed above was evaluated.

The base instance has a single SU and $N = 4$ channels, with parameters $p = (0.03, 0.01, 0.05, 0.01)$, $q = (0.01, 0.03, 0.05, 0.04)$, $\delta = (0.01, 0.005, 0.01, 0.015)$, $\epsilon = (0.02, 0.01, 0.01, 0.05)$, $\zeta = 0.05$, and $b = (5, 1, 3, 1)$. Sensing costs are taken to be zero. This base instance was modified to obtain three instances. In the first, only the first $N = 2$ channels are used. In the second, only the first $N = 3$ channels are used. In the third instance, all $N = 4$ channels are used.

The MP index was computed off-line for each channel at a grid of x values having width 10^{-3}, and was then retrieved during the simulation as needed, using linear interpolation to approximate intermediate values.

The experiment focused on the average criterion. For each instance, 10^3 independent simulation runs were performed on a horizon of $T = 10^4$ time slots. The initial state for each channel n was taken to be equal to the steady-state mean channel availability $x_0^{(n)} = q^{(n)}/(p^{(n)} + q^{(n)})$. Table 1 reports the resulting average throughput (Mbs/slot) under each policy, including 95 % confidence intervals around the mean, along with the upper bound obtained from the relaxation.

The results show that the MP index policy outperforms the myopic index policy by 9.96 % for $N = 2$, by 7.7 % for $N = 3$, and by 9.4 % for $N = 4$, which are significant amounts. The random policy performed rather poorly.

As for the MP index policy's suboptimality gap, we can bound it above using the relaxation's upper bound, by 7.09% for $N = 2$, by 10.30% for $N = 3$, and by 9.35% for $N = 4$.

References

1. Ai, J., Abouzeid, A.A.: Opportunistic spectrum access based on a constrained multi-armed bandit formulation. J. Commun. Networks 11(2), 134–147 (2009)
2. Chen, Y., Zhao, Q., Swami, A.: Joint design and separation principle for opportunistic spectrum access in the presence of sensing errors. IEEE Trans. Inf. Theory 54(5), 2053–2071 (2008)
3. Gittins, J.C.: Bandit processes and dynamic allocation indices. J. Roy. Statist. Soc. Ser. B 41(2), 148–177 (1979); With discussion
4. Hoang, A.T., Liang, Y.C., Wong, D.T.C., Zeng, Y., Zhang, R.: Opportunistic spectrum access for energy-constrained cognitive radios. IEEE Trans. Wireless Commun. 8(3), 1206–1211 (2009)
5. Johnston, L.A., Krishnamurthy, V.: Opportunistic file transfer over a fading channel: a POMDP search theory formulation with optimal threshold policies. IEEE Trans. Wireless Commun. 5(2), 394–405 (2006)
6. Liu, K., Zhao, Q.: A restless bandit formulation of opportunistic access: indexability and index policy. In: Proc. 5th IEEE Conf. Sensor, Mesh and Ad Hoc Commun. Networks, pp. 1–5 (2008)
7. Niño-Mora, J.: Restless bandits, partial conservation laws and indexability. Adv. Appl. Probab. 33(1), 76–98 (2001)
8. Niño-Mora, J.: Dynamic priority allocation via restless bandit marginal productivity indices. TOP 15(2), 161–198 (2007); Followed by discussions by Adan, I.J.B.F., Boxma, O.J., Altman, E., Hernández-Lerma, O., Weber, R., Whittle, P., Yao, D.D.
9. Niño-Mora, J.: An index policy for dynamic fading-channel allocation to heterogeneous mobile users with partial observations. In: Proc. NGI 2008, 4th Euro-NGI Conf. Next Generation Internet Networks, Krakow, Poland, pp. 231–238. IEEE, Los Alamitos (2008)
10. Niño-Mora, J., Villar, S.S.: Multi-target tracking via restless bandit marginal productivity indices and Kalman filter in discrete time. In: Proc. 2009 CDC/CCC, Joint 48th IEEE Conf. Decision and Control and 28th Chinese Control Conf., Shanghai, China. IEEE, Los Alamitos (in press, 2009)
11. Whittle, P.: Restless bandits: Activity allocation in a changing world. In: Gani, J. (ed.) A Celebration of Applied Probability. J. Appl. Probab. spec. Applied Probability Trust, Sheffield, UK, vol. 25A, pp. 287–298 (1988)
12. Zhao, Q., Tong, L., Swami, A., Chen, Y.: Decentralized cognitive MAC for opportunistic spectrum access in ad hoc networks: a POMDP framework. IEEE J. Sel. Areas Commun. 25(3), 589–600 (2007)

Content-Based Routing in Networks with Time-Fluctuating Request Rates

Folkert van Vliet[1], Richard J. Boucherie[1], and Maurits de Graaf[2,*]

[1] University of Twente
[2] Thales Nederland B.V., Division Land and Joint Systems, Netherlands
maurits.degraaf@nl.thalesgroup.com

Abstract. In large-scale distributed applications, a loosely-coupled e-vent-based style of communication as in publish-subscribe systems eases the integration of autonomous, heterogeneous components. In a publish-subscribe system, content-based routing - where routing is based on the content of the messages - is an alternative to address-based delivery. In this paper we provide a time-dependent analysis of the identity-based routing scheme. Our analytical approach is based on continuous-time Markov chains and extends the steady-state approach by Jaeger and Mühl [7] to systems with time-fluctuating parameters. For m-ary trees with k levels, with a single publisher at the root and subscribers at the leaves, we obtain explicit closed form solutions for the time-dependent distribution of the traffic rates in the network. The results allow us to investigate, for example, the impact of time-fluctuating request rates versus time-independent request rates, and the switching point between optimality of flooding and identity-based routing.

Keywords: content-based routing, publish-subscribe mechanisms, transient behavior.

1 Introduction

1.1 Motivation

In many computer networks, independently created applications have to be integrated into a complex information system. Especially in large-scale distributed applications, a loosely-coupled event-based style of communication has many advantages.

In publish/subcribe systems, individual processing entities, called *publishers*, publish information, called *notifications*, without specifying a particular destination. Similarly, *subscribers* express their interest in receiving certain types of information by subscribing. The messages are asynchronously exchanged over the network.

---

* Supported by the Netherlands Organization for Scientific Research (NWO) Casimir 2005 programme (grant: 018.001.037).

R. Núñez-Queija and J. Resing (Eds.): NET-COOP 2009, LNCS 5894, pp. 75–90, 2009.

Content-based routing is used in publish-subscribe systems to distribute the messages. Routing decisions are based on the content of the messages (as opposed to the addresses of the messages). In this paper, we present an analytical approach for performance evaluation of content-based routing. Our model is based on networks of infinite-server queues with time-varying parameters. In this model, a heterogeneous population of publishers (distributed over the system) serves a heterogeneous population of subscribers. The subscribers initiate requests according to an arrival process that fluctuates over time. Subscribers remain active for a random amount of time that may also fluctuate over time. Our model explicitly takes into account the influence of the time-varying subscription process on the amount of data and control traffic. The analysis allows us to compare the total amount of messages (subscriptions and notifications) flowing through the network with time-fluctuating request rates and with time-independent request rates. In addition, the total amount of messages under flooding and identity-based routing can be compared. This is mainly important in distributed systems where bandwidth is a limitation (due to e.g. wireless connections).

In the remaining part of Section 1 we describe content-based routing algorithms in more detail. In Section 2 we present our contribution: a time-dependent analysis of the traffic under flooding and identity-based routing. Section 3 presents two examples allowing to compare a time-dependent to a steady state setting, and to compare identity-based routing to flooding. Section 4 presents the conclusions of this work.

1.2   Statement of Contribution

Jaeger and Mühl [7] present an analytical approach to analyze an identity-based routing system using a stochastic approach involving continuous-time birth-death Markov chains in equilibrium. The contribution of the present paper is the extension to allow the rate at which subscribers initiate content requests to depend on time (e.g. due to time of day effects). The importance of such a time-dependent analysis - as opposed to steady-state analysis - is discussed below. As in [7], our analysis is done for m-ary trees with k levels, where a single publisher is connected to the root of the tree and subscribers are connected to the leaf nodes of the tree.

Our model falls in the class of networks of infinite-server queues. For such networks, the limiting distribution of the number of customers in the queues is known to have a so-called multivariate Poisson distribution [9]. Surprisingly, the equilibrium results of Jaeger and Mühl [7] show that for identity-based routing, the amount of toggle traffic, and traffic due to notifications and subscriptions, depends only on the load and arrival rate parameters of this time-dependent distribution. This allows us to extend their results to the time-dependent case.

In contrast with the direct correspondence of our results with those of Jaeger and Mühl, we stress that the reasoning for obtaining explicit results for the time-dependent performance measures is not based on equilibrium methods. Instead, we use a new method that avoids the use of regenerative and insensitivity arguments, and hence generalizes to the time-dependent setting.

1.3 Example: The Added Value of a Time-Varying Analysis

The approach presented in this paper allows us to analyze the impact of varying rates at which subscribers initiate content requests (e.g. due to time of day
effects). One may wonder why this is important: one could imagine performing
various equilibrium-based analysis based on various regimes to account for the
effects of the time of the day. We will call this 'piecewise stationary approximation'. Below we show that -depending on the system parameters- a time-
dependent analysis much better captures the behavior of a queueing system than
piecewise stationary approximation. To that order consider the following simple
example. Suppose a time-dependent queueing system consists of a single queue
with a Poisson arrival rate (denoting the number of customers arriving per time
unit) that oscillates between 0 and 1 as given by: $\lambda(t) = 1$ for $t \in [3i, 3(i+1)]$,
$i = 0, 2, 4$, and $\lambda(t) = 0$, for $t \in [3i, 3(i+1)]$, $i = 1, 3, 5$. Here, the periods where
$\lambda(t) = 1$ represent the busy periods, the periods where $\lambda(t) = 0$ represent the
quiet periods, when no new customers are entering the system. The exponential
completion rate (i.e., the number of customers served per time unit) is a constant
$\mu = 1$.

With regimes chosen appropriately, the approximation method, yields the
following time-dependent system load $\rho(t) = \frac{\lambda}{\mu} = 1$, when $\lambda(t) = 1$ and $\rho(t) = 0$
otherwise.

A time varying (or transient) analysis using the methods in [9], shows that
in this case the time-dependent system load is composed of functions $\rho_i(t)$ for
$t \in [3i, 3(i+1)]$ and $i = 0, 1, 2, \ldots$. The time-dependent system load for the
period $t \in [3i, 3(i+1)]$, is then given as:

$$\rho_i(t) = 1 + e^{-t}(\rho_{0,i} - 1) \text{ when } i \in \{0, 2, 4\}$$

and

$$\rho_i(t) = \rho_{0,i}e^{-t} \text{ when } i \in \{1, 3, 5\}.$$

Here $\rho_{0,i}$ denotes the initial value for period $[3i, 3(i+1)]$ which is recursively
defined as $\rho_{0,i} = \rho_{i-1}(3(i+1))$ for $i = 1, 2, \ldots$ and $\rho_{0,0} = 0$. (So we start with
an empty system). Both the piecewise stationary approximation and the exact
solution are displayed in Figure 1. Here the dashed lines indicate the system
load ρ as calculated by the approximation. The bold lines indicate the system
load $\rho(t)$ as calculated by a transient analysis. The figure makes clear that the
exact analysis and the piecewise linear approximation yield different results. For
example, assume that for dimensioning purposes it is important to have insight in
the fraction of time that the system load exceeds the value 0.8 (which is called: a
high load period). The approximation would conclude that this system is half the
time in a high load period. The time-dependent analysis shows that the fraction
of time that system is in a high load period is much less: only about one quarter
of the time. Similarly, from the approximative analysis we would conclude that
the system is only half the time having a strictly positive probability for at least
one customer. However, the time-dependent analysis shows that the system has
all the time a strictly positive probability for at least one customer.

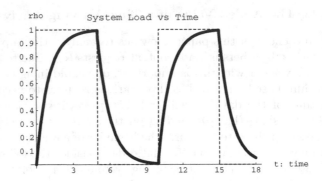

Fig. 1. Exact solution vs piecewise stationary approximation: a simple example

Note however, that the accuracy of the piecewise stationary approximation improves when increasing the length of the intervals for which $\lambda(t) = 1$ or 0, or increasing the value of μ. In practical language: if the time of day effects are about the same order of magnitude as the average holding time of a subscription, then the time-dependent analysis is needed. Otherwise, with much shorter subscription holding times, the piecewise stationary approximation will do fine.

1.4   Content-Based Routing Algorithms

The simplest content-based routing algorithm is *flooding*. In this method, publisher notifications are flooded to all *brokers* (content-based routers) in the network. The only content-based aspect is the fact that subscribers interests are saved at the local broker (i.e., the content-based router to which the client is directly attached). Only notifications corresponding to the subscribers' interest are then forwarded to the subscriber. A more sophisticated content-based routing algorithm is *identity-based routing*. Here, subscriptions are forwarded between the brokers and saved in the routing tables at the brokers. The routing tables at the brokers are set up so that notifications are sent only to local brokers that have subscribers attached. To reduce the amount of traffic in the network, a subscription is not forwarded over a link if previously the same subscription (of another subscriber) was forwarded over that link, and an unsubscription is not forwarded over a link, if there is still another subscription on the same content active.

Under flooding, there is no subscription-traffic, but a lot of notification-traffic, whereas under identity-based routing there usually will be less notification-traffic at the cost of additional subscription traffic. In this paper, we analyze the total network traffic for flooding and identity-based routing. Alternative content-based routing algorithms, are *simple routing*, where each subscription is treated independently from the other subscriptions, *covering-based routing* (where it is exploited that subscriptions can cover other subscriptions on a smaller part of that information) and *filter merging* (a technique that combines filters into a covering filter to reduce the number of propagated filters and thus the size of distributed state).

1.5 Literature

A lot of research is focused on the design of a properly working publish/subscribe systems in practice. Examples are the SIENA system (Carzaniga, Rosenblum and Wolf [3]), the ELVIN system (Segall and Arnold [14]) and the REBECA system (Mühl [10]). Mühl [10] and Eugster et al. [6] provide an extensive overview of a publish/subscribe system. Mühl et al. [11] evaluated the traffic of several routing algorithms in a working prototype. In [4] it is argued that Content-Based Routing (CBR) has the potential of becoming the technology to address both global service retrieval and large-scale asynchronous interaction in service oriented architectures. In Takoma [17] filter merging is investigated.

Baldoni et al. [1] present a formal modelling framework for content-based routing. Their approach focuses on the correctness of the system when it is evolving in time. Another approach for modelling a fault tolerant publish/subscribe system is proposed by Mühl et al. [12]. They define a self-stabilizing algorithm that enables the system to automatically recover from faults and is implementable in highly dynamical environments. Tarkoma [16] investigates the cost and safety of handoff protocols for subscribers and publishers in mobility aware content-based routing systems.

There is a large body of theoretical literature studying queueing networks in equilibrium. For networks with other than infinite-server queues there seem to be very few analytical results concerning transient behavior. The relevant theory on Markov chains and transient behavior is largely developed in [2],[5] and [9]. These also refer to further material on transient behavior of open networks.

2   Main Results

In order to provide a time-dependent analysis of the amount of traffic generated under identity-based routing and flooding, we consider an m-ary tree with k levels where one publisher is active at the root broker and the only possible subscribers are at the end brokers. The m denotes the number of children of each node and the k denotes the depth of the tree. The choice for using this tree-shaped network is motivated by the fact that many underlying multicast routing protocols are based on underlying tree-like (logical) structures. An m-ary tree is chosen as the simple representant of such a tree. Figure 2 shows this structure where $m = 2$ and $k = 4$. We assume subscriptions only have to be propagated towards the root (there is a prior knowledge where the publisher is located). The nodes without clients are the brokers. The number of brokers on the i-th level equals m^i. Hence, the total number of end brokers is $N = m^{k-1}$. The brokers $B_{i,j}$ are numbered as indicated in the figure. We refer to the brokers at level $k-1$ (these are: $B_{k-1,j}$, $j = 1, 2, ..., N$), as the *end brokers* $1, 2, ..., N$ (numbered from left to right). Let l denote the number of links in the network.

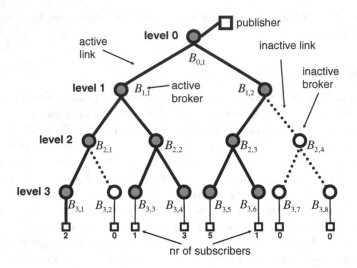

Fig. 2. Example of m-ary tree with k levels, with $m = 2$ and $k = 4$ and broker numbering. The figure shows $L((2, 0, 1, 3, 5, 1, 0, 0)) = 10$. The number of active brokers is 11.

For an m-ary tree with k levels: $l = \sum_{i=0}^{k-1} m^i - 1 = \frac{m^k - m}{m - 1}$. The random variable $X_j(t)$ denotes the number of active subscribers at end broker j, $j = 1, \ldots, N$, at time t with state space $S = \{0, 1, 2, 3, \ldots\}$. Let $\mathbf{X}(t) = (X_1(t), \ldots, X_N(t))$ and let $\mathbf{n} = (n_1, \ldots, n_N)$. We assume the system starts empty, i.e., $\mathbf{X}(0) = \mathbf{0}$. Consider the stochastic process in *state* $\mathbf{n}$, i.e., under the condition that $\mathbf{X}(t) = \mathbf{n}$. (Figure 2 displays the process in state $\mathbf{n} = (2, 0, 1, 3, 5, 1, 0, 0)$). Given a state, we call a link or a broker *active* if it is on the path from the root to an end broker j with $n_j > 0$. An end broker j is called active if $n_j > 0$. Let $L(\mathbf{n})$ denote the number of links that are active in state $\mathbf{n}$. With $y(t)$ we denote the average number of active links at time t, averaged over all instances. We assume the state of a broker j at level i equals either 0 or 1 according to: $B_{i,j} = 1$ if $B_{i,j}$ is active, and $B_{i,j} = 0$, otherwise. As the number of vertices with $B_{i,j} = 1$ induces a subtree of the m-ary tree, for each state $\mathbf{n}$, the number of active links $L(\mathbf{n})$ is:

$$L(\mathbf{n}) = -1 + \sum_{i=0}^{k-1} \sum_{j=1}^{m^i} B_{i,j}. \tag{1}$$

The publisher frequently publishes notifications according to an exponentially distributed inter-arrival time between consecutive notifications with an expected length of ω^{-1}. We assume that subscribers independently arrive at an end broker and become active for a while until leaving again. When a subscriber becomes active, it sends a subscription message. We assume each notification message contains the same type of content. Analogously, we have one subscription-message, which indicates whether or not there is interest for the notification.

Active subscribers will frequently update their subscription by sending a re-subscription each period r. Then, the local broker of the subscriber will re-new the routing entry by removing the old subscription and replacing it with the re-subscription. Next it forwards the re-subscription to its neighbor brokers which will perform the same tasks. In this manner all routing entries in the network for this subscription are refreshed. When a subscriber switches to the inactive state an unsubscription is sent. The size of a message is 1 unit and the cost for sending one message over one link equals 1 unit of traffic. A final assumption is that messages sent over the links between subscriber and the brokers they are attached to is free, because we are only interested in the traffic between the brokers. Furthermore, we assume that there is no delay when messages are propagated over the links.

We consider a non-homogeneous Poisson arrival rate of subscribers $\lambda_j(t)$ at end broker j which depends on the time t. The time a subscriber is active at time t is exponentially distributed with completion rate $\mu_j(t)$ at time t.

The message rate by *flooding* is given by $A_f(t) = \omega l$. Thus, the total traffic over a time interval T follows as:

$$A_f^T = \int_T A_f(t)dt = T\omega l. \tag{2}$$

In order to calculate the traffic in the system for *identity-based routing*, we distinguish between the *toggle traffic* rate $A_t(t)$ and *state-dependent traffic* rate $A_{sdt}(t)$, at time t. Toggle traffic only originates when new subscribers arrive or when subscribers leave: this traffic is caused by subscriptions and unsubscriptions. The state-dependent traffic consists of the notifications and re-subscriptions that are flowing through the network in a specific state of the system. Notice that in a certain state $\mathbf{n}$ the state-dependent traffic is easily calculated as $\left(\omega + \frac{1}{r}\right) L(n)$. The difficulty lies in determining the number of active links $y(t)$ averaged over all states. Our main result provides an explicit expression for this. The difficulty in determining the toggle traffic rate lies in determining the number of links that carry new subscription or unsubscription messages. For example, considering Figure 2, when $B_{3,7}$, the number of subscribers of end broker 7, increases from 0 to 1, a subscription message is carried over 2 links. For the toggle traffic, our main result provides an explicit expression for the number of links affected by a toggle.

Theorem 1. *The message rate at time t for identity-based routing is $A_{ibr}(t) = A_{sdt}(t) + A_t(t)$, where*

$$A_{sdt}(t) = \left(\omega + \frac{1}{r}\right) y(t), \tag{3}$$

where $y(t)$ is defined as:

$$y(t) = \left(l - \sum_{h=0}^{k-2} \sum_{j=1}^{m^{k-1-h}} \prod_{i=m^h(j-1)+1}^{jm^h} p_{0,i}(t)\right), \tag{4}$$

and

$$A_t(t) = \sum_{j=1}^{N} \left(p_{0,j}(t) + \sum_{h=1}^{k-2} \prod_{i=m^h\left(\left\lceil \frac{j}{m^h}\right\rceil - 1\right)+1}^{m^h\left\lceil \frac{j}{m^h}\right\rceil} p_{0,i}(t) \right) (\lambda_j(t) + \mu_j(t)\rho_j(t)), \quad (5)$$

where $p_{0,i}(t) = P(X_i(t) = 0)$, $i = 1, \ldots, N$.

So, the total amount of traffic in a time-interval of length T can be expressed as:

$$A_{ibr}^T = \int_T A_{ibr}(t)dt. \quad (6)$$

Note that compared to [7] our formulation is slightly more complex, because we allow $\lambda_i(t)$, $\mu_i(t)$, $i = 1, \ldots, N$, to be different. With $\lambda_i(t) = \lambda$, and $\mu_i(t) = \mu$ the results coincide. We prove Theorem 1 by means of the following results.

Lemma 1. *For the system with Poisson arrival rate $\lambda_j(t)$ and exponential completion rate $\mu_j(t)$ at end broker j, the time-dependent multivariate distribution is expressed by:*

$$P(\mathbf{X}(t) = \mathbf{n}) = \prod_{j=1}^{N} \frac{\rho_j(t)^{n_j}}{n_j!} e^{-\rho_j(t)} \; (n_j \in S, \; j = 1, \ldots, N, \; t \geq 0), \quad (7)$$

where $\rho_j(t)$ *is the solution of :*

$$\frac{d\rho_j(t)}{dt} = \lambda_j(t) - \mu_j(t)\rho_j(t), \; j = 1, \ldots, N, \; t \geq 0;$$
$$\rho_j(0) = 0, \; j = 1, \ldots, N. \quad (8)$$

Proof. Notice that the stochastic process $\mathbf{X}(t) = (X_1(t), \ldots, X_N(t))$ corresponds to a network of infinite-server queues with arrival rates $\lambda_j(t)$ and completion rates $\mu_j(t)$, at time t. Now the lemma follows from [9].   □

Note that (7) implies that $\rho_i(t)$ is the expected number of subscribers at end broker i at time t. Moreover, $p_{0,i}(t) = e^{-\rho_i(t)}$. The following theorem provides an expression for the total traffic as an expectation with respect to the time-dependent distribution (7).

Theorem 2. *The total traffic rate for identity-based routing equals $A_{ibr}(t) = A_{sdt}(t) + A_t(t)$, where*

$$A_{sdt}(t) = \left(\omega + \frac{1}{r}\right) \sum_{\mathbf{n}} L(\mathbf{n})P(\mathbf{X}(t) = \mathbf{n}), \quad (9)$$

and

$$A_t(t) = \sum_{j=1}^{N} \left[\lambda_j(t) \sum_{(\mathbf{n}_{j,0}, \mathbf{n}_{j,1})} b(\mathbf{n}_{j,0}, \mathbf{n}_{j,1})P(\mathbf{X}(t) = \mathbf{n}_{j,0}) + \right.$$

$$+ \mu_j(t) \sum_{(\mathbf{n}_{j,1}, \mathbf{n}_{j,0})} b(\mathbf{n}_{j,1}, \mathbf{n}_{j,0}) P(\mathbf{X}(t) = \mathbf{n}_{j,1}) \Bigg], \tag{10}$$

where $b(\mathbf{n}, \mathbf{n}') = |L(\mathbf{n}) - L(\mathbf{n}')|$ and the vectors $\mathbf{n}_{j,0} = (n_1, ..., n_{j-1}, 0, n_{j+1}, ..., n_N)$ and $\mathbf{n}_{j,1} = (n_1, ..., n_{j-1}, 1, n_{j+1}, ..., n_N)$ indicate all possible states of the system with the state at end broker j being resp. 0 and 1.

Proof. Let $a : S^N \to \mathbb{N}$ indicate the traffic rate in state $\mathbf{n}$. As notifications are sent according to an average rate ω and re-subscriptions according to a rate $1/r$ over all active links in that state, we find,

$$A_{sdt}(t) = \sum_{\mathbf{n}} a(\mathbf{n}) P(\mathbf{X}(t) = \mathbf{n}) = \sum_{\mathbf{n}} (\omega + 1/r) L(\mathbf{n}) P(\mathbf{X}(t) = \mathbf{n}). \tag{11}$$

The toggle traffic rate at time t, is the expected rate for $\mathbf{X}(t)$ of traffic originating from transitions between states $\mathbf{n}$ and $\mathbf{n}'$. Let the function $b : (S^N, S^N) \to \mathbb{N}$ be the amount of messages in the network caused by a transition between $\mathbf{n}$ and $\mathbf{n}'$. The toggle traffic rate is:

$$A_t(t) = \sum_{(\mathbf{n}, \mathbf{n}')} b(\mathbf{n}, \mathbf{n}') P(\mathbf{X}(t) = \mathbf{n}) q(\mathbf{n}, \mathbf{n}'; t), \tag{12}$$

where $q(\mathbf{n}, \mathbf{n}'; t)$ is the transition rate from state $\mathbf{n}$ to $\mathbf{n}'$ at time t. For our model, the transition rates at time t, $q(\mathbf{n}, \mathbf{n}'; t)$ are given by: $q(\mathbf{n}, \mathbf{n}+\mathbf{e}_j; t) = \lambda_j(t)$, corresponding to an arrival at end broker j, and $q(\mathbf{n}, \mathbf{n}-\mathbf{e}_j; t) = \mu_j(t)$, corresponding to a departure from end broker j, where $\mathbf{e}_j$ equals the j-th unit vector of length N with value 1 on place j and value 0 elsewhere. Other transitions cannot occur.

To derive the toggle traffic rate we need to express the function $b(\mathbf{n}, \mathbf{n}')$. First observe that a toggle between states only affects the amount of traffic when there is a transition between states 0 and 1 at an end broker. Transitions between higher states (e.g. 1 and 2) will not add toggle traffic due to the identity-based routing algorithm. For this reason, a subscription needs to be forwarded over a link if and only if that link goes from inactive to active (and an unsubscription if and only if that link goes from active to inactive). Therefore, the number of links that carries an (un)subscription upon a toggle between states $\mathbf{n}$ and $\mathbf{n}'$, is expressed by:

$$b(\mathbf{n}, \mathbf{n}') = |L(\mathbf{n}) - L(\mathbf{n}')| . \tag{13}$$

Thus, the toggle traffic rate $A_t(t)$ is given by (10), as the sum over all possible transitions at all end brokers j, where the first expression indicates the subscription traffic caused by an arrival of a subscriber at a 0-state of end broker j and the second expression indicates the unsubscription traffic when the last subscriber leaves end broker j. □

Now with (1), (7), (9), and (10) we can find recursive expressions for $A_{ibr}(t)$ for given $\lambda_j(t)$ and $\mu_j(t)$ and given m and k describing the m-ary tree network with k levels. However, the equilibrium results of Jaeger and Mühl [7] allow us also to obtain a closed form for $A_{ibr}(t)$.

Lemma 2 ([7]). *Consider the network with $\lambda_i(t) = \lambda_i$, $\mu_i(t) = \mu_i$, $i = 1, \ldots, N$, independent of t, and assume that the system is in equilibrium. The state-dependent traffic rate equals:*

$$A_{sdt} = \left(\omega + \frac{1}{r}\right)\left[l - \sum_{h=0}^{k-2}\sum_{j=1}^{m^{k-1-h}}\prod_{i=m^h(j-1)+1}^{jm^h} p_{0,i}\right].\tag{14}$$

Note that according to (7) and (8) it follows that $p_{0,i} = e^{-\rho_i}$, and $\rho_i = \lambda_i/\mu_i$, $i = 1, \ldots, N$.

Lemma 3 ([7],[18]). *Consider the network with $\lambda_i(t) = \lambda_i$, $\mu_i(t) = \mu_i$, $i = 1, \ldots, N$, independent of t, and assume that the system is in equilibrium. The toggle traffic rate equals:*

$$A_t = 2\sum_{j=1}^{N}\left(p_{0,j} + \sum_{h=1}^{k-2}\prod_{i=m^h(\lceil\frac{j}{m^h}\rceil-1)+1}^{m^h\lceil\frac{j}{m^h}\rceil} p_{0,i}\right)\lambda_j.\tag{15}$$

Notice that the proof of Theorem 1 builds upon the results of [7]. However, the arguments used in [7], in particular in the proof of the result corresponding to Lemma 3 cannot directly be extended to the time-dependent setting. In [18] we present a complete proof of this lemma, with the applied insensitivity and the regenerative arguments explicitly pointed out. These arguments are not valid for processes with time-dependent transition rates. Below, in the proof of Theorem 1, we use a different method that avoids the use of insensitivity and regenerative arguments, and hence generalizes to the time-dependent setting.

Proof of Theorem 1. Theorem 2 provides an expression for the traffic rate: $A_{ibr}(t) = \sum_{\mathbf{n}} a(\mathbf{n})P(\mathbf{X}(t) = \mathbf{n}) + \sum_{(\mathbf{n},\mathbf{n}')} b(\mathbf{n},\mathbf{n}')P(\mathbf{X}(t) = \mathbf{n})q(\mathbf{n},\mathbf{n}';t)$. The expression for A_{sdt} provided in Lemma 2 is a function of ρ_j, $j = 1, \ldots, N$, only and hence for each fixed t, we may replace ρ_j by $\rho_j(t)$, and find $A_{sdt}(t)$ as expressed in (3), (4).

For each fixed t, and for each j, $j = 1, \ldots, N$, the derivation of (15) as provided in equilibrium in [7],[18] yields, conditioning on the event that there are no subscriptions at broker j, that the expected path length $d_j(t)$ at time t for a toggle message at end-broker j is

$$d_j(t) = 1 + \sum_{h=1}^{k-2}\prod_{i=m^h(\lceil\frac{j}{m^h}\rceil-1)+1}^{m^h\lceil\frac{j}{m^h}\rceil} p_{0,i}(t)\prod_{k=i+1}^{j-1} p_{0,k}(t).$$

For new subscriptions, the rate at which toggle messages are generated at broker j at time t is the fraction of arrivals that find no subscriptions at end broker j, i.e., $\lambda_j(t)p_{0,j}(t)$. As a consequence, we find that, for $j = 1, \ldots, N$,

$$\sum_{(\mathbf{n}_{j,0},\mathbf{n}_{j,1})} b(\mathbf{n}_{j,0}, \mathbf{n}_{j,1})P(\mathbf{X}(t) = \mathbf{n}_{j,0})q(\mathbf{n}_{j,0}, \mathbf{n}_{j,1}; t) = \lambda_j(t)p_{0,j}(t)d_j(t).$$

Observe that from (7)

$$P(\mathbf{X}(t) = \mathbf{n}_{j,1}) = \rho_j(t)P(\mathbf{X}(t) = \mathbf{n}_{j,0}),$$

and that from (13) $b(\mathbf{n}_{j,0}, \mathbf{n}_{j,1}) = b(\mathbf{n}_{j,1}, \mathbf{n}_{j,0})$, so that

$$\sum_{(\mathbf{n}_{j,1},\mathbf{n}_{j,0})} b(\mathbf{n}_{j,1}, \mathbf{n}_{j,0})P(\mathbf{X}(t) = \mathbf{n}_{j,1})q(\mathbf{n}_{j,1}, \mathbf{n}_{j,0}; t) =$$

$$\sum_{(\mathbf{n}_{j,0},\mathbf{n}_{j,1})} b(\mathbf{n}_{j,0}, \mathbf{n}_{j,1})\rho_j(t)P(\mathbf{X}(t) = \mathbf{n}_{j,0})\mu_j(t) = \mu_j(t)\rho_j(t)p_{0,j}(t)d_j(t)$$

This completes the proof. □

3 Examples

3.1 Influence of a Varying Arrival Rate

Consider the situation with an infinite population and $\lambda_j(t) = \lambda(t)$ and $\mu_j(t) = \mu(t)$ for $j = 1, \ldots, N$. For the non-homogeneous arrival process we use: $\lambda(t) = c + b \sin at$ with $0 \leq b \leq c$. This choice is made for evaluation purposes only and is not meant to represent actual user behavior. A particular advantage of this arrival process is that a closed form expression for (8) can be obtained. For the service time we use: $\mu(t) = \mu$. Using Laplace integration of (8) we find:

$$\rho(t) = \frac{c}{\mu} + \left(\rho(0) + \frac{ba}{a^2+\mu^2} - \frac{c}{\mu}\right)e^{-\mu t} + \left(\frac{b\mu}{a^2+\mu^2}\right)\sin at - \left(\frac{ba}{a^2+\mu^2}\right)\cos at.$$

With Theorem 1, we calculate the total traffic for identity-based routing in the time-dependent process (see Figure 3). The parameters in this example are chosen as follows: $b = c = 1$, and $\rho(0) - 0$ so we start with an empty system. For the remaining parameters we use, $k = 5$, $m = 3$, $\omega = 1$, $r = 1$ and $\mu = 1$. For these parameters we clearly have $A_f = 240$ for the flooding traffic. Figure 3 shows the influence of a by choosing $a = 4\pi/100$ and $a = 4\pi/10$. The figure shows for each value of a the curves for A_{ibr} (total traffic), A_{sdt} (state-dependent traffic) and A_t (toggle traffic) for the time-dependent arrival process. At the start of the process, a lot of toggle traffic is generated as all messages arrive in an empty system. Actual values are: $A_t(0) = 324$, $A_{sdt}(0) = 0$. Then the process finds a periodic behavior according to the arrival process. The figure shows clearly the increasing of the toggle traffic when the system fills up, or when it empties, according to the arrival process. For the stationary arrival process with corresponding parameters $\rho = 1$, i.e., on average one subscriber per end-broker. The stationary process does not depend on a. Calculation yields that $A_{ibr} = 245.39$, $A_{sdt} = 177.71$ and $A_t = 67.68$ (these are not shown in the graph). After integration of $A_{ibr}(t)$, we find that in the time-dependent setting the average traffic rate for $a = 4\pi/10$ equals 200.62 (integration over 1000 time-units), for $a = 4\pi/100$ the average traffic rate 232.36 (integration over 200 time-units). So, for this system, a stationary analysis would lead to the conclusion that the additional messages in identity based routing do not outweigh

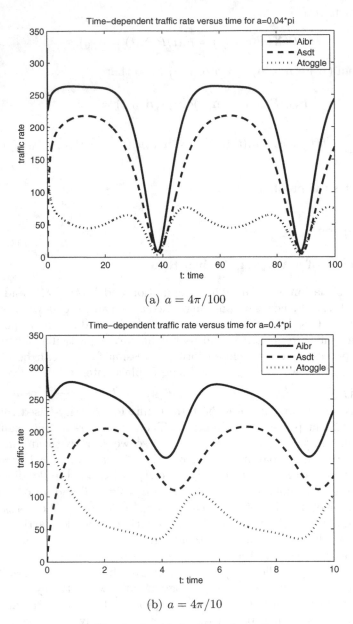

(a) $a = 4\pi/100$

(b) $a = 4\pi/10$

Fig. 3. $A_{ibr}(t)$ for two values of a

the extra efficiency in the algorithm. However, by the time-dependent analysis, we come to the opposite conclusion: identity-based routing generates less traffic than flooding, over extended periods of time. This shows that already in this simple setting, a careful analysis by a time-dependent process yields valuable additional information.

3.2   Example: Impact of Local Interest

With the next example, we also describe a model extension to include also finite populations of clients per end-broker. Consider a finite population of N_i clients at end-broker i, that independently switch between an exponentially distributed off-period with time varying intensity $\lambda_i(t)$ and an exponentially distributed on-period with time varying intensity $\mu_i(t)$. Now the time-dependent distribution for the number of active subscribers at time t is given by:

$$P(X_i(t) = n_i) = \binom{N_i}{n_i} \rho_i(t)^{n_i} (1 - \rho_i(t))^{N_i - n_i}, \tag{16}$$

with $\rho_i(t)$ following from: $\frac{d\rho_i(t)}{dt} = \lambda_i(t)(1 - \rho_i(t)) - \mu_i(t)\rho_i(t)$. Using $p_{0,i}(t) = P(X_i(t) = 0)$ from (16) in (4), we find the amount of traffic that originates in a time-interval of length T, when there is a finite population at each single end-broker.

As an example, consider stationary traffic in tree rooted at $(0, 1)$ with 3 levels, with one publisher, located at $(3, 1)$, publishing at rate ω (see Figure 4).

To investigate the impact of local interest, we assume three distinct types of behavior among subscribers, based on the distance from the publisher. We define three groups as: *Local* (L): The members located in the subtree rooted at $(2, 1)$, with arrival rate λ. *Average* (A): the non-local members located in the tree rooted at $(1, 1)$ with arrival rate $\frac{\lambda}{q}$ and *Far* (F): all remaining subscribers with arrival rate $\frac{\lambda}{q^2}$. By varying parameter q we are able to express a stronger local interest. For fixed $\mu = 1$, $\omega = 6$ and $r = 1/6$ we compared A_f with A_{ibr} for $q = 1$ (uniform), $q = 10$ and $q = 100$. By relatively straightforward extensions for non-root publishers (see [18]) and 'almost' m-ary trees we find the results of Figure 5. Here the traffic is plotted against Ψ, where Ψ indicates the total

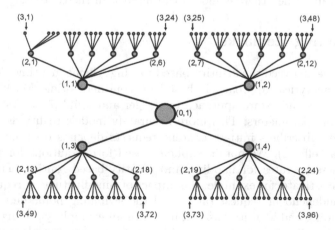

Fig. 4. The content based routing network used in investigating the impact of local interest

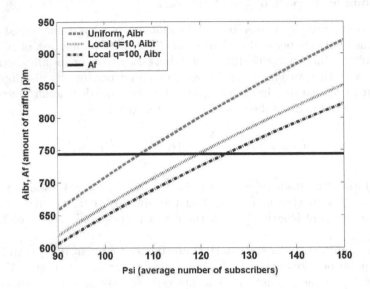

Fig. 5. Flooding compared with identity-based routing for different uniform and local behavior. The y-axis indicates the traffic amount in messages per minute. Aibr denotes the amount of messages generated by identity based routing. Af denotes the amount of messages generated by flooding.

expected number of active subscribers in the network, which can be calculated from (16). The intervals correspond to an area around the break even points (where A_{ibr} crosses A_f). When q is higher, identity-based routing improves in comparison with flooding. This corresponds to the intuition that identity based routing is suitable when there is more local interest in the content.

4   Concluding Remarks

In this paper we analyzed the identity-based routing scheme in a time-dependent setting. Our analytical approach is based on continuous-time Markov chains and extends the steady-state approach by Jaeger and Mühl [7] to systems with time-fluctuating parameters. This more accurately models reality as often the rate at which subscribers initiate content requests depends on time (e.g. due to time of day effects). We obtain explicit closed form solutions for the time-dependent message rates for flooding and identity-based routing. The results allow us to investigate, for example, the impact of time-fluctuating request rates versus time-independent request rates, and the switching point between optimality of flooding and identity-based routing. In an exemplary setting, we have compared the traffic generated by the identity-based routing algorithm for a time-dependent arrival process to a stationary arrival process with the same load. This shows that the time-dependent process models the traffic behavior more accurately than a time-independent approximation would do, and leads to different conclusions when compared to flooding. In a stationary situation we have compared identity-based routing to flooding, showing that identity based routing is suitable when there is more local interest in the content.

Extensions of this work to other forms of content-based routing like covering and filter merging, would be interesting. Additional model features, such as finite numbers of clients, roaming clients, arbitrary (i.e., not at the root) locations of (multiple) publishers and subscribers in the network and the use of advertisements, are worth a further investigation as well. (Advertisements are used by publishers to indicate which information they contain and are willing to send over network. By using advertisements, the subscriptions can be propagated on the path established by the advertisements and future notifications will travel the same path.) Some of these extensions are included in [18].

References

1. Baldoni, R., Beraldi, R., Tucci Piergiovanni, S., Virgillito, A.: On the modelling of publish/subscribe communication systems. Concurrency Computat.: Pract. Exper. 17, 1471–1495 (2005)
2. Boucherie, R.J., Taylor, P.G.: Transient Product Form Distributions in Queuing networks. Discrete Event Dynamic Systems: Theory and Applications 3, 375–396 (1993)
3. Carzaniga, A., Rosenblum, D.S., Wolf, A.L.: Design and Evaluation of a Wide-Area Event Notification Service. ACM Transactions on Computer Systems 19(3), 332–383 (2001)
4. Cugola, G., Di Nitto, E.: On adopting Content-Based Routing in service-oriented architectures. Information and Software Technology (50), 22–35 (2008)
5. van Dijk, N.M.: Queueing Networks and Product Forms: a system's approach. Wiley, New York (1993)
6. Eugster, P.T., Felber, P.A., Guerraoui, R., Kermarrec, A.: The Many Faces of Publish/Subscribe. ACM Computing Surveys 35(2), 114–131 (2003)
7. Jaeger, M.A., Mühl, G.: Stochastic analysis and comparison of self-stabilizing routing algorithms for publish/subscribe systems. In: The 13th IEEE/ACM International Symposium on Modelling, Analysis and Simulation of Computer and Telecommunication Systems (MASCOTS 2005), Atlanta, Georgia, pp. 471–479. IEEE Press, Los Alamitos (2005)
8. Kurose, J.F., Ross, K.W.: Computer Networking: A Top-Down Approach Featuring the Internet, 2nd edn. Addison-Wesley, Reading (2003)
9. Massey, W.A., Whitt, W.: Networks of infinite-server queues with non-stationairy Poisson input. Queueuing Systems 13, 183–250 (1993)
10. Mühl, G.: Large-Scale Content-Based Publish/Subscribe Systems. PhD thesis, Darmstadt University of Technology (2002)
11. Mühl, G., Fiege, L., Gärtner, F.C., Buchmann, A.: Evaluating Advanced Routing Algorithms for Content-Based Publish/Subscribe Systems. In: The 10th IEEE/ACM International Symposium on Modelling, Analysis and Simulation of Computer and Telecommunication Systems (MASCOTS 2002), pp. 167–176. IEEE Press, Los Alamitos (2002)

12. Mühl, G., Jaeger, M.A., Herrmann, K., Weis, T., Fiege, L., Ulbrich, A.: Self-stabilizing publish/subscribe systems: Algorithms and evaluation. In: Cunha, J.C., Medeiros, P.D. (eds.) Euro-Par 2005. LNCS, vol. 3648, pp. 664–674. Springer, Heidelberg (2005)
13. Rhea, S., Geels, D., Roscoe, T., Kubiatowicz, J.: Handling Churn in a DHT. In: Proceedings of the annual conference on USENIX, Boston (2004)
14. Segall, B., Arnold, D.: Elvin has left the building: A publish/subscribe notification service with quenching. In: Proceedings of the Australian UNIX and Open System User Group Conference (AUUG 1997), Brisbane, Australia (1997)
15. Stutzbach, D., Rejaie, R.: Understanding churn in peer-to-peer networks. In: Proceedings of the 6th ACM SIGCOMM conference on Internet Measurement, Rio de Janeiro, pp. 189–202 (2006)
16. Tarkoma, S., Kangasharju, J.: On the cost and safety of handoffs in content-based routing systems. Computer Networks 51, 1459–1482 (2007)
17. Tarkoma, S.: Dynamic filter merging and mergeability detection for publish/subscribe. Pervasive and Mobile Computing 4(5), 681–696 (2008)
18. van Vliet, F., Boucherie, R.J., de Graaf, M.: Content based routing in networks with time-fluctuating request rates. Memorandum 1888, Department of Applied Mathematics, University of Twente, Enschede, ISSN 1874-4850,
    http://www.math.utwente.nl/publications

A Queueing-Based Approach to Overload Detection

Michel Mandjes[1] and Piotr Żuraniewski[2,*]

[1] University of Amsterdam, Science Park 904, 1098 XH Amsterdam, The Netherlands
[2] AGH University of Science and Technology, Kraków, Poland

Abstract. The control of communication networks critically relies on procedures capable of detecting unanticipated load changes. In this paper we develop such techniques, in a setting in which each connection consumes roughly the same amount of bandwidth (with VoIP as a leading example). For the situation of exponential holding times an explicit analysis can be performed in a large-deviations regime, leading to approximations of the test statistic of interest (and, in addition, to results for the transient of the $M/M/\infty$ queue, which are of independent interest). This procedure being applicable to exponential holding times only, and also being numerically rather involved, we then develop an approximate procedure for general holding times. In this procedure we record the number of trunks occupied at equidistant points in time $\Delta, 2\Delta, \ldots$, where Δ is chosen sufficiently large to safely assume that the samples are independent; this procedure is backed by results on the transient of the $M/G/\infty$ queue. The validity of the testing procedures is demonstrated through an extensive set of numerical experiments.

Keywords: Overload detection, infinite-server queues, transient, VoIP.

1 Introduction

When sizing communication networks, probably still the most frequently used tool is the celebrated *Erlang loss formula*, dating back to the early 1900s. This formula was originally developed for computing the blocking probability for circuit-switched (for instance voice) traffic sharing a trunk group of size, say $C \in \mathbb{N}$, and is often used for *dimensioning* purposes: it enables the selection of a value of C such that the blocking probability is below some tolerable level ε. Despite the fact that the formula has been around for a rather long time, it is still a cornerstone when resolving dimensioning issues, owing to its general applicability and its explicit, manageable form. Also, notice that it can in principle be used in any setting in which each connection requires (roughly) the same amount of bandwidth. As a consequence, it is also applicable in non-circuit-switched technologies, e.g. when considering voice-over-IP (VoIP).

In more detail, the Erlang loss formula is based on the (realistic) assumption of a Poisson arrival stream of flows (say, with intensity λ, expressed in Hertz or

* The authors thank COST action TMA (IC0703) and Polish Ministry of Science and Higher Education, grant no. 10.420.03, for financial support.

R. Núñez-Queija and J. Resing (Eds.): NET-COOP 2009, LNCS 5894, pp. 91–106, 2009.

s^{-1}). The call durations are independent and identically distributed, with mean $1/\mu$ (in s), and the load ϱ is defined as the unit-less number $\varrho := \lambda/\mu$. If there are C lines available, the probability of blocking in this model is

$$p(C \mid \varrho) := \left(\frac{\varrho^C}{C!}\right) \Big/ \left(\sum_{c=0}^{C} \frac{\varrho^c}{c!}\right).$$

Importantly, this formula shows that for dimensioning the trunk group, no information on λ and μ is needed apart from their ratio $\varrho = \lambda/\mu$. Observe that no assumption on the distribution of the call holding times was imposed; the above formula applies for all holding-time distributions with mean $1/\mu$. We denote by $\bar{\varrho}$ the maximum load ϱ such that $p(C \mid \varrho)$ is below some predefined tolerance ε. The underlying queueing model is often referred to as the $M/G/C/C$ queue; a useful approximation of $p(C \mid \varrho)$ is the probability that the number of busy servers in the corresponding infinite-server queue (i.e., $M/G/\infty$) exceeds C.

When operating a network one has to constantly check the validity of the input assumptions the dimensioning decision was based upon. More concretely, one has to check whether the load ϱ has not reached the maximum allowable load $\bar{\varrho}$. Clearly, if the load has increased beyond $\bar{\varrho}$, measures have to be taken to deal with the overload, perhaps by rerouting the excess calls, or, on a longer timescale, by increasing the available capacity.

This motivates why it is of crucial importance to design procedures to (statistically) assess whether the load has changed. In statistical terms we would call this a 'changepoint detection problem' [9]: from observations of the number of lines used, we wish to infer whether a load change has taken place. Also, one would like to know *when* the change has occurred; then an alarm can be issued that triggers traffic management measures (overload control, such as rerouting, or temporary adaptations of the amount of bandwidth available to the calls).

Empirical guidelines for the problem described above have been developed in e.g., [5], but there is a clear need for more rigorously supported procedures. Without aiming to give an exhaustive overview, we mention here related work on a fractal model [12], and also [3,11]. An application of the celebrated cusum technique [9] in the networking domain can be found in [7]. Several valuable contributions to the changepoint detection problem are due to Tartakovsky and co-authors, cf. [10].

The main contributions of the present paper are the following. (i) We first consider the case in which the call durations have an exponential distribution. We show how a likelihood-based cusum-type of test can be set up. The crucial complication is that the number of trunks occupied does *not* constitute a sequence of i.i.d. random variables (as there will be dependence between subsequent observations). Therefore the 'traditional' cusum result does not apply here, and a new approach had to be developed. Setting up our test requires knowledge of the transient probabilities in the corresponding $M/M/\infty$ system. We first show how, in a large-deviations setting, these transient probabilities can be determined. These have interesting features, such as a so-called bifurcation, as in [8]. The test also requires the computation of the probability that a sum of likelihoods exceeds some threshold. We show how this can be done, relying on calculus-of-variations techniques.

(ii) The findings above being only applicable to the case of exponentially distributed call durations, and given the high numerical complexity of the resulting procedure, we then look for an approach that works for the $M/G/\infty$ in general, and that requires substantially less computational effort. We explain how we can use classical changepoint-detection, which rely on the assumption of independent observations (where the observations correspond to samples of the number of calls in progress, at equidistant points in time, say $\Delta, 2\Delta, \ldots$). This independence assumption is clearly not fulfilled in our model, at least not formally, but evidently for Δ sufficiently large the dependence will have a minor impact. We develop new estimates on the relaxation time of the $M/G/\infty$ queue, which tell us how large Δ should be in order to be able to safely assume independence.

(iii) The third contribution is that we show how accurately the proposed procedures can detect overload. This we do through a series of simulation experiments. Special attention is paid to the trade-off between the detection ratio and the false alarm rate. The experiments indicate that our procedure, after some tuning, provides a powerful technique for changepoint detection.

We have organized the paper as follows. In Section 2 we present our model and some preliminaries, and define our goal in terms of a changepoint detection problem. Section 3 presents a framework for changepoint detection for the $M/M/\infty$ model, whereas Section 4 presents the approximate analysis for the $M/G/\infty$ model. The last section is devoted to numerical experimentation.

2   Model, Preliminaries, and Goals

In this section we describe the goals of the paper, and the underlying mathematical model. Our analysis will be based on the $M/G/\infty$ queue, that is, a service system in which calls arrive according to a Poisson process (with rate, say, λ), where it is assumed that the call durations form an i.i.d. sequence $B_1, B_2, \ldots$, and infinitely many servers. With $1/\mu$ denoting the mean value of a generic call duration B, the load of the system is defined as $\varrho := \lambda/\mu$. It is well-known that the stationary distribution of the number of calls simultaneously present, say Y, is Poisson with mean ϱ. Also the transient distribution of this system can be dealt with fairly explicitly. Suppose that $Y(t)$ denotes the number of trunks occupied at time t, and assuming that the queue is in stationarity at time 0, the following decomposition applies. Conditioning on $Y(0) = k$, with '$=_d$' denoting equality in distribution, we have that

$$Y(t) =_d \mathbb{Bin}(k, p_t) + \mathbb{Pois}(\lambda t q_t), \tag{1}$$

where $\mathbb{Bin}(k, p)$ denotes a binomial random variable with parameters k and p, and $\mathbb{Pois}(\lambda)$ as Poisson random variable with mean λ; in addition, the binomial and Poisson random variables in the right-hand side of (1) are independent. Here, p_t is the probability that an arbitrary call that is present at time 0 is still present at time t, which equals $\mathbb{P}(B^\star > t) = \mathbb{E}B^{-1} \int_t^\infty \mathbb{P}(B > s)\mathrm{d}s$, where $B^\star$

denotes the excess life-time distribution of B. Likewise, q_t is the probability that an arbitrary call that arrives in $(0, t]$ is still present at time t; using the fact that the arrival epoch of such an arbitrary call is uniformly distributed on $(0, t]$, conditioning on the arrival epoch $s \in (0, t]$ yields that

$$q_t = t^{-1} \int_0^t \mathbb{P}(B > t - s)\mathrm{d}s = t^{-1} \int_0^t \mathbb{P}(B > s)\mathrm{d}s = \mathbb{E}B \cdot t^{-1} \cdot \mathbb{P}(B^* \leq t).$$

Observe that the mean of the Poissonian term in the right-hand side of (1), $\lambda t q_t$, equals $\varrho \mathbb{P}(B^* < t)$. It is readily verified that the correlation coefficient of $Y(0)$ and $Y(t)$ equals $\mathbb{Corr}(Y(0), Y(t)) = \mathbb{P}(B^* > t)$; here it is used that $Y(0)$ has a Poisson distribution with mean ϱ.

As mentioned in the introduction, the goal of the paper is to detect changes in the load imposed on a M/G/∞ queue. More specifically, with ϱ the load imposed on the queueing resource, and $\bar{\varrho}$ the maximum allowable load (in order to meet a given performance criterion, for instance in terms of a blocking probability), we want to test whether all samples correspond to load ϱ (which we associate with hypothesis H_0), or whether there has been a changepoint within the data set, such that before the changepoint the data were in line with load ϱ, and after the changepoint with $\bar{\varrho}$ (which is hypothesis H_1).

3   Analysis for M/M/∞

In this section we consider the case that the calls are i.i.d. samples from an exponential distribution with mean $1/\mu$; the model is then known as M/M/∞. We consider the discrete-time Markovian model describing the dynamics of the number of trunks occupied, by recording the continuous-time process at the embedded epochs at which this number changes.

Let, for $i = 1, 2, \ldots$, $Y_i := \sum_{j=1}^i X_i$, where the probabilities $\mathbb{P}(X_i = \pm 1 \mid Y_{i-1})$ are defined through, for given numbers λ_m and μ_m,

$$(X_i \mid Y_{i-1} = m) = \begin{cases} 1 & \text{with probability } \lambda_m \\ -1 & \text{with probability } \mu_m = 1 - \lambda_m. \end{cases}$$

As mentioned above, in this section we assume that the dynamics of the number of trunks occupied is described by the M/M/∞ model, i.e., $\lambda_m \equiv \lambda_m(\varrho) = \lambda/(\lambda + m\mu) = \varrho/(\varrho + m)$, with $\varrho := \lambda/\mu$. We consider the model with an infinite number of trunks available; then the (steady-state) probability of C calls present can be used as an approximation of the blocking probability in the model with C lines.

In this section, our analysis relies on applying the so-called *many-flows scaling*. Under this scaling the load is renormalized by n (that is, we replace $\varrho \mapsto n\varrho$), and at the same time the number of trunks is inflated by a factor n, as motivated in [8, Ch. 12]. It effectively means that we can use *large-deviations theory* to asymptotically (large n) determine the distribution of the number of calls simultaneously present. Under this scaling the steady-state number of calls present has a Poisson distribution with mean $n\varrho$, i.e., $\mathbb{P}(Y = k) = (n\varrho)^k e^{-n\varrho}/k!$. A straightforward application of Stirling's formula yields the following expression for the exponential decay rate of $\mathbb{P}(Y = \lfloor n\beta \rfloor)$:

$$\lim_{n\to\infty} \frac{1}{n} \log \mathbb{P}(Y = \lfloor n\beta \rfloor) = -\varrho + \beta + \beta \log \left(\frac{\varrho}{\beta} \right) =: \xi(\beta);$$

here we recognize the large-deviations rate function of the Poisson distribution [8, Example 1.13]. Using Cramér's theorem, we also have that the probability $\mathbb{P}(Y \geq n\beta)$ has the same exponential decay rate.

Goal: changepoint. We want to test whether there is a 'changepoint', that is, during our observation period the load parameter ϱ (which we let correspond to the probability model $\mathbb{P}$) changes into $\bar{\varrho} \neq \varrho$ (the model $\mathbb{Q}$). More formally, we consider the following (multiple) hypotheses.

H_0: $(X_i)_{i=1}^n$ is distributed according to the above described birth-death chain with parameter ϱ.

H_1: For some $\delta \in \{1/n, 2/n, \ldots, (n-1)/n\}$, it holds that $(X_i)_{i=1}^{\lfloor n\delta \rfloor}$ is distributed according to the birth-death chain with parameter ϱ, whereas $(X_i)_{i=\lfloor n\delta \rfloor+1}^n$ is distributed according to the birth-death chain with parameter $\bar{\varrho} \neq \varrho$.

Inspired by the Neyman-Pearson lemma, see e.g. [2, Ch. V.E and Appendix E], we consider the following likelihood-ratio test statistic:

$$T_n := \max_{\delta \in [0,1)} T_n(\delta), \text{ with } T_n(\delta) := \frac{1}{n} \sum_{i=\lfloor n\delta \rfloor+1}^n L_i - \varphi(\delta), \quad L_i := \log \frac{\mathbb{Q}(X_i \mid Y_{i-1})}{\mathbb{P}(X_i \mid Y_{i-1})},$$

for some function $\varphi(\cdot)$ we will specify later. If $T_n > 0$, then H_0 is rejected.

To enable statistical tests, we wonder what the probability is, under H_0, that the above test statistic is larger than 0. For reasons of tractability, we consider its exponential decay rate (asymptotic in the scaling parameter n):

$$\eta(\varphi) := \lim_{n\to\infty} \frac{1}{n} \log \mathbb{P}(T_n > 0), \quad \eta(\varphi \mid \beta_0) := \lim_{n\to\infty} \frac{1}{n} \log \mathbb{P}(T_n > 0 \mid Y_0 = n\beta_0)$$

These decay rates can be evaluated as follows. We define $\eta(\varphi, \delta \mid \beta_0)$, $\bar{\eta}(\varphi, \delta \mid \beta_\delta)$, and $\xi(\beta_\delta \mid \beta_0)$, as the exponential decay rates of, respectively,

$$\mathbb{P}(T_n > 0 \mid Y_0 = n\beta_0), \quad \mathbb{P}(T_n > 0 \mid Y_{\lfloor n\delta \rfloor} = n\beta_\delta), \quad \mathbb{P}(Y_{\lfloor n\delta \rfloor} = n\beta_\delta \mid Y_0 = n\beta_0).$$

Standard large-deviations argumentation yields that

$$\eta(\varphi \mid \beta_0) = \sup_{\delta \in [0,1)} \eta(\varphi, \delta \mid \beta_0) = \sup_{\delta \in [0,1)} \sup_{\beta_\delta > 0} (\xi(\beta_\delta \mid \beta_0) + \bar{\eta}(\varphi, \delta \mid \beta_\delta))$$

('principle of the largest term'), and also

$$\eta(\varphi) = \sup_{\delta \in [0,1)} \sup_{\beta_\delta > 0} (\xi(\beta_\delta) + \bar{\eta}(\varphi, \delta \mid \beta_\delta)).$$

The decay rate of the transient probabilities, that is, $\xi(\beta_\delta \mid \beta_0)$, will be analyzed in Section 3.1, and the decay rate of the exceedance probabilities $\bar{\eta}(\varphi, \delta \mid \beta_\delta)$ (which we will sometimes refer to as 'likelihood probabilities') in Section 3.2.

3.1   Transient Probabilities

To analyze the decay rate of $\mathbb{P}(Y_{\lfloor n\delta \rfloor} = n\beta_\delta \mid Y_0 = n\beta_0)$, we rely on *Slow Markov Walk* theory [2, Ch. IV.C]. As this technique has been described in detail in [2] we restrict ourselves to sketching the main steps. Then we show how to apply this theory to determine the transient probabilities $\xi(\beta_\delta \mid \beta_0)$.

Slow Markov Walk. A prominent role in Slow Markov Walk theory is played by the so-called 'local large deviations rate function' $I_x(u)$, defined as

$$\sup_\theta \left(\theta u - \log \left(e^\theta \lambda_{nx}(n\varrho) + e^{-\theta}(1 - \lambda_{nx}(n\varrho)) \right) \right) = \sup_\theta \left(\theta u - \log \left(\frac{\varrho e^\theta + x e^{-\theta}}{\varrho + x} \right) \right).$$

Intuitively reasoning, $I_x(u)$ measures the 'effort the process has to make' (per time unit), starting in state x, to move into direction u. It follows that

$$\theta^\star \equiv \theta^\star_x(u) = \frac{1}{2} \log \left(\frac{x}{\varrho} \cdot \frac{1+u}{1-u} \right), \tag{2}$$

$\theta^\star$ denoting the optimizing θ; if $\theta^\star$ is positive (negative) the process has to 'speed up' ('slow down') to be moving into direction u. Slow Markov Walk theory yields the exponential decay rates of the empirical mean process $n^{-1} \cdot Y_{\lfloor nt \rfloor}$ to be in a certain set, or close to a given function f. Loosely speaking, it says that

$$\lim_{n \to \infty} \frac{1}{n} \log \mathbb{P} \left(\frac{1}{n} \cdot Y_{\lfloor nt \rfloor} \approx f(t), t \in [0, \delta) \right) = -\int_0^\delta I_{f(t)}(f'(t)) dt;$$

sometimes the right-hand side of the previous display is referred to as the 'cost' of the path f in the interval $[0, \delta)$. In this sense, we can determine also the 'average path' of $Y_{\lfloor nt \rfloor}/n$, which is the path with *zero* cost: it consists of pairs $(f(t), f'(t))$ for which $I_{f(t)}(f'(t)) = 0$, or, put differently, $\theta^\star_{f(t)}(f'(t)) = 0$. It can be calculated that this average path is given through the differential equation

$$\frac{f(t)}{\varrho} \cdot \frac{1 + f'(t)}{1 - f'(t)} = 1, \quad \text{or} \quad f'(t) = \frac{\varrho - f(t)}{\varrho + f(t)}; \tag{3}$$

This path converges to the 'mean' $f(\infty) = \varrho$ as $t \to \infty$, as was expected. Inserting $\theta^\star$, as given in (2), we find after tedious computations that $I_x(u)$ equals

$$\frac{1}{2} u \log \left(\frac{1+u}{1-u} \right) + \frac{1}{2} u \log \left(\frac{x}{\varrho} \right) - \frac{1}{2} \log \left(\frac{x\varrho}{(\varrho + x)^2} \right) - \log 2 + \frac{1}{2} \log(1 - u^2).$$

Determining the decay rate of $\xi(\beta_\delta \mid \beta_0)$. We now reduce the search for the decay rate $\xi(\beta_\delta \mid \beta_0)$ to a variational problem. Slow Markov Walk theory says that

$$\xi(\beta_\delta \mid \beta_0) = -\inf_{f \in \mathscr{A}} \int_0^\delta I_{f(t)}(f'(t)) dt,$$

where the set $\mathscr{A}$ consists of all paths f such that $f(0) = \beta_0$ and $f(\delta) = \beta_\delta$. This variational problem can be solved by applying elementary results from calculus of variations; see for instance [8, Appendix C]. The optimizing path is characterized by the so-called DuBois-Reymond equation [8, Eq. (C.3)]:

$$I_{f(t)}(f'(t)) - f'(t) \cdot \frac{\partial}{\partial u} I_x(u)\Big|_{x=f(t),u=f'(t)} = K,$$

or, equivalently,

$$\log\left((1 - (f'(t))^2) \cdot \frac{(\varrho + f(t))^2}{4f(t)\varrho}\right) = K;$$

the K is to determined later on (and essentially serves as a 'degree-of-freedom', to be chosen such that $f(\delta) = \beta_\delta$). After some elementary algebraic manipulations we find the ordinary differential equation

$$f'(t) = \pm\sqrt{1 - e^K \cdot \frac{4f(t)\varrho}{(\varrho + f(t))^2}}; \tag{4}$$

notice that for $K = 0$ we retrieve the 'average path' (3), as expected.

Interestingly, we can explicitly find the inverse of the solution of (4) (that is, t in terms of f, rather than f in terms of t). Recalling that $\varrho + f(t) > 0$, by separating variables we obtain

$$t = \pm \int \frac{(\varrho + f)}{\sqrt{f^2 + (2\varrho - 4\varrho e^K)f + \varrho^2}}\, df.$$

With $b_\varrho := 2\varrho - 4\varrho e^K$, standard calculus eventually gives that $t \equiv t(f)$ equals

$$\pm\left(\sqrt{f^2 + b_\varrho f + \varrho^2} + 2\varrho e^K \log\left(f + \varrho - 2\varrho e^K + \sqrt{f^2 + b_\varrho f + \varrho^2}\right) + \gamma\right), \tag{5}$$

where γ is chosen such that the boundary condition, i.e., $f(0) = \beta_0$, is met.

Numerical evaluation. To obtain the path $f(t)$, for a given value of K, (5) needs to be solved, but obviously there are alternatives. One could for instance solve the differential equation (4) iteratively starting in $f(0) = \beta_0$, by applying techniques of the Runge-Kutta type. This is not entirely standard, though, as the path may be horizontal at some point between 0 and δ (so that the most straightforward numerical procedures do not work). Figures 1-2 serve as examples, and show the paths for specific monotone and non-monotone cases. Both β_0 and β_δ are larger than ϱ, so there is a bifurcation point T. In the left graph, $\delta < T$ and hence the path is monotone, whereas in the right graph $\delta > T$ and hence the path has a minimum in $(0, \delta)$. In both figures $\delta = 0.95$, $\varrho = 1.05$, and $\beta_\delta = 1.6$, but in the left panel $\beta_0 = 1.48$, whereas in the right panel $\beta_0 = 1.58$.

3.2   Likelihood Probabilities

In this section we analyze the decay rate $\bar{\eta}(\varphi, \delta \mid \beta_\delta)$, using the same methodology as in Section 3.1. As the line of reasoning is very similar to the one followed in Section 3.1, we just sketch the basic steps.

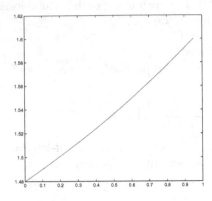 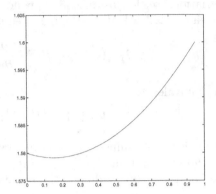

Fig. 1. Monotone path   **Fig. 2.** Nonmonotone path

First observe that we can shift time so that we obtain

$$\bar{\eta}(\varphi, \delta \mid \beta_\delta) = \lim_{n\to\infty} \frac{1}{n} \log \mathbb{P}\left(\bar{T}_n(\delta) > 0 \mid Y_0 = n\beta_\delta\right), \ \bar{T}_n(\delta) := \frac{1}{n} \sum_{i=1}^{\lfloor n(1-\delta)\rfloor} L_i - \varphi(1-\delta);$$

if this is indeed a large deviation probability, then we can replace the inequality '$> \varphi(1 - \delta)$' by an equality '$= \varphi(1 - \delta)$'. We again want to use Slow Markov Walk theory, in that we wish to evaluate

$$\bar{\eta}(\varphi, \delta \mid \beta_\delta) = -\inf_{f \in \mathscr{B}} \int_0^{1-\delta} I_{f(t)}(f'(t))\mathrm{d}t,$$

where $\mathscr{B}$ are the paths (with $f(0) = \beta_\delta$) such that $\lim_{n\to\infty} n^{-1} \cdot Y_{\lfloor nt\rfloor} = f(t)$, for $t \in [0, \delta)$, implies that $\lim_{n\to\infty} \bar{T}_n(\delta) = \varphi(1 - \delta)$. Let us characterize the paths with this property. To this end, first rewrite

$$g_f(\delta) := \lim_{n\to\infty} \frac{1}{n} \sum_{i=1}^{\lfloor n(1-\delta)\rfloor} L_i = \lim_{n\to\infty} \frac{1}{n} \sum_{k=1}^{(1-\delta)/\varepsilon} \sum_{i=n(k-1)\varepsilon+1}^{nk\varepsilon} L_i.$$

For i in $\{n(k-1)\varepsilon + 1, \ldots, nk\varepsilon\}$ we have that

$$\frac{\mathbb{Q}(X_i \mid Y_{i-1})}{\mathbb{P}(X_i \mid Y_{i-1})} = \frac{\bar{\varrho}}{\varrho} \cdot \frac{\varrho + f(k\varepsilon)}{\bar{\varrho} + f(k\varepsilon)} + O(\varepsilon) \text{ and } \frac{\mathbb{Q}(X_i \mid Y_{i-1})}{\mathbb{P}(X_i \mid Y_{i-1})} = \frac{\varrho + f(k\varepsilon)}{\bar{\varrho} + f(k\varepsilon)} + O(\varepsilon)$$

if $X_i = 1$ and $X_i = -1$, respectively. Let $U_{k,n}$ be the number of steps upwards in $\{n(k-1)\varepsilon+1, \ldots, nk\varepsilon\}$, and $D_{k,n}$ the number of steps downwards. Then trivially $U_{k,n} + D_{k,n} = n\varepsilon$, but on the other hand $U_{k,n} - D_{k,n} = n\varepsilon f'(k\varepsilon) + O(\varepsilon^2)$. From these relations we can solve $U_{k,n}$ and $D_{k,n}$. We end up with

$$\sum_{k=1}^{(1-\delta)/\varepsilon} \left(\frac{\varepsilon}{2} f'(k\varepsilon) \log\left(\frac{\bar{\varrho}}{\varrho}\right) - \frac{\varepsilon}{2} \log\left(\frac{\bar{\varrho}}{\varrho}\right) + \varepsilon \log\left(\frac{\varrho + f(k\varepsilon)}{\bar{\varrho} + f(k\varepsilon)}\right) + O(\varepsilon^2)\right).$$

Letting $\varepsilon \downarrow 0$, we obtain

$$g_f(\delta) = \int_0^{1-\delta} \frac{1}{2} \log\left(\frac{\bar{\varrho}}{\varrho}\right) \cdot f'(t)\, dt - \frac{1-\delta}{2} \log\left(\frac{\bar{\varrho}}{\varrho}\right) + \int_0^{1-\delta} \log\left(\frac{\varrho + f(t)}{\bar{\varrho} + f(t)}\right) dt$$

$$= h_f(\delta) + \int_0^{1-\delta} \log\left(\frac{\varrho + f(t)}{\bar{\varrho} + f(t)}\right) dt,$$

with $h_f(\delta) := \frac{1}{2} \log(\bar{\varrho}/\varrho) \cdot (f(1-\delta) - f(0)) - \frac{1}{2}(1-\delta) \log(\bar{\varrho}/\varrho)$. Hence we are left with a variational problem, with Lagrange multiplier L:

$$\inf_{f \in B} \left(\int_0^{1-\delta} \left(I_{f(t)}(f'(t)) - L \log\left(\frac{\varrho + f(t)}{\bar{\varrho} + f(t)}\right) \right) dt - L h_f(\delta) \right). \tag{6}$$

The DuBois-Reymond equation reads

$$I_{f(t)}(f'(t)) - f'(t) \cdot \left. \frac{\partial}{\partial u} I_x(u) \right|_{x=f(t), u=f'(t)} - L \log\left(\frac{\varrho + f(t)}{\bar{\varrho} + f(t)}\right) = K,$$

which reduces to

$$f'(t) = \pm\sqrt{1 - e^K \left(\frac{\varrho + f(t)}{\bar{\varrho} + f(t)}\right)^L \frac{4f(t)\varrho}{(\varrho + f(t))^2}}.$$

We again need to numerically solve this, under $f(0) = \beta_\delta$. K and L should be chosen such that $g_f(\delta) = \varphi(1 - \delta)$ and (6) is minimal. In more detail, a procedure could be the following. For given K, L, solve the differential equation, to obtain the path $f^\star_{K,L}(\cdot)$. For given L, determine the $K \equiv K(L)$ such that $g_{f^\star_{K,L}}(\delta) = \varphi(\delta)$. Then minimize, over L,

$$\int_0^{1-\delta} I_{f^\star_{K(L),L}(t)}((f^\star_{K(L),L})'(t)) dt.$$

It is clear, however, that such procedures are, from a numerical standpoint, in general quite involved. A substantial simplification can be achieved by approximating the functions involved by polynomial functions (cf. Ritz method).

3.3   Discussion

Now that we have derived in Sections 3.1 and 3.2 expressions for the decay rate of interest, it remains to select an appropriate function $\varphi(\cdot)$. We can choose, for a given value of β_0, $\varphi(\cdot)$ such that $\eta(\varphi, \delta \mid \beta_0) \equiv \alpha$ for all $\delta \in [0, 1)$. As argued in [2, Ch. V.E], this choice gives the best type-II error rate performance.

The procedure described above is a natural counterpart for the 'usual' change-point detection procedures that were designed for i.i.d. increments; importantly, we recall the fact that in our model the increments are dependent made it necessary to develop a new method. The most significant drawbacks of the above procedure are: (i) it only applies to the case of exponentially distributed call durations; (ii) its computational complexity is high. In the next section we present an approach with is somewhat more crude, but overcomes these two problems.

4   Analysis for M/G/∞

In this section we present an approach to do changepoint detection in an M/G/∞ queue. Clearly, the observations $Y(0), Y(\Delta), Y(2\Delta), \ldots$ are *not* independent; remember from Section 2 that the correlation coefficient between $Y(0)$ and $Y(\Delta)$ is given by $\mathbb{P}(B^\star > \Delta)$. It is evident, however, that this dependence is negligible for Δ sufficiently large. In Section 4.1 we analyze how large Δ should be to be able to safely assume independence – as a useful by-product, we derive insight into the so-called relaxation times in the M/G/∞ queue (which can be interpreted as a measure of the speed of convergence to the stationary distribution). Then Section 4.2 describes a changepoint detection procedure, which again relies on Slow Markov Walk theory [2, Ch. IV.C]; however, where we used this framework for *dependent* observations in Section 3, we now focus on the case in which the observations are i.i.d. (and sampled from a Poisson distribution).

4.1   Transient Probabilities

We first focus on the question: for a given number of calls present at time 0, how fast does the (transient) distribution of the number of calls present at time t, converge to the stationary distribution? This speed of convergence is often referred to as *relaxation time*, cf. [1]. We now identify $u_{k,\ell}(\cdot)$ such that

$$\lim_{t\to\infty} (u_{k,\ell}(t))^{-1} \cdot (\mathbb{P}(Y(t) = \ell \mid Y(0) = k) - \mathbb{P}(Y = \ell)) = 1. \qquad (7)$$

We first observe that, due to (1),

$$\mathbb{P}(Y(t) = \ell \mid Y(0) = k) = \sum_{m=0}^{\min\{k,\ell\}} \mathbb{P}(\mathbb{Bin}(k, p_t) = m)\, \mathbb{P}(\mathbb{Pois}(\lambda t q_t) = \ell - m).$$

Take the term corresponding to $m = 0$ in the summation in the right-hand side of the previous display, and subtract $\mathbb{P}(Y = \ell)$. We then obtain that $\varrho(r_{\ell-1} - r_\ell) \cdot \mathbb{P}(B^\star > t) \cdot (1 + o(1))$ as $t \to \infty$, recalling that $\lambda t q_t = \varrho\,\mathbb{P}(B^\star < t) = \varrho - \varrho\,\mathbb{P}(B^\star > t)$ and denoting $r_\ell := e^{-\varrho}\varrho^\ell/\ell!$; here we used that

$$\lim_{t\to\infty} \frac{f(\varrho) - f(\varrho(1 - \mathbb{P}(B^\star > t)))}{\varrho\,\mathbb{P}(B^\star > t)} = f'(\varrho).$$

The term corresponding to $m = 1$ obeys $k r_{\ell-1} \cdot \mathbb{P}(B^\star > t) \cdot (1 + o(1))$. Finally observe that the terms corresponding to $m \geq 2$ are $o(\mathbb{P}(B^\star > t))$. Combining the above findings, we conclude that (7) indeed applies, with

$$u_{k,\ell}(t) = U_{k,\ell} \cdot \mathbb{P}(B^\star > t), \quad U_{k,\ell} := \varrho(r_{\ell-1} - r_\ell) + k r_{\ell-1}.$$

Suppose our goal is to enforce 'approximate independence' between $Y(0)$ and $Y(t)$ by choosing t sufficiently large that for all $k, \ell \in \{0, \ldots, C\}$ we have that $|U_{k,\ell}| \cdot \mathbb{P}(B^\star > t) < \varepsilon_{\max}$. Observe that $U_{k,\ell} \leq (\varrho + k) r_{\ell-1}$. Now use that the mode of the Poisson distribution lies close to ϱ: for all $i = 0, 1, \ldots$

$$r_i \leq g(\varrho) := r_{\varrho m}, \quad \varrho m := \lfloor \varrho \rfloor \text{ if } \varrho \notin \mathbb{N}, \text{ and } \varrho \text{ else.}$$

We conclude that $U_{k,\ell} \leq (\varrho + C)g(\varrho)$ for all $k,\ell \in \{0,\ldots,C\}$. Likewise, $U_{k,\ell} \geq -\varrho r_\ell \geq -\varrho g(\varrho)$. It is now straightforward to choose t such that for all $k,\ell \in \{0,\ldots,C\} \mid U_{k,\ell} \mid \cdot \mathbb{P}(B^\star > t) < \varepsilon_{\max}$.

4.2 Changepoint Detection Procedure

As described above, we can now choose Δ so large that $u_{k,\ell}(\Delta) < \varepsilon_{\max}$, for all $k,\ell \in \{1,\ldots,C\}$ and $\varepsilon_{\max}$ some given small positive number. In this way we enforced 'approximate independence', thus justifying the use of procedures for i.i.d. observations, as in [2, Section VI.E].

Goal: changepoint. Again, we wish to detect a changepoint, that is, during our observation period the load parameter ϱ (which we let again correspond to the probability model $\mathbb{P}$) changes into $\bar{\varrho} \neq \varrho$ (the model $\mathbb{Q}$). More formally, we consider the following (multiple) hypotheses. Let $Y_i := Y(i\Delta)$ be the sequence of observations of the number of calls present at time $i\Delta$.

H_0: $(Y_i)_{i=1}^n$ are distributed $\mathbb{P}ois(\varrho)$.
H_1: For some $\delta \in \{1/n, 2/n, \ldots, (n-1)/n\}$, it holds that $(Y_i)_{i=1}^{\lfloor n\delta \rfloor}$ is distributed $\mathbb{P}ois(\varrho)$, whereas $(Y_i)_{i=\lfloor n\delta \rfloor +1}^n$ is distributed $\mathbb{P}ois(\bar{\varrho})$, with $\bar{\varrho} \neq \varrho$.

Again, in view of the Neyman-Pearson lemma, we consider the following likelihood-ratio test statistic: for some function $\varphi(\cdot)$ we will provide later,

$$T_n := \max_{\delta \in [0,1)} T_n(\delta), \quad \text{with } T_n(\delta) := \frac{1}{n} \sum_{i=\lfloor n\delta \rfloor +1}^n L_i - \varphi(\delta),$$

$L_i := \log \mathbb{Q}(Y_i)/\mathbb{P}(Y_i) = e^{\varrho-\bar{\varrho}} \left(\bar{\varrho}/\varrho\right)^{Y_i}$. If T_n is larger than 0, we reject H_0. We can now use the machinery of [2, Section VI.E] to further specify this test. We first introduce the moment generating function and its Legendre transform:

$$M(\vartheta) = \sum_{k=0}^{\infty} \left(\frac{\bar{\varrho}^k}{k!} e^{-\bar{\varrho}}\right)^{\vartheta} \left(\frac{\varrho^k}{k!} e^{-\bar{\varrho}}\right)^{1-\vartheta} = e^{-\varrho} e^{(\varrho-\bar{\varrho})\vartheta} \exp\left(\varrho \left(\frac{\bar{\varrho}}{\varrho}\right)^{\vartheta}\right);$$

$$I(u) = \sup_{\vartheta}(\vartheta u - \log M(\vartheta)) = \vartheta^\star(u)\,u - \log M(\vartheta^\star(u)), \quad \text{where}$$

$$\vartheta^\star(u) := \frac{\log(u + \bar{\varrho} - \varrho) - \log(\varrho \log(\bar{\varrho}/\varrho))}{\log(\bar{\varrho}/\varrho)}.$$

From [2, Section VI.E, Eqn. (46)–(48)], we can compute the decay rate of issuing an alarm under H_0, for a given threshold function $\varphi(\cdot)$:

$$\lim_{n\to\infty} \frac{1}{n} \log \mathbb{P}\left(\max_{\delta \in [0,1)} T_n(\delta) > 0\right) = \max_{\delta \in [0,1)} (1-\delta) \cdot \lim_{n\to\infty} \frac{1}{n(1-\delta)} \log \mathbb{P}\left(\frac{T_n(\delta)}{1-\delta} > 0\right)$$

$$= \max_{\delta \in [0,1)} \psi(\delta) \quad \text{with } \psi(\delta) := (1-\delta) \cdot I\left(\frac{\varphi(\delta)}{1-\delta}\right).$$

To get an essentially uniform alarm rate, choose $\varphi(\cdot)$ such that $\psi(\delta) = \alpha^\star$ for all $\delta \in [0,1)$; here $\alpha^\star = -\log \alpha/n$, where α is a measure for the likelihood of false alarms (for instance 0.05). Unfortunately, $\varphi(\cdot)$ cannot be solved in closed form, but it can be obtained numerically (e.g. by bisection).

5   Numerical Evaluation

In this section we present the results of our numerical experimentation. We first focus on testing the procedures proposed for M/G/∞ in Section 4.2, and then shift to the setting of Section 3.

Changepoint detection for nearly independent Poisson samples. As mentioned above, we start by presenting numerical results for the setting of Section 4.2.

— *Experiment A1.* We then consider the situation that Y_1 up to Y_{100} are sampled from the evolution of the M/M/∞ queue, at epochs $\Delta, 2\Delta, \ldots, 100\Delta$; $Y_0 = Y(0)$ is sampled according to the equilibrium distribution $\mathrm{Pois}(\varrho)$. For these first 100 observations we chose $\lambda = 200$ and $\mu = 1$, leading to $\varrho = 200$. Then Y_{101} up to Y_{200} are generated in an analogous way, but now with $\lambda = 250$, and hence $\bar{\varrho} = 250$. Assuming a maximum allowable blocking probability of 0.1%, the value $\bar{\varrho} = 250$ corresponds with $C = 291$ lines. It is easily verified that choosing $\Delta = 10$ makes sure that $\mid U_{k,\ell} \mid \cdot \mathbb{P}(B^\star > t) < \varepsilon_{\max}$, for an $\varepsilon_{\max}$ of 0.01, using the procedures developed in Section 4.1.

We take windows of length 50, that is, we test whether H_0 should be rejected based on data points $Y_i, \ldots, Y_{i+49}$, for $i = 1$ up to 151. The first window in which the influence of $\bar{\varrho}$ is noticeable is therefore window 52. 500 runs are performed. Figure 3 shows the detection ratio as a function of the window id. It indeed hardly shows false alarms up to id 52, and then the detection ratio grows to 1 quite rapidly, as desired.

Clearly, from window 101 on all observations have been affected by the load change. For window i between 52 and 101, one could (within the window that consists of 50 observations) detect a load change at the earliest at the $(101-i)$-th observation — this is what could be called the 'true changepoint'; in addition, we call the ratio of $101 - i$ and the window length 50, which is a number between 0 and 1, the 'true delta', in line with the meaning of δ in Section 4.2. Figure 4 provides insight into the spread of the time of detection. It shows that the detection takes place always somewhat later than the true changepoint (as could be expected, as it takes a few observations to 'gather enough statistical evidence'), but the delay is fairly short. In 50% of the cases the delay is less than 8 observations, in 75% less than 12 observations, as can be seen from the graph.

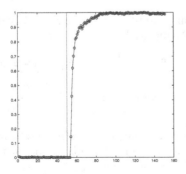   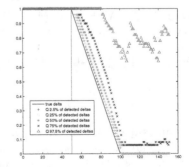

Fig. 3. Detection ratio Exp. A1   **Fig. 4.** Detection epoch Exp. A1

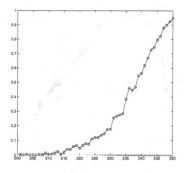

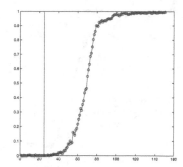

Fig. 5. Detection ratio Exp. A2   **Fig. 6.** Detection ratio Exp. A3

— *Experiment A2.* In Exp. A1 we instantaneously changed ϱ into $\bar{\varrho}$ (which is the value tested against). We now study the effect of a load change to a value $\hat{\varrho} < \bar{\varrho}$. The main question is: despite the fact that $\hat{\varrho}$ is not the value of the load we test against, do we still detect a load change? The experiment is done in a similar fashion as Exp. A1: there is a load change from $\varrho = 200$ to $\hat{\varrho} \in \{201, \ldots, 250\}$ from time 100Δ on, and we test against $\bar{\varrho} = 250$. Figure 5 shows that values of $\hat{\varrho}$ up to 225 are hardly detected. For $\hat{\varrho}$ larger than 235 in at least 50% of the runs an alarm has been issued. Only for $\hat{\varrho}$ larger than 245 the changepoint has been detected with high probability (more than, say 85%).

— *Experiment A3.* In Exp. A1 we instantaneously changed ϱ into $\bar{\varrho}$, but a next question is what happens when ϱ *gradually* increases to $\bar{\varrho}$. We repeated Exp. A1, but now the load first has value 200, then increase from observation 76 on in a linear way, to reach value 250 at observation 125 (and hence only from window id 76 on part of the observations were under $\bar{\varrho}$). Figs. 6 and 7 are the counterparts of Figs. 3 and 4. Compared to Fig. 3, the detection ratio in Fig. 6 is considerably less steep; note that this could be expected from Exp. A2, as we saw there that only if the load is close to $\bar{\varrho}$ load changes are detected.

Changepoint detection for jump process of $M/M/\infty$. The function $\varphi(\cdot)$ can be determined by executing the computations proposed in Section 3, but due to their intrinsic complexity we chose for the obvious alternative of determining it empirically (that is, by simulation). For $\varrho = 200$ and $\bar{\varrho} = 250$, we thus obtained the curve shown in Fig. 8. We performed the following experiments:

— *Experiment B1.* We consider the following setting, in which we start with Y_0 being $\mathrm{Pois}(\varrho)$, then sample 2500 times according to $\mathbb{P}$, and then 2500 times according to $\mathbb{Q}$. The window size is 2000, so that from window id 501 on the measure $\mathbb{Q}$ has impact on the test statistic. Fig. 9 shows that we indeed detect the changepoint after window id 1501, but the plot also shows that the chance of false alarms (that is, alarms before window id 501) is substantially higher than the 5% that was aimed for, viz. about 87%. The main reason for this phenomenon is that $\varphi(\cdot)$ was (empirically) determined by making $\mathbb{P}(T_n(\delta) > 0)$ equal to α for all $\delta \in [0, 1)$. The probability of an alarm under H_0, however, is

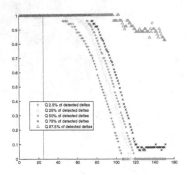

Fig. 7. Detection epoch Exp. A3

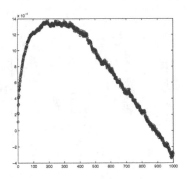

Fig. 8. $\varphi(\cdot)$ for $\varrho = 200$, $\bar{\varrho} = 250$, $\alpha = 0.05$

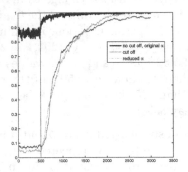

Fig. 9. Detection ratio Exps. B1, B2, B3

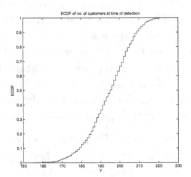

Fig. 10. Detection epoch Exp. B4

the probability that $T_n(\delta) > 0$ *for some* $\delta \in [0, 1)$, which is then evidently larger than α. Apparently this difference can be quite large (although all probabilities involved have the same exponential decay rate, when n grows large).

— *Experiment B2.* There are several ways to make reduce the fraction of false positives. We first consider the effect of changing the criterion $\max_{\delta \in [0,1)} T_n(\delta) > 0$ into $\max_{\delta \in [0,\delta_{\max})} T_n(\delta) > 0$. Fig. 9 shows what happens when imposing such a 'cut off'; we took $\delta_{\max} = 0.9$. The false alarm rate is indeed reduced to a number close to 5%, but at the expense of detecting load changes after window id 501.

— *Experiment B3.* We now study an alternative to imposing a 'cut off', viz., using an α' which is smaller α; see Fig. 9 for $\alpha' = 0.15\%$ (where it is noted that $\varphi(\cdot)$ had to be recomputed). The effect is very similar to that of Experiment B2: reduction of the false alarm rate, at the expense of loss of detection. It seems that tuning either $\delta_{\max}$ or α' is necessary to control the false alarm rate.

— *Experiment B4.* Now we start at $Y_0 = 200$ and simulate the first 2500 slots under ϱ, and the last 2500 under $\bar{\varrho}$. The window length is 2000, and $\delta_{\max} = 0.8$. In

Fig. 10 we show the empirical cumulative distribution function of the first epoch that an alarm is issued. Interestingly, its mean is 236, i.e., considerably less than 250. In other words: the alarm is early detected in that the 'new equilibrium', that is, 250, has not been reached yet. This aspect is a significant advantage of this approach over that of Section 4.

6   Concluding Remarks and Discussion

In this paper we developed procedures that are capable of detecting load changes, in a setting in which each connection consumes roughly the same amount of bandwidth (think of VoIP). We designed testing procedures, relying on large-deviations theory. In passing, we found results for the transient of the $M/M/\infty$ and $M/G/\infty$ systems, which are of independent interest. The last part of the paper was devoted to numerical experimentation. It was shown that the procedures that we developed were, after elementary tuning, capable of tracking load changes. Special attention was paid to managing the trade-off between the detection ratio and the false alarm rate.

We considered traffic generated by applications that require per connection (roughly) the same amount of bandwidth. A next step would be to extend this to a setting where the aggregate traffic stream is the result of many more heterogeneous users. Then one could model the traffic by Gaussian processes [4, 6], and to develop changepoint detection procedures for these; observe, however, that we again have to resolve the issue of dependence between the observations. A second issue for future research relates to applying the procedures developed in this paper in a real network, by using real traces.

References

1. Blanc, J., van Doorn, E.: Relaxation times for queueing systems. In: de Bakker, J., Hazewinkel, M., Lenstra, J.K. (eds.) Mathematics and Computer Science. CWI Monograph, vol. 1, pp. 139–162. North-Holland, Amsterdam (1984)
2. Bucklew, J.: Large Deviation Techniques in Decision, Simulation, and Estimation. Wiley, New York (1990)
3. Ho, L., Cavuto, D., Papavassiliou, S., Zawadzki, A.: Adaptive/automated detection of service anomalies in transaction-oriented WANS: Network analysis, algorithms, implementation, and deployment. IEEE Journal of Selected Areas in Communications 18, 744–757 (2000)
4. Mandjes, M.: Large Deviations of Gaussian Queues. Wiley, Chichester (2007)
5. Mandjes, M., Saniee, I., Stolyar, A.: Load characterization, overload prediction, and load anomaly detection for voice over IP traffic. IEEE Transactions on Neural Networks 16, 1019–1028 (2005)
6. van de Meent, R., Mandjes, M., Pras, A.: Gaussian traffic everywhere? In: Proc. 2006 IEEE International Conference on Communications, Istanbul, Turkey (2006)
7. Münz, G., Carle, G.: Application of forecasting techniques and control charts for traffic anomaly detection. In: Proc. 19th ITC Specialist Seminar on Network Usage and Traffic, Berlin, Germany (2008)
8. Shwartz, A., Weiss, A.: Large Deviations for Performance Analysis. Chapman and Hall, London (1995)

9. Siegmund, D.: Sequential Analysis. Springer, Berlin (1985)
10. Tartakovsky, A., Veeravalli, V.: Changepoint detection in multichannel and distributed systems with applications. In: Applications of Sequential Methodologies, pp. 331–363. Marcel Dekker, New York (2004)
11. Thottan, M., Ji, C.: Proactive anomaly detection using distributed intelligent agents. IEEE Network 12, 21–27 (1998)
12. Żuraniewski, P., Rincón, D.: Wavelet transforms and change-point detection algorithms for tracking network traffic fractality. In: Proc. NGI 2006, pp. 216–223 (2006)

Rare-Event Simulation for Tandem Queues: A Simple and Efficient Importance Sampling Scheme*

Denis Miretskiy[1], Werner Scheinhardt[1], and Michel Mandjes[2]

[1] University of Twente, Enschede, The Netherlands
[2] University of Amsterdam, Amsterdam, The Netherlands

Abstract. This paper focuses on estimating the rare event of overflow in the downstream queue of a tandem Jackson queue, relying on importance sampling. It is known that in this setting 'traditional' state-independent schemes perform poorly. More sophisticated state-dependent schemes yield asymptotic efficiency. Their drawback, however, is that they require a per-state computation of the new measure, so that it still consumes considerable machine time.

The contribution of this paper is a scheme that combines asymptotic efficiency with low complexity. It retains the quality of the original state-dependent scheme, but its implementation is almost as simple as for state-independent analogues.

1 Introduction

Importance sampling (IS) is a powerful and flexible technique to speed up Monte Carlo simulations of rare events. The main idea behind IS is the simulation of a system under a new probability measure which guarantees more frequent occurrence of the rare event of interest. To compensate for the influence of the new measure (i.e., to obtain an unbiased estimator), the simulation outputs need to be corrected by appropriate likelihood ratios. The challenge is to construct a 'good' new measure, by which we mean that the likelihood ratios of the rare event in which we are interested are 'small'. If this is not the case, the variance of the resulting estimator can blow up, or even become infinite. We refer to [1,8] and [13], for more background.

In the current paper, we consider a tandem Jackson network and our interest is in the rare event of collecting a large number of jobs in the second buffer before the system becomes empty. A first, naïve approach could be to consider *state-independent* IS schemes, that is, schemes in which the change of measure is static. In this context we mention the landmark paper by Parekh and Walrand [12], where the authors show the appealing result that for overflow in

---

* Part of this research has been funded by the Dutch BSIK/BRICKS project. This article is also the result of joint research in the 3TU Centre of Competence NIR-ICT (Netherlands Institute for Research on ICT) within the Federation of Three Universities of Technology in The Netherlands.

R. Núñez-Queija and J. Resing (Eds.): NET-COOP 2009, LNCS 5894, pp. 107–120, 2009.

a single M/M/1 queue a swap of the arrival and service rate works excellently. Later Sadowsky [14] proved that this type of new measure was asymptotically efficient (or: asymptotically optimal) even for the (multi-server) GI/GI/m queue (with light-tailed service times), where asymptotic efficiency effectively means that the variance of the estimator behaves approximately as the square of its first moment. Application of a similar new measure to a two-node Jackson network (swapping the arrival rate with the slowest service rate) was not so encouraging – the method was asymptotically efficient for a specific set of parameter values, but led to unbounded variance for other values [7,2].

It was clear that the class of state-independent new measures was not rich enough to obtain asymptotic efficiency, and therefore one started considering *state-dependent* IS, where the new measure is *not* uniform over the state space. In [3,15] such measures were constructed, and asymptotic efficiency was empirically concluded, but without any analytic proofs. The first provably asymptotically efficient scheme (even for considerably more general networks) was proposed by Dupuis *et al.* [5], relying on a control-theoretical approach. In this approach, a first element is to find the exponential decay rate of the probability of interest, by relying on a large-deviations formulation (i.e., solving a variational problem). Understanding of this large-deviations behavior is a crucial step in the construction of an asymptotically efficient scheme, but, as argued in [6], in general not sufficient. To make the scheme work, the large-deviations-based new measure has to be subtly modified, as demonstrated in [5].

In the present paper, our aim is to analyze the probability of the population of the downstream queue in a tandem Jackson network exceeding some predefined threshold, before the system idles. It is noted that [5] focuses on overflow in either of the buffers during a busy cycle. A crucial difference (on the technical level) between these two settings, is that in our setting the states space (that is, the set of states the process can visit before one can determine whether the threshold has been reached before the system idle) is infinite, as in principle the first queue can grow beyond any value during such a run. The present paper is a follow-up to [9], where for this problem a state-independent scheme was proposed that worked well for just a limited set of parameter values, and [11], where an asymptotically efficient state-dependent scheme was presented. It is also stressed that [11] is more general than most of the previous papers, in that it considers the event of exceeding a threshold in the second buffer before emptying the system, starting from *any* given state, in contrast to all previous research where the origin was chosen as the starting state.

Importantly, the IS scheme of [11] has a substantial drawback as well: the state-dependence entails that one has to compute the new measure for any state in the state space, which may be time-consuming. Therefore one would like to device an IS algorithm that combines the attractive features of state-dependent and state-independent schemes. The present paper provides such a scheme: it is asymptotically efficient, but at the same time of low complexity (as determining the new measure requires minimal computational effort). Numerical experiments provide further insight in the performance of our method (including a comparison with existing methods). We remark that we could have cast our approach in a control-theoretic framework, in line with, e.g., [5,6], but we have refrained from doing so with the intention to make the paper accessible to an audience as broad as possible.

As a last remark we should note that the type of probability that we consider is primarily of academic interest, in the sense that the task of designing a good new measure for IS is already highly nontrivial, even in our specific setting (Poisson arrivals and exponential services, only two queues, no feedback). Whether similar techniques as we present here will also work well for more general networks (that may be more suitable for applications), is not clear in general, although they can in principle be applied to general Jackson networks.

We finish this introduction with a description of the paper's structure. We describe the model of interest in detail in Section 2. Section 3 contains, in addition to a brief review of IS, the IS schemes themselves. The analytic proof of asymptotic efficiency is given in Section 4. Supporting numeric results are presented in Section 5. We end the paper with some final remarks in Section 6.

2   Model

We consider two $M/M/1$ queues in tandem, with jobs arriving at the first queue according to a Poisson process of rate λ, and the queues having service rates μ_1 and μ_2 respectively. Both stations have infinitely large waiting room. Moreover, we assume that the system is stable, i.e., $\lambda < \min\{\mu_1, \mu_2\}$. As we are interested in the probability that the number of jobs at the second station exceeds a given (typically high) level B before the system gets empty, we may rescale time; in the sequel we assume $\lambda + \mu_1 + \mu_2 = 1$ without loss of generality. It is also clear that all information required is captured by the embedded discrete-time Markov chain $Q_j = (Q_{1,j}, Q_{2,j})$, where $Q_{i,j}$ is the number of jobs in queue i after the j-th transition. The possible transitions of the latter Markov chain are $v_0 = (1, 0)$, $v_1 = (-1, 1)$ and $v_2 = (0, -1)$ with corresponding probabilities λ, μ_1 and μ_2. However, note that the transition v_k is impossible while queue k is empty, and to resolve this issue we introduce self-transitions:

$$\mathbb{P}(Q_{j+1} = Q_j | Q_{k,j} = 0) = \mu_k, \text{ for } k = 1, 2.$$

For convenience we also introduce the scaled process $X_j = Q_j / B$. The main benefit of this is that X_j's state space does not depend on B: it is $\bar{D} = D \cup \partial_e \cup \partial_1 \cup \partial_2$, where

$$D := \{(x_1, x_2) : x_1 > 0, 0 < x_2 < 1\}, \quad \partial_1 := \{(0, x_2) : 0 < x_2 < 1\},$$
$$\partial_2 := \{(x_1, 0) : x_1 > 0\}, \qquad\qquad \partial_e := \{(x_1, 1) : x_1 > 0\},$$

see Figure 1. Note that the probability of our interest is equal to the probability that process X_j reaches the exiting boundary ∂_e before reaching the origin. To define it more formally, we first introduce the stopping time τ_B^s, which denotes

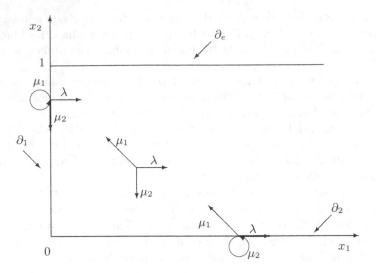

Fig. 1. State space and transition structure for scaled process X_j

the first entrance of the process X_j to the exit boundary ∂_e starting from the state $s = (s_1, s_2)$ without visits to the origin:

$$\tau_B^s = \inf\{k > 0 : X_k \in \partial_e, X_j \neq 0 \text{ for } j = 1, \dots, k-1\}, \tag{1}$$

where $\tau_B^s := \infty$ if X_j reaches the origin before ∂_e. Denote by $I_B(A^s)$ the indicator of the event $\{\tau_B^s < \infty\}$ for the path $A^s = (X_j, j = 0, \dots : X_0 = s)$, as in [11]. Consequently the probability of interest reads

$$p_B^s := \mathbb{P}(\tau_B^s < \infty) = \mathbb{E}I_B(A^s). \tag{2}$$

3   Importance Sampling

This section has two goals: (i) a brief description of IS, (ii) the presentation of our IS scheme for estimating the probability p_B^s.

IS is one of the most popular and powerful tools to efficiently estimate rare-event probabilities. For example in our case, due to the rarity of the event under consideration, simulating the system under the original measure to estimate p_B^s is inefficient. In IS this problem is resolved by simulating the system under a *different* measure, under which the event of interest occurs frequently.

To estimate p_B^s, IS generates samples under a new probability measure $\mathbb{Q}$, with respect to which $\mathbb{P}$ is absolutely continuous. It is elementary that p_B^s can now alternatively be expressed as an expectation under $\mathbb{Q}$, viz. $p_B^s = \mathbb{E}^{\mathbb{Q}}[L(A^s)I_B(A^s)]$, where $L(\omega)$ is the likelihood ratio (also known as Radon-Nikodým derivative) of a realization ('path') ω, i.e., $L(\omega) = \frac{d\mathbb{P}}{d\mathbb{Q}}(\omega)$. Performing n independent runs, with observations $(L_i(A^s), I_{B,i}(A^s)), i = 1, \dots, n$ an unbiased estimator is

$$\frac{1}{n}\sum_{i=1}^{n} L_i(A^s)I_{B,i}(A^s).$$

A notion developed to measure the efficiency of the new measure $\mathbb{Q}$ is *asymptotic efficiency*, which roughly requires that the second moment of the estimate behaves approximately as the square of its first moment (thus essentially minimizing the variance of the estimator). Since we know that $-B^{-1} \cdot \log p_B^s$ converges to a positive constant as B grows large (see [11]; this constant, the exponential decay rate of p_B^s, will be denoted by $\gamma^s(s)$ in the sequel), we can write the definition of asymptotic efficiency in our case as follows.

Definition 1. *The IS scheme is asymptotically efficient if*

$$\limsup_{B \to \infty} \frac{1}{B} \log \mathbb{E}[L(\Lambda^s) I_B(A^s)] \leq 2 \lim_{B \to \infty} \frac{1}{B} \log p_B^s. \tag{3}$$

If the probability of interest decays exponentially in the 'rarity parameter' (B in our case), which holds for our p_B^s, asymptotic efficiency effectively means that the number of replications needed to obtain an estimate of given accuracy grows subexponentially in the rarity parameter.

We now propose the new measure to be used in this paper, distinguishing between the cases $\mu_2 < \mu_1$ and $\mu_1 \leq \mu_2$. Like the measure proposed in [11], it is state-dependent, but its computation is substantially less demanding, as we will see.

3.1   IS Scheme for the Case $\mu_2 < \mu_1$

Recall that our goal is to modify the IS scheme described in [11], such that the scheme's complexity is reduced, but without compromising the asymptotic efficiency. Again, the scheme is based on the most probable path to overflow, that we identified in [11, Section 3.2], as well as the new measure that ensures that 'on average' the process follows this optimal trajectory. To ease the exposition of the new measures, we partitioned the state space as shown in Figure 2 into A_1, A_2 and A_3; here, $\alpha_1 := (\mu_1 - \mu_2)/(\mu_1 - \lambda)$. The same figure also provides some examples (solid lines) of the most probable path to the exit boundary for various starting states s.

We now proceed by giving the new measure for starting points in A_1, A_2, and A_3. Let $(\lambda^{(\text{line})}, \mu_1^{(\text{line})}, \mu_2^{(\text{line})})$ solve

$$\begin{cases} \lambda^{(\text{line})} = \mu_1^{(\text{line})} - s_1(\mu_1^{(\text{line})} - \mu_2^{(\text{line})})/(1 - s_2) \\ \lambda^{(\text{line})} + \mu_1^{(\text{line})} + \mu_2^{(\text{line})} = \lambda + \mu_1 + \mu_2 \\ \lambda^{(\text{line})} \mu_1^{(\text{line})} \mu_2^{(\text{line})} = \lambda \mu_1 \mu_2 \\ \lambda^{(\text{line})} \leq \mu_1^{(\text{line})} \text{ and } \mu_1^{(\text{line})} > \mu_2^{(\text{line})} \\ \lambda^{(\text{line})}, \mu_1^{(\text{line})}, \mu_2^{(\text{line})} > 0. \end{cases} \tag{4}$$

The superscript "(line)" indicates that the solution is in fact the optimal change of measure to reach the exit boundary following a straight line starting in s. Now we can define the (overall) optimal new measure $(\tilde{\lambda}, \tilde{\mu}_1, \tilde{\mu}_2)$ through

$$(\tilde{\lambda}, \tilde{\mu}_1, \tilde{\mu}_2) = \begin{cases} (\mu_2, \mu_1, \lambda), & \text{if } s \in A_1, \\ (\lambda^{(\text{line})}, \mu_1^{(\text{line})}, \mu_2^{(\text{line})}), & \text{if } s \in A_2, \\ (\lambda, \mu_1, \mu_2), & \text{if } s \in A_3. \end{cases} \tag{5}$$

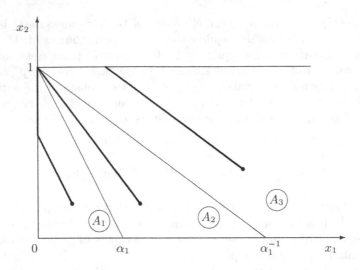

Fig. 2. Partition of $\bar{D}$ and some optimal paths to overflow when $\mu_2 < \mu_1$

Note that the dependence of $\tilde{\lambda}$ etc. on s is suppressed in the notation. Next we define

$$\gamma^s(x) := -x_1 \log \frac{\tilde{\lambda}}{\lambda} - (1 - x_2) \log \frac{\tilde{\mu}_2}{\mu_2}. \tag{6}$$

In the context of [11], when x is on the optimal path to overflow that started in s, $\gamma^s(x)$ can be interpreted as the residual 'cost' of moving from state x to ∂_e along that path. In particular $\gamma^s(s)$, the total cost of moving from s to ∂_e, is equal to the exponential decay rate of p_B^s, i.e., $B^{-1} \cdot \log p_B^s \to -\gamma^s(s)$, see Theorem 4.5 in [11].

Notice that the function $\gamma^s(x)$ is simply linear in x, since the new 'tilde-measure', i.e., $(\tilde{\lambda}, \tilde{\mu}_1, \tilde{\mu}_2)$, depends only on the fixed initial state s, and *not* on the current state x. This is the main difference with the new measure studied in [11], where we used the optimal new measure for each current state x with its cost $\gamma^x(x)$. Therefore a cubic equation (corresponding to system (4) with s replaced by x) had to be solved for each state x in the sample path. In our current approach, computation of the tilde-measure requires the (numerical) solution of just a single cubic equation.

It is known, e.g. from [9], that the new measure $(\tilde{\lambda}, \tilde{\mu}_1, \tilde{\mu}_2)$, which makes a sample path 'on average' follow the optimal trajectory to the rare set, is not necessarily asymptotically efficient; this is due to the possibility of several visits to the horizontal axis, which inflate the likelihood ratio, cf. [2,12]. In order to resolve this, we first introduce a measure $(\hat{\lambda}, \hat{\mu}_1, \hat{\mu}_2)$ as in [5], to be used when the current state is on or near the horizontal axis, through

$$(\hat{\lambda}, \hat{\mu}_1, \hat{\mu}_2) := (\tilde{\lambda}, \mu_1 \lambda / \tilde{\lambda}, \tilde{\mu}_2). \tag{7}$$

The primary idea behind this 'hat-measure' is to make the likelihood ratios of the loops around the horizontal axis not greater than 1 (by ensuring $\hat{\mu}_2 = \mu_2$).

Having introduced the 'tilde-measure' and the 'hat-measure', we are now ready to define the (state-dependent) measure $(\bar{\lambda}(x), \bar{\mu}_1(x), \bar{\mu}_2(x))$, of which we will prove asymptotic efficiency, and which is a combination of the two measures defined above and the original measure:

$$\bar{\lambda}(x) = \tilde{\lambda}^{\rho_1(x)} \hat{\lambda}^{\rho_2(x)} \lambda^{\rho_3(x)} M(x),$$
$$\bar{\mu}_1(x) = \tilde{\mu}_1^{\rho_1(x)} \hat{\mu}_1^{\rho_2(x)} \mu_1^{\rho_3(x)} M(x), \qquad (8)$$
$$\bar{\mu}_2(x) = \tilde{\mu}_2^{\rho_1(x)} \hat{\mu}_2^{\rho_2(x)} \mu_2^{\rho_3(x)} M(x).$$

Here $M(x)$ is a normalization function, and the $\rho_i(x)$ are positive weights, adding up to unity, such that $\rho_1(x)$ is close to 1 on almost all of the state space (leaving the other weights to be close to zero), while $\rho_2(x)$ is close to 1 only near the horizontal axis; the reason that we include the original measure with a weight $\rho_3(x)$ that should be close to 1 near the origin, is that applying the 'hat measure' there would also lead to high likelihood ratios. For the precise definition of the weights we have some freedom; here we follow the convenient choice in [5, Equation (3.15)],

$$\rho_i(x) = \frac{e^{-W_i(x)/\epsilon}}{\sum_{j=1}^3 e^{-W_j(x)/\epsilon}}, \quad i = 1, 2, 3, \qquad (9)$$

where

$$W_1(x) := 2\gamma^s(x) - \delta, \quad W_2(x) := W_1(x_1, \delta/2\gamma^s(0)), \quad W_3(x) := 2\gamma^s(0) - 3\delta. \quad (10)$$

Not only does this choice ensure that the new measure (8) has the 'appropriate' form, in that $(\bar{\lambda}(x), \bar{\mu}_1(x), \bar{\mu}_2(x)) \approx (\tilde{\lambda}, \tilde{\mu}_1, \tilde{\mu}_2)$ if $x \in D$, or $(\bar{\lambda}(x), \bar{\mu}_1(x), \bar{\mu}_2(x)) \approx (\hat{\lambda}, \hat{\mu}_1, \hat{\mu}_2)$ if $x \in \partial_2$, etc.; it is also possible to express the new measures (5) and (7), and the original measure in terms of the gradients of the functions $W_1(x), W_2(x)$ and $W_3(x)$ respectively (see Proposition 3.2 and Section 3.8.4 in [5]). This will be useful in the proof of asymptotical efficiency in Section 4.

3.2   IS Scheme for the Case $\mu_1 \leq \mu_2$

In this subsection we present the IS scheme for the case when $\mu_1 \leq \mu_2$. Again, we start by partitioning the state space $\bar{D}$ as in [11], see Figure 3. To see whether a starting state s belongs to B_1 or B_2 we again need to solve system (4). Then s belongs to B_1 if and only if $f(s) \leq 0$, where

$$f(s) := \log \frac{\mu_2}{\lambda} + s_1 \log \frac{\lambda^{\text{(line)}}}{\mu_1} + (1 - s_2) \log \frac{\mu_2^{\text{(line)}}}{\mu_2}.$$

The constant β is the solution to $f(0, s_2) = 0$, while $\alpha_2 := (\mu_2 - \mu_1)/(\mu_2 - \lambda)$.

In the previous subsection, we arrived at a 'uniform' new measure $(\bar{\lambda}(x), \tilde{\mu}_1(x), \tilde{\mu}_2(x))$ for all s, but in the case $\mu_1 \leq \mu_2$, we have to distinguish between two measures, depending on the starting state.

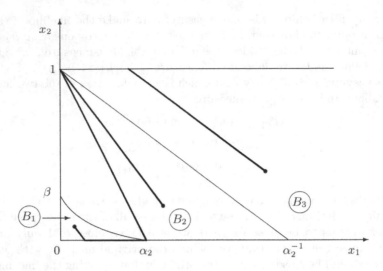

Fig. 3. Partition of $\bar{D}$ and some optimal paths to overflow when $\mu_1 \leq \mu_2$

– At first, let us consider the case $s \in B_2 \cup B_3$. Then we define

$$(\tilde{\lambda}, \tilde{\mu}_1, \tilde{\mu}_2) = \begin{cases} (\lambda^{(\text{line})}, \mu_1^{(\text{line})}, \mu_2^{(\text{line})}), & \text{if } s \in B_2, \\ (\lambda, \mu_2, \mu_1), & \text{if } s \in B_3. \end{cases} \qquad (11)$$

The function $\gamma^s(x)$ is again defined by (6), but of course its shape is different from that in the previous subsection, since the 'tilde-measure' is now different. Similarly, for the IS simulations we propose to use the state-dependent new measure $(\bar{\lambda}(x), \bar{\mu}_1(x), \bar{\mu}_2(x))$ again defined by (8) (with the 'tilde-measure' given by (11)), and the weights $\rho_i(x)$ given through (9) in conjunction with (10).

– Now consider $s \in B_1$. We know from [11, Section 3.3] that the optimal trajectory for this case consist of three straight subpaths, see also Figure 3. In our new measure, we need the stopping time $\tau^\star$, defined as the first time X_k visits $B_2 \cap \partial_2$, or, formally,

$$\tau^\star := \min\{k : X_{1,k} \geq \alpha_2 \text{ and } X_{2,k} = 0\}. \qquad (12)$$

Now we define the new measure as (μ_1, λ, μ_2) before time $\tau^\star$ and as (μ_1, μ_2, λ) after it, by

$$(\tilde{\lambda}, \tilde{\mu}_1, \tilde{\mu}_2) = (\mu_1, \lambda I_{\{k<\tau^\star\}} + \mu_2 I_{\{k \geq \tau^\star\}}, \mu_2 I_{\{k<\tau^\star\}} + \lambda I_{\{k \geq \tau^\star\}}); \qquad (13)$$

note that the new measure depends on time k, but (as with the starting state s) we omit this dependence in the notation. The residual cost $\gamma^s(x)$ is not given by (6) anymore, but rather by

$$\gamma^s(x) := \log \frac{\mu_2}{\lambda} - x_1 \log \frac{\tilde{\lambda}}{\lambda} + x_2 \log \frac{\tilde{\mu}_2}{\mu_2}, \quad \text{if } s \in B_1, \qquad (14)$$

which is again a simple linear function in x; also $\gamma^s(s)$ is again the exponential decay rate of p_B^s, see Theorem 4.5 in [11].

With the function $\gamma^s(x)$ defined by (14), the proposed state-dependent new measure $(\bar{\lambda}(x), \bar{\mu}_1(x), \bar{\mu}_2(x))$ is given by (8) (with the 'tilde-measure' given by (13)), and the weights $\rho_i(x)$, as before, through (9) and (10).

3.3   Overview of the Is Scheme

For convenience we summarize the resulting IS scheme for the different cases.

- When $\mu_2 < \mu_1$ one needs to
  1. define the 'primary' new measure (5);
  2. define the 'hat'-measure (7);
  3. define weights $\rho_i(x)$ by (9), based on (10) and (6);
  4. apply (8).
- When $\mu_1 \le \mu_2$ and $s \in B_2 \cup B_3$, the same procedure is followed, only replacing the 'primary' new measure (5) by (11) in step 1.
- When $\mu_1 \le \mu_2$ and $s \in B_1$, again the same procedure is followed, this time replacing the 'primary' new measure by that in (13) *and* replacing (6) by (14) when determining the $W_i(x)$ and $\rho_i(x)$ in step 3.

Note that in the last case we always have $(\hat{\lambda}, \hat{\mu}_1, \hat{\mu}_2) = (\mu_1, \lambda, \mu_2)$, both before and after time τ^*. In particular this means that when $k < \tau^*$, the hat measure coincides with the tilde measure (and hence $\rho_1(x) = \rho_2(x)$).

4   Asymptotic Efficiency

We now prove the asymptotic efficiency of the IS scheme proposed in the previous section; the approach is due to [4].

Theorem 1. *If we choose the strictly positive parameters $\delta \equiv \delta_B$ and $\epsilon \equiv \epsilon_B$ such that as $B \to \infty$: (i) $\epsilon_B \to 0$, (ii) $\delta_B \to 0$, (iii) $B\epsilon_B \to \infty$, (iv) $\epsilon_B/\delta_B \to 0$, then the IS scheme defined by (8) is asymptotically efficient.*

Proof. Our first step is the decomposition of the likelihood $L(A)$ of any path $A = (X_j, j = 0, \ldots, \sigma)$ in three terms, cf. Lemma 5.4 in [11] or Lemma 1 in [4]. For this we define the following function

$$W(x) := -\epsilon \log \sum_{i=1}^{3} e^{-W_i(x)/\epsilon}, \tag{15}$$

which was firstly introduced in [5, Equation (3.13)]. It is not difficult to see that its gradient satisfies

$$DW(x) = \sum_{i=1}^{3} \rho_i(x) DW_i(x), \tag{16}$$

where the weights $\rho_i(x)$ are defined by (9). Combining the definition of the likelihood ratio with (15) and (16) one obtains

$$
\log L(A) = \frac{B}{2} \sum_{j=0}^{\sigma-1} \langle DW(X_j), X_{j+1} - X_j \rangle
$$

$$
+ \sum_{k=1}^{2} \frac{1}{2} \sum_{j=0}^{\sigma-1} \langle DW(X_j), v_k \rangle I\{X_j = X_{j+1} \in \partial_k\} \qquad (17)
$$

$$
- \sum_{j=0}^{\sigma-1} \log M(X_j).
$$

Now we bound all three sums in (17) and show that only the first sum has a significant impact on the log-likelihood.

(a) We start by analyzing the first term. For any path $A = (X_j, j = 0, ..., \sigma)$ and some positive constant C we can, in self-evident notation, construct the following bound:

$$
\left| \sum_{j=0}^{\sigma-1} \langle DW(X_j), X_{j+1} - X_j \rangle - (W(X_\sigma) - W(X_0)) \right| \leq \frac{C}{B^2\epsilon}\sigma + \frac{C}{B} I_{\{\mu_1 \leq \mu_2\} \cap \{s \in B_1\}}.
$$

$$
(18)
$$

The proof of the above inequality is based on the approximation of the increment of the function $W(x)$ in terms of its gradient $DW(x)$, analogous to Lemma 5.5 in [11]. The accuracy of this representation can be shown by bounding the absolute value of any element of the corresponding Hessian matrix from above. The first term in the right-hand side of (18) corresponds to the sum of these contributions over all σ steps. The second term appears only if $\mu_1 \leq \mu_2$ and $s \in B_1$, as a consequence of the non-smoothness of $\gamma^s(x)$ as a function of k, see (13), and therefore also of $W(x)$, after the τ^*-th transition; note that a similar problem was treated in Lemma 4.4 of [10]. Bearing in mind the definition of the function $W(x)$, see (15), we obtain

$$
W(s) \geq 2\gamma^s(s) - \epsilon \log(3) - 3\delta \quad \text{and} \quad W(X_{\tau_B^s}) \leq -\log \frac{\tilde{\lambda}}{\lambda} X_{1,\tau_B^s} - \delta \leq -\delta.
$$

Combining the two last inequalities with (18), we derive an upper bound for the first term in (17):

$$
\sum_{j=0}^{\tau_B^s-1} \langle DW(X_j), X_{j+1} - X_j \rangle \leq -2\gamma^s(s) + \eta(B) + \frac{C}{B^2\epsilon}\tau_B^s, \qquad (19)
$$

where $\eta(B)$ is such that $\lim_{B \to \infty} \eta(B) = 0$.

(b) We now proceed with the second term. For any path $A = (X_j, j = 0, ..., \sigma)$ and some positive constant γ^* we obtain by routine computations, as were done in [11, Equation (41)] and [4, Lemma 5.4],

$$\sum_{k=1}^{2} \frac{1}{2} \sum_{j=0}^{\sigma-1} \langle DW(X_j), v_k \rangle I_{\{X_j = X_{j+1} \in \partial_k\}} \leq \gamma^\star e^{-\delta/\epsilon} \sigma.$$

(c) We finally consider the third term. For any $x \in D$ we have $\log M(x) \geq 0$. We skip the proof of the result as it consists of lengthy but basic computations that can be found in [11] (where $M(x)$ is denoted as $N(DW(x))$, see also Lemma 5.3 and Equation (38) there).

Upon combining (a), (b) and (c), we obtain the following upper bound on the likelihood ratio:

$$\log L(A^s) \leq -B\gamma^s(s) + B\eta(B) + \chi(B)\tau_B^s, \qquad \text{where} \qquad \chi(B) := \gamma^\star e^{-\delta/\epsilon} + \frac{C}{B\epsilon}.$$

After some elementary algebra this leads to

$$\frac{1}{B} \log \mathbb{E}\left[L(A^s)I_B(A^s)\right] = \frac{1}{B} \log \mathbb{E}\left[L(A^s)|I_B(A^s) = 1\right] \mathbb{P}\left[I_B(A^s) = 1\right]$$

$$\leq -\gamma^s(s) + \eta(B) + \frac{1}{B} \log \mathbb{E}\left[e^{\chi(B)\tau_B^s}|I_B(A^s) = 1\right] + \frac{1}{B} \log p_B^s.$$

Using that $\lim_{B \to \infty} \chi(B) = 0$, due to assumptions (iii) and (iv), in conjunction with

$$\lim_{B \to \infty} \frac{1}{B} \log \mathbb{E}(e^{\chi(B)\tau_B^s}|I_B(A^s) = 1) = 0, \qquad \text{when} \qquad \lim_{B \to \infty} \chi(B) = 0,$$

see Lemma 5.6 in [11], we can neglect the penultimate item in the last expression. Now recalling that $B^{-1} \cdot \log p_B^s \to -\gamma^s(s)$, we conclude that

$$\limsup_{B \to \infty} \frac{1}{B} \log \mathbb{E}\left[L(A^s)I_B(A^s)\right] \leq 2 \lim_{B \to \infty} \frac{1}{B} \log p_B^s,$$

which completes the proof.

5   Numerical Results

In this section we present two types of results. We start with some estimates of p_B^s obtained using our IS-scheme (8), see Table 1. In the rest of the section we compare the performance of the current scheme with that of the existing methods, in particular with [11]; see Table 2.

In Table 1 we present simulation results for three different parameter settings using the IS scheme defined in (8). We compute the weights $\rho_i(x)$ as in (9), choosing $\epsilon = 0.005$ and $\delta = -\epsilon \log \epsilon$ to enable comparison with [11]; see also [5] for the motivation of this choice. Each time we perform a fixed number of 10^6 simulation runs. In Table 1 we present the resulting estimates of p_B^s with 95%-confidence intervals. In the first two columns we have $\mu_2 < \mu_1$ while the third

Table 1. Simulation results: 95%-confidence intervals for p_B^s

B	$(\lambda, \mu_1, \mu_2) = (0.3, 0.36, 0.34)$ $s = (0, 0)$	$(\lambda, \mu_1, \mu_2) = (0.1, 0.55, 0.35)$ $s = (0.6\,B, 0)$	$(\lambda, \mu_1, \mu_2) = (0.3, 0.33, 0.37)$ $s = (0, 0)$
20	$5.96 \cdot 10^{-2} \pm 3.65 \cdot 10^{-4}$	$2.00 \cdot 10^{-5} \pm 5.19 \cdot 10^{-8}$	$3.05 \cdot 10^{-2} \pm 2.27 \cdot 10^{-3}$
50	$1.52 \cdot 10^{-3} \pm 1.17 \cdot 10^{-5}$	$3.12 \cdot 10^{-12} \pm 9.70 \cdot 10^{-15}$	$6.15 \cdot 10^{-5} \pm 9.54 \cdot 10^{-6}$
100	$2.93 \cdot 10^{-6} \pm 2.37 \cdot 10^{-8}$	$1.82 \cdot 10^{-23} \pm 6.48 \cdot 10^{-26}$	$1.52 \cdot 10^{-9} \pm 4.01 \cdot 10^{-10}$

Table 2. Comparison of different schemes

	st.-indep. [9]		st.-dep. old [11]			st.-dep. new		straightforward	
B	RE	time	RE	virtual time	time	RE	time	RE	time
20	$6.08 \cdot 10^{-3}$	12	$2.61 \cdot 10^{-3}$	$5 \cdot 10^6$	$55 + 16$	$3.12 \cdot 10^{-3}$	28	$3.95 \cdot 10^{-3}$	6
50	$2.21 \cdot 10^{-2}$	37	$3.12 \cdot 10^{-3}$	$9 \cdot 10^6$	$132 + 100$	$3.94 \cdot 10^{-3}$	80	$2.18 \cdot 10^{-2}$	9
100	$1.37 \cdot 10^{-2}$	77	N/A	N/A	N/A	$4.74 \cdot 10^{-3}$	168	$5.70 \cdot 10^{-1}$	9

Table 2.1: $(\lambda, \mu_1, \mu_2) = (0.3, 0.36, 0.34)$ and $s = (0, 0)$

B									
20	N/A	N/A	$7.01 \cdot 10^{-4}$	$1 \cdot 10^6$	$42 + 11$	$1.32 \cdot 10^{-3}$	7	$2.42 \cdot 10^{-1}$	3
50	N/A	N/A	$7.67 \cdot 10^{-4}$	$3 \cdot 10^6$	$104 + 68$	$1.58 \cdot 10^{-3}$	18	N/A	N/A
100	N/A	N/A	N/A	N/A	N/A	$1.81 \cdot 10^{-3}$	35	N/A	N/A

Table 2.2: $(\lambda, \mu_1, \mu_2) = (0.1, 0.55, 0.35)$ and $s = (0.6\,B, 0)$

B									
20	$4.59 \cdot 10^{-2}$	15	$3.10 \cdot 10^{-2}$	$9 \cdot 10^6$	$46 + 11$	$3.79 \cdot 10^{-2}$	28	$5.40 \cdot 10^{-3}$	9
50	$3.67 \cdot 10^{-1}$	53	$6.73 \cdot 10^{-2}$	$22 \cdot 10^6$	$123 + 68$	$7.91 \cdot 10^{-2}$	84	$1.25 \cdot 10^{-1}$	11
100	$2.33 \cdot 10^{-1}$	116	N/A	N/A	N/A	$13.4 \cdot 10^{-2}$	189	N/A	N/A

Table 2.3: $(\lambda, \mu_1, \mu_2) = (0.3, 0.33, 0.37)$ and $s = (0, 0)$

column has $\mu_1 < \mu_2$. In columns 1 and 3 we chose $s = (0, 0)$ and the parameters λ, μ_1, μ_2 lie close together; the latter is challenging in the sense that such values are often problematic for IS. A comparison with Tables 1 and 2 in [9], where the same parameters were simulated using state-*in*dependent IS, indeed shows similar estimates, but with smaller confidence intervals. Column 2 shows a scenario in which the starting state is not the origin. The results may be compared with those in Table 1 in [11], showing similar results.

We now turn to comparing the performance of three different IS schemes (as well as straightforward simulations). In Table 2 we present the results for the same three scenarios as in Table 1. For the same fixed number of replications (10^6) we compare the relative errors (RE) and machine running times (time; in seconds) of the different schemes. In the first column we always use the state-independent IS scheme designed in [9]; for the second column we use the state-dependent scheme described in [11], and the third column contains the outcomes of the current scheme. We also applied straightforward simulations to obtain the same estimates, see the fourth column.

The *virtual time* in the second column is an estimate of the time it would take to actually follow the IS scheme from [11], recalculating the path to overflow and the corresponding new measure after each transition. When the current state x is in subspace A_2 (or B_2) this means solving system (4) many times (with s replaced by x). To estimate the virtual time needed to do this, we multiplied the number of transitions in A_2 (or B_2) with the time needed to solve (4). However, when we did the simulations in [11] we actually used a method which is less time consuming, namely we precalculated the new measure for each state inside A_2

in advance. The real computation time therefore consists of two parts, which can be found under 'time' in the second column: the simulation time itself (first term) and the time needed to pre-compute the new measure (second term). Note that the pre-computation time grows as a square of the overflow level B.

From Tables 2.1 and 2.3 it becomes clear that both the scheme in [11] and the current scheme provide a relative error that is smaller than with the state-independent scheme from [9]. (Note that the latter is not available in Table 2.2 since we only allowed the origin as starting state in [9]). This is due to our choice of the parameters: we chose the values of the parameters λ, μ_1 and μ_2 very close to each other, since this is the most difficult case. Therefore, the IS scheme performs even better when arrival and service rates are clearly distinctive, as in Table 2.2, but this may also hold when we apply a state-independent scheme for these parameter values.

When we compare the current scheme with the old state-dependent scheme in [11], it becomes apparent that the relative error is slightly larger than in the old scheme, but of the same order. The big advantage is of course that running times are much lower, and the scheme is easier to implement.

6 Conclusions

In this work we designed an asymptotically efficient IS scheme for estimating the probability of overflow in the second buffer of a tandem Jackson network. The IS scheme presented in this paper is the result of an investigation started in [9,11]. The scheme constructed in [9] is easy to implement, but it is not always asymptotically efficient. The scheme from [11] *is* asymptotically efficient, but it has the drawback that it is difficult to use in practice, and simulation times are high. The IS scheme designed in this paper provides a good compromise: it is asymptotically efficient for all parameter values, giving relative errors that are comparable to those from the 'fully state-dependent' counterpart in [11] (although slightly larger), and at the same time it is almost as simple to implement and as fast as the state-independent schemes in [9].

References

1. Bucklew, J.: Introduction to Rare Event Simulation. Springer, New York (2004)
2. de Boer, P.T.: Analysis of state-independent importance-sampling measures for the two-node tandem queue. ACM Transactions on Modeling and Computer Simulation 16, 225–250 (2006)
3. de Boer, P.T., Nicola, V., Rubinstein, R.: Adaptive importance sampling simulation of queueing networks. In: Proceedings of the 2000 Winter Simulation Conference, pp. 646–655 (2000)
4. de Boer, P.T., Scheinhardt, W.: Alternative proof with interpretations for a recent state-dependent importance sampling scheme. Queueing Systems: Theory and Applications 57, 61–69 (2007)
5. Dupuis, P., Sezer, A., Wang, H.: Dynamic importance sampling for queueing networks. Annals of Applied Probability 17, 1306–1346 (2007)

6. Dupuis, P., Wang, H.: Importance sampling, large deviations and differential games. Stochastic and Stochastics Reports 76, 481–508 (2004)
7. Glasserman, P., Kou, S.: Analysis of an importance sampling estimator for tandem queues. ACM Transactions on Modeling and Computer Simulation 1, 22–42 (1995)
8. Heidelberger, P.: Fast simulation of rare events in queueing and reliability models. ACM Transactions on Modeling and Computer Simulation 5, 43–85 (1995)
9. Miretskiy, D., Scheinhardt, W., Mandjes, M.: Efficient simulation of a tandem queue with server slow-down. Simulation 83, 751–767 (2007)
10. Miretskiy, D., Scheinhardt, W., Mandjes, M.: State-dependent importance sampling for a slow-down tandem queue. See also Memorandum 1879, Dept. of Applied Mathematics, University of Twente (2008) (submitted),
    http://eprints.eemcs.utwente.nl/13251/
11. Miretskiy, D., Scheinhardt, W., Mandjes, M.: State-dependent importance sampling for a Jackson tandem network. Accepted for publication in ACM Transactions on Modeling and Computer Simulation. See also Memorandum 1867, Dept. of Applied Mathematics, University of Twente (2008),
    http://eprints.eemcs.utwente.nl/12734/
12. Parekh, S., Walrand, J.: A quick simulation method for excessive backlogs in networks of queues. IEEE Transactions on Automatic Control 34, 54–66 (1989)
13. Rubino, G., Tuffin, B.: Rare Event Simulation using Monte Carlo Methods. Wiley, New York (2009)
14. Sadowsky, J.: Large deviations theory and efficient simulation of excessive backlogs in a $GI/GI/m$ queue. IEEE Transactions on Automatic Control 36, 1383–1394 (1991)
15. Zaburnenko, T., Nicola, V.: Efficient heuristics for simulating population overflow in tandem networks. In: Proceedings of the Fifth St. Petersburg Workshop on Simulation, pp. 755–764 (2007)

An Anonymous Sequential Game Approach for Battery State Dependent Power Control

Piotr Więcek[1], Eitan Altman[2], and Yezekael Hayel[3]

[1] Institute of Mathematics and Computer Science, Wrocław University of Technology,
Wybrzeże Wyspiańskiego 27, 50-370 Wrocław, Poland
[2] INRIA, 2004 Route des Lucioles, P.B. 93, 06902 Sophia Antipolis Cedex, France
[3] LIA, Université d'Avignon, Agroparc BP 1228, 84911 Avignon, France

Abstract. The sensitivity of mobile terminals to energy and power limitations keeps posing challenges to wireless technology. The ratio between the useful signal's power and that of noise and interferences has a crucial impact on the achievable throughputs and on outage aspects, little has been done concerning another central challenge that limited energy poses: that of limitation on battery life. In this paper we study power control in a way that combines the two aforementioned aspects. We propose a modeling approach which extends the Anonymous Sequential Game framework introduced in 1988 by Jovanovic and Rosenthal. The approach is designed for systems that have a very large number of interacting decision makers, so large that they can be modeled as a continuum of players. We introduce an appropriate equilibrium concept for this game (which extends the Wardrop equilibrium by including random individual states with controlled transitions), characterize the structure of the equilibrium policies and provide two efficient equilibrium computation procedures.

1 Introduction

We consider a game among a large population of mobiles competing for wireless access. Each terminal attempts transmission over a sequence of time slots. At each attempt, a mobile m has to take a decision on the transmission power based on m's battery energy state. A higher power provides larger throughput, but reduces the life of the battery. The transmission ends when the battery empties. The aim of each player is to maximize his throughput minus the transmission cost, over the whole lifetime of his battery taking into account that all the other mobiles do the same. As we consider competition among a large population of mobiles, we find it convenient to model the set of mobiles as continuum so that actions of an individual have a negligible impact on the performance of other mobiles. This is then a non-atomic game, for which the notion of Wardrop equilibrium has been used (in the context of road traffic) since 1952 [7].

The dependence on the battery state adds another dimension to the modeling: each mobile has to take into consideration the battery state in the decision. This may seem to be like any other state dependence, such as the dependence on the radio channel. However a mobile's battery state, unlike the radio channel state,

R. Núñez-Queija and J. Resing (Eds.): NET-COOP 2009, LNCS 5894, pp. 121–136, 2009.
© Springer-Verlag Berlin Heidelberg 2009

is influenced only by the choices of transmission power of the mobile. A mobile that is interested in maximizing the amount of information during its lifetime, has to constantly balance the impact of using more energy for achieving better performance in the present and having energy available for future transmissions. Each mobile is thus playing a sequential (stochastic) game.

We consider a CDMA type cellular system in which all mobiles transmit simultaneously to a common base station. Thus (i) the performance of a mobile is determined by the distribution of the actions used by other mobiles. Moreover, (ii) the other mobiles are indistinguishable – all mobiles with the same battery state and using the same powers are interchangeable in terms of their impact on the interference. Non-atomic sequential games with these features are called Anonymous Sequential Games and have been introduced in 1988 by Jovanovic and Rosenthal [3]. We generalize this framework, developed for the discounted cost criterion, to our setting by extending it to the more involved total expected cost criterion.

When applying this theory to our problem, we are able to identify the equilibria in our game. This, together with monotonicity results that we obtain, enables us to establish efficient procedures for computing them.

Structure of the paper. In the next section we present the model and define formally the solution we shall be looking for. In Section 3 we give a characterization of the equilibria in our model, and in Section 4 the numerical methods to compute them. Further, in Section 5, we present a simple example of the game, providing both analytic computations of the solution and numerical illustrations of it. Finally the last section contains the conclusions.

2   Mathematical Model

2.1   Model for Individual Player

We associate with each player a Markov Decision Process (MDP) with the following parameters:

State space: $S = \{0, 1, \ldots, N\}$ is a finite set of states.

Action space: $Q = \{q_1, \ldots, q_K\}$, $q_1 < q_2 < \ldots < q_K$, is a finite set of actions.

Transitions. P is the transition probability law. Namely, $p(s'|s, q)$ is the probability that the next state is s' given that the actual state is s and the action taken is q.

Below we define some specific characteristics of our model.

Individual state s^i of player i (the battery energy state) belongs to the set S, where state 0 corresponds to the situation of empty battery when no transmission is possible.

Set of actions available to players (energy levels at which they transmit) is Q. We assume that at individual state $s \neq 0$ the set of actions available to a player is $Q_s = \{q_1, \ldots, q_s^+\} \subset Q$ and for any two $s_1 < s_2$, the maximal transmission levels $q_{s_1}^+$, $q_{s_2}^+$ satisfy $q_{s_1}^+ \leq q_{s_2}^+$, so that if the energy level increases, the player has more actions available.

Transitions. The transitions are defined for individual states of the players with the following rule: the probability of staying in any given state s by a player who takes the action q is $p(q)$. We assume that $p(q) = 1 - \alpha q - \gamma$, where α and γ are some fixed positive coefficients satisfying $\alpha q_K + \gamma \leq 1$.

We assume that at any given time a mobile whose battery is empty may have it recharged. This is reflected by a fixed probability p_{0N} of moving from state 0 (empty battery) to N (full battery).

In the sequel we also use the notation $\tilde{p}(q) = 1 - p(q)$ (the probability of moving one battery state down) and $\tilde{p}_{0N} = 1 - p_{0N}$ (the probability of no battery recharge).

2.2 Model of Interactions

Global state. The global state of the system at time t is the $N + 1$-tuple $X^t = (X_0^t, \ldots, X_N^t)$, such that $\sum_{n=0}^{N} X_n^t = 1$, where X_s^t denotes the fraction of mobiles with battery state s.

Proportion of actions. For each action $q_k \in Q$ we define the proportion of mobiles using action q_k at time t as w_k^t.

Reward. Now the reward at time t for a user in state s^t playing action q_k^t when the vector of proportions of players using different actions is w^t is

$$R^t(q_k^t, s^t; w^t) = \frac{q_k^t}{\sigma^2 + C \sum_{l=1}^{K} q_l^t w_l^t} - \beta q_k^t, \qquad (1)$$

where C is the non-orthogonality constant that captures the interference caused by other mobiles, σ^2 is the noise power and β is the energy cost. This function is the difference between the *global* signal to interference and noise ratio (SINR) and the energy cost. It is widely used to measure the performance of wireless transmission in decentralized multiple access channels [2].

Stationary policies. A stationary policy of an individual player u is defined as a map from the set of possible individual states S to the set of probability measures over Q, $P(Q)$. It prescribes to use actions with distribution $u(s)$ whenever the player is in state s and does not depend on t, nor on w^t. Then the action taken at time t is $q_k \in Q_s$ which depends on the state s at time t.

To make the notation shorter we often write u_s and u_s^k to denote the distribution of the actions in state s and the probability of choosing the action q_k in state s respectively. If all the probability distributions u_s prescribe to take a single action with probability 1, we say that policy u is deterministic (or non-randomized). The set of all the stationary policies in our game will be denoted by $\mathcal{U}$.

Suppose that all of the remaining players apply the same stationary policy, say policy u. Then, at any time t sufficiently large, for any state s, using [4], the proportion of the population in state s can be approximated by the expected frequency of the system in this state X_s. Then, at any given time t, the fraction of players using action q_k does not depend on t and can now be given by

$$w_k(u) = \sum_{s=1}^{N} X_s u_s^k, \quad w(u) = (w_1(u), \ldots, w_K(u)).$$

This enables to compute the expected reward at time t of a player in state s^t using policy v against policy u of the others:

$$R^t(v, u) = \sum_{k=1}^{K} R^t(q_k, s^t; w(u)) v_{s^t}^k, = \sum_{k=1}^{K} \frac{q_k v_{s^t}^k}{\sigma^2 + C \sum_{l=1}^{K} q_l w_l(u)} - \sum_{k=1}^{K} \beta q_k v_{s^t}^k. \quad (2)$$

The objective of any player is to maximize his expected reward over the whole lifetime of his battery:

$$J(X^0, v, u) = E^{p, X^0} \sum_{t=1}^{\tau} R^t(v, u).$$

Here τ is a random variable denoting his lifetime with the assumption that it starts in state N, while X^0 denotes the initial distribution of the states of all other mobiles. If the initial distribution X^0 is the stationary distribution corresponding to u (a player joins the game when it reached the stationary regime), we would simply write $J(v, u)$.

Equilibrium. Since the number of players in this game is infinite, the solution we will be looking for will be a variant of stationary equilibrium designed for our class of games.

Definition 1. *A stationary policy u is in a Stationary Equilibrium if*

$$J(u, u) = \max_{v \in \mathcal{U}} J(v, u).$$

This kind of equilibrium concept, where each player maximizes his own payoff against others using the equilibrium policy and being in a stationary regime was designed by Jovanovic and Rosenthal [3] in their paper on anonymous sequential games. Here we adapt it to the total reward case.

3   Existence and Characterization of Equilibrium

Next, we characterize the equilibria of the game. We first provide some general characterization of all possible stationary equilibria, and then we give a more detailed description of the equilibria belonging to a set of particularly simple stationary policies.

3.1   General Characterization of Equilibrium Policies

We start by introducing some additional notation. Let $A(u)$ denote the inter-ference perceived by one player, generated by all the other users and by the background noise, when all the players apply policy u and the game is in sta-tionary regime, that is:

$$A(u) = \sigma^2 + C \sum_{k=1}^{K} w_k(u) q_k.$$

The following theorem provides a general characterization of the equilibria in our game.

Theorem 1. *Let $u^+(s) = \delta[q_s^+]$ and $u^-(s) = \delta[q_1]$[1]. Then the following three statements are true:*

(i) u^+ is an equilibrium in the game iff $A(u^+) \leq 1/\beta$.
(ii) u^- is an equilibrium in the game iff $A(u^-) \geq 1/\beta$.
(iii) Any stationary policy u^* that satisfies $A(u^*) = 1/\beta$ is an equilibrium.

The equilibria in cases (i) and (ii) are unique if the inequalities in (i) and (ii) are strict.

Before we prove this theorem, we need to make the following observation: for each state s and stationary policy v the average amount of time units a user is in a state s is given by

$$T_s(v) = \frac{1}{\sum_{l=1}^{K} \tilde{p}(q_l) v_s^l}. \tag{3}$$

Each player starts in state N, stays in this state an expected amount of time $T_N(v)$ depending on his policy v, and moves to the next state $N-1$. This behavior is repeated until the player reaches the state 0. For each time t, the reward at time t for a user in state s^t playing action q_k^t when the action distribution of other players is w^t, is given by equation (2). Thus, the expected reward of a player using policy v when all other users apply policy u and the game is in stationary regime is given by:

$$J(v, u) = \sum_{s=1}^{N} \sum_{k=1}^{K} T_s(v) R^t(q_k, s) v_s^k$$

$$= \sum_{s=1}^{N} \sum_{k=1}^{K} T_s(v) \left[\frac{q_k v_s^k}{\sigma^2 + C \sum_{l=1}^{K} q_l w_l(u)} - \beta q_k v_s^k \right]$$

$$= \sum_{s=1}^{N} \sum_{k=1}^{K} \frac{v_s^k q_k}{\sum_{l=1}^{K} \tilde{p}(q_l) v_s^l} \left[\frac{1}{\sigma^2 + C \sum_{l=1}^{K} q_l w_l(u)} - \beta \right]. \tag{4}$$

---

[1] Here and in the sequel $\delta[q]$ denotes a probability distribution that puts all the mass on action q.

Now we are ready for the proof.

Proof of Thm 1: We need to find u such that $J(u, u) = \max_{v \in \mathcal{U}} J(v, u)$. To do this we first rewrite $J(v, u)$ adding to (4) some of the notation introduced earlier:

$$
J(v, u) = \sum_{s=1}^{N} \sum_{k=1}^{K} \frac{v_s^k q_k}{\sum_{l=1}^{K} \tilde{p}(q_l) v_s^l} \left(\frac{1}{A(u)} - \beta \right) = \left(\frac{1}{A(u)} - \beta \right) \sum_{s=1}^{N} \frac{\sum_{k=1}^{K} v_s^k q_k}{\sum_{l=1}^{K} \tilde{p}(q_l) v_s^l}.
$$
(5)

Now note that

$$
\frac{\sum_{k=1}^{K} v_s^k q_k}{\sum_{l=1}^{K} \tilde{p}(q_l) v_s^l} = \frac{\sum_{k=1}^{K} v_s^k q_k}{\sum_{l=1}^{K} v_s^l (\alpha q_l + \gamma)} = \frac{1}{\alpha} - \frac{\gamma}{\alpha(\alpha \sum_{k=1}^{K} v_s^k q_k + \gamma)}
$$

achieves its maximum when $v_s = u_s^+$ and minimum when $v_s = u_s^-$, hence policy $v = u^+$ maximizes $J(v, u)$ whenever $\frac{1}{A(u)} - \beta > 0$ and $v = u^-$, when $\frac{1}{A(u)} - \beta < 0$. Therefore u^+ is an equilibrium for our model iff $\frac{1}{A(u^+)} - \beta \geq 0$ and u^- is an equilibrium iff $\frac{1}{A(u^-)} - \beta \leq 0$, which is equivalent to the statements (i) and (ii) of the theorem. The uniqueness of these equilibria when the inequalities are strict is straightforward.

Next, suppose that $A(u^*) = 1/\beta$. This means that by (5), $J(v, u^*) = 0$ for every stationary policy v and thus $J(u^*, u^*) = \max_{v \in \mathcal{U}} J(v, u^*)$. And so u^* is an equilibrium in the game. □

3.2   Extreme Stationary Policies

We proceed with introducing subsets of the set of stationary policies to which we will show that some of the equilibria belong. Let

$$
\mathcal{U}_0 = \left\{ u \in \mathcal{U} : \exists s_0 \in S, \exists r \in [0, 1], u_s = \begin{cases} \delta[q_1], & s < s_0 \\ r\delta[q_1] + (1 - r)\delta[q_s^+], & s = s_0 \\ \delta[q_s^+], & s > s_0 \end{cases} \right\}.
$$

As one can easily see, these policies are not necessarily nonrandomized, but randomization appears in at most one state. That kind of policies often appears in different MDP problems. They are called threshold policies.

In the remainder of the paper we shall also consider policies belonging to a larger set: $\mathcal{U}_1 = \{ u \in \mathcal{U} : \exists r_1, \ldots, r_N \in [0, 1], u_s = r_s \delta[q_1] + (1 - r_s)\delta[q_s^+] \}$. Here the randomization is possible in any state, but also only the maximum and minimum power are employed.

Now we can pass to the first of our main results of this section, which emphasizes the importance of the set $\mathcal{U}_0$, giving also some precise conditions under which each of the three cases considered in Thm 1 apply.

Theorem 2. *The game under consideration always possesses a stationary equilibrium $u \in \mathcal{U}_0$. Moreover:*

(i) *This equilibrium is unique in the set $\mathcal{U}_0$.*

(ii) u^+ is this equilibrium if

$$\beta C N > \frac{N\alpha(1 - \beta\sigma^2) + N\gamma}{\alpha q_1^+ + \gamma} \quad and \quad p_{0N} \le \frac{\alpha(1 - \beta\sigma^2)}{\beta C N - \frac{N\alpha(1-\beta\sigma^2)+N\gamma}{\alpha q_1^+ + \gamma}} \quad (6)$$

(iii) u^- is this equilibrium if and only if

$$\beta C q_1 > 1 - \beta\sigma^2 \quad and \quad p_{0N} \ge \frac{(\alpha q_1 + \gamma)(1 - \beta\sigma^2)}{N(\beta C q_1 - (1 - \beta\sigma^2))} \quad (7)$$

Two lemmata will be used to prove this theorem.

Lemma 1. *The stationary (ergodic) state of the system, when players apply the stationary policy u is given by:*

$$X_s(u) = \frac{1}{a_s \sum_{j=0}^{N} \frac{1}{a_j}}, \quad (8)$$

where $a_0 = \tilde{p}_{0N}$ and $a_s = \sum_{k=1}^{K} \tilde{p}(q_k) u_s^k$ for $s > 0$.

Proof. The stationary state $X(u)$ has to satisfy the following matrix equation:

$$\begin{bmatrix} a_0 & -a_1 & 0 & \cdots & 0 & 0 \\ 0 & a_1 & -a_2 & \cdots & 0 & 0 \\ 0 & 0 & a_2 & \cdots & 0 & 0 \\ \vdots & \vdots & \vdots & \ddots & \vdots & \vdots \\ 0 & 0 & 0 & \cdots & a_{N-1} & -a_N \\ 1 & 1 & 1 & \cdots & 1 & 1 \end{bmatrix} X(u) = \begin{bmatrix} 0 \\ 0 \\ 0 \\ \vdots \\ 0 \\ 1 \end{bmatrix}$$

with a_i defined as in the lemma. (Here the first N rows correspond to stationarity conditions, while the last one is the condition for it to be a probability distribution). We can solve this equation using the standard Cramer formula, obtaining (8). □

We proceed by introducing a linear ordering in the set $\mathcal{U}_0$. Take two elements of $\mathcal{U}_0$, say u' and u'' defined by:

$$u'_s := \begin{cases} \delta[q_1], & s < s'_0 \\ r'\delta[q_1] + (1-r')\delta[q_s^+], & s = s'_0 \\ \delta[q_s^+], & s > s'_0 \end{cases} \quad u''_s := \begin{cases} \delta[q_1], & s < s''_0 \\ r''\delta[q_1] + (1-r'')\delta[q_s^+], & s = s''_0 \\ \delta[q_s^+], & s > s''_0 \end{cases}. \quad (9)$$

We would write that $u' \preceq u''$ if and only if $s'_0 > s''_0$ or $s'_0 = s''_0$ and $r' \ge r''$.

Remark 1. $\mathcal{U}_0$ with the order topology induced by $\preceq$ is homeomorphic with the interval $[0, N]$ with standard topology. The homeomorphism can be defined for any $u \in \mathcal{U}_0$,

$$u := \begin{cases} \delta[q_1], & s < s_0 \\ r\delta[q_1] + (1-r)\delta[q_s^+], & s = s_0 \\ \delta[q_s^+], & s > s_0 \end{cases} \quad (10)$$

as follows:

$$h(u) = N + 1 - s_0 - r. \tag{11}$$

One of the consequences of it is that any real valued function defined on $\mathcal{U}_0$ which is continuous has the intermediate value property.

Lemma 2. *The function A is monotonously increasing and continuous on the set $\mathcal{U}_0$ with the linear ordering $\preceq$.*

Proof: The continuity of A in the product topology on $\mathbb{R}^N$ implies the continuity in topology induced by $\preceq$, so the proof of continuity is immediate. To prove the monotonicity we take $u \in \mathcal{U}_0$ defined by (10) and consider three cases.

Case 1: For a fixed s_0 we show that $A(u)$ is decreasing in r.

In this case and using the expression of the stationary state described in Lemma 1, $A(u)$ can be rewritten as:

$$A(u) = \sigma^2 + C \left[\sum_{s=1}^{s_0-1} q_1 X_s(u) + (rq_1 + (1-r)q_{s_0}^+) X_{s_0}(u) + \sum_{s=s_0+1}^{N} q_s^+ X_s(u) \right]$$

$$= \sigma^2 + C \frac{\frac{(s_0-1)q_1}{\tilde{p}(q_1)} + \frac{rq_1+(1-r)q_{s_0}^+}{r\tilde{p}(q_1)+(1-r)\tilde{p}(q_{s_0}^+)} + \sum_{s=s_0+1}^{N} \frac{q_s^+}{\tilde{p}(q_s^+)}}{\frac{s_0-1}{\tilde{p}(q_1)} + \frac{1}{r\tilde{p}(q_1)+(1-r)\tilde{p}(q_{s_0}^+)} + \sum_{s=s_0+1}^{N} \frac{1}{\tilde{p}(q_s^+)} + \frac{1}{p_0 N}}. \tag{12}$$

Note now that $\tilde{p}(q_1) \le \tilde{p}(q_{s_0}^+)$ and so the denominator of (12) is nondecreasing in r. On the other hand

$$\frac{rq_1 + (1-r)q_{s_0}^+}{r\tilde{p}(q_1) + (1-r)\tilde{p}(q_{s_0}^+)} = \frac{q_{s_0}^+ - r(q_{s_0}^+ - q_1)}{\tilde{p}(q_{s_0}^+) - r(\tilde{p}(q_{s_0}^+) - \tilde{p}(q_1))}$$

$$= \frac{q_{s_0}^+ - r(q_{s_0}^+ - q_1)}{\alpha q_{s_0}^+ + \gamma - r\alpha(q_{s_0}^+ - q_1)} = \frac{1}{\alpha} - \frac{\gamma}{\alpha[\alpha q_{s_0}^+ + \gamma - r\alpha(q_{s_0}^+ - q_1)]},$$

which is decreasing in r, and thus the numerator of (12) is decreasing in r. But since both the numerator and the denominator are positive this implies that $A(u)$ is decreasing in r or equivalently increasing in u.

Case 2: For a fixed $r = 1$ we show that $A(u)$ is decreasing in s_0.

First we consider a simple subcase with $s_0'' = s_0' + 1$, $r' = r'' = 1$ and u' and u'' defined by (9). Note that u' can be represented in another way, namely we can take $s_0' = s_0''$ and $r'' = 0$. Then the monotonicity will follow from Case 1.

Now the general case is obtained through repeated use of the subcase above.

Case 3: Neither r nor s_0 is fixed. Then the thesis follows as a combination of Cases 1 and 2. $\qquad \square$

Knowing this we may pass to the proof of the theorem.

Proof of Thm 2: (i) By (i) and (ii) of Thm 1 the game may have no equilibria in $\mathcal{U}_0$ only if $A(u^-) < 1/\beta < A(u^+)$. (Note that u^+ and u^- both are elements of $\mathcal{U}_0$. In fact u^+ is its biggest and u^- its smallest element with respect to the ordering

$\preceq$). By Lemma 2, the function A is continuous on $\mathcal{U}_0$ and thus (as stated in Remark 1) has the intermediate value property, which means that there exists a $u^* \in \mathcal{U}_0$ such that $A(u^*) = \frac{1}{\beta}$, which is an equilibrium by (iii) of Thm 1. Moreover, since (by Lemma 2) A is increasing, u^* is the unique equilibrium in the set $\mathcal{U}_0$. The uniqueness of u^+ and u^- in $\mathcal{U}_0$ is already guaranteed by Thm 1.

(ii) Suppose now that (6) holds. It implies that

$$\frac{1 - \beta\sigma^2}{p_{0N}} \geq \frac{\beta CN}{\alpha} + \left(\beta\sigma^2 - 1 - \frac{\gamma}{\alpha}\right)\frac{N}{\alpha q_1^+ + \gamma} \geq \frac{\beta CN}{\alpha} + \left(\beta\sigma^2 - 1 - \frac{\gamma}{\alpha}\right)\sum_{s=1}^{N}\frac{1}{\alpha q_s^+ + \gamma}.$$

Since $\frac{q}{\alpha q + \gamma} = \frac{1}{\alpha} - \frac{\gamma}{\alpha(\alpha q + \gamma)}$, this is equal to

$$(\beta\sigma^2 - 1)\sum_{s=1}^{N}\frac{1}{\alpha q_s^+ + \gamma} + \beta C\sum_{s=1}^{N}\frac{q_s^+}{\alpha q_s^+ + \gamma}.$$

After some algebra this yields

$$\sigma^2 + C\frac{\sum_{s=1}^{N}\frac{q_s^+}{\alpha q_s^+ + \gamma}}{\sum_{s=1}^{N}\frac{1}{\alpha q_s^+ + \gamma} + \frac{1}{p_{0N}}} \leq \frac{1}{\beta} \tag{13}$$

which is exactly equivalent (note (12)) to $A(u^+) \leq \frac{1}{\beta}$.

(iii) Now suppose (7) holds. We can rewrite it as

$$p_{0N}(N\beta\sigma^2 + \beta CNq_1 - N) \geq (\alpha q_1 + \gamma)(1 - \beta\sigma^2)$$

and further as

$$\sigma^2 + C\frac{Nq_1 p_{0N}}{Np_{0N} + \alpha q_1 + \gamma} \geq \frac{1}{\beta}.$$

But this is equivalent to

$$\frac{1}{\beta} \leq \sigma^2 + \frac{C\frac{Nq_1}{\alpha q_1 + \gamma}}{\frac{N}{\alpha q_1 + \gamma} + \frac{1}{p_{0N}}} = A(u^-),$$

which is exactly what we wanted to prove. $\qquad\square$

Remark 2. (6) is, unlike (7), only a sufficient condition for policy u^+ to be the equilibrium. The necessary and sufficient condition for u^+ to be in equilibrium is (13).

Remark 3. Note that for a low cost of transmission (or more formally if the unit cost of transmission β approaches 0) it is always profitable to use the high power policy u^+, regardless of all the other parameters of the model. Similarly, when the cost is high (namely when $\beta \geq \frac{1}{\sigma^2}$) it is always profitable to use the lowest power possible.

Remark 4. Although one of the statements of Thm 2 is that the equilibrium is *unique*, this is only uniqueness in the class $\mathcal{U}_0$. In fact usually when neither u^+ nor u^- is the equilibrium in our model, there exist multiple equilibria in randomized stationary policies (some of them will be characterized by Thm 3). However, the equilibrium from Thm 2 is the only one in a class that we believe is the class of the simplest possible randomized policies in this game. Another reason for why it is reasonable to consider the equilibrium policies from $\mathcal{U}_0$ is given in Thm 4.

In the next theorem we characterize the equilibria from the wider set $\mathcal{U}_1$.

Theorem 3. *Suppose neither u^+ nor u^- is an equilibrium in our game and $S_0 := \{s \in S : |Q_s| > 1\}$ has at least two elements. Then there exist a continuum of equilibria in $\mathcal{U}_1$. Moreover, $u^* \in \mathcal{U}_1$ is an equilibrium iff it satisfies*

$$\sum_{s=1}^{N} \bar{r}_s \left(\frac{1}{\tilde{p}(q_1)} - \frac{1}{\tilde{p}(q_s^+)} \right) = \frac{C\beta(Np_{0N} + \gamma)}{p_{0N}(\alpha - \alpha\beta\sigma^2 + C\beta\gamma)} - \sum_{s=1}^{N} \frac{1}{\tilde{p}(q_s^+)} - \frac{1}{p_{0N}}, \quad (14)$$

$$\text{where } \bar{r}_s := \frac{r_s \tilde{p}(q_1)}{r_s \tilde{p}(q_1) + (1 - r_s)\tilde{p}(q_s^+)} \quad (15)$$

and r_s are such that $u_s^* = r_s \delta[q_1] + (1 - r_s)\delta[q_s^+]$.

We precede the proof of the theorem by a more general characterization of equilibrium policies.

Lemma 3. *Suppose that neither u^- nor u^+ is an equilibrium in our game. Then $u^* \in \mathcal{U}$ is an equilibrium iff it satisfies*

$$\sum_{s=1}^{N} \frac{1}{\sum_{k=1}^{K} \tilde{p}(q_k)u_s^{*k}} = \frac{C\beta(Np_{0N} + \gamma)}{p_{0N}(\alpha - \alpha\beta\sigma^2 + C\beta\gamma)} - \frac{1}{p_{0N}}. \quad (16)$$

Proof: By (iii) of Thm 1, u^* has to satisfy $A(u^*) = 1/\beta$. $A(u^*)$ can be written here as

$$A(u^*) = \sigma^2 + C\sum_{s=1}^{N}\sum_{k=1}^{K} q_k u_s^{*k} X_s(u^*) = \sigma^2 + C\frac{\sum_{s=1}^{N} \frac{\sum_{k=1}^{K} q_k u_s^{*k}}{\sum_{l=1}^{K} \tilde{p}(q)u_s^{*l}}}{\sum_{s=1}^{N} \frac{1}{\sum_{l=1}^{K} \tilde{p}(q_l)u_s^{*l}} + \frac{1}{p_{0N}}}$$

$$= \sigma^2 + C\frac{\sum_{s=1}^{N} \frac{\sum_{k=1}^{K} q_k u_s^{*k}}{\alpha\sum_{l=1}^{K} q_l u_s^{*l} + \gamma}}{\sum_{s=1}^{N} \frac{1}{\alpha\sum_{l=1}^{K} q_l u_s^{*l} + \gamma} + \frac{1}{p_{0N}}}$$

$$= \sigma^2 + C\frac{\sum_{s=1}^{N} \frac{1}{\alpha} + \frac{\gamma}{\alpha p_{0N}} - \frac{\gamma}{\alpha}\left(\sum_{s=1}^{N} \frac{1}{\alpha\sum_{l=1}^{K} q_l u_s^{*l} + \gamma} + \frac{1}{p_{0N}}\right)}{\sum_{s=1}^{N} \frac{1}{\alpha\sum_{l=1}^{K} q_l u_s^{*l} + \gamma} + \frac{1}{p_{0N}}}$$

$$= \sigma^2 + C\left[\frac{Np_{0N} + \gamma}{\alpha p_{0N}\left(\sum_{s=1}^{N} \frac{1}{\alpha\sum_{l=1}^{K} q_l u_s^{*l} + \gamma} + \frac{1}{p_{0N}}\right)} - \frac{\gamma}{\alpha} \right].$$

Now condition (iii) of Thm 1 takes the form:

$$\frac{1}{\beta} = \sigma^2 + C\left[\frac{Np_{0N} + \gamma}{\alpha p_{0N}\left(\sum_{s=1}^{N}\frac{1}{\alpha\sum_{l=1}^{K}q_l u_s^{*l} + \gamma} + \frac{1}{p_{0N}}\right)} - \frac{\gamma}{\alpha}\right].$$

This can be rewritten as

$$\frac{\alpha - \alpha\beta\sigma^2 + C\beta\gamma}{\alpha\beta} = \frac{C(Np_{0N} + \gamma)}{\alpha p_{0N}\left(\sum_{s=1}^{N}\frac{1}{\alpha\sum_{l=1}^{K}q_l u_s^{*l} + \gamma} + \frac{1}{p_{0N}}\right)}$$

and further as

$$\sum_{s=1}^{N}\frac{1}{\alpha\sum_{l=1}^{K}q_l u_s^{*l} + \gamma} = \frac{C\beta(Np_{0N} + \gamma)}{p_{0N}(\alpha - \alpha\beta\sigma^2 + C\beta\gamma)} - \frac{1}{p_{0N}},$$

which is equivalent to (16).   □

Proof of Thm 3: Suppose $u^* \in \mathcal{U}_1$ is an equilibrium policy given in Thm 3. By Lemma 3 it has to satisfy (16). The LHS of (16) takes the form:

$$\sum_{s=1}^{N}\frac{1}{\sum_{k=1}^{K}\tilde{p}(q_k)u_s^k} = \sum_{s=1}^{N}\frac{1}{r_s\tilde{p}(q_1) + (1 - r_s)\tilde{p}(q_s^+)}.$$

By simple computations one can show that for any $r_s \in [0,1]$, the $\bar{r}_s \in [0,1]$ defined by (15) satisfies:

$$\frac{1}{r_s\tilde{p}(q_1) + (1 - r_s)\tilde{p}(q_s^+)} = \frac{\bar{r}_s}{\tilde{p}(q_1)} + \frac{1 - \bar{r}_s}{\tilde{p}(q_s^+)}.$$

Now we can rewrite (16) using $\bar{r}_s$ in the form:

$$\sum_{s=1}^{N}\left(\frac{\bar{r}_s}{\tilde{p}(q_1)} + \frac{1 - \bar{r}_s}{\tilde{p}(q_s^+)}\right) = \frac{C\beta(Np_{0N} + \gamma)}{p_{0N}(\alpha - \alpha\beta\sigma^2 + C\beta\gamma)} - \frac{1}{p_{0N}},$$

which is clearly equivalent to (14).

What we have left to show is that there is a continuum of equilibria in $\mathcal{U}_1$, or in other words that there is a continuum of solutions to (14) (whenever $|S_0| > 1$). By Thm 2 we know that there exists at least one solution to this equation, and it is such that $\bar{r}_s = r_s = 1$ for $s < s_0$, $r_{s_0} \in (0,1)$, and consequently also $\bar{r}_{s_0} \in (0,1)$, and $\bar{r}_s = r_s = 0$ for $s > s_0$. (14) is a single linear equation with at least two variables and as such has an infinite number (a continuum) of solutions. Next, since $\bar{r}_{s_0} \in (0,1)$, also an infinite number of its solutions satisfy $r_s \in [0,1]$ for all $s \in S$.   □

Remark 5. Though the expression characterizing the equilibria given in Thm 3 is not a very easy one, it is a significant simplification of the conditions given in Thm 1, since it is linear (note that the function A, in terms of which the characterization of equilibria in Thm 1 is given, is not linear). This simplifies the analysis of some features of the equilibrium strategies, and at the same time gives a possibility to compute them numerically.

4   Computation of Equilibrium Policies

In the next section we present a simple example of the game of the type we are discussing in this paper, and give closed-form solutions for it. However, in most of the cases finding the equilibrium policies in closed form would be difficult. Fortunately, proved properties of function A allow us to compute an arbitrarily good approximation of the equilibrium policies lying in the set $\mathcal{U}_0$ in any case.

Theorem 4. *The equilibrium $u^* \in \mathcal{U}_0$ in the game under consideration can be computed using bisection applied to the function $\phi(a) = A(h^{-1}(a)) - \frac{1}{\beta}$ on the interval $[0, N]$, where A is given by (12) and h by (11). The approximation of u^* will be given by $h^{-1}(a^*)$, where a^* is the (approximate) zero of function ϕ. If the zero does not exist then either u^+ (when $\phi < 0$) or u^- (when $\phi > 0$) is the equilibrium.*

Proof: The result follows immediately from the fact that A is continuous and the characterization of the equilibrium policies in Thm 1. $\qquad\square$

Some of the equilibria lying in $\mathcal{U}_1$ (including the ones in $\mathcal{U}_0$) can also be computed using linear programming.

Theorem 5.   *(i) The following procedure gives an equilibrium $u^* \in \mathcal{U}_1$, such that the randomization occurs in no more than one state:*

(a) *Check whether the parameters of the game satisfy (13) or (7). If they satisfy (13), put $u^* := u^+$, if they satisfy (7), let $u^* := u^-$. If it does not satisfy any pass to (b).*

(b) *Using the simplex method solve the LP:*

$$maximize \quad f(\bar{r}_1, \ldots, \bar{r}_N)$$

$$subject\ to \quad \sum_{s=1}^{N} \bar{r}_s \left(\frac{1}{\tilde{p}(q_1)} - \frac{1}{\tilde{p}(q_s^+)} \right) = D - \sum_{s=1}^{N} \frac{1}{\tilde{p}(q_s^+)} \qquad (17)$$

$$0 \le \bar{r}_s \le 1 \quad \forall s \in S, \qquad (18)$$

f is a linear function from $\mathbb{R}^N$ to $\mathbb{R}$ and $D := \frac{C\beta(Np_{0N}+\gamma)}{p_{0N}(\alpha-\alpha\beta\sigma^2+C\beta\gamma)} - \frac{1}{p_{0N}}$.

(c) *For each $s \in S$ compute $r_s := \frac{\bar{r}_s \tilde{p}(q_s^+)}{\bar{r}_s \tilde{p}(q_s^+) + (1-\bar{r}_s)\tilde{p}(q_1)}$ and $u_s^* := r_s \delta[q_1] + (1-r_s)\delta[q_s^+]$.*

(ii) *If we take*

$$f(\bar{r}_1, \ldots, \bar{r}_N) = \sum_{s=1}^{N} M^{N-s} \left(\frac{1}{\tilde{p}(q_1)} - \frac{1}{\tilde{p}(q_s^+)} \right) \bar{r}_s,$$

where $M > 1$ is a fixed constant, then the u^* obtained will be the unique equilibrium in $\mathcal{U}_0$.

Proof: (i) According to Thm 1 and 2 and Remark 2, (13) and (7) are sufficient and necessary conditions for u^+ and u^- (respectively) to be in equilibrium. In any other case, by Thm 3 the equilibria in $\mathcal{U}_1$ have to satisfy the conditions given as constraints in the above LP, moreover these conditions are sufficient for u^* to be an equilibrium policy. This implies that the solution (if it exists) to the above LP is an equilibrium. Next, since the set of vectors $(\bar{r}_1, \ldots, \bar{r}_N)$ satisfying (18) is bounded, and by Thm 2 the set of vectors satisfying (17, 18) is nonempty, this LP has a solution.

What we are left with to show is that the u^* obtained randomizes only in one state. By well known results form the theory of linear programming, the solution obtained $(\bar{r}_1, \ldots, \bar{r}_N)$ has to admit equality in $N-1$ of the $2N$ constraints (18). Since none of the $\bar{r}_s$ can be equal to 0 and to 1 at the same time, it has to be either $\bar{r}_s = 0$ or $\bar{r}_s = 1$ for every state s except one, say s^*, and consequently also either $r_s = 0$ or $r_s = 1$ for every $s \neq s^*$.

(ii) First note that a policy from $\mathcal{U}_1$ which randomizes at most in one state belongs to $\mathcal{U}_0$ iff $\bar{r}_1 \geq \bar{r}_2 \geq \cdots \geq \bar{r}_N$ and suppose this condition is not satisfied for the solution $\bar{r} = (\bar{r}_1, \ldots, \bar{r}_N)$ of the LP described in part (ii) of the theorem. This is equivalent to saying that there exist $s_1 < s_2$ such that $\bar{r}_{s_1} < \bar{r}_{s_2}$ for this solution. Then there exists an $\varepsilon > 0$ such that

$$\bar{r}_{s_1}^* = \bar{r}_{s_1} + \frac{\varepsilon}{1/\tilde{p}(q_1) - 1/\tilde{p}(q_{s_1}^+)} \leq 1 \text{ and } \bar{r}_{s_2}^* - \frac{\varepsilon}{1/\tilde{p}(q_1) - 1/\tilde{p}(q_{s_2}^+)} \geq 0.$$

If we take $\bar{r}_s^* = \bar{r}_s$ for $s \neq s_1, s_2$ then obviously $\bar{r}^* = (\bar{r}_1^*, \ldots, \bar{r}_N^*)$ would satisfy the constraints (17,18). At the same time

$$f(\bar{r}^*) = f(\bar{r}) + M^{N-s_1} \left(\frac{1}{\tilde{p}(q_1)} - \frac{1}{\tilde{p}(q_{s_1}^+)} \right) (\bar{r}_{s_1}^* - \bar{r}_{s_1})$$

$$+ M^{N-s_2} \left(\frac{1}{\tilde{p}(q_1)} - \frac{1}{\tilde{p}(q_{s_2}^+)} \right) (\bar{r}_{s_2}^* - \bar{r}_{s_2}) = f(\bar{r}) + M^{N-s_1}\varepsilon - M^{N-s_2}\varepsilon > f(\bar{r}),$$

contradicting the assumption that $\bar{r}$ was maximizing f. $\square$

5   An Example

We next present an example, similar to [1]. There, an evolutionary game model was used to model the pairwise interaction between mobiles. We adopt that problem to a problem with global interaction.

5.1   Analytic Computations

An individual is characterized by one of three possible individual states of its battery: empty (E), almost empty (A) and full (F). Whenever the player is in state F he has two actions possible: to transmit at high power h or to transmit at low power l. If he is in state A, he can only transmit at low power.

According to Thm 2 and Remark 2, we can compute when strategy u^- (always to use low power) is the equilibrium. It is when the following condition is satisfied:

$$\beta Cl > 1 - \beta\sigma^2 \quad \text{and} \quad p_{EF} \geq \frac{(\alpha l + \gamma)(1 - \beta\sigma^2)}{2(\beta Cl - (1 - \beta\sigma^2))}.$$

Next, as noticed in Remark 2, the necessary and sufficient condition for u^+ to be an equilibrium is (13), which for our example can be written as:

$$\sigma^2 + C\frac{\frac{l}{\alpha l+\gamma} + \frac{h}{\alpha h+\gamma}}{\frac{1}{\alpha l+\gamma} + \frac{1}{\alpha h+\gamma} + \frac{1}{p_{EF}}} \leq \frac{1}{\beta}.$$

After some computation this can be rewritten as

$$\beta\sigma^2(\alpha(l+h)+2\gamma) > (l+h)(C\beta\gamma - \alpha) + 2(C\beta\alpha h l - \gamma)$$

$$\text{or} \quad p_{EF} \leq \frac{(\alpha l+\gamma)(\alpha h+\gamma)(1-\beta\sigma^2)}{(l+h)(C\beta\gamma-\alpha) + 2(\beta\alpha h l-\gamma) - \beta\sigma^2(\alpha(l+h)+2\gamma)}$$

Next, if none of the above two conditions is satisfied, by Thm 2, the game has another equilibrium u^* in $\mathcal{U}_0$. Since the randomization in our example is only possible in state H, this will be of the form

$$u^*(s) = \begin{cases} \delta[l], & s = A \\ r\delta[l] + (1-r)\delta[h], & s = F \end{cases}$$

As we have already shown, it will be an equilibrium if $A(u^*) = 1/\beta$. This means that the following equation needs to be satisfied (here we again use (12)):

$$\frac{1}{\beta} = \sigma^2 + C\frac{\frac{l}{\alpha l+\gamma} + \frac{rl+(1-r)k}{\alpha(rl+(1-r)h)+\gamma}}{\frac{1}{\alpha l+\gamma} + \frac{1}{\alpha(rl+(1-r)h)+\gamma} + \frac{1}{p_{EF}}}.$$

After some computation we obtain the following expression for r:

$$\frac{Cp_{EF}[2\alpha l h + \gamma(l+h)] - (1-\beta\sigma^2)[\alpha p_{EF}(l+h) + 2p_{EF}\gamma + (\alpha l+\gamma)(\alpha h+\gamma)]}{(l-h)[(1-\beta\sigma^2)\alpha(p_{EF}+\alpha l+\gamma) - Cp_{EF}(2\alpha l+\gamma)]}.$$

5.2   Numerical Illustrations

Choose: $p_{EF} = 0.5$, $\gamma = 0.05$, $h = 1$, $l = 0.5$ and $\sigma^2 = 0.00001$. In Figure 1 we show the dependence of the equilibrium policy u^* on the interference parameter C and the power cost β for a fixed value of $\alpha = 0.8$. The left figure shows the regions in which respectively policies u^- and u^+ are equilibria, while on the right one we see the dependence of parameter r on C and β. We observe that when the costs are small, individuals are more aggressive. On the other hand, we see that all the strategies from $\mathcal{U}_0$ are employed for some values of C and β.

In Figure 2 we see the dependence on α of the areas where respectively u^- and u^+ are equilibrium policies. This is a crucial parameter in our model, as it decides the speed at which the battery depletes. We see that as α increases, the region of u^+ gets bigger, while the one of u^- shrinks. This may seem counterintuitive at first sight, however notice that bigger α means shorter life of all the batteries (without affecting the time after which the batteries are recharged), so any mobile trying to transmit perceives less interference, and thus increases its throughput at higher rate by increasing the transmission power.

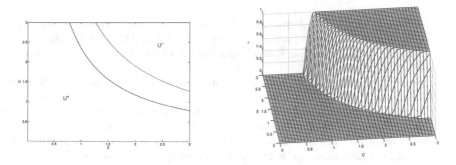

Fig. 1. The dependence of equilibrium strategies on C and β for a fixed value of $\alpha = 0.8$

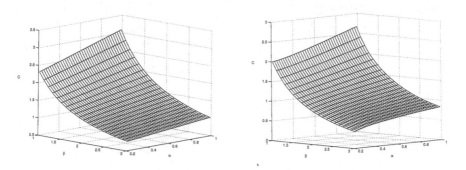

Fig. 2. The dependence of equilibrium strategies on C, β and α. The area above the surface on the left is the region where u^- is in equilibrium, while the area below the surface on the right is the region where u^+ is in equilibrium.

6   Conclusions

We considered a battery state-dependent power control which we formulated as an extension of the anonymous sequential game introduced in [3]. In contrast to the setting in our previous work [1] of local interactions in a sparse network, we have modeled here the situation of global interactions - each mobile interacts with all other. We consider the total expected (non-discounted) utility accumulated over the battery life time, which is not covered by the Theory in [3]. We have characterized the structure of the equilibrium strategies and investigated their properties analytically and numerically. We intend to extend the theoretical framework of anonymous sequential games to other payoff criteria of individual mobiles, such as the limiting expected time average payoff.

Acknowledgements. This work has been partially supported by the European Commission within the framework of the BIONETS project, IST-FET-SAC-FP6-027748, www.bionets.eu. It was also supported in part by the Arc Popeye collaborative project of INRIA.

References

1. Altman, E., Hayel, Y.: A Stochastic Evolutionary Game Approach to Energy Management in a Distributed Aloha Network. In: IEEE INFOCOM (2008)
2. Cover, T., Thomas, J.: Elements of Information Theory, 2nd edn. Wiley Interscience, Hoboken (2006)
3. Jovanovic, B., Rosenthal, R.W.: Anonymous Sequential Games. J. Math. Econ. 17, 77–87 (1988)
4. Mannor, S., Tsitsiklis, J.N.: On the Empirical State-Action Frequencies in Markov Decision Processes Under General Policies. Math. Oper. Res. 30(3), 545–561 (2005)
5. Maynard Smith, J.: Game Theory and the Evolution of Fighting. In: Maynard Smith, J. (ed.) On Evolution, pp. 8–28. Edinburgh University Press (1972)
6. Proakis, J.G.: Communication Systems Engineering. Prentice Hall International Editions, Englewood Cliffs (1994)
7. Wardrop, J.G.: Some theoretical aspects of road traffic research. Proc. Inst. Civil Eng. 2, 325–378 (1952)

Probabilistic Analysis of Hierarchical Cluster Protocols for Wireless Sensor Networks

Ingemar Kaj

Department of Mathematics
Uppsala University
Box 480, SE 751 06 Uppsala, Sweden
Tel.: +4618-471 3287
ikaj@math.uu.se

Abstract. Wireless sensor networks are designed to extract data from the deployment environment and combine sensing, data processing and wireless communication to provide useful information for the network users. Hundreds or thousands of small embedded units, which operate under low-energy supply and with limited access to central network control, rely on interconnecting protocols to coordinate data aggregation and transmission. Energy efficiency is crucial and it has been proposed that cluster based and distributed architectures such as LEACH are particularly suitable. We analyse the random cluster hierarchy in this protocol and provide a solution for low-energy and limited-loss optimization. Moreover, we extend these results to a multi-level version of LEACH, where clusters of nodes again self-organize to form clusters of clusters, and so on.

Keywords: LEACH, Cluster head, Hierarchical protocol, Voronoi cluster, Low-energy sensor network.

1 Introduction

Wireless sensor networks combine sensing, data processing and wireless communication into an ensemble of hundreds or thousands of small embedded units. Interconnecting protocols are designed to extract data from the network environment and provide efficient forwarding of useful information to a central processing center. Successful systems in the future are bound to meet a number of requirements of functionality, size, cost, energy handling, etc, to enable reliable monitor information to its users, possibly over the internet. An important challenge for research is to make sensor networks self-configuring, robust and maintenance-free.

Each node in a wireless sensor network is a battery driven tiny device equipped with sensing and wireless communication capabilities. The devices enable extraction of data in the spatial environment of the nodes as well as transmission of data between the nodes in the network and between a network node and a base station. The base station could be located at a distance away from the region of deployment of the sensor devices, or in the direct vicinity of these units

R. Núñez-Queija and J. Resing (Eds.): NET-COOP 2009, LNCS 5894, pp. 137–151, 2009.

and uses the arriving aggregated and recorded data for continuous monitoring or detection of special events. The nodes contain sophisticated layers of electronics, with a radio transceiver, antenna, computer, memory, batteries, sensors, and possibly solar panels, functionality for sensor calibration, etc. Yet, current research efforts envision a regular wireless sensor unit in the future to reach an integration size of $5 \times 5 \times 5$ mm and a manufacturing cost down to 1 euro, c.f.[7].

It is usually not an option to replace or reload battery driven sensor units. Thus, a particularly important feature for long life time sensor networks is energy efficiency. The most energy demanding part of a node is the wireless communication. Since the power consumption for transmission of data increases greatly with distance, it is important to reduce data transmission between nodes far apart and crucial to minimize the amount of upload traffic from sensor nodes to a distant base station. It has been proposed that cluster-based architectures are favorable for this purpose. Under a hierarchical clustering algorithm all nodes of the network are organized in a number of clusters, each with a designated cluster head node. The nodes within a cluster only communicate with their cluster head, which ideally is a short distance away if clusters are suitably chosen. The aggregated data from each cluster is then forwarded to the base station. In this way any substantial energy dissipation in the system is limited to the nodes currently serving as cluster heads. To avoid draining the power supply of individual sensor devices, the task of being a cluster head must rotate over time among the nodes. Also, to avoid costly central processing overheads, an effective cluster architecture protocol should be distributed in nature, so that clusters are formed only based on information already available in the nodes.

The architecture LEACH (Low-Energy Adapted Clustering Hierarchy) introduced by Heinzelman, Chandrakasan, and Balakrishnan, [4], [5], is a randomized, distributed clustering protocol, which is widely proposed and tested in wireless sensor networks. A number of variations and extensions have been discussed, see e.g. [6], [1]. Our contributions in this work include a refined probabilistic analysis of the LEACH protocol under the energy dissipation model in [5], based on a renewal-reward argument. As a further novelty, we introduce a suitable loss probability as control criteria. In addition, our approach extends the scope of modeling to a wider class of scenarios where the base station is located either inside or away from the sensor network. As in [1], stochastic geometric results of [3] are applied as a tool. From a network control perspective, our analyses yield added insight as to the role of the basic protocol parameters for minimizing energy consumption without jeopardizing functionality, hence optimizing the network life length. A similar study based on a different approach has been announced in [2]. These authors consider a scaling scenario where the sensor coverage region and the distance to the base station increase and study the energy dissipation in a scaling limit scenario.

As a main novelty in this work we propose a multi-level hierarchy version of LEACH, where the cluster head nodes of the original protocol form clusters of cluster heads, etc. Only the heads of the highest level clusters communicate directly with the base station. Our analysis shows, for example, that under loss-free conditions the one-level protocol remains competitive in comparison with the two-level version, whereas the benefits of multilevel hierarchies begin to show in lossy systems.

2   The Protocol Architecture LEACH

We first recall the basic ideas of low-energy adaptive clustering hierarchies as presented in [5]. Consider a system of sensor nodes in a given spatial region. The nodes are linked with each other and with a central base station, essentially using a single-hop mode of communication. The operation of LEACH is managed over consecutive *cycles* where each cycle consists of a fixed number of *rounds*. Each round has a set-up phase and a steady-state phase. The set-up phase begins with a selection process where randomized announcements among all nodes result in a random number of cluster heads (CH). This is followed by the formation of randomly sized clusters of Voronoi type, where each non-cluster head (nonCH) node makes a decision based on minimum distance to join exactly one of the available CH nodes. During the subsequent steady-state phase, the CH coordinates the transmission of data from all sensors in its cluster to the base station. In this way, the main energy load of the system is concentrated to CH nodes. In order to distribute the energy dissipation evenly over nodes, it is essential that the nodes take turns acting as CHs. Thus, in consecutive rounds of a cycle the self-selection of CHs involves only nonCHs of previous rounds. Also, to make its decision a node does not need to have knowledge of the remaining number nonCHs in the system. The design of LEACH guarantees that for each integer r, it is possible to operate the protocol as a sequel of independent cycles each consisting of r rounds, such that each node has the burden of acting as CH exactly once in a cycle.

2.1   Probabilistic Aspects of Cluster Selection in LEACH

Consider a network of n identical nodes deployed randomly and uniformly in some spatial region, such as a set in two-dimensional space or along a straight line. Fix an integer r, known in advance to all nodes in the network. The result of the CH selection algorithm is a sequential list $X_1, \ldots, X_r$, where

$$X_i = \text{the number of cluster head nodes in round } i, \quad i = 1, \ldots, r.$$

During the set-up of the first round in a cycle each node decides with probability $1/r$ to be a CH, so that $X_1 \sim \text{Bin}(n, 1/r)$, a binomially distributed random variable with parameters n and $1/r$. The remaining $n - X_1$ nonCH nodes are potential CHs for the second round in which the selection probability is modified to $1/(r-1)$ in order to keep the average number of CHs constant at n/r. By repeating the process r times, we may recast the LEACH selection algorithm in terms of the conditional distributions

$$X_1 \sim \text{Bin}(n, \frac{1}{r})$$

$$X_2|X_1 \sim \mathrm{Bin}(n - X_1, \frac{1}{r-1})$$

$$X_3|X_1, X_2 \sim \mathrm{Bin}(n - X_1 - X_2, \frac{1}{r-2})$$

$$\vdots$$

$$X_r|X_1, \ldots, X_{r-1} \sim \mathrm{Bin}(n - X_1 - \ldots - X_{r-1}, 1) = n - X_1 - \ldots - X_{r-1}$$

For comparison, note that [5] uses network size n and expected cluster size $k = n/r$ as the basic parameters.

The above conditional scheme is known in statistical sampling theory to be a property of the multinomial distribution. However, it appears that the following reformulation of the cluster selection algorithm has not been observed in the context of LEACH. Since we could not find a direct reference for this particular statistical fact we also give a proof.

Proposition 1. *The joint distribution of the number of cluster heads in consecutive rounds of a cycle is given by the multinomial distribution*

$$(X_1, \ldots, X_r) \sim \mathrm{Multnom}\left(n, \left\{\frac{1}{r}, \ldots, \frac{1}{r}\right\}\right)$$

Moreover, letting $Z_1, \ldots, Z_r$ be i.i.d. Poisson distributed random variables with parameter n/r,

$$(X_1, \ldots, X_r) \overset{d}{=} \left(Z_1, \ldots, Z_r \,\middle|\, \sum_{i=1}^{r} Z_i = n\right)$$

Proof. The conditioning scheme implies, in particular, that $X_1 + \ldots + X_r = n$, which is the property that each node serves as cluster head exactly once per cycle. The generating function of the cluster head counting variables thus have the form

$$g(s_1, \ldots, s_r) = E(s_1^{X_1} \cdots s_r^{X_r}) = s_r^n \, E((s_1/s_r)^{X_1} \cdots (s_{r-1}/s_r)^{X_{r-1}}).$$

Next,

$$E((s_{r-1}/s_r)^{X_{r-1}}|X_1, \ldots, X_{r-2}) = \left(\frac{s_{r-1} + s_r}{2s_r}\right)^{n - X_1 - \ldots - X_{r-2}},$$

so

$$g(s_1, \ldots, s_r) = \left(\frac{s_{r-1} + s_r}{2}\right)^n E\left(\left(\frac{2s_1}{s_{r-1} + s_r}\right)^{X_1} \cdots \left(\frac{2s_{r-2}}{s_{r-1} + s_r}\right)^{X_{r-2}}\right).$$

By repeating these steps, conditioning on $(X_1, \ldots, X_k)$ for $k = r - 3$ down to $k = 1$, we obtain

$$g(s_1, \ldots, s_r) = \left(\frac{s_2 + \ldots + s_r}{r-1}\right)^n E\left(\left(\frac{(r-1)s_1}{s_2 + \ldots + s_r}\right)^{X_1}\right) = \left(\frac{s_1 + \ldots + s_r}{r}\right)^n,$$

which is the generating function of the uniform multinomial distribution with parameters n and $1/r$. It is a basic property of the multivarate distribution that it is also obtained by conditioning independent Poisson random variables on their sum.

Remark 1. To see heuristically that the dynamics of LEACH is consistent with the multivariate distribution in Proposition 1, one may consider the outcome of randomly distributing n balls uniformly and without replacement in r boxes. Let X_1 denote the number of balls in box 1. Given X_1, the remaining $n - X_1$ balls are distributed uniformly over $r - 1$ boxes. In particular, $\mathrm{Bin}(n - X_1, 1/(r - 1))$ balls fall in box 2, which given round 1 is the number of CH nodes X_2 in the second round according to LEACH. Now, $n - X_1$ is $\mathrm{Bin}(n, 1 - 1/r)$-distributed. Thus, the number of balls in box 2 is binomially distributed with parameters n and $(1 - 1/r)/(r - 1) = 1/r$. An iteration of this argument shows that the CH distribution in LEACH agrees with the stated multivariate distribution.

It is sometimes an advantage for energy efficiency to run the algorithm with large values of r. This will limit the average number of CHs and thus the number of costly data transmissions to the base station. As a consequence, during start-up of a round none of the potential nodes may choose to announce its intention to be a CH. The fact that LEACH does not guarantee a CH in each round may then become an issue of practical importance. In our treatment we interpret the case $X_i = 0$ for some i as the complete loss of data in the entire network in this round. To deal with such lost rounds, suppose that the network user is willing to accept a loss probability $\alpha > 0$, in the sense that the proportion of rounds over long time where no clusters form is at most α. Since $P(X_i = 0) = (1 - 1/r)^n$ it follows that the admissible range of values for r is limited to integers $1 \leq r \leq r_\alpha$ where

$$r_\alpha = [(1 - \alpha^{1/n})^{-1}]. \tag{1}$$

It might be argued that rather than incorporating lost rounds, LEACH should be altered so that each round results in the formation of at least one CH. This could be achieved by adding to the set-up phase a distributed control mechanism, which is activated if a nonCH node at the end of a short time-out period has not received any CH announcements from other nodes. If this happens to one node it happens to all. Upon activation of the control in round i, the natural consequence is to restart the cluster formation phase so that eventually $X_i \geq 1$. This modification will cause a random time delay and a conditioning of the binomial distributions to be positive. However, in this work we stay with the original LEACH protocol and analyze its performance by using lost rounds as a means to optimizing and tuning the model parameters.

2.2   Renewal-Reward Analysis

We begin by analyzing the energy usage in the network under the assumption that the nodes have fixed locations $\xi = (\xi_j)_{1 \leq j \leq n}$ in a planar region Λ. Suppose each round lasts a constant period of time of length μ. This includes the set-up of clusters in addition to the steady-state phase, which typically is the predominant mode of operation for the network. Thus, time intervals of length $r\mu$ naturally form independent cycles of a renewal process, which counts the number of complete LEACH cycles over time. With the jth such renewal cycle we associate the total energy R_j that the system must use during the entire cycle for communication and data aggregation. Now, the energy load on the network during a cycle is symmetric over rounds. In fact, as will be clarified in the next section the energy usage pattern only depends on the size and shape of clusters. It then follows from Proposition 1 that each R_j may be represented as a sum $R_j = T_{j1} + \ldots + T_{jr}$ of identically distributed (dependent) random variables $(T_{ji})_{1 \leq i \leq r}$ where T_{ji} is the energy dissipated in the network during round i of cycle j.

Let R and T represent the distributions of the rewards (R_j) and (T_{ji}), respectively, and let $R(t)$ denote the total energy consumed by the network up to time t. We write $\mathbf{E}_\xi$ for expectation with respect to the conditional probability $\mathbf{P}_\xi$ given spatial location ξ. Since the cycles have fixed length $r\mu$ and the rewards are nonnegative and satisfy $\mathbf{E}_\xi R \leq r\mathbf{E}_\xi T$, the prerequisites for the renewal-reward theorem are satisfied as soon as $\mathbf{E}_\xi T < \infty$. In this case the average energy consumption per time unit is given asymptotically by the cycle average

$$\lim_{t \to \infty} \frac{1}{t} R(t) = \frac{\mathbf{E}_\xi(R)}{r\mu} = \frac{1}{\mu} \mathbf{E}_\xi(T), \quad \mathbf{P}_\xi - a.s.$$

As the basic measure of performance of the wireless sensor network under LEACH we take the corresponding energy dissipation per time unit averaged over the random locations of the nodes, that is $\mathbf{E}(T)/\mu$. Our next goal is to model T and compute or estimate $\mathbf{E}(T)$ by means of the cluster distribution properties.

2.3   Energy Dissipation Model

The energy model in [5] refers to sensors randomly distributed over the square $\Lambda_M = M \times M$ in the plane. The data is transmitted in the form of messages with fixed size ℓ bits. Data aggregation takes place in CH sensors and radio communication within the network follows the free-space model where power loss is proportional to squared distance between sender and receiver. We consider two scenarios for communication with the base station:

distBS: (model of [5]) Data transmission between CH nodes and a distant base station located outside of Λ_M follows the multipath fading model of power loss proportional to the fourth power of the distance;

nearBS: The base station is placed at a point within Λ_M, such as the center point $(M/2, M/2)$ and operates under the free-space model.

The relevant energy constants are summarized in Table 1, with values that are used for some numerical illustrations.

We have demonstrated above, that LEACH is completely symmetric over rounds. Moreover, the performance metric does not involve the dependence between rounds within a cycle. Thus, for a given round let T_{within} be the energy

Table 1. Energy model in Ref [5]

energy coefficient	notation	numerical value and unit
electronic	E_{elec}	50 nJ/bit
data aggregation	E_{DA}	5 nJ/bit/signal
free-space amplifier	$\mathcal{E}_{\text{fs}}$	10 pJ/bit/m^2
multipath amplifier	$\mathcal{E}_{\text{mp}}$	0.0013 pJ/bit/m^4

loss for communication within clusters and T_{toBS} the additional energy dissipation due to uploading data from CHs to the base station. We are interested in the total energy loss $T = T_{\text{within}} + T_{\text{toBS}}$ per round and, in particular, in the expected energy dissipation $E(T)$ per round as a function of the protocol parameters n and r. In Proposition 2 below we give an approximate expression $\psi_n(r) \approx E(T)$, which is obtained by analyzing the separate parts of T. For given size n and an acceptable loss rate α in the network, LEACH should operate with the parameter r, $1 \leq r \leq r_\alpha$, tuned so that $\psi_n(r)$ is minimal.

2.4   Estimated Energy Loss in Two Versions of LEACH

Let X be the number of clusters in a given round and write $L_1, \ldots, L_X$ for the number of nonCH nodes in each of these clusters. For a nonCH node to transmit an ℓ-bit message to its CH distance d away, the radio expends the power $\ell(E_{\text{elec}} + \mathcal{E}_{\text{fs}}d^2)$. To receive this message the CH expends another ℓE_{elec}. In addition, the aggregation of data in the CH will consume ℓE_{DA} per node involved. Thus, in a cluster consisting of one CH located at ξ^{CH} and L nonCH nodes at locations $\xi_1, \ldots, \xi_L$, the power expenditure adds to

$$\ell E_{\text{elec}}(L + L) + \ell E_{\text{DA}}(L + 1) + \ell\mathcal{E}_{\text{fs}}\chi^2, \quad \chi^2 = \sum_{l=1}^{L} |\xi^{CH} - \xi_l|^2.$$

Since $\sum_{m=1}^{X} L_m = n - X$,

$$T_{\text{within}} = \ell E_{\text{elec}}2(n - X) + \ell n E_{\text{DA}} + \ell\mathcal{E}_{\text{fs}} \sum_{m=1}^{X} \chi_m^2, \quad \chi_m^2 = \sum_{l=1}^{L_m} |\xi_m^{CH} - \xi_{lm}|^2$$

where ξ_m^{CH} and (ξ_{lm}) indicate the locations of the CH and nonCH nodes of the relevant cluster. The last term in T_{within} involves the cluster head selection distribution in Proposition 1 and the Voronoi tessalation of Λ_M, which decides the cluster size variables (L_j) and the length of the edges between nodes and cluster head in each cluster. To obtain an estimate of

$$\mathbf{E}\left(\sum_{m=1}^{X} \chi_m^2\right) = \mathbf{E}\sum_{m=1}^{X} \mathbf{E}(\chi_m^2 | X),$$

we note that given X, for each m,

$$\chi_m^2 = \sum_{j=1}^{L_m} d^2(\cdot, \cdot), \quad \sum_{\nu=1}^{X} L_\nu = n - X.$$

By alluding to the Poisson representation in Proposition 1, we may compare this situation to that in [3] for Voronoi clusters in a bivariate Poisson point process in the plane. These authors obtain the expected value over edge lengths in a typical Voronoi cell, in the precise sense of Palm distribution, in terms of the corresponding Poisson intensities. If the intensities λ_0 and λ_1 are taken to represent nonCH and CH nodes per unit area, respectively, then the expected sum of squared edge lengths in a typical Voronoi cell is given by

$$\lambda_0 \int_{R^2} |x|^2 e^{-\lambda_1 \pi |x|^2}\, dx = \frac{\lambda_0}{\pi \lambda_1^2}.$$

To make the connection to our model, conditional on $X = k$ we may compare the cluster functional χ_m^2 to the sum of squares of the edge lengths which arise in a bivariate spatial Poisson process with intensities corresponding to $\lambda_0 = (n - k)/M^2$ and $\lambda_1 = k/M^2$. Hence

$$E(\chi_m^2 | X = k) \approx \frac{n - k}{\pi k^2} M^2, \quad 1 \le m \le k,$$

and

$$\mathbf{E}\Big(\sum_{m=1}^{X} \chi_m^2 \Big) \approx \mathbf{E}\Big(\frac{n - X}{X} \Big) \frac{M^2}{\pi} = H_n(r) \frac{M^2}{\pi}, \tag{2}$$

where

$$H_n(r) = \sum_{k=1}^{n} \frac{n - k}{k} \binom{n}{k} \Big(\frac{1}{r} \Big)^k \Big(1 - \frac{1}{r} \Big)^{n-k}. \tag{3}$$

It follows that

$$E(T_{\text{within}}) \approx \ell E_{\text{elec}} 2n(1 - 1/r) + \ell E_{\text{DA}}\, n + \ell \mathcal{E}_{\text{fs}} \pi^{-1} H_n(r)\, M^2.$$

Next we turn to the energy loss associated with transmitting the data in the system from CH nodes to the base station, which we assume is located in the point $\xi_{BS} = (u, v)M$. For the case $(u, v) \notin [0, 1]^2$ that is $\xi_{BS} \notin \Lambda_M$, we adopt the model $distBS$ so that multipath transmission of an ℓ-bit message requires the additional energy dissipation

$$T_{\text{distBS}} = \ell E_{\text{elec}} X + \ell \mathcal{E}_{\text{mp}} \sum_{k=1}^{X} |\xi_k^{CH} - \xi_{BS}|^4.$$

Since the CH locations (ξ_k^{CH}) are uniformly scattered over Λ_M and independent of the number of CH nodes, the expected energy loss is

$$E(T_{\text{distBS}}) = \ell E_{\text{elec}} \frac{n}{r} + \ell \mathcal{E}_{\text{mp}} \frac{n}{r} M^4 d_{\text{distBS}}^4(u, v),$$

with

$$d_{\text{distBS}}^4(u, v) = \int_{[0,1]^2} ((x - u)^2 + (y - v)^2)^2 \, dx dy.$$

For the case $\xi_{BS} \in \Lambda_M$, the modeling assumption $nearBS$ stipulates free-space transmission for which the energy dissipation per ℓ-bit message amounts to

$$T_{\text{nearBS}} = \ell E_{\text{elec}} X + \ell \mathcal{E}_{\text{fs}} \sum_{k=1}^{X} |\xi_k^{CH} - \xi_{\text{BS}}|^2,$$

with expected value

$$E(T_{\text{nearBS}}) = \ell E_{\text{elec}} \frac{n}{r} + \ell \mathcal{E}_{\text{fs}} \frac{n}{r} M^2 d_{\text{nearBS}}^2(u, v),$$

and now

$$d_{\text{nearBS}}^2(u, v) = \int_{[0,1]^2} ((x - u)^2 + (y - v)^2) \, dx dy.$$

In particular, if the base station is placed at the middle point of the deployment region, $u = v = 1/2$, then $d_{\text{nearBS}}^2(u, v) = 1/6$.

By summing up the terms for energy consumption within clusters and between cluster heads and base, we obtain an approximate expression for the performance measure $E(T)$ in terms of network size n and the protocol parameter r. Based on the above arguments we summarize these findings as follows.

Proposition 2. *Consider the sensor network model as above with n nodes deployed uniformly within the square $[0, M]^2$, the base station placed in the point (uM, vM), and with energy use specified by the parameters in Table 1. Asymptotically over many cycles of LEACH, the average energy dissipation per round and per ℓ-bit message is given approximately by*

$$\psi_n(r) = \ell \left(E_{\text{elec}} n \left(2 - \frac{1}{r} \right) + E_{\text{DA}} n + \pi^{-1} \mathcal{E}_{\text{fs}} M^2 H_n(r) + C_M \frac{n}{r} \right), \quad 1 \le r \le n,$$

where $H_n(r)$ is introduced in (3) and

$$C_M = \begin{cases} \mathcal{E}_{\text{mp}} M^4 \int_{[0,1]^2} ((x - u)^2 + (y - v)^2)^2 \, dx dy & \text{for distBS,} \\ \mathcal{E}_{\text{fs}} M^2 \int_{[0,1]^2} ((x - u)^2 + (y - v)^2) \, dx dy. & \text{for nearBS.} \end{cases} \quad (4)$$

To optimize LEACH for energy efficiency while accepting lost rounds at a rate of α, use

$$\tilde{r} = \arg\min \{\psi_n(r) : 1 \le r \le r_\alpha\},$$

with r_α defined in (1).

Remark 2. *The following series expansion for $H_n(r)$, which is extracted from [8], Corollary 1, is accurate for not too large values of r:*

$$H_n(r) = (r - 1) \left(1 + \frac{r}{n} + \frac{r(2r - 1)}{n^2} + \mathcal{O}\left(\frac{r^3}{n^3} \right) \right).$$

Remark 3. The analysis in [5] involves the (lower bound) approximation

$$\mathbf{E}(X^{-1}) \approx \frac{r}{n} = \frac{1}{\mathbf{E}(X)}$$

and corresponds to taking $H_n(r) \approx r$ in our setting. By ignoring one additional term we obtain for the case *distBS*

$$\psi_n(r) \approx \ell \left(2E_{\text{elec}} n + E_{\text{DA}} n + \pi^{-1} \mathcal{E}_{\text{fs}} M^2 r + \mathcal{E}_{\text{mp}} M^4 d^4_{\text{distBS}}(u,v) \frac{n}{r} \right).$$

In their study [5] takes $(u,v) = (1/2, 7/4)$ and varies d_{BS} over min and max distance to the CHs. We obtain $d_{\text{distBS}}(1/2, 7/4) \approx 1.3699$. Apart from this and from their choice of prefactor of the free-space transmission term, $1/(2\pi)$ instead of our $1/\pi$, we recover the corresponding expression in [5] by setting $k = n/r$. It leads to the conclusion that k, the expected number of clusters in the system, should be proportional to the square root of n.

2.5   Numerical Illustration

To illustrate the optimization problem in Proposition 2, we consider again the experimental and numerical setup in [5]. Thus, we take $M = 100$, $\xi_{BS} = (1/2, 7/4)M = (50, 175)$, $\ell = 4\,200$, and adopt the energy parameter values listed in Table 1. By Proposition 1 for *distBS*,

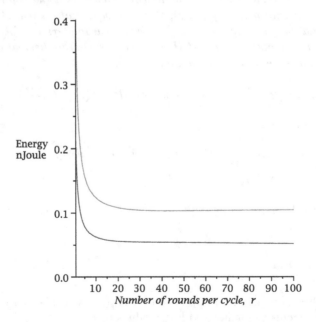

Fig. 1. Energy loss per round as function of cycle length r, distant base station and energy model of [5], lower curve: $n = 100$, upper curve: $n = 200$

$$\psi_n(r) = \ell\left(E_{\text{elec}}n\left(2-\frac{1}{r}\right) + E_{\text{DA}}n + \pi^{-1}\mathcal{E}_{\text{fs}}M^2 H_n(r) + \mathcal{E}_{\text{mp}} M^4 3.522\frac{n}{r}\right)$$

$$= 4.2\cdot 10^{-4}\left(\frac{n}{2}\left(2-\frac{1}{r}\right) + \frac{n}{20} + \pi^{-1}H_n(r) + 4.5785\frac{n}{r}\right)\quad\text{(Joule)}$$

The example in [5] is $n = 100$. Figure 1, lower curve, shows the graph of $\psi_{100}(r)$. For comparison, the upper curve represents the energy loss with twice as many nodes in the same region, $\psi_{200}(r)$. These curves have no distinct minimum point. If the number of rounds per cycle is less than 15 or so, then the multipath fading term is dominant with increased risk of draining the energy supply in the nodes. Cycles of length $r \approx 20$ and above appear to be equivalent energy wise. However, with increasing r there is a trade-off in terms of losses. By (1), a 5% loss rate in the network of size $n = 100$ will limit the length of cycles to $r_{0.05} = 33$ and a loss rate of 1% implies a maximum of $r_{0.01} = 22$. Hence for this example, LEACH achieves its optimal performance at $n/r \approx 5$.

In case the base station can be placed in the same region as the sensors themselves, the energy balance shifts. It is no longer obvious that short cycles - many cluster heads on average - is a disadvantage. Indeed, if the base station is a conveniently located centre point of the network region, it may be counterproductive to use only a few cluster heads. Figure 2 applies to fixed size $n = 100$ and the same situation as above except that we use *nearBS* in Proposition 1 with the base station either in a corner point $(0,0)$ (upper curve) or the middle point, that is $u = v = 1/2$ (lower curve). It is noteworthy that if the base station is right in the middle of the network then optimal performance of LEACH

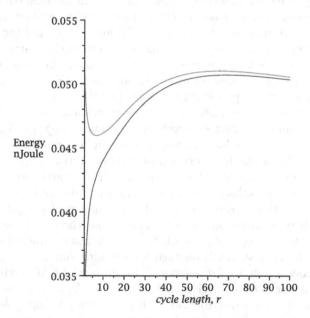

Fig. 2. Energy loss per round for nearby base station at a corner point (upper curver) or middle point (lower curve)

is obtained for $r = 1$, which is the case when each node forms its own cluster of size one. If instead the CHs must establish data transmission with a corner point, then the upper curve shows that the optimal (integer) value is $r = 7$.

3   A Multi-level Hierarchical Algorithm

A limiting assumption in LEACH is that all nodes are in within communication range of each other and the base station. As discussed already in [5], to relax the impact of this assumption one alternative is to develop further the hierarchy of clusters by forming "super clusters" out of the CH nodes. It is natural to follow up on this line of thought and investigate the possible gain in terms of energy consumption if we let the cluster heads which have been selected in a round, again act according to the same protocol principles and form new clusters of cluster heads. This will require a node to store further information about its prehistory as CH and prolonge the set-up phase, but should not impose any significant additional work in the system since the same mechanisms as in the one-level version are iterated.

We introduce m-level LEACH by specifying m parameters $r_1, \ldots, r_m$ and an m-level CH selection algorithm as follows. In setting up the first round, the ensemble of n nodes make m decisions. First of all, as in regular 1-level LEACH, the nodes pick $X_{1,1}$ CHs according to $\mathrm{Bin}(N, 1/r_1)$. These selected CHs immediately go on to announce among themselves with probability $1/r_2$ their willingness to be CH-heads (2-CH). Given $X_{1,1}$, the resulting number, $X_{2,1}$, of 2-CH nodes is $\mathrm{Bin}(X_{1,1}, 1/r_2)$. This is repeated m times and yields in the final step $X_{m.1}$ m-CH nodes. The network is now ready to enter the steady state phase in which data will be transmitted from nonCH to CH to 2-CH and so on, until the m-CH nodes complete the round by handling data transmission to the base station. In setting up round 2, the cluster heads of levels 1 to $m - 2$ remain the same. Only the (m-1)-CH nodes must select a new set of m-CHs among the $X_{m-1,1} - X_{m,1}$ available candidates. The selection probability changes to $1/(r_m - 1)$ and we obtain $X_{m,2}$ mCH nodes in charge of exchange with the base station in round 2. After completion in this manner of the first sub-cycle of r_m rounds, all $\sum_{j=1}^{r_m} X_{m,j} = X_{m-1,1}$ CHs on level $m - 1$ are considered used up and will be replaced in the beginning of round $r_m + 1$. The suitable selection probability is $1/(r_{m-1} - 1)$. After $r_m r_{m-1}$ rounds it is time to go one level further down in the hierarchy and make the appropriate update. The subsequent decisions and updates of CHs at the various levels follow the path of a contour around the branches of a regular rooted tree of depth m where all tree-nodes at distance j from the root have r_j branches. Finally, after a total of $r_1 \cdots r_m$ rounds the system has completed a full cycle in which each node has been a CH on each level exactly once.

The analogous result to Proposition 1 for m-level LEACH yields that the collection of cluster sizes on level j, that is $(X_{j,1}, \ldots X_{j,r_1\cdots r_j})$, $j = 1, \ldots, m$ has the uniform multinomial distribution with parameters n and $\frac{1}{r_1\cdots r_j}$. Since the full cycles of length $r_1 \cdots r_m$ are independent, we may apply the renewal-reward theorem as before and measure performance of the system as the expected energy loss per round.

Theorem 1. *Suppose a network with n nodes is deployed uniformly in $[0, M]^2$. The base station is located in (uM, vM), and the energy model in Proposition 2 applies. For the m-level LEACH model introduced above with parameters $\mathbf{r} = (r_1, \ldots, r_m)$, the average energy dissipation per round and ℓ-bit message is given approximately by*

$$\psi_n^{(m)}(\mathbf{r}) = \ell\Big(2E_{\text{elec}}\Big(1 - \frac{1}{r_1 \cdots r_m}\Big)n + E_{\text{elec}} \sum_{j=1}^{m} \frac{n}{r_1 \cdots r_j}$$

$$+ E_{\text{DA}}\Big(1 + \sum_{j=1}^{m-1} \frac{1}{r_1 \cdots r_j}\Big)n + \pi^{-1}\mathcal{E}_{\text{fs}}M^2 H_n^{(m)}(\mathbf{r}) + C_M \frac{n}{r_1 \cdots r_m}\Big),$$

where

$$H_n^{(m)}(\mathbf{r}) = \sum_{j=1}^{m} \frac{r_j - 1}{r_1 \cdots r_j - 1} H_n(r_1 \cdots r_j), \quad H_n^{(1)} = H_n \qquad (5)$$

$H_n(r)$ is introduced in (3), and C_M is defined in Proposition 2.

For a given acceptable loss rate α, optimal performance of m-LEACH is achieved by minimizing $\psi_n^{(m)}(\mathbf{r})$ over all m-tuples $\mathbf{r} = (r_1, \ldots, r_m)$ of integers such that

$$r_1 \cdots r_m \leq r_\alpha.$$

Proof. The total expected energy dissipation is obtained by adding over all m levels and each time use Proposition 2 with the appropriate parameter values r_j inserted. In this way all terms in $\psi_n^{(m)}$ arise straightforwardly, except the free-space energy within clusters which has the form

$$\frac{1}{\pi}\mathcal{E}_{\text{fs}}M^2 \sum_{j=1}^{m} \mathbf{E}\Big(\frac{X_{j-1,1} - X_{j,1}}{X_{j,1}}\Big),$$

where we use the cluster size variables $(X_{j,1})$ which arise in the first r_1 rounds of m-LEACH and we have put $X_{0,1} = n$. To verify (5) we must show

$$\mathbf{E}\Big(\frac{X_{j-1,1} - X_{j,1}}{X_{j,1}}\Big) = \frac{r_j - 1}{r_1 \cdots r_j - 1} H_n(r_1 \cdots r_j), \quad 2 \leq j \leq m.$$

Fix a j, $2 \leq j \leq m$, and write $p = 1/r_1 \cdots r_{j-1}$ and $q = 1/r_j$. We have

$$X_{j-1,1} \sim \text{Bin}(n, p), \qquad X_j | X_{j-1,1} \sim \text{Bin}(X_{j-1,1}, q)$$

so that

$$\mathbf{E}\Big(\frac{X_{j-1,1} - X_{j,1}}{X_{j,1}}\Big) = \sum_{k=1}^{n} \sum_{\ell=1}^{k} \frac{k - \ell}{\ell} \binom{n}{k} p^k (1-p)^{n-k} \binom{k}{\ell} q^\ell (1-q)^{k-\ell}$$

$$= \frac{p(1-q)}{1 - pq} \sum_{\ell=1}^{n} \frac{n - \ell}{\ell} \binom{n}{\ell} (pq)^\ell (1 - pq)^{n-\ell}$$

$$= \frac{p(1-q)}{1 - pq} H_n\Big(\frac{1}{pq}\Big) = \frac{r_j - 1}{r_1 \cdots r_j - 1} H_n(r_1 \cdots r_j),$$

which is (5). The loss probability is given by

$$P(X_{1,1} = 0) + P(X_{1,1} > 0, X_{2,1} = 0) + \ldots$$
$$\ldots + P(X_{1,1} > 0, \ldots, X_{m-1,1} > 0, X_{m,1} = 0)$$
$$= \sum_{j=1}^{m} (P(X_{j,1} = 0) - P(X_{j-1,1} = 0)) = \left(1 - \frac{1}{r_1 \cdots r_m}\right)^n,$$

which completes the proof.

3.1 Numerical Illustration of 2-Level LEACH

To evaluate the performance of m-level LEACH with that of the original one-level protocol under comparable loss conditions, it is natural to consider the difference in energy dissipation, which according to Theorem 1 is given by

$$\psi_n^{(m)}(r_1, \ldots, r_m) - \psi_n^{(1)}(r_1 \cdots r_m) = \ell\bigg((E_{\text{elec}} + E_{\text{DA}}) \sum_{j=1}^{m-1} \frac{n}{r_1 \cdots r_j}$$
$$+ \pi^{-1} \mathcal{E}_{\text{fs}} M^2 \, H_n^{(m-1)}(r_1, \ldots, r_{m-1}) - \frac{r_1 \cdots r_m - r_m}{r_1 \cdots r_m - 1} H_n(r_1 \cdots r_m)\bigg).$$

In particular, if we compare 1-level and 2-level LEACH applied to the same numerical example as above, this yields

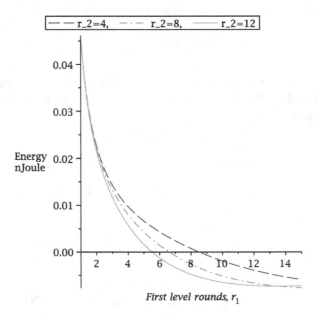

Fig. 3. Energy difference according to (6)

$$\psi_n^{(2)}(r_1, r_2) - \psi_n(r_1 \cdot r_2)$$

$$= 4.2 \cdot 10^{-4} \left(0.55 \frac{n}{r_1} + \pi^{-1} H_n(r_1) - \pi^{-1} \frac{(r_1 - 1)r_2}{r_1 \cdot r_2 - 1} H_n(r_1 \cdot r_2) \right). \quad (6)$$

Figure 3 shows the differencing energy dissipation for the case $n = 200$, for which loss rates of 1% and 5% yield $r_{0.01} = 43$ and $r_{0.05} = 67$. The merits of 2-level LEACH begin to show in the approximate range of parameters $r_1 r_2 \geq 50$, which as we have seen is also the parameter regime where lost rounds come into play regularly.

References

1. Bandyopadhyay, S., Coyle, E.J.: An energy efficient hierarchical clustering algorithm for wireless sensor networks. In: Proceedings of IEEE INFOCOM (2003)
2. Banerjee, P., Lahiri, S.N.: Optimal configuration of the LEACH: A statistical analysis, http://www.samsi.info/200708/sensor/presentations/Tue/Soumen_Lahiri.pdf
3. Foss, S.G., Zuyev, S.A.: On a Voronoi aggregative process related to a bivariate Poisson process. Adv. Appl. Probab. 28(4), 965–981 (1996)
4. Heinzelman, W.B., Chandrakasan, A.P., Balakrishnan, H.: Energy-efficient communication protocol for wireless microsensor networks. In: Proceedings of the Hawaii International Conference on System Sciences, Maui, Hawaii (January 2000)
5. Heinzelman, W.B., Chandrakasan, A.P., Balakrishnan, H.: An application-specific protocol architecture for wireless microsensor networks. IEEE Trans. Wireless Commun. 1(4), 660–670 (2002)
6. Yang, H., Sikdar, B.: Optimal Cluster Head Selection in the LEACH Architecture. In: Proceedings of IPCCC 2007, IEEE Performance, Computing, and Communications Conference, pp. 93–100 (2007)
7. WISENET, Uppsala VINN Excellence Center for Wireless Sensor Networks, Uppsala University, Vision statement, http://www.wisenet.uu.se
8. Wuyungaowa, Wang, T.: Asymptotic expansions for inverse moments of binomial and negative binomial. Statistics and Probability Letters 78, 3018–3022 (2008)

Performance of the Sleep-Mode Mechanism of the New IEEE 802.16m Proposal for Correlated Downlink Traffic

Koen De Turck, Stijn De Vuyst, Dieter Fiems, Sabine Wittevrongel, and Herwig Bruneel

Ghent University, Department of Telecommunications and Information Processing, St. Pietersnieuwstraat 41, B-9000 Ghent, Belgium

Abstract. There is a considerable interest nowadays in making wireless telecommunication more energy-efficient. The sleep-mode mechanism in WiMAX (IEEE 802.16e) is one of such energy saving measures. Recently, Samsung proposed some modifications on the sleep-mode mechanism, scheduled to appear in the forthcoming IEEE 802.16m standard, aimed at minimizing the signaling overhead. In this work, we present a performance analysis of this proposal and clarify the differences with the standard mechanism included in IEEE 802.16e. We also propose some special algorithms aimed at reducing the computational complexity of the analysis.

1 Introduction

Great hopes are pinned on the IEEE 802.16e standard (WiMAX) [1], which is poised to be the next big standard in wireless communications. It regulates the communication between mobile stations (MS) and base stations (BS) in a metropolitan area wireless network. Energy-saving mechanisms in wireless communications are currently a hot topic. Short battery life is one of the main impediments to a more widespread use of wireless devices. Hence, understandably, a lot of research is directed at solving or at least mitigating this problem. In the first place, this can be done by making more efficient batteries, but lately there is also a lot of interest in including energy-saving measures in the communication protocols themselves. On that account, it is no wonder that the WiMAX committee has opted to incorporate various energy-saving elements which are commonly referred to as 'sleep mode' and 'idle mode'. Power saving is generally achieved by turning off parts of the MS in a controlled manner when there is neither traffic from the MS (uplink traffic) nor to the MS (downlink traffic). Whereas a MS in sleep mode is still registered to a BS and still performs hand-off procedures, idle mode operation (which is optional in current WiMAX standards) goes further and allows the MS to be completely switched off and unregistered with any BS, while still receiving broadcast traffic.

In this paper, we mainly consider the sleep-mode mechanism, in which the MS turns itself off for predetermined periods of time which are negotiated with the

R. Núñez-Queija and J. Resing (Eds.): NET-COOP 2009, LNCS 5894, pp. 152–165, 2009.

BS. For the new upcoming IEEE 802.16m standard [2], two companies have proposed a new sleep-mode mechanism, Samsung [3] and Nokia Siemens Networks [4]. The difference between the customary WiMAX sleep-mode mechanism and the new proposals is that the former must be renegotiated every time the traffic volume is low, while in case of the latter mechanisms, traffic is organized in a structure of cycles, and when the system goes into sleep mode, it does so for the rest of the cycle. This requires very few signaling messages. As the Nokia Siemens proposal is a special case of the one championed by Samsung, we will mainly consider the latter.

Sleep-mode operation has received quite some attention lately from the performance modeling community. In [5], the average energy consumption of the MS is obtained in case of downlink traffic only, as well as an approximate expression for the mean packet delay. The energy consumption of the MS in case of both downlink and uplink traffic is considered in [6]. Both [5] and [6] model the incoming (and outgoing) traffic as a Poisson process. An accurate assessment of the delay experienced at the BS buffer however, requires a queueing model. For IEEE 802.16e, in [7] the BS buffer is modeled as a continuous-time finite-capacity queue with a Poisson arrival process and deterministic service times. A semi-Markov chain analysis leads to expressions for the mean packet delay and the mean energy consumption by the MS. The analysis in [8] is based on an $M/G/1/K$ queueing model with multiple vacations and exhaustive service, where the vacations represent the sleep intervals. Similar work can also be found in [9], where the length of a vacation is assumed to depend on the previous vacation length. In [10], the sleep-mode operation in Cellular Digital Packet Data (CDPD) services is evaluated. The difference with IEEE 802.16e is that the subsequent sleep intervals do not increase in length. The system can thus be modeled as a queueing system with multiple vacations and exceptional first vacation. The loss probability in both [8] and [10] is obtained as well. A simulation study of CDPD sleep-mode performance is found in [11]. An alternative to the exponential increase of the sleep interval lengths is evaluated by simulation in [12]. Finally, in our previous work on the sleep-mode mechanism [14] [13], we considered a general D-BMAP arrival process, and we found that traffic correlation, which was hitherto neglected in almost every study, has an important influence on the sleep-mode performance.

Along with every other paper published on this topic, we assume that the base station has a dedicated buffer for each mobile station that is connected to it, as well as a dedicated amount of bandwidth. It is thus sufficient to consider only a single mobile user. In our opinion, the advantage of modeling a multi-user scenario does not outweigh the significant increase in complexity. The only advantage we see is that one might model to some degree the typical variations in bandwidth that are observed when the number of mobile active users is variable, but this is already a challenging and ongoing research topic without any form of sleep-mode mechanism.

The structure of this paper is as follows. In Section 2, we describe Samsung's proposal and design a mathematical model for it. The analysis is spelled out in Section 3, where we reduce the problem to a matrix-analytical problem. We develop a computationally efficient variant in Section 4, specifically tailored to this model. We employ our analysis for a WiMAX scenario in Section 5 together with some numerical results. Finally, we draw some conclusions in Section 6.

2   Model

Let us first sketch the sleep-mode mechanism that is included in the current IEEE 802.16e protocol. Whenever there is no data to be transmitted between the mobile station (MS) and the base station (BS), the MS can negotiate to go into sleep mode, that is, it will switch off its radio interface for some time, so that the BS cannot transmit packets during this time. There are three types of sleep mode foreseen in the protocol. The simplest is the so-called class III sleep mode, in which a single sleep interval is negotiated. For class II sleep mode, the MS checks at the end of the first sleep interval if the BS has already packets to be transmitted to the said MS, if not, then automatically a new sleep interval of the same length is started. The last, and perhaps the most well-known is the class I sleep-mode mechanism, which is very similar to class II, except that the subsequent sleep intervals do not stay the same but double each time in length until a certain maximum is reached.

In principle, sleep-mode parameters must be renegotiated every time when there is no data traffic between BS and MS (i.e. at the end of each busy period, in queueing parlance). This results in a certain signaling overhead, and it is this shortcoming that the new proposal attempts to address. To this end, data transmission is organized in cycles, consisting of a number of frames. When at a certain point during the cycle, the traffic between BS and MS is interrupted, then a so-called *closedown* interval is started, and if during this closedown interval no new traffic appears, then the mobile station goes into sleep mode until the end of the current cycle. If packets arrive during the closedown interval, then they are transmitted without delay. The advantage of this scheme is that once this sleep mode is in order, it does not have to be renegotiated.

We model the buffer in the base station (from now on denoted as simply 'the buffer') as a discrete-time queue with infinite capacity and a first-come-first-served (FCFS) server discipline. This buffer is fed by the traffic in the downlink direction (i.e. from the base station to the mobile station). In this work, as in several other papers on sleep-mode operation, we do not take into account the uplink traffic. We adhere to queueing terminology and denote by a *slot*, what is in the IEEE community usually referred as a frame. The durations of a cycle, of a listening interval at the beginning of a cycle, and of a closedown interval are denoted by N, L, and C respectively. In our analysis, we will further assume that $0 \leq L \leq C < N$, which is conform to most practical situations. Packets arrive at the buffer according to a discrete-time batch Markovian arrival process (D-BMAP). That is, the arrival process is determined by a finite-state Markov chain (with M states), which is usually referred to as the background Markov chain. The arrival process is defined by the values $a(k, j|i); \; k \geqslant 0; \; i, j \in \{1, \cdots, M\}$, denoting the probability that if the background state is i during a slot, there are k arrivals during this slot and the background state during the next slot is j. We put these probabilities in a matrix generating function $\mathbf{A}(z)$ with dimension $M \times M$, which is defined as follows:

$$\mathbf{A}(z) \doteq \sum_{k=0}^{\infty} \mathbf{A}_k z^k, \text{ where } [\mathbf{A}_k]_{ij} \doteq a(k, j|i). \tag{1}$$

Delayed access is assumed, i.e. arriving packets do not enter the buffer until the end of their arrival slot. Packets are transmitted one by one according to a FCFS discipline. The model at hand differs from a normal single-server queueing model when the buffer gets empty, as in that case a closedown interval of duration C is started. When during the closedown interval new packets arrive at the BS side, then the closedown interval is abandoned and the packets are served during the next slot. Otherwise, the system goes into sleep mode for the rest of the cycle, and newly arriving packets accumulate in the buffer, waiting to be transmitted during the next cycle. If the closedown interval gets interrupted at the beginning of the next cycle, it gets abandoned as well. At the beginning of each cycle there is a listening interval of L slots, which behaves identical to a closedown interval. An example of how the system might evolve under the model as described above is depicted in Fig. 1.

The difference between the proposal of Samsung[3] and the one of Nokia Siemens Networks[4] is that the latter does not have a closedown mechanism, and hence corresponds to the special case $C = 0$. We conclude this section with some terminology: slots during which a transmission takes place are called 'active'. Furthermore we distinguish listening slots, closedown slots, and sleep slots, with obvious semantics.

3   Analysis

We determine the probability generating function $U(z)$ of the buffer content during an arbitrary slot. The first step in the analysis is the choice of a convenient set of embedded points and the corresponding Markovian state description. After some trial and error, we settled for the following embedded points: either the beginning of the first slot of a cycle, or the end of a departure slot, that is, a slot in which the packet is transmitted. As there is a fairly large number of possible transitions, we will walk through them, one by one. The Markov state space consists of the buffer content u, the background state s and the position n within the cycle, where we denote the beginning of the cycle with 0, and the end of the different slots with $1, 2, \cdots, N - 1$. In the next paragraphs, we detail all possible transitions from system state (u, n, s) to (u', n', s'), along with the corresponding transition probabilities. These steps take a certain amount of care, as 'off-by-one' errors are easily committed.

The first case concerns the functioning of the system in active mode : when there are packets available to be sent $(u > 0)$, then one of them is sent and the embedded Markov chain jumps to the next cycle position (that is, we add one modulo N)

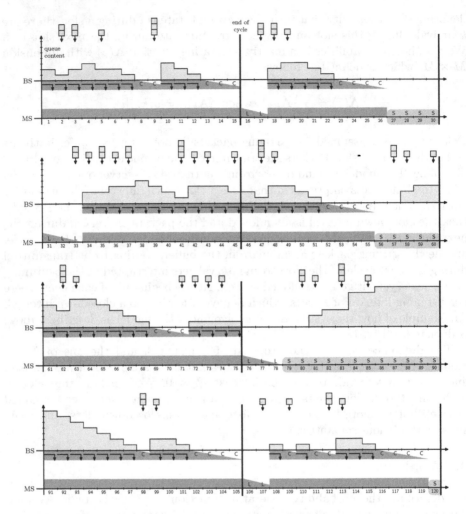

Fig. 1. System evolution in case $N = 15, C = 4$ and $L = 3$

From	To	Probability
(u, n, s)	$(u + k - 1, n + 1 \mod N, s')$	$[\mathbf{A}_k]_{ss'}$ if $u > 0$

For the second case, we look at the closedown intervals, more specifically at closedown intervals that are interrupted because of a packet arrival. For this to happen, we must start from an empty buffer, then there must be a number of slots i in which no arrivals occur, followed by a slot during which there is at least one arrival. The next embedded instant is at the end of the slot thereafter.

From	To	Probability
$(0, n, s)$	$(k, n + i + 2, s')$	$[z^{k+1}][\mathbf{A}_0^{i-1}(\mathbf{A}(z) - \mathbf{A}_0)\mathbf{A}(z)]_{ss'}$ if $0 < n < N - i - 2, 0 \leq i < C$

The notation $[z^k]F(z)$ denotes the coefficient of power series $F(z)$ in z^k. Now we turn our attention to situations where the system enters sleep mode. In that case, we again start from an empty buffer ($u = 0$), followed by a period of C slots in which no arrivals occur. Then we have a sleep interval of $N - n - C$ slots in which arrivals accumulate. The next embedded instant is at the cycle boundary.

From	To	Probability
$(0, n, s)$	$(k, 0, s')$	$[z^k][\mathbf{A}(0)^C \mathbf{A}(z)^{N-n-C}]_{ss'}$ if $N - C < n < N$

If the cycle boundary is reached during a closedown interval, then it is not continued, but rather a listening interval is started. Hence the embedded process just jumps to the cycle boundary.

From	To	Probability
$(0, n, s)$	$(0, 0, s')$	$[\mathbf{A}(0)^{N-n}]_{ss'}$ if $0 < n \le N - C$

The last two cases concern the listening interval at the beginning of a cycle. As already noted in the previous section, a listening interval functions in exactly the same way as a closedown interval, except that it occurs only at the beginning of a cycle. Due to that reason, we need not consider the interruption of a listening interval by a cycle boundary. This leads to the last two cases:

From	To	Probability
$(0, 0, s)$	$(k, 0, s')$	$[z^k][\mathbf{A}(0)^L \mathbf{A}(z)^{N-L}]_{ss'}$
$(0, 0, s)$	$(k, i + 2, s')$	$[z^{k+1}][\mathbf{A}(0)^i(\mathbf{A}(z) - \mathbf{A}(0))\mathbf{A}(z)]_{ss'}$ if $0 \le i < L$

Note that the buffer content u decreases at most by one, i.e. it is skip-free to the left in u, which means that the Markov chain can be written as an $M/G/1$ process with level set $\{u : u \ge 0\}$ and phase set $\{(n, s) : 0 \le n < N, 1 \le s \le M\}$. We give a short account of the solution method in the next section, along with some improvements that are tailored to this specific model.

We now derive relations between the buffer content distribution at embedded points and the distributions during closedown, sleep and listening intervals, in order to eventually establish the distribution at an arbitrary time instant. Essentially, we must 'fill in the gaps' that can occur between two embedded time instants. Let us first give some definitions. The (row) vector generating function $\mathbf{U}_n^A(z)$ records the buffer content distribution at embedded time instant n for each background state. Specifically, the ith entry of this vector is the partial pgf

$$[\mathbf{U}_n^A(z)]_i = \sum_{k=0}^{\infty} z^k \Pr[u = k, s = i, n, \mathbf{A}]. \tag{2}$$

As active slots are just one type of slots, this means that $\sum_n \mathbf{U}_n^A(z)$ is a partial generating function, i.e. $\sum_n \mathbf{U}_n^A(1)\mathbf{1} < 1$.

By means of the $M/G/1$-technique, we will calculate this vector generating function. Likewise, let $\mathbf{U}_n^{\mathsf{S}(j)}(z)$, $\mathbf{U}_n^{\mathsf{C}(j)}(z)$ and $\mathbf{U}_n^{\mathsf{L}(j)}(z)$ denote the vector generating functions at the end of the jth slot of a sleep, closedown and listening interval respectively. From the description of the model, we find the following equations:

$$\mathbf{U}_j^{\mathsf{L}(j)}(z) = \mathbf{U}_0^{\mathsf{A}}(0)\mathbf{A}(0)^{j-1}\mathbf{A}(z) \text{ for } 1 \le j \le L, \tag{3}$$

$$\mathbf{U}_n^{\mathsf{C}(j)}(z) = \mathbf{U}_{n-j}^{\mathsf{A}}(0)\mathbf{A}(0)^{j-1}\mathbf{A}(z) \text{ for } 1 \le j \le C, j < n < N, \tag{4}$$

$$\mathbf{U}_n^{\mathsf{S}(j)}(z) = \begin{cases} \mathbf{U}_0^{\mathsf{A}}(0)\mathbf{A}(0)^L\mathbf{A}(z)^j, & \text{for } n = j+L, 0 < j < N-L, \\ \mathbf{U}_{n-j-C}^{\mathsf{A}}(0)\mathbf{A}(0)^C\mathbf{A}(z)^j & \text{for } j+C < n < N, j > 0. \end{cases} \tag{5}$$

By taking the summation of the generating functions over all types of slots, we find the following generating function $U(z)$ for the buffer content.

$$U(z) = \sum_{n=0}^{N-1} \mathbf{U}_n^{\mathsf{A}}(z)\mathbf{1} + \mathbf{U}_0^{\mathsf{A}}(0)\big(\mathbf{X}^{(L)}(0) + \mathbf{A}(0)^L\mathbf{X}^{(N-L-1)}(z)\big)\mathbf{1}$$
$$+ \sum_{j=1}^{N-C-1} \mathbf{U}_j^{\mathsf{A}}(0)\big(\mathbf{X}^{(C)}(0) + \mathbf{A}(0)^C\mathbf{X}^{(N-C-j)}(z)\big)\mathbf{1}$$
$$+ \sum_{j=N-C}^{N-1} \mathbf{U}_j^{\mathsf{A}}(0)\mathbf{X}^{(N-j)}(0)\mathbf{1}, \tag{6}$$

where $\mathbf{1}$ denotes a column vector with all entries equal to 1 and matrix generating function $\mathbf{X}^{(k)}(z)$ is defined as

$$\mathbf{X}^{(k)}(z) = \sum_{i=1}^k \mathbf{A}(z)^i = \mathbf{A}(z)(\mathbf{I} - \mathbf{A}(z)^k)(\mathbf{I} - \mathbf{A}(z))^{-1}. \tag{7}$$

We apply the normalization condition $U(1) = 1$. Apart from the buffer behavior, the other quantity that is important for a proper evaluation of the sleep-mode mechanism is the expected power consumption E over a slot. Let external parameters E_{A}, E_{L}, E_{C}, E_{S} denote the power consumption during an active, listening, closedown and sleeping slot respectively, then we find that

$$E = E_{\mathsf{A}} \sum_n \big(\mathbf{U}_n^{\mathsf{A}}(1)\mathbf{1} - \mathbf{U}_n^{\mathsf{A}}(0)\mathbf{1}\big) + \mathbf{U}_0^{\mathsf{A}}(0)\big(E_{\mathsf{L}}\mathbf{X}^{(L)}(0) + E_{\mathsf{S}}\mathbf{A}^{(L)}(0)\mathbf{X}^{(N-L-1)}(1)\big)\mathbf{1}$$
$$+ \sum_{j=1}^{N-C-1} \mathbf{U}_j^{\mathsf{A}}(0)\big(E_{\mathsf{C}}\mathbf{X}^{(C)}(0) - E_{\mathsf{S}}\mathbf{A}^{(C)}(0)\mathbf{X}^{(N-C-j)}(1)\big)\mathbf{1}$$
$$+ E_{\mathsf{C}} \sum_{j=N-C}^{N-1} \mathbf{U}_j^{\mathsf{A}}(0)\mathbf{X}^{(N-j)}(0)\mathbf{1}, \tag{8}$$

4   Computational Method

In the previous section, we showed that, by choosing the set of embedded points carefully, we can reduce the problem to an $M/G/1$-type Markov chain, which has a transition matrix with the following block structure:

$$
\mathbf{P} = \begin{pmatrix}
\mathcal{B}_0 & \mathcal{B}_1 & \mathcal{B}_2 & \cdots \\
\mathcal{A}_0 & \mathcal{A}_1 & \mathcal{A}_2 & \cdots \\
 & \mathcal{A}_0 & \mathcal{A}_1 & \mathcal{A}_2 & \cdots \\
 & & \mathcal{A}_0 & \mathcal{A}_1 & \mathcal{A}_2 & \cdots \\
 & & & \ddots & \ddots & \ddots
\end{pmatrix}. \tag{9}
$$

The block matrices $\mathcal{A}_k$ and $\mathcal{B}_k$ can be found using the tables in the previous section. Numerical solutions of this type of Markov chain revolve since the pioneering work of Neuts [15] around the computation of the fundamental matrix $\mathbf{G}$, which is the smallest nonnegative solution of the matrix equation

$$
\mathbf{G} = \sum_{k=0}^{\infty} \mathcal{A}_k \mathbf{G}^k \tag{10}
$$

The stationary probability vector $\boldsymbol{\pi} = [\boldsymbol{\pi}_0, \boldsymbol{\pi}_1, \cdots]$ that satisfies $\boldsymbol{\pi} = \boldsymbol{\pi}\mathbf{P}$, can subsequently be found by the equations

$$
\boldsymbol{\pi}_0 = \boldsymbol{\pi}_0 \mathcal{B}_0^* \text{ and } \boldsymbol{\pi}_n = \left(\boldsymbol{\pi}_0 \mathcal{B}_n^* + \sum_{i=1}^{n-1} \boldsymbol{\pi}_i \mathcal{A}_{n-i+1}^* \right) (\mathbf{I} - \mathcal{A}_0^*)^{-1}, \text{ for } n > 0, \tag{11}
$$

where

$$
\mathcal{A}_{n+1}^* = \sum_{i=n+1}^{\infty} \mathcal{A}_i \mathbf{G}^{i-n-1}, \quad \mathcal{B}_n^* = \sum_{i=n}^{\infty} \mathcal{B}_i \mathbf{G}^{i-n}. \tag{12}
$$

These last expressions are known as Ramaswami's formula, after another pioneer of the matrix-analytic method. There exist a lot of algorithms that aid in computing the desired quantities of interest. Even a straightforward translation of formula (10) constitutes a solid and numerically stable computational method, especially when the Markov chain possesses a strong negative drift. There exist more sophisticated methods as well, for an overview see e.g. [16]. For all these methods, the computational complexity increases very fast with respect to the size of the phase set (here equal to MN). Indeed, as we discern a lot of matrix-matrix multiplications of size MN in the above formulas, the complexity will most often be cubic in MN, that is $O(M^3 N^3)$. As the cycle length N can be substantial, this would seem bad news for the scalability of our approach. However, the structure that is present in the block matrices $\mathcal{A}_k$, allow us to formulate variants of the customary algorithms that are significantly more efficient. Indeed, block matrices $\mathcal{A}_k$ have the following form:

$$\mathbfcal{A}_k = \begin{pmatrix} 0 & \mathbf{A}_k & 0 & \cdots & 0 \\ 0 & 0 & \mathbf{A}_k & \ddots & \vdots \\ \vdots & \ddots & \ddots & \ddots & 0 \\ 0 & \ddots & \ddots & 0 & \mathbf{A}_k \\ \mathbf{A}_k & 0 & \cdots & 0 & 0 \end{pmatrix} = \mathbf{C}_N \otimes \mathbf{A}_k, \qquad (13)$$

where $\mathbf{C}_N$ is the cyclic permutation matrix that maps the vector $(v_1, v_2, \cdots, v_{N-1}, v_N)$ to $(v_N, v_1, v_2, \cdots, v_{N-1})$. Hence the matrix $\mathbfcal{A}_k$ is block circulant, which means that there exists a block row vector $\mathbf{a}$ such that $[\mathbfcal{A}_k]_{ij} = [\mathbf{a}]_{i-j \bmod N}$. In this case, the block vector $\mathbf{a}$ is equal to $[0, \mathbf{A}_k, 0, \cdots, 0]$. Apart from being efficiently storable (only the first block row or block column must be stored), block circulant matrices are closely related to the discrete Fourier transform, and that fact speeds up the basic operations considerably.

Consider two block circulant matrices $\mathbf{M}_1$ and $\mathbf{M}_2$ with first block rows equal to resp. $\mathbf{m}_1$ and $\mathbf{m}_2$. The product $\mathbf{M}_1\mathbf{M}_2$ is again block circulant [19] with first block row equal to $\mathsf{IDFT}(\mathsf{DFT}(\mathbf{m}_1) * \mathsf{DFT}(\mathbf{m}_2))$, where $\mathsf{DFT}(.)$ and $\mathsf{IDFT}(.)$ denote the discrete Fourier transform and the inverse discrete Fourier transform respectively, and the operation $*$ denotes the component-wise product of the blocks: let $\mathbf{c} = [\mathbf{C}_1, \cdots, \mathbf{C}_N]$ and $\mathbf{d} = [\mathbf{D}_1, \cdots, \mathbf{D}_N]$ denote two block vectors of length N, with $M \times M$ block sizes, then $\mathbf{c} * \mathbf{d}$ is equal to

$$\mathbf{c} * \mathbf{d} = [\mathbf{C}_1\mathbf{D}_1, \cdots, \mathbf{C}_N\mathbf{D}_N]. \qquad (14)$$

In order to derive an efficient procedure to compute the fundamental matrix $\mathbf{G}$, we first note that because the matrices $\mathbfcal{A}_k$ are block circulant, $\mathbf{G}$ is block circulant as well. This can be intuited from the stochastic interpretation of the matrix $\mathbf{G}$. Entry $[\mathbf{G}]_{ij}$ denotes the probability that, starting from level n in phase i, the process returns to level $n-1$ in finite time, and that j is the first phase visited in level $n-1$. This probability does not depend on the cycle positions at the beginning and end of such excursions, but merely on the difference (modulo N) between the cycle positions.

All this means we can perform the iterative computation of $\mathbf{G}$ entirely in the DFT domain. Indeed, let $\hat{\mathbf{g}}$ denote the DFT transform of the first block row of $\mathbf{G}$, and let $\hat{\mathbf{a}}_k$ denote the DFT of $[0, \mathbf{A}_k, 0, \cdots, 0]$, then we find from relation (10):

$$\hat{\mathbf{g}} = \sum_{k=0}^{\infty} \hat{\mathbf{a}}_k * \hat{\mathbf{g}}^{*k} \qquad (15)$$

This leads to an iterative procedure whose computational complexity is much better than that of the customary algorithms, as the $*$-operation costs NM^3 floating point operations, a huge contrast with the N^3M^3 floating point operations of the original iteration. This variant of the standard M/G/1 technique may have applications beyond the ones in this paper.

There are some faint correspondences between the technique developed in this section and the paper by Gail et al. [17] for structured Markov chains with limited displacement, in that in both cases there is a two-tier block structure, and the fundamental matrix has a special structure as well, although in our case it is block circulant and in the latter case it is the power of a block companion matrix. The use of DFT transforms in the matrix-analytic method became popular with Meini's work [18].

5 Practical Example

In this section, we show some examples of what is possible with the model developed in the present article. In all examples, we will use an interrupted Poisson arrival process, conform to guidelines of the IEEE community [21] for the 802.11 standard. This is a two-state (on/off) Markov model with Poissonian arrivals with rate λ in the on-state and no arrivals in the off-state. The Markov chain spends a fraction σ of the time in the on-state. The coefficient of correlation between the states in two subsequent slots is $1 - \frac{1}{K}$, where K is a measure for the mean lengths of both on and off periods, given by $\frac{K}{1-\sigma}$ and $\frac{K}{\sigma}$ respectively. It can easily be verified that the matrix generating function $\mathbf{A}(z)$ for this traffic model equals

$$\mathbf{A}(z) = \begin{pmatrix} e^{\lambda(z-1)} & 0 \\ 0 & 1 \end{pmatrix} \begin{pmatrix} 1 - \frac{1-\sigma}{K} & \frac{1-\sigma}{K} \\ \frac{\sigma}{K} & 1 - \frac{\sigma}{K} \end{pmatrix}. \tag{16}$$

The case of uncorrelated states from slot to slot clearly corresponds to $K = 1$. Larger values of K imply that on-slots and off-slots occur more clustered together in time and the arrival process is more bursty. The correlation parameter K is therefore also referred to as the burstiness factor or the burst-length factor of the arrival process [24], [25]. As transmission times have a fixed length of 1 slot, the load ρ is equal to $\rho = \lambda\sigma$.

For the power consumption during the different types of slots we use the values summarized in Table 1. As there are as yet no consumer-end WiMAX devices, we have used the corresponding WiFi data [23] as a guideline. The performance measures we will look at are the mean packet delay and the mean power consumption.

In the first pair of plots, Fig. 2 and Fig. 3, we look at the influence of the traffic correlation on the mean packet delay and mean power consumption. We see a confirmation of the well-known fact that traffic correlation deteriorates the queueing performance tremendously. Also note that the system performance gets worse for very light loads. On the other hand, correlation has a small but marked improvement on the average power consumption. Also note that the

Table 1. Power consumption parameters

Parameter	Value	Description
E_S	0.045 W	Sleep mode power
E_L	1.15 W	Listening mode power
E_C	1.15 W	Power during closedown
E_A	1.65 W	Transmit mode power

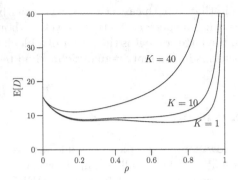

Fig. 2. Mean packet delay versus the load for different levels of correlation, where $N = 32, L = 1, C = 8$, and $\sigma = 0.2$

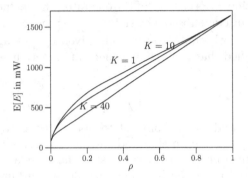

Fig. 3. Energy consumption versus the load for different levels of correlation, where $N = 32, L = 1, C = 8$, and $\sigma = 0.2$

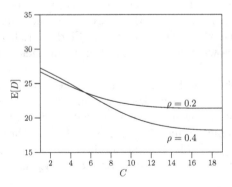

Fig. 4. Mean packet delay versus the closedown time for different values of the load, where $N = 64, L = 1$, and $\sigma = 0.2$

delay gets larger for very light loads, which is intuitively clear from the fact that in that case the system goes into sleep mode for longer time periods, and hence incoming packets must wait for a longer time.

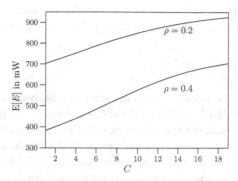

Fig. 5. Energy consumption versus the closedown time for different values of the load, where $N = 64, L = 1$, and $\sigma = 0.2$

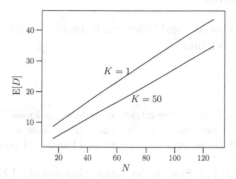

Fig. 6. Mean packet delay versus the cycle length for different levels of correlation, where $L = 1, C = 8, \rho = 0.2, \sigma = 0.2$

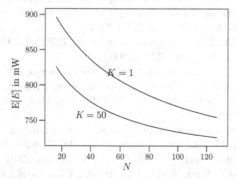

Fig. 7. Energy consumption versus the cycle length for different levels of correlation, where $L = 1, C = 8, \rho = 0.2, \sigma = 0.2$

The next pair of plots, Fig. 4 and Fig. 5 shows the influence of the length C of the closedown interval on the performance measures, for loads $\rho = 0.2$ and $\rho = 0.4$. As can be expected, larger values of C signify an increase of the power consumption and a decrease of the mean delay.

We see the same story, but to a larger degree, in the last two plots, Fig. 6 and Fig. 7, where we show the influence of the cycle length on the performance N.

6 Conclusion

We analyzed Samsung's proposal of a new sleep-mode mechanism to be included in the next version of IEEE 802.16m WiMAX protocol, by means of a queueing model. From the preliminary numerical results, we see that the proposal shows the same qualitative behavior as the customary (802.16e) sleep-mode mechanism, and thus provides the same room for optimization of the parameters C, L and N. This optimization forms the focus of our planned further work.

Acknowledgements

The third author is a Postdoctoral Fellow with the Research Foundation–Flanders (FWO–Vlaanderen), Belgium.

References

1. IEEE 802.16e-2005, Part 16: Air interface for fixed and mobile broadband wireless access systems — Amendment 2: physical and medium access control layers for combined fixed and mobile operation in licensed bands — Corrigendum 1 (February 2006)
2. The Draft IEEE 802.16m System Description Document, IEEE 802.16m-08/003r4 (July 2008)
3. Sleep mode operation for IEEE802.16m, C802.16m-08/721r1 (July 2008)
4. Keep-awake mechanism for 802.16m sleep mode, C802.16m-08/718 (July 2008)
5. Xiao, Y.: Energy saving mechanism in the IEEE 802.16e wireless MAN. IEEE Communications Letters 9(7), 595–597 (2005)
6. Zhang, Y., Fujise, M.: Energy management in the IEEE 802.16e MAC. IEEE Communications Letters 10(4), 311–313 (2006)
7. Han, K., Choi, S.: Performance analysis of sleep mode operation in IEEE 802.16e mobile broadband wireless access systems. In: Proceedings of the IEEE 63rd Vehicular Technology Conference, VTC 2006-Spring, Melbourne, May 7-10, vol. 3, pp. 1141–1145 (2006)
8. Park, Y., Hwang, G.U.: Performance modelling and analysis of the sleep-mode in IEEE 802.16e WMAN. In: Proceedings of the IEEE 65th Vehicular Technology Conference, VTC 2007-Spring, Dublin, April 22-25, pp. 2801–2806 (2007)
9. Seo, J.-B., Lee, S.-Q., Park, N.-H., Lee, H.-W., Cho, C.-H.: Performance analysis of sleep mode operation in IEEE 802.16e. In: Proceedings of the 60th Vehicular Technology Conference, VTC 2004-Fall, Los Angeles, September 26-29, vol. 2, pp. 1169–1173 (2004)
10. Kwon, S.-J., Chung, Y.W., Sung, D.K.: Queueing model of sleep-mode operation in cellular digital packet data. IEEE Transactions on Vehicular Technology 52(4), 1158–1162 (2003)
11. Lin, Y.-B., Chuang, Y.-M.: Modeling the sleep mode for cellular digital packet data. IEEE Communications Letters 3(3), 63–65 (1999)

12. Lee, N.-H., Bahk, S.: MAC sleep mode control considering downlink traffic pattern and mobility. In: Proceedings of the IEEE 61st Vehicular Technology Conference, VTC 2005-Spring, Stockholm, 30 May – 1 June 2005, vol. 3, pp. 2076–2080 (2005)
13. De Turck, K., De Vuyst, S., Fiems, D., Wittevrongel, S.: An analytic model of IEEE 802.16e sleep mode operation with correlated traffic. In: Koucheryavy, Y., Harju, J., Sayenko, A. (eds.) NEW2AN 2007. LNCS, vol. 4712, pp. 109–120. Springer, Heidelberg (2007)
14. De Turck, K., De Vuyst, S., Fiems, D., Wittevrongel, S.: Performance analysis of the IEEE 802.16e sleep mode for correlated downlink traffic. Telecommunication Systems 39(2), 145–156
15. Neuts, M.F.: Structured stochastic matrices of $M/G/1$ type and their applications. Probability: Pure and Applied, vol. 5. Marcel Dekker Inc., New York (1989)
16. Bini, D.A., Latouche, G., Meini, B.: Numerical Methods For Structured Markov Chains. Oxford University Press, Oxford (2005)
17. Gail, H.R., Hantler, S.L., Taylor, B.A.: Non-skip-free $M/G/1$ and $G/M/1$ type Markov chains. Advances in Applied Probability 29(3), 733–758 (1997)
18. Meini, B.: An improved FFT-based version of Ramaswami's formula. Stochastic Models 13(2), 223–238 (1997)
19. Van Loan, C.: Computational frameworks for the fast Fourier transform. Frontiers in Applied Mathematics, vol. 10. Society for Industrial and Applied Mathematics (SIAM), Philadelphia (1992)
20. Berlemann, L., Hoymann, C., Hiertz, G.R., Mangold, S.: Coexistence and interworking of IEEE 802.16 and IEEE 802.11(e). In: IEEE 63rd Vehicular Technology Conference (VTC), vol. 1, pp. 27–31 (2006)
21. Baugh, C.R., Huang, J., Schwartz, R., Trinkwon, D.: Traffic model for 802.16 tg3 mac/phy simulations. Technical report, IEEE 802.16 Broadband Wireless Access Working Group (2001)
22. Sivchenko, D., Xu, B., Rakocevic, V., Habermann, J.: Internet traffic performance in IEEE 802.16 networks. In: European Wireless 2006, Athens, Greece, April 2-5 (2006)
23. Jung, E.-S., Vaidya, N.H.: Improving IEEE 802.11 power saving mechanism. Wireless Networks 14(3), 375–391 (2004)
24. Wittevrongel, S., Bruneel, H.: Discrete-time queues with correlated arrivals and constant service times. Computers & Operations Research 26(2), 93–108 (1999)
25. De Vuyst, S., Wittevrongel, S., Bruneel, H.: Mean value and tail distribution of the message delay in statistical multiplexers with correlated train arrivals. Performance Evaluation 48(1-4), 103–129 (2002)

User Association to Optimize Flow Level Performance in Wireless Systems with Dynamic Interference*

Balaji Rengarajan[1] and Gustavo de Veciana[2]

[1] IMDEA Networks
balaji.rengarajan@gmail.com
[2] University of Texas at Austin
gustavo@ece.utexas.edu

Abstract. We study the impact of user association policies on flow-level performance in interference limited wireless networks. Most research in this area has used static interference models (neighboring base stations are always active) and resorted to intuitive objectives such as load balancing. In this paper, we show that this can be counterproductive in the presence of dynamic interference which couples the transmission rates to users at various base stations. We propose a methodology to optimize the performance of a class of coupled systems, and apply it to study the user association problem. We show that by properly inducing load asymmetries, substantial performance gains can be achieved relative to a load balancing policy (e.g., 15 times reduction in mean delay). Systematic simulations establish that our optimized static policy substantially outperforms various dynamic policies and that these results are robust to changes in file size distributions, channel parameters, and spatial load distributions.

Keywords: User association, flow-level performance, coupled queues, semidefinite programming.

1 Introduction

The high demand for wireless capacity and the increasing volume of traffic mandates the efficient use of available radio resources. Wireless capacity can be substantially enhanced by reusing the entire frequency spectrum at every transmitter instead of sacrificing individual peak and overall system capacity by partitioning it. This increased system capacity and spectral efficiency is achieved at the expense of increased interference. Even in the case of WLANs with frequency reuse, high densities of users in large scale networks could lead to high interference due to the limited number of orthogonal frequencies available under the present standards.

The bursty nature of traffic in typical wireless systems results in dynamic interference which couples performance in the system in a complex manner. For such coupled systems, stability is fairly difficult to establish, and performance is particularly hard to optimize. The capacity of such a system as well as the actual performance that users perceive can be very different from that predicted by a saturated model that assumes

---

* This research was supported by NSF Award CNS-0917067, an Intel Research Council Grant, and IMDEA Networks.

R. Núñez-Queija and J. Resing (Eds.): NET-COOP 2009, LNCS 5894, pp. 166–188, 2009.

that transmitters are always on, see for example [1,2,3]. Without having access to good performance models, many researchers have resorted to intuitive objectives such as load balancing across system resources. In this paper, we show that such load balancing, be it greedily done by users or across the system, may be counter productive when there is dynamic coupling due to interference.

Let us consider some examples where dynamic coupling impacts network functions. Consider the user association problem exhibited in Fig. 1a. Assume that the base stations share the same spectrum, so they interfere with each other when they are concurrently active, which in turn reduces their transmission capacity to users. For simplicity, assume user requests to download files arrive uniformly between base stations 1 and 2. A basic problem in such networks is to decide which base station should serve a new user request. If both the network and traffic demands are *symmetric*, one might intuitively expect that a static policy that associates arrivals with the closest base station, i.e., the one that delivers the strongest signal, and thus balances the offered load, would be 'optimal'. Surprisingly, we will see that this is not the case.

A second example is exhibited in Fig. 1b where wireless nodes relay traffic. Assume nodes contend at random for a shared channel. Depending on the amount of traffic and interference they see, one might optimize nodes' contention probability for the channel so as to minimize overall packet delays. Clearly, performance here is a complex function of the dynamic traffic loads, contention probabilities, and interference seen by nodes. The third example, also shown in the same figure, concerns routing traffic across paths that are link/node disjoint. Unfortunately, transmissions along the paths may directly (or even indirectly) interfere with each other. Should a packet flow with rate λ be split across the two paths, or is it better to route traffic on a single path?

The above exemplify the relevance of dynamic coupling in optimizing network functions at various layers. In the above cases, assuming symmetry in loads and/or the network, one might imagine load balancing might be a good objective, but this need not be the case. For example, it may be preferable to route traffic on a single path so as to avoid interference across paths. In this paper, we focus on the terminal association problem which, as we will see, is already fairly complex. As mentioned earlier, when the channels and traffic load are symmetric, one might expect that associating users'

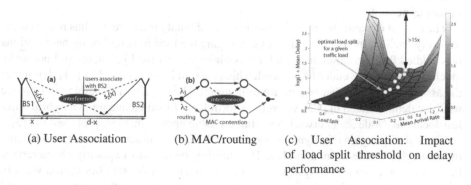

(a) User Association

(b) MAC/routing

(c) User Association: Impact of load split threshold on delay performance

Fig. 1. Examples of network functions impacted by dynamic coupling

requests with the closest base station might be a good strategy. This corresponds to splitting the load evenly between the two base stations. Fig. 1c shows the simulated delay performance (explained in more detail in the sequel) when load split between the base stations is varied from 0.5 (even division of load) to 0.1 (highly asymmetric load division). The results show that the optimal load division depends on the intensity of the offered load, and is not balanced but significantly asymmetric. As exhibited in the figure, where mean delays are plotted on a logarithmic scale, the performance implications can be substantial; load balancing may achieve mean delays 15 times higher versus an optimal asymmetric split. This result is surprising, and reveals the complexity and substantial impact that dynamic coupling can have in the context of wireless networks. This motivates the need for careful analysis that we will carry out in this paper, as well as comparisons with more complex user and system greedy dynamic policies.

Related Work. Various dynamic policies that split load among base stations have been proposed for different contexts. For example, load balancing schemes have been proposed for the scenario where frequency reuse is used to protect against inter-cell interference, and where the traffic carried by the network is voice [4,5,6]. The objective in these works has been to ensure that load is balanced among base stations.

This philosophy has also been used in addressing the case of best effort traffic. When the wireless network is subject to spatially heterogeneous traffic loads, emphasis has been placed on the development of schemes that try to balance the load across base stations. Centralized schemes to jointly balance loads and schedule packets are presented in [7]. Such centralized schemes however, incur excessive communication and computational overhead. In [8], a load balancing scheme that requires much less coordination is considered. The scheme tries to explicitly balance the load across base stations, taking into consideration both the long term rate at which users can be served, and their load. Another idea that was proposed, also in [8], is to lower the strength of the pilot signals that heavily loaded base stations broadcast, so as to discourage users from joining them. A scheme that is similar in spirit is proposed in [9], called MAC-cell breathing, that attempts to balance the load in all base stations. The above mentioned schemes however, assume implicitly that the base stations in the network are always transmitting and thus interfering with transmissions in their neighboring cells. The focus in these schemes is to ensure that the load being served by different base stations in a neighborhood is as similar as possible.

The case of dynamic traffic, with the associated bursty interference, has not been extensively studied. In [10], the effect of equalizing the load in neighboring base stations was studied through simulation, and it was observed that load balancing did not make much of a difference under heavy load. This problem is also studied in [11], but under the assumption that transmissions are orthogonal. The impact of dynamic interference was also demonstrated in [12], wherein the problem of load balancing in a hybrid wireless local area/wide area network was studied using approximations proposed in [13].

The stability region of a dynamic system with interacting servers under load balancing strategies was examined in [14]. The stability region was explicitly characterized in the case of a two server system, and a lower bound on the stability region was obtained for systems with multiple servers. The stability region in the case of static load balancing policies and a class of dynamic policies was also studied in [15]. A surprising result is that the stability region of the system is not always maximized by perfect load balancing across servers. While the above papers address the question of determining the network capacity, they do not provide insight into designing user association policies to optimize performance perceived by users in a system serving a load that is in the interior of the stability region. In contrast, the focus of this paper is on flow level performance, i.e., the actual file transfer delays experienced by users. We obtain bounds on the mean delay experienced by users in coupled systems and use these bounds to design user association policies that optimize flow level performance.

Our contributions. We study a static load allocation scheme that takes into account the long term spatial load being served by the base stations and attempts to minimize the average file transfer delay perceived by users. In addition to short-term, unpredictable variations in the load caused by individual user arrivals and departures, there are predictable long-term variations in the aggregate traffic load depending on the day-of-week, hour-of-day, etc. [16,11]. The proposed scheme is adapted to these long-term traffic patterns, and does not depend on the instantaneous loads or short-term variations. Such a scheme is potentially simpler than dynamic schemes which require knowledge of the instantaneous loads being served, but might be sensitive to errors in the long term traffic estimates. Our contributions in this context include:

1. We propose a methodology to optimize the performance of wireless systems coupled through dynamic interference and apply it to study networks with base stations distributed on a line and on a two dimensional plane. To our knowledge, prior to this work, no closed-form or good approximations were available for general systems with 3 or more coupled queues.
2. For a dynamic model of the user association problem in one dimension, we show that delay optimal static policies are threshold based. Surprisingly, we find that even for a symmetric network, a policy which balances load can be highly suboptimal. Moreover, we find that asymmetric policies can improve average delays seen by users at *all* spatial locations.
3. We show that an optimized static policy (asymmetric) can substantially outperform dynamic policies which are greedy from the user's or system's points of view and achieves performance close to that of a 'repacking' policy. This suggests that an important objective for protocol and network design will be to achieve such asymmetries.
4. We demonstrate through extensive simulations that the proposed policy consistently outperforms conventional, load balancing based approaches under both spatially homogeneous and heterogeneous loads. These results also show that the performance of conventional dynamic schemes is highly dependent on the spatial load, and no single best scheme can be identified.

Organization of paper. The system model is described in detail in Sec. 2. The optimal static association policy is characterized in Sec. 3, while Sec. 4 explores the impact of asymmetric static association policies. The methodology used to pick the optimal static policy is presented in Sec. 5. Simulation results comparing the performance of the static policy to various dynamic strategies is presented in Sec. 6, and the effect of non-homogeneous spatial loads is explored in Sec. 6.4. The sensitivity of delay performance to file size distributions and system and channel parameters is considered in Sec. 6.5, and Sec. 7 concludes the paper.

2   System Model

In Secs. 3-4, we consider two base stations, BS1 and BS2, located a distance d apart on a line, as shown in Fig. 1a. User requests are distributed on the line segment joining the two base stations. We identify a user request by the distance between the user and BS1, denoted by $x \in [0, d]$. The distance between the user and BS2 is then given by $d - x$. User requests arrive according to a spatial Poisson process with mean measure $\lambda(\cdot)$ which is absolutely continuous with respect to the Lebesgue measure, i.e., the rate at which user requests arrive into a set X is $\lambda(X)$. We assume that each user request corresponds to a downlink file transfer which is assumed to be exponentially distributed with mean 1, and the position of the user remains fixed for the duration of the transfer. Once the file transfer is completed, the user leaves the system.

The capacity to users from their serving base station depends on the received signal strength and the strength of the received interference, and is assumed to be monotonically increasing in the perceived signal to interference plus noise ratio (SINR). The base stations transmit, and thereby cause interference only when they are serving users. We assume that the base stations use the processor sharing mechanism to serve active users, i.e., the base station splits time evenly among all users currently being served. Thus, a degree of temporal 'fairness' is imposed.

We classify user association policies into static and dynamic policies. *Dynamic* policies use information about the current loads being served at the candidate base stations when deciding the base station to which a new user is assigned. A *static* user association policy is one that does not take into account the current state of the system when making this decision. A static load allocation policy π partitions the line segment into regions X_1^π and X_2^π, served by BS1 and BS2 respectively. The base station that serves a user at location x under policy π is denoted by $\beta^\pi(x)$. Thus, if $x \in X_1^\pi$ then $\beta^\pi(x) = 1$, otherwise $\beta^\pi(x) = 2$. Base stations transmit at maximum power when there are active associated users, and turn off otherwise. The signal strengths received by a user at location x from BS1 and BS2 are denoted by $s_1(x)$ and $s_2(x)$ respectively. For $i = 1, 2$, we denote the worst and best received signals in $A \subset [0, d]$ by $\underline{s_i}(A) = \inf_{x \in A} s_i(x)$ and $\overline{s_i}(A) = \sup_{x \in A} s_i(x)$. Let N_0 denote the average power of the additive Gaussian noise.

Under a given policy π, we let $\mathbf{U}^\pi(t) = (\mathcal{U}_1^\pi(t), \mathcal{U}_2^\pi(t))$ where $\mathcal{U}_i^\pi(t)$ is the set of locations for users being served at base stations $i = 1, 2$ at time t. Note that since $\lambda(\cdot)$ is non-atomic, users' locations will be distinct with probability 1. Given our assumptions on arrivals and file sizes, $\mathbf{U}^\pi(t)$ is a Markov process since, given all the users locations, one can determine their service capacities and thus departure rates. Note however that its state space is uncountable. By contrast, the process $\mathbf{Q}^\pi(t) = (Q_1^\pi(t), Q_2^\pi(t))$ defined by $Q_i^\pi(t) = |\mathcal{U}_i^\pi(t)|$ for $i = 1, 2$ is on a countable state space, but not Markovian.

This model is similar to that of optimally routing n classes of users to m non-identical queues studied in [17], with an infinite number of classes. However, in our case the problem is further complicated by the fact that the queues at the base stations are coupled (through interference) and the system is non-work conserving. Systems of coupled queues have been analyzed in the past [18,19,20,21], but the problem is extremely diffi-cult and only asymptotic results and closed form expressions in the case of some simple work-conserving scenarios with two coupled queues are known. Even the problem of characterizing the stability of coupled queues which was addressed in [22] is difficult, and one has to employ numerical methods.

2.1 Simulation Model

In the bulk of the simulation results, we consider two base stations located 500m apart with users arriving according to a Poisson process.The three base station network stud-ied in Sec. 6.3 consists of three facing sectors in a hexagonal layout of base stations with cell radius 250m, with users again arriving according to a Poisson process.In Secs. 3-6, where we develop and study the semidefinite programming based method-ology, we assume that the user distribution is spatially homogeneous. In the two base station case, users are assumed to be distributed uniformly on the line joining the two base stations, and in the three base station network, users are assumed to be distributed uniformly within the hexagon formed by the three interfering sectors. We consider non-homogeneous spatial load distributions in the simulation results presented in Sec. 6.4. and the exact load profiles simulated are described therein.

A carrier frequency of 1GHz, and a bandwidth of 10MHz are assumed. The maxi-mum transmit power is restricted to 10W. Additive white Gaussian noise with power -55dBm is assumed. We consider a log distance path loss model[23], with path loss exponent 2. Shadowing, and fading are not considered in these preliminary results. File sizes are assumed to be exponentially distributed, with mean 5MB. The data rate at which users are served is calculated based on the perceived SINR using Shannon's ca-pacity formula. The maximum rate at which a user can be served is capped at 54 Mbps. The base stations transmit at maximum power when they have active users, share ca-pacity across users using a processor sharing mechanism, and turn off otherwise. The mean user perceived delay is estimated within a relative error of 2%, at a confidence level of 95%. Note that the sensitivity of the delay performance to the channel and sys-tem model is examined in Sec. 6.5 where a system with a higher path loss exponent, and cell-edge SNR of 10 dB is simulated.

3   Optimal Static Policies

We begin by considering static association policies in the one dimensional, two base station system. Such policies are defined by the service regions corresponding to each base station, which in turn may depend on the long term offered load $\lambda(\cdot)$. The key result is that under our system model, the service regions are contiguous and thus are defined by a single threshold between the two base stations. The following lemma provides a partial characterization of optimal static policies. Note at the outset that, while this result appears straightforward, the challenge lies in the dynamic nature of the model; specifically, in dealing with the spatial arrivals and departures, the dynamic (on/off) nature of the interference from the neighboring base station, and thus the coupling of delay performance between the two base stations.

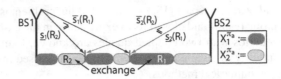

Fig. 2. A sub-optimal load allocation policy

Lemma 1. *Consider the two base station model defined in Sec. 2. For any static load allocation policy π_a with $\mathcal{R}_1 \subseteq X_1^{\pi_a}$, $\mathcal{R}_2 \subseteq X_2^{\pi_a}$ with $\lambda(\mathcal{R}_1) = \lambda(\mathcal{R}_2)$, and such that $\underline{s_1}(\mathcal{R}_2) \geq \overline{s_1}(\mathcal{R}_1)$ and $\overline{s_2}(\mathcal{R}_2) \leq \underline{s_2}(\mathcal{R}_1)$, the policy π_b with $X_1^{\pi_b} = (X_1^{\pi_a} \cup \mathcal{R}_2) \setminus \mathcal{R}_1$, $X_2^{\pi_b} = (X_2^{\pi_a} \cup \mathcal{R}_1) \setminus \mathcal{R}_2$ achieves lower (or equal) average user delay.*

The insight underlying this lemma can be grasped by considering Fig. 2. It illustrates a policy π_a which satisfies the lemma's conditions if signal strength decays monotonically with distance from the serving base station – although part of our system model, this is not required to prove the lemma. Policy π_b is constructed by merely exchanging service regions $\mathcal{R}_1, \mathcal{R}_2$ between the two base stations. The constraints on the best and worst case signal strengths ensure that this exchange is favorable for both base stations at all the associated user locations, which implies the following straightforward fact.

Fact 1. *Under the assumptions on $\mathcal{R}_1$ and $\mathcal{R}_2$ in Lemma 1, and the assumption that capacity is monotonically increasing in SINR, the capacity from BS1 to any user in $\mathcal{R}_2$ is greater than that to any user in $\mathcal{R}_1$ under the same interference regime, i.e., BS2 is transmitting or not. Similarly, the capacity from BS2 to any user in $\mathcal{R}_1$ is greater than that to any user in $\mathcal{R}_2$, whether BS1 is transmitting or not.*

So, the exchange leaves the intensity of arrivals to BS1 and BS2 unchanged, and associates users to them which then can be served at higher capacity under the same interference regime. This allows us to construct a spatial coupling (i.e., by associating users in different regions) for networks under the two policies, showing that the average queue lengths are not increased. The details of this argument are in the appendix, and can be extended to other service disciplines, e.g., FCFS and LCFS.

Theorem 1. *For the two base station model defined in Sec. 2, there exists a static load allocation policy minimizing mean delay corresponding to a spatial threshold $x^* \in [0,d]$ such that a user at location x is served by BS1 if $x \leq x^*$ and by BS2 otherwise. This can also be expressed as a threshold on the ratio of received signal strengths from the two base stations.*

Proof Sketch: Since traffic intensity measure $\lambda(\cdot)$ is non-atomic, if the service regions associated with the BS1 and BS2 are not contiguous, one can construct regions $\mathcal{R}_1$ and $\mathcal{R}_2$ satisfying Lemma 1. Thus, a new policy can be constructed by exchanging regions $\mathcal{R}_1$ and $\mathcal{R}_2$ between the base stations' service regions without increasing the mean delay. This exchange operation can be repeated as long as the service areas are not contiguous. Thus an optimal policy must be defined by contiguous regions, i.e., specified by a spatial threshold. Since the ratio of the received signal strengths is strictly decreasing or increasing with the received signal strength (or distance) from a base station, the policy also be implemented as a threshold on this ratio.

Note that optimal static load allocation policies need not necessarily be unique. For example, consider the case when user requests are distributed homogeneously on the line segment joining the two base stations. If the optimal threshold does not correspond to the midpoint, then by symmetry, the policies that divide the service areas using thresholds at a distance d^* from BS1 and d^* from BS2 will result in identical mean user delays.

4 Optimal Threshold Trends

As a consequence of Theorem 1, we need only consider threshold-based static allocation policies. Fig. 1c exhibits the simulated mean user delay for varying thresholding policies as the (spatially homogeneous) arrival rate between the base stations increases. The policies are characterized by the fraction of load served by BS1 with 0.5 corresponding to load balancing and 0.1 to only 10% of the load. As noted earlier, due to symmetry, the delay performance would be identical if the threshold were moved closer to BS2. For each arrival rate, the optimal load split, i.e., roughly achieving the minimum mean delay, is highlighted. We make the following observations:

1. The location of the optimal threshold is a function of the load on the system.

2. Except at very low loads, delay performance is improved by moving the threshold away from the mid-point, thus inducing asymmetrical loads on the two base stations.

Why does this happen? Load balancing increases parallelism, i.e., base stations are more likely to be simultaneously active. In our model, load balancing associates users with close by base stations providing them a stronger signal. Finally, it would appear that load balancing might be beneficial in terms of statistical multiplexing at the two base stations. If capacity users see were fixed, these points would provide the right insight. Yet, when dynamic interference is present, the capacity users see (particularly those far from either base station) can be substantially reduced by interference, and the fraction of time that base stations interfere with each other depends on the traffic and the load allocation policy. Thus, when arrival rate is low, the probability of the base stations being simultaneously active is low; the base stations operate in an interference-free environment, and load balancing is roughly optimal. For higher arrival rates, performance is strongly impacted by interference, and skewing the load is beneficial. Intuitively, this skew reduces the utilization of one of the base stations, say BS1, and thus the interference it causes on BS2's users, which reduces BS2's utilization, in turn benefiting BS1. However, one cannot overdo this skew as serving users that are far away, and thus have poor received signal, is also detrimental. Finally, it is tempting to assume that as load increases, base stations are always busy and the role of dynamic coupling reduces. Yet, as can be seen, at high loads performance sensitivity is also high, and the gains of an optimal asymmetric split increase further. The optimal threshold reflects a complex tradeoff among dynamic interference, statistical multiplexing, and users' signal strengths.

5 Optimizing the Threshold

In this section, we propose an approximation methodology for optimizing static load allocation policies for the wireless network model in Sec. 2, naturally extended to N base stations serving a possibly higher dimensional region. A policy π partitions the service area such that base station n has service area $\mathcal{X}_n^\pi$ and overall arrival rate $\lambda_n = \lambda(\mathcal{X}_n^\pi)$. Several technical challenges will be addressed. First, we approximate the Markovian model with uncountable state space by one with a countable state space, i.e., we will no longer keep track of the locations of users associated with each base station. This involves introducing an 'effective' rate for *all* users associated with a base station which depends on the busy state of the remaining base stations. Thus, the model preserves the dynamic interference characteristics. Second, we propose an approach to upper/lower bound the performance for the approximated model. Finally, we propose optimizing performance over families of static policies that can be easily parametrized, e.g., for our one dimensional example, one need only determine the threshold. The subsequent section shows the accuracy of the proposed methodology is excellent. We also note that the approach is applicable to a broader set of problems with coupled queues or dynamic interference.

5.1   Countable State-Space Approximation

We let $\vec{Q}(t) = (Q_n(t), n = 1, \ldots, N)$ denote the number of active users at each base station at time t for our approximated process. For notational simplicity, we have suppressed its dependency on π. As mentioned earlier, the capacity to a user depends on *both* its current location and the interference profile it sees from neighboring base stations. We let $\vec{\Delta}(t) = (\Delta_n(t), n = 1, \ldots, N)$ where $\Delta_n(t) = \mathbf{1}(Q_n(t) > 0)$ denotes the status (idle or busy) or the 'interference profile' of the base stations. Note that $\vec{\Delta}(t)$ can take 2^N possible values which we denote $\vec{\delta}^i, i = 1, \ldots, 2^N$. Let $c_n(x, \vec{\delta}^i)$ denote the actual capacity at which base station n can serve a user at location $x \in \mathcal{X}_n^\pi$ under interference profile $\vec{\delta}^i$.

The incremental time users spend in the system is inversely proportional to their service capacity. Thus, the mean rate at which users in a cell can be served depends on the steady state distribution of users that is induced in the cell (which differs from the distribution of arrivals). As shown in [24], the effective service capacity of a base station is given by the harmonic mean of the user capacities, when these are not time varying. In our approximate model, the effective capacity under interference profile $\vec{\delta}^i$ depends *only* on $\vec{\delta}^i$ and is given by

$$c_n^{\vec{\delta}^i} = \left(\int_{\mathcal{X}_n^\pi} \frac{1}{c_n(x, \vec{\delta}^i)} \frac{\lambda(dx)}{\lambda_n} \right)^{-1},$$

the *harmonic mean* of the users service capacities under $\vec{\delta}^i$ weighted by the spatial distribution of arrivals to the base station, i.e., $\frac{\lambda(dx)}{\lambda_n}$. Since, in reality, each user does observe different rates over the course of time depending on the activity level of the neighboring base station, these effective capacities are an approximation. However, users with low received signal strength tend to be located near the cell edge, and are also typically subject to high levels of inter-cell interference. Thus, in most cases, we expect this approximation to be reasonable. Since files have mean size of 1, the total service rate $\mu_n^{\vec{\delta}^i}$ at base station n under interference profile $\vec{\delta}^i$ is given by $\mu_n^{\vec{\delta}^i} = c_n^{\vec{\delta}^i}$. We assume that the system is stable and let μ^* denote an upper bound for the maximum service rate for any base station.

Our approximation is given by a continuous-time Markov chain with transition rate bounded by $\eta = \sum_{n=1}^{N} \lambda_n + N\mu^*$, so it can be uniformized. This will be of use in the sequel. With a slight abuse of notation, we let $\vec{Q}(k)$ denote the state for the uniformized discrete time Markov chain and $\vec{\Delta}(k)$ the associated interference profile at discrete time step k. The transition probabilities for the uniformized Markov chain are as follows. Suppose $\vec{Q}(k) = \vec{q}$ has associated interference profile $\vec{\delta}^i$, i.e., $\delta_n^i = \mathbf{1}(q_n > 0)$ then

$$\mathbf{P}(\text{arrival to queue } n | \vec{Q}(k) = \vec{q}) = \frac{\lambda_n}{\eta},$$

$$\mathbf{P}(\text{departure from queue } n | \vec{Q}(k) = \vec{q}) = \frac{\mu_n^{\vec{\delta}^i}}{\eta} \delta_n^i,$$

$$\mathbf{P}(\text{no change} | \vec{Q}(k) = \vec{q}) = 1 - \frac{\sum_{n=1}^{N} \lambda_n + \mu_n^{\vec{\delta}^i} \delta_n^i}{\eta}.$$

Note that, if it exists, the uniformized chain's stationary distribution is identical to that of the original. Also, its evolution can be represented as a stochastic recursion

$$\vec{Q}(k+1) = \vec{Q}(k) + \vec{X}(k), \quad k = 0, 1, \ldots,$$

where $\vec{X}(k) = (X_n(k), n = 1, 2, \ldots, N)$ denotes increments in the queues. An arrival into queue n at iteration k is represented by $X_n(k) = 1$, a departure by $X_n(k) = -1$ and if the transition corresponds to the self-loop, $\vec{X}(k) = \vec{0}$. Note that $\vec{X}(k)$ and $\vec{Q}(k)$ are not independent, e.g., one can not have a departure from an empty queue. When the system is stable [25,26], there is a stationary distribution for $(\vec{Q}, \vec{X})$ such that

$$\vec{Q} \stackrel{d}{=} g(\vec{Q}, \vec{X}) := \vec{Q} + \vec{X} \tag{1}$$

where $\stackrel{d}{=}$ denotes equality in distribution.

5.2 Performance Bounds

Below, we describe our approach to bounding the system's mean sum-queue length. The approach extends the work of [27] to coupled queuing systems and can also be used to bound other performance metrics, see [28] for more details. Bounds on the mean queue lengths in turn translate to bounds on the mean delay via Little's Law.

Let ψ denote a joint distribution for $(\vec{Q}, \vec{X})$ on $S = S_{\vec{Q}} \times S_{\vec{X}} \subseteq \mathbb{Z}_+^N \times \mathbb{Z}_+^N$ satisfying (1) and with marginals $\psi_{\vec{Q}}$ and $\psi_{\vec{X}}$. Eq. (1) can in this case be rewritten as

$$\psi_{\vec{Q}} = \psi g^{-1}. \tag{2}$$

We partition $S_{\vec{Q}}$ into 2^N regions where the *same* set of queues are non-zero, i.e., $S_{\vec{\delta}^i} := \{\vec{q} : \delta_n^i = \mathbf{1}(q_n > 0), n = 1, \ldots, N\}$ for $i = 1, \ldots, 2^N$. Let $\psi^{\vec{\delta}^i}$ and $\psi_{\vec{Q}}^{\vec{\delta}^i}$, $\psi_{\vec{X}}^{\vec{\delta}^i}$ be the conditional distributions for $(\vec{Q}, \vec{X})$ and its marginals given $\vec{Q} \in S_{\vec{\delta}^i}$. Note that for all states in

$S_{\vec{\delta}i}$ the queues share the same service rates, so follows $\vec{Q}$ is conditionally independent of $\vec{X}$ given $\vec{Q} \in S_{\vec{\delta}i}$, i.e.,

$$\psi^{\vec{\delta}i} = \psi_{\vec{Q}}^{\vec{\delta}i} \psi_{\vec{X}}^{\vec{\delta}i}, \; i = 1, \ldots, 2^N. \tag{3}$$

We shall use multi-index notation in formulating our bounds. For $\vec{\alpha} \in \mathbb{Z}_+^N$ and $\vec{Y} \in \mathbb{R}^N$ we let $\vec{Y}^{\vec{\alpha}}$ denote the term $Y_1^{\alpha_1} \ldots Y_N^{\alpha_N}$, and let $|\vec{\alpha}| = \sum_{n=1}^N \alpha_n$. For $r \in \mathbb{N}$ we define

$$m_{\vec{\delta}i}^{\vec{\beta}} = \mathbf{E}_{\psi_{\vec{X}}^{\vec{\delta}i}} \left[\vec{X}^{\vec{\beta}} \right], \; |\vec{\beta}| \leq 2r \text{ and } i = 1, \ldots, 2^N. \tag{4}$$

Given the transition probabilities on each region $S_{\vec{\delta}i}$ these can be easily computed. Bounds on mean sum-queue length can be obtained by optimizing distributions ψ satisfying the following constraints:

Problem 1. Given $S, S_{\vec{Q}}$ and $S_{\vec{X}}$ solve:

$$\sup / \inf_{\psi} \; \mathbf{E}_{\psi_{\vec{Q}}} \left[\sum_{n=1}^N Q_n \right]$$

$$\text{s.t. } (2), (3), (4),$$

$$\mathbf{E}_{\psi}[1] = \mathbf{E}_{\psi_Q}[1] = \mathbf{E}_{\psi_X}[1] = 1, \tag{5}$$

$$\psi \in \mathbb{M}(S), \psi_Q \in \mathbb{M}(S_Q), \psi_X \in \mathbb{M}(S_X). \tag{6}$$

Here, $\mathbb{M}(S)$, $\mathbb{M}(S_{\vec{Q}})$, and $\mathbb{M}(S_{\vec{X}})$ are sets of positive Borel measures supported on S, S_Q, and S_X respectively, and (5) ensures they are probability measures. The parameter r controls the degree of accuracy of such bounds [29]. As $r \to \infty$ the distribution of $\vec{X}$ is specified exactly, in turn uniquely determining the distributions of $\vec{Q}$ and $(\vec{Q}, \vec{X})$.

To allow numerical computation, we further relax Problem 1 based on joint moments of degree no higher than $2r$. For all $\vec{\alpha}, \vec{\beta}$ such that $|\vec{\alpha}| + |\vec{\beta}| \leq 2r$ and $k = 1, \ldots, 2^N$ we define decision variables:

$$x_k^{\vec{\alpha}\vec{\beta}} := \mathbf{E}[\vec{Q}^{\vec{\alpha}} \vec{X}^{\vec{\beta}} | \vec{Q} \in S_{\vec{\delta}k}] \, \mathbf{P}(\vec{Q} \in S_{\vec{\delta}k}).$$

Note that the mean sum queue length can now be expressed as $\sum_{n=1}^N \sum_{k=1}^{2^N} x_k^{\vec{e}_n, 0}$, where $\vec{e}_n$ is the unit vector with a 1 for queue n.

Eq. (2), or equivalently (1), implies equality for all moments on the left and right hand sides. Note that

$$g(\vec{Q}, \vec{X})^{\vec{\alpha}} = (\vec{Q} + \vec{X})^{\vec{\alpha}} = \sum_{|\vec{\gamma}_1| + |\vec{\gamma}_2| \leq \alpha} g_{\vec{\alpha}}^{(\vec{\gamma}_1, \vec{\gamma}_2)} \vec{Q}^{\vec{\gamma}_1} \vec{X}^{\vec{\gamma}_2},$$

with Binomial coefficients $\{g_{\vec{\alpha}}^{(\vec{\gamma}_1, \vec{\gamma}_2)}\}$. So, we can relax the distributional constraint (2) to a constraint on moments of order no higher than $2r$ giving

$$\sum_{k=1}^{2^N} x_k^{\vec{\alpha}, 0} = \sum_{k=1}^{2^N} \sum_{|\vec{\gamma}_1| + |\vec{\gamma}_2| \leq \alpha} g_{\vec{\alpha}}^{(\vec{\gamma}_1, \vec{\gamma}_2)} x_k^{\vec{\gamma}_1 \vec{\gamma}_1}, \; \forall |\vec{\alpha}| \leq 2r. \tag{7}$$

We also relax constraint (3) by equating the moments of the product distribution to the products of the moments

$$x_k^{\vec{\alpha}\vec{\beta}} = m_{\delta_k}^{\vec{\beta}} x_k^{\vec{\alpha},0}, \ \forall |\vec{\alpha}| + |\vec{\beta}| \le 2r, \ k = 1, \dots, 2^N,$$
(8)

which also subsumes (4). Constraint (5) can be directly expressed as:

$$\sum_{k=1}^{2^N} x_k^{0,0} = 1.$$
(9)

Finally we need to ensure constraints (6) are satisfied by the moments/decision variables. Let $x_k = \{x_k^{\vec{\alpha}\vec{\beta}}, |\vec{\alpha}| + |\vec{\beta}| \le 2r\}$, a moment sequence associated with the set $S_{\vec{\delta}_k}$ for $k = 1, \dots, 2^N$. We denote the cone of moments supported on $S_k = S_{\vec{\delta}_k} \times S_X$ by $\mathcal{M}_{2r}(S_k)$, and it's closure by $\overline{\mathcal{M}_{2r}(S_k)}$. So (6) translates to a moment constraint $x_k \in \overline{\mathcal{M}_{2r}(S_k)}, \ \forall k = 1, \dots, 2^N$. Such constraints can in turn be expressed as certain matrices being positive semidefinite. In general, a necessary condition for the sequence $y = \{y^{\vec{\alpha}\vec{\beta}}, |\vec{\alpha}| + |\vec{\beta}| \le 2r\}$ to be a valid truncated sequence of moments is that the associated moment matrix, denoted $\mathbf{M}_r(y)$, be positive semidefinite, i.e., $\mathbf{M}_r(y) \succeq 0$ – see [27,29] for details. Such constraints must be satisfied by the truncated moment sequences, i.e.,

$$\mathbf{M}_r(x_k) \succeq 0, \ k = 1, \dots, 2^N.$$
(10)

Additionally, note that $S_{\vec{\delta}_k}$ can be specified by an intersection of linear inequalities and so can S_k, i.e.,

$$S_k = \cap_{h \in H_k} \{h(\vec{q}, \vec{x}) \ge 0\},$$

where H_k denotes a set linear functions defining S_k. Clearly $\{x_k\}$ should also be a valid truncated moment sequence when restricted to each half plane $\{h(\vec{q}, \vec{x}) \ge 0\}$. Again it can be shown that a necessary condition for this to be the case is that an associated (localizing) moment matrix, denoted $\mathbf{M}_{r-1}(h, x_k)$, depending on the coefficients of the hyperplane h and x_k be positive semidefinite, see [27,29] for details. The corresponding set constraints is given by

$$\mathbf{M}_{r-1}(h, x_k) \succeq 0, \ \forall h \in H_k, k = 1, \dots, 2^N.$$
(11)

Substituting our relaxed moment and semidefinite constraints into Problem 1 we obtain :

Problem 2. Given $m_{\vec{\delta}_i}^{\vec{\beta}}, |\vec{\beta}| \le 2r$ and $i = 1, \dots, 2^N$, the moments of X, solve:

$$\sup / \inf_{\{x_k | k=1,\dots,2^N\}} \sum_{k=1}^{2^N} \sum_{n=1}^{N} x_k^{\vec{e}_n,0}$$
$$\text{s.t. } (7),(8),(9),(10),(11).$$

Solving this semidefinite optimization problem also yields tighter bounds as r is increased, i.e., more information about X is used, yet at an increased complexity. We shall see that small r suffice in the sequel.

5.3   Determining Optimal Thresholds

As mentioned earlier, when policies can be easily parameterized, one can use these bounds to optimize performance. For our two base-station scenario, Theorem 1 shows the optimal static load allocation policy is a simple threshold. So for any threshold, Problem 2 can be solved to determine bounds on the mean delay, and a simple line search can be used to determine the threshold giving the smallest lower bound on the mean delay. In the case of the three base station network considered in the sequel, we parametrize policies based on weights associated with the base stations, as described in Sec. 6.3.

Fig. 3a exhibits the computed approximate optimal thresholds versus those obtained via brute force simulation for our two base station model. Semidefinite optimization problems associated with relaxations of order 2 were solved using [30] and [31] to determine the necessary bounds. As can be seen both load splits (thresholds) and resulting mean delay performance are very close, supporting the accuracy of our optimization methodology. The optimization approach however provides the flexibility to address complex traffic loads as well as systems with a larger number of base stations.

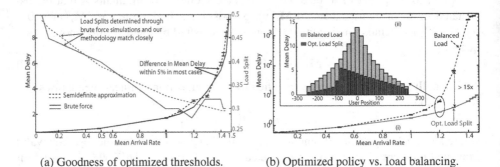

(a) Goodness of optimized thresholds.   (b) Optimized policy vs. load balancing.

Fig. 3. Performance of the optimized static user association policy

6   Performance Comparison

6.1   Comparing Static Policies

Fig. 3b-i again illustrates the impact that the choice of threshold location has on delay performance. The user distribution is spatially homogeneous, so locating the threshold at the midpoint between the base stations corresponds to a static load balancing approach. As can be seen, the resultant mean user delays are greatly decreased by choosing an optimal threshold, particularly at moderate to high system loads. Fig. 3b-ii further exhibits the spatial distribution of user delays under the two schemes when the rate at which user requests arrive in the network is 1.2 per second. Surprisingly, skewing the load towards one base station does not result in a trade off where a subset of the users, e.g., at the heavily loaded base station, experience poor performance. Instead, under the optimal policy, the overall impact of inter-cell interference is reduced such that all users, irrespective of their spatial location or perceived signal strength, see improved performance on average.

6.2 Optimized Policy vs. Dynamic Strategies

Next we compare the performance of the optimal static policy versus the following three dynamic policies:

Greedy User. each new user joins the base station which offers the highest current service rate. This requires knowledge of the new user's capacity to each base station when the neighbor is active/idle and the number of users each is serving.

Greedy System. each new user is assigned to the base station so as to maximize the resulting current sum service rate of the base stations. This policy is more complex than the Greedy User policy as in addition it requires knowledge of the capacity for *all* ongoing users with and without interference.

Repacking. each time a user arrives or leaves, the assignments of *all* users are chosen so as to maximize sum service rate of the base stations via a brute force search – the overheads and complexity of such a scheme would be unrealistically high, yet we hypothesize that it results in the best delay performance among non-anticipative dynamic schemes.

Fig. 4a illustrates the mean delay (logarithmic scale) for varying traffic loads under the above-mentioned greedy policies. Surprisingly, the optimal static policy substantially outperforms the two greedy polices at moderate to high loads. Indeed, at high load, the mean delay of the static policy is 6 times lower than the greedy system policy which itself is orders of magnitude lower than the greedy user policy. As expected, the repacking policy shown in Fig. 4b (linear scale) is the best, but indeed very close to the optimal static policy.

Fig. 4c exhibits the spatial delay distribution under the system-level greedy scheme vs. the static policy. While the greedy policy exhibits perhaps desirable spatially symmetric performance, it is still the case that the optimal static policy gives better performance to all user locations.

6.3 Three Base Station Network

The three base station case can be used as a building block to develop a load allocation policy in a larger network. The number of base stations that can potentially serve a particular user request is unlikely to be very large. A load association policy that decides only between the three strongest base stations for each user request seems to be a

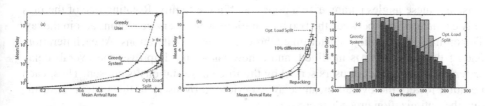

Fig. 4. Mean delay under optimized policy vs. (a) greedy schemes (log scale); (b) repacking scheme (linear scale); (c) greedy system in terms of spatial distribution

reasonable tradeoff between complexity and performance. For the 2 dimensional three base station network described in Sec. 2.1, the form of the optimal static association policy is difficult to characterize. We compute the 'optimal' static association policy within a family of policies that can be easily parametrized.

Weighted Signal Strengths. The first family of policies we consider is parametrized by base station weights. Each base station is assigned a weight and a user is associated with the base station that offers the maximum weighted received signal strength. The weight associated with one of the base stations is set to 1, and a simple gradient descent is used to determine weights for the remaining base stations. The bounding methodology described in Sec. 5.2 is used to approximate the mean delay at each step of the gradient descent algorithm.

Pairwise Optimization. As an alternative to the methodology proposed above, we consider a family of policies where modifying a single parameter while keeping the rest constant allows the load division between two base stations to be modified without affecting the set of users served by the other base station. Note that the policy presented in Sec. 6.3 does not possess this property as changing the weight associated with any base station potentially changes the load served by all three base stations. This property allows the sequential optimization of the policy parameters, and the optimal policy can be determined using a sequence of iterations where one parameter is adjusted in each iteration.

The vector of received signal strengths from the three base stations, $\vec{s}(x) = (s_1(x), s_2(x), s_3(x))$, is projected down on to the two dimensional hyperplane that passes through the origin and is orthogonal to the vector $(1,1,1)$. The family of static policies that we consider divide this hyperplane into regions, and a base station serves all users whose projected signal strength vector falls in its region. The hyperplane is chosen such that users with identical relative received signal strengths from the base stations are mapped to the same point. The projected vector, after an orthogonal transformation is given by $\vec{z} = \{z_1, z_2\}$, where

$$z_1 = \frac{1}{\sqrt{6}}(2s_1(x) - s_2(x) - s_3(x)) \text{ and } z_2 = \frac{1}{\sqrt{2}}(s_2(x) - s_3(x)).$$

The hyperplane is divided into three regions by three rays extending from the origin, as shown in Fig. 5a. Each base station serves the region between two rays as illustrated in the figure. The rays are specified by the angles α, β, and γ that they subtend with the z_1 axis, and these angles parametrize a policy within the family. Rotating one of the rays only exchanges load between the two base stations whose service regions adjoin the ray. The optimal static policy is determined through a series of iterations. At each iteration, one of the parameters is modified, and a new value that improves the overall delay experienced by the set of users served by the three base stations is chosen. Thus, each iteration lowers the overall mean delay experienced by users in the system, ensuring that the optimization procedure converges.

Fig. 5b exhibits the mean delay performance in a three base station network. The repacking policy for this case is a hard combinatorial problem to be solved upon each arrival/departure and so was infeasible. The static load balancing and the greedy user

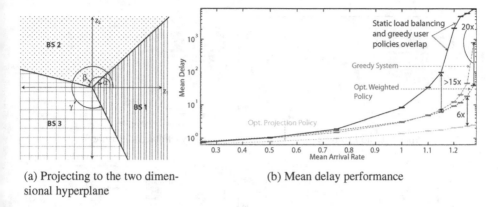

(a) Projecting to the two dimensional hyperplane

(b) Mean delay performance

Fig. 5. Three base station network

policies exhibit similar performance, i.e., overlap, while the optimized static (asymmetric) policy exhibits substantial performance gains. Even the greedy system policy (itself unrealistic in practice) achieves mean delays up to 20 times higher than the weighted signal strength based policy. The projection based policy performs significantly better than even the weighted signal strength policy, reducing the user perceived mean delay further by 6-10 times at high loads.

6.4 Heterogeneous Spatial Traffic Loads

Thus far, all the simulation results exhibited performance under spatially homogeneous user (load) distributions. In this section, we additionally consider various spatially non-homogeneous load profiles for the two base station scenario, as shown in Fig. 6a-6d. The line segment joining the two base stations is split into four quarters, and the load distribution is varied by varying the proportion of users in each quarter. Users in a particular quarter are uniformly distributed within that quarter. Load profiles 2 and 4 are symmetric with respect to the midpoint between the base stations. The users are concentrated near the base stations in profile 2, and the impact of inter-cell interference is diminished. The effective load on the network under this profile is lighter at a fixed user arrival rate compared to profile 4, where users are concentrated close to the midpoint and are strongly impacted by inter-cell interference. The load distribution under profiles 3 and 5 is asymmetric.

The optimized static policy performs consistently well under all spatial load profiles, and performs as well as or outperforms all the dynamic policies. This demonstrates its robustness to spatially heterogeneous traffic loads. Under load profile 3, for example, the optimized static policy outperforms all the other schemes by a wide margin. None of the other schemes perform well under all profiles, while our proposed scheme is able to infer the nature of the spatial load and adapt to it. The relative performance of the dynamic schemes can vary dramatically with the distribution of the spatial load. The greedy system scheme performs well under profiles 1 and 4. However, it is the worst among the schemes under load profile 2. Since the greedy system scheme tries to maximize the average throughput realized by all users in the system, it might deviate from a

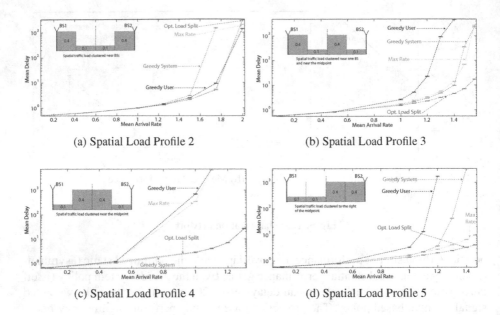

(a) Spatial Load Profile 2   (b) Spatial Load Profile 3

(c) Spatial Load Profile 4   (d) Spatial Load Profile 5

Fig. 6. Delay performance under spatially heterogeneous traffic

load balancing policy so as to ensure that a base station stays idle. However, since users cannot be reassigned, such decisions adversely affect long-term delay performance. The static max rate scheme performs well under load profile 2, where the effect of interference is minimal and under profile 4, where the spatial load is inherently asymmetric. It performs very poorly under the other spatial profiles.

6.5   Performance Sensitivity

Channel Model.   We use parameters that model cellular base stations in an urban environment. We simulate a system consisting of two base stations 2800 meters apart, and compare the performance of the schemes presented earlier using a path loss exponent 3.5, and a cell-edge signal to noise ratio of 10 dB. The data rate at which users are served is calculated using Shannon's capacity formula, after a 6dB backoff is applied to the perceived SINR. Fig. 7a demonstrates that the optimized static policy significantly outperforms the dynamic schemes. The mean delay under the greedy system scheme, for example, is over 50 times the mean delay under the optimized static scheme at high loads. These results demonstrate that the performance trends observed earlier do not depend on the particular channel model used and are a consequence of the dynamics introduced by inter-cell interference.

Long Tailed File Size Distributions.   In the process of determining the optimized static threshold, we still assume that file sizes are exponentially distributed. We assume that the users' file size requirements are log normally distributed with mean 5 MB, and variance 12.276×10^6. The performance of the various schemes under a spatially homogeneous user distribution is shown in Fig. 7b. The relative performance of the

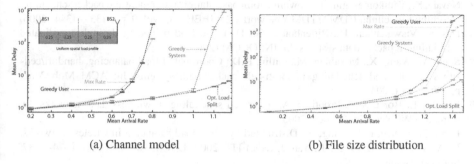

(a) Channel model   (b) File size distribution

Fig. 7. Performance Sensitivity

different schemes is very similar to the case of exponential file sizes. The optimized static policy again results in the best performance, and appears to be robust to variations in the distribution of users' file size requirements.

7   Conclusion

We considered a user-base station association problem in wireless networks serving dynamic loads and thus coupled through interference and proposed a methodology to bound and optimize performance of such systems. For the one and two dimensional models considered, the performance gain from optimized static policies is substantial, even outperforming natural greedy user and system dynamic policies. The load-balancing static policy was shown to be very poor, showing that the critical aspect is inducing asymmetry in the load, even when the network and loads are symmetric. Our simulation results demonstrated that our proposed policy performs consistently well under all spatial loads and is robust to variations in file size distributions and channel parameters. The performance of the conventional dynamic policies was found to vary dramatically with the load distribution, and no one policy performed consistently well. This work suggests the possibility that substantial gains might be achieved if network functions (see e.g., Sec. 1) coupled through interference (or otherwise) are optimized for dynamic loads.

References

1. Borst, S., Hegde, N., Proutière, A.: Capacity of wireless data networks with intra- and inter-cell mobility. In: INFOCOM (2006)
2. Borst, S.: User-level performance of channel-aware scheduling in wireless data networks. In: INFOCOM (2003)
3. Bonald, T., Borst, S., Proutière, A.: Inter-cell coordination in wireless data networks. European Transactions on Telecommunications 17, 303–312 (2006)
4. Das, S.K., Sen, S.K., Jayaram, R.: A dynamic load balancing strategy for channel assignment using selective borrowing in cellular mobile environment. Wirel. Netw. 3(5), 333–347 (1997)
5. Bianchi, G., Tinnirello, I.: Improving load balancing mechanisms in wireless packet networks. In: IEEE ICC, vol. 2 (2002)
6. Yanmaz, E., Tonguz, O.K., Rajkumar, R.: Is there an optimum dynamic load balancing scheme? In: IEEE GTC, vol. 1 (2005)

7. Navaie, K., Yanikomeroglu, H.: Downlink joint base-station assignment and packet scheduling algorithm for cellular CDMA/TDMA networks. In: IEEE ICC, vol. 9, pp. 4339–4344 (2006)
8. Das, S., Viswanathan, H., Rittenhouse, G.: Dynamic load balancing through coordinated scheduling in packet data systems. In: INFOCOM (2003)
9. Sang, A., Wang, X., Madihian, M., Gitlin, R.D.: Coordinated load balancing, handoff/cell-site selection, and scheduling in multi-cell packet data systems. In: ACM MobiCom., pp. 302–314 (2004)
10. Bonald, T., Borst, S.C., Proutière, A.: Inter-cell scheduling in wireless data networks. In: European Wireless Conference (2005)
11. Borst, S., Saniee, I., Whiting, A.: Distributed dynamic load balancing in wireless networks. In: Mason, L.G., Drwiega, T., Yan, J. (eds.) ITC 2007. LNCS, vol. 4516, pp. 1024–1037. Springer, Heidelberg (2007)
12. Zemlianov, A., et al.: Load balancing of best effort traffic in wirel. sys. supporting end nodes with dual mode capabilities. In: CISS (2005)
13. Bonald, T., Borst, S.C., Hegde, N., Proutière, A.: Wireless data performance in multicell scenarios. In: SIGMETRICS (2004)
14. Borst, S., Hegde, N., Proutiere, A.: Interacting queues with server selection and coordinated scheduling - application to cellular data networks. Annals of Operations Research 170(1), 59–78 (2009)
15. Jonckheere, M.: Stability of two interfering processors with load balancing. In: Third International Conference on Performance Evaluation Methodologies and Tools (2008)
16. Borst, S.C., Buvaneswari, A., Drabeck, L.M., Flanagan, M.J., Graybeal, J.M., Hampel, K.G., Haner, M., MacDonald, W.M., Polakos, P.A., Rittenhouse, G., Saniee, I., Weiss, A., Whiting, P.A.: Dynamic optimization in future cellular networks. Bell Labs Technical Journal 10(2), 99–119 (2005)
17. Borst, S.C.: Optimal probabilistic allocation of customer types to servers. In: ACM SIGMETRICS, pp. 116–125 (1995)
18. Fayolle, G., Iasnogorodski, R.: Two coupled processors: The reduction to a Riemann–Hilbert problem. Wahrscheinlichkeitstheorie (3), 1–27 (1979)
19. Guillemin, F., Pinchon, D.: Analysis of generalized processor sharing systems with two classes of customers and exponential services. J. Appl. Prob. 41(3), 832–858 (2004)
20. Borst, S.C., Boxma, O.J., Jelenkovic, P.R.: Coupled processors with regularly varying service times. In: IEEE INFOCOM, vol. 1, pp. 157–164 (2000)
21. Borst, S.C., Boxma, O.J., Van Uitert, M.J.G.: The asymptotic workload behavior of two coupled queues. Queueing Systems 43(1-2), 81–102 (2003)
22. Borst, S., Jonckheere, M., Leskelä, L.: Stability of parallel queueing systems with coupled service rates. Discrete Event Dynamic Systems 18(4), 447–472 (2008)
23. Rappaport, T.S.: Wireless Communications: Principles and Practice. Prentice-Hall, Englewood Cliffs (2002)
24. Rengarajan, B., de Veciana, G.: Architecture and abstractions for environment and traffic aware system-level coordination of wireless networks: The downlink case. In: INFOCOM, pp. 502–510 (2008)
25. Borovkov, A., Foss, S.: Stochastically recursive sequences and their generalizations. Siberian Adv. in Math. 2(1), 16–81 (1992)
26. Loynes, R.: The stability of a queue with non-independent inter-arrival and service times. Proc. Cambr. Phil. Soc. 58, 497–520 (1962)
27. Bertsimas, D., Natarajan, K.: A semidefinite optimization approach to the steady-state analysis of queueing systems. Queueing Syst. Theory Appl. 56(1), 27–39 (2007)
28. Rengarajan, B., Caramanis, C., de Veciana, G.: Analyzing queueing systems with coupled processors through semidefinite programming (2008),
http://users.ece.utexas.edu/~gustavo/papers/SdpCoupledQs.pdf

29. Lasserre, J.: Bounds on measures satisfying moment conditions. Annals of Applied Probability 12, 1114–1137 (2002)
30. Henrion, D., Lasserre, J.: Gloptipoly: global optimization over polynomials with matlab and sedumi. ACM Transactions on Mathematical Software 29(2), 165–194 (2003)
31. Sturm, J.F.: The Advanced Optimization Laboratory at McMaster University: Sedumi version 1.1r3 (2006), http://www.sedumi.mcmaster.ca
32. Marshall, A., Olkin, I.: Inequalities: Theory of Majorization and its Applications. Academic Press, New York (1979)
33. Stoyan, D.: Comparison Methods for Queues and Other Stochastic Models. John Wiley, New York (1983)

Appendix

The following definitions provide a characterization of the stochastic ordering relationship between two process, and will be used in the proof of Lemma 1.

Definition 1 ([32]). *Let* $\mathbf{l}, \mathbf{m} \in \mathbb{R}^n$, *and let* $l_{[1]} \geq \cdots \geq l_{[n]}$ *denote the components of* $\mathbf{l}$ *arranged in descending order.*

$$\mathbf{l} \prec_w \mathbf{m} \ if \ \sum_{i=1}^{k} l_{[i]} \leq \sum_{i=1}^{k} m_{[i]}, \ k = 1, \ldots, n$$

The vector $\mathbf{l}$ *is then said to be* weakly majorized *by* $\mathbf{m}$.

Definition 2 ([33]). *Let* $\mathbf{L}, \mathbf{M}$ *be random vectors taking values in* $\mathbb{R}^n$. $\mathbf{L}$ *is* stochastically weak-majorized *by* $\mathbf{M}$, *written* $\mathbf{L} \prec_w^{st} \mathbf{M}$, *if there exist random vectors* $\tilde{\mathbf{L}}$ *and* $\tilde{\mathbf{M}}$ *taking values in* $\mathbb{R}^n$ *with the same probability laws as* $\mathbf{L}$ *and* $\mathbf{M}$ *respectively, with* $\tilde{\mathbf{L}} \prec_w \tilde{\mathbf{M}}$ *a.s.*

Proof of Lemma 1. We will demonstrate that the policy π_b, which is obtained from π_a by exchanging service regions $\mathcal{R}_1$ and $\mathcal{R}_2$ between the base stations, obtains a lower (or equal) mean delay, see Section 3. This is shown by constructing a pair of coupled processes $\tilde{\mathbf{U}}^{\pi_a}(t)$ and $\tilde{\mathbf{U}}^{\pi_b}(t)$, such that

$$\tilde{\mathcal{U}}_1^{\pi_b}(t) \subseteq \tilde{\mathcal{U}}_1^{\pi_a}(t) \text{ and } \tilde{\mathcal{U}}_2^{\pi_b}(t) \subseteq \tilde{\mathcal{U}}_2^{\pi_a}(t), \tag{12}$$

and such that $\tilde{\mathbf{U}}^{\pi_a}(t) \sim \mathbf{U}^{\pi_a}(t)$ and $\tilde{\mathbf{U}}^{\pi_b}(t) \sim \mathbf{U}^{\pi_b}(t)$. It follows that associated queue length processes $\tilde{\mathbf{Q}}^{\pi_a}(\mathbf{t})$ and $\tilde{\mathbf{Q}}^{\pi_b}(\mathbf{t})$ satisfy similar properties with containment replaced with an inequality. By standard arguments, see [33], this construction suffices to show that $\mathbf{Q}^{\pi_b}(t)$ is *stochastically weak-majorized* by $\mathbf{Q}^{\pi_a}(t)$. As $t \to \infty$ this implies π_b achieves a lower (or equal) mean queue length, and thus, by Little's Law, a lower (or equal) mean delay.

Note that the arrival rates associated with the exchanged service regions are equal so the arrival rate to each base station under the two policies are the same, i.e., $\lambda_1 = \lambda(\mathcal{X}_1^{\pi_a}) = \lambda(\mathcal{X}_1^{\pi_b})$ and $\lambda_2 = \lambda(\mathcal{X}_2^{\pi_a}) = \lambda(\mathcal{X}_2^{\pi_b})$. We couple arrivals of the two processes $\tilde{\mathbf{U}}^{\pi_a}(t)$ and $\tilde{\mathbf{U}}^{\pi_b}(t)$, as generated by a common Poisson process with intensity $\lambda_1 + \lambda_2$. For convenience, we index user requests based on arrival times (including those in the system at $t = 0$), i.e., $1, 2, \ldots$ While arrival times for users to the two systems are identical, their locations may not be, whence we let $x_i^{\pi_a}$ and $x_i^{\pi_b}$ denote the locations of the ith request under policy π_a and π_b respectively.

Suppose $x \in \tilde{U}_1^{\pi_a}(t)$ then let $c_x^{\pi_a}(t)$ be the capacity to the user under policy π_a at time t taking into account the state of the neighboring base station. Since users share capacity via processor sharing, effective service rate to users at locations x and y under the two policies is given by $\mu^{\pi_a}(t,x) = \frac{c_x^{\pi_a}(t)}{Q_{\beta^{\pi_a}(x)}^{\pi_a}(t)}$ and $\mu^{\pi_b}(t,y) = \frac{c_y^{\pi_b}(t)}{Q_{\beta^{\pi_b}(y)}^{\pi_b}(t)}$. So the departure rate of users from BS1 under policy π_a is given by

$$\mu_1^{\pi_a}(t) = \sum_{x \in \tilde{U}_1^{\pi_a}(t)} \mu^{\pi_a}(t,x).$$

We define the overall departure rates $\mu_2^{\pi_a}(t), \mu_1^{\pi_b}(t)$, and $\mu_2^{\pi_b}(t)$ analogously.

Let $\tilde{U}^{\pi_a}(0) = \tilde{U}^{\pi_b}(0)$ so (12) holds at time $t = 0$. Our construction will be such that if (12) holds at some time t then it is satisfied after the next arrival/departure, while maintaining marginal dynamics that are consistent with systems associated with policies π_a and π_b. Although the two systems see the same overall arrival rates they may see different overall departure rates. In our construction we let

$$\nu(t) = \lambda_1 + \lambda_2 + \max(\mu_1^{\pi_a}(t), \mu_1^{\pi_b}(t)) + \max(\mu_2^{\pi_a}(t), \mu_2^{\pi_b}(t))$$

denote the current rate of events for the *coupled processes* and allow fictitious events to ensure the marginal system processes have the correct dynamics. Let the time at which the next event occurs be t' and z be a realization of a random variable Z, which is uniformly distributed on $[0, \nu(t)]$. The coupled process events are constructed as follows:

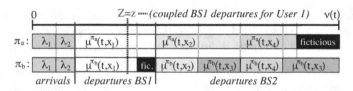

Fig. 8. Example coupling construction for arrivals/deparartures based on realization of Z

Arrivals. If $0 \leq z \leq \lambda_1$, the next event is an arrival, say of user n, to BS1 under both policies. We let random variables $X_n^{\pi_a}$ and $X_n^{\pi_b}$ denote the position of this user under policies π_a and π_b respectively. The distribution $X_n^{\pi_a}$ is given by $\mathbf{P}(X_n^{\pi_a} \in A) = \frac{\lambda(A)}{\lambda_1}$, for a measurable set $A \subseteq X^{\pi_a}$. The position of the user under policy π_b is identical, except if $X_n^{\pi_a} \in \mathcal{R}_1$. In this case, the user's location falls within $\mathcal{R}_2$ with a distribution $\mathbf{P}(X_n^{\pi_b} \in B | X_n^{\pi_a} \in \mathcal{R}_1) = \frac{\lambda(B)}{\lambda(\mathcal{R}_2)}$, where $B \subseteq \mathcal{R}_2$. The states of the processes are updated accordingly. If $\lambda_1 \leq z \leq \lambda_1 + \lambda_2$, the next event is an arrival to BS2 under both policies, with the user's location generated analogously to the above. In either case, arrivals to BS1 or BS2 occurs simultaneously for both policies, so (12) holds at time t'. Also under the above construction the spatial distribution of Poisson arrivals is maintained.

Departures. If $\lambda_1 + \lambda_2 \leq z \leq \lambda_1 + \lambda_2 + \max(\mu_1^{\pi_a}(t), \mu_1^{\pi_b}(t))$, the event is a potential departure from BS1. Consider any user k such that $x_k^{\pi_b} \in \tilde{U}_1^{\pi_b}(t)$. Since (12) holds, user k is also in the system under policy π_a, i.e., $x_k^{\pi_a} \in \tilde{U}_1^{\pi_a}(t)$. Since (12) holds there are only three cases to consider:

1. $\tilde{\mathcal{U}}_2^{\pi_b}(t) = \tilde{\mathcal{U}}_2^{\pi_a}(t) = \emptyset$: BS2 is idle under both policies. If $x_k^{\pi_a} = x_k^{\pi_b}$, $c_{x_k^{\pi_b}}^{\pi_b}(t) = c_{x_k^{\pi_a}}^{\pi_a}(t)$.
Otherwise, $x_k^{\pi_a} \in R_1$ and $x_k^{\pi_b} \in R_2$, so Fact 1 implies $c_{x_k^{\pi_b}}^{\pi_b}(t) \geq c_{x_k^{\pi_a}}^{\pi_a}(t)$.

2. $\tilde{\mathcal{U}}_2^{\pi_b}(t) \neq \emptyset$, $\tilde{\mathcal{U}}_2^{\pi_a}(t) \neq \emptyset$: BS2 is transmitting under both policies, and, as in the previous case, we can argue that $c_{x_k^{\pi_b}}^{\pi_b}(t) \geq c_{x_k^{\pi_a}}^{\pi_a}(t)$.

3. $\tilde{\mathcal{U}}_2^{\pi_b}(t) = \emptyset$, $\tilde{\mathcal{U}}_2^{\pi_a}(t) \neq \emptyset$: In this case, users in BS1 see no interference under policy π_b while they see interference from BS2 under policy π_a. Combining our conclusion in case 1 with the fact that the data rate at which users can be served is an increasing function of the received signal to interference plus noise ratio, we see that $c_{x_k^{\pi_b}}^{\pi_b}(t) \geq c_{x_k^{\pi_a}}^{\pi_a}(t)$.

Also, by assumption $\tilde{Q}_1^{\pi_b}(t) \leq \tilde{Q}_1^{\pi_a}(t)$, thus $\mu^{\pi_b}(t, x_k^{\pi_b}) \geq \mu^{\pi_a}(t, x_k^{\pi_a})$. This permits us to couple User k's departure such that if it leaves under policy π_a, it also leaves under policy π_b. To see this, consider Fig. 8 where $[0, \nu(t)]$ has been subdivided based on the arrival rates and service rates of the users in the system under the two policies. If a user is present in both systems then a set of length $\mu^{\pi_a}(t, x_k^{\pi_a})$ for policy π_a is contained within one of length $\mu^{\pi_b}(t, x_k^{\pi_b})$ for policy π_b. If the user has already left the system under policy π_a, the corresponding set for policy π_b can be arranged arbitrarily (need not be contiguous) within $[0, \nu(t)]$. Unused intervals correspond to dummy events. Which departures (if any) occur for the two systems depend on which sets contain z. However, clearly a departure of User k from BS1 under policy π_a results in the same under policy π_b unless it has already left the system, and (12) still hold at time t'. If $(\lambda_1 + \lambda_2 + \max(\mu_1^{\pi_a}(t), \mu_1^{\pi_b}(t))) \leq z$, the event is a potential departure from BS2, and is treated analogously to departures from BS1.

Since relationship (12) holds after any future event, by induction the relationship holds for all times in the future. We show that the following relationship hold at any given time

1. $\tilde{Q}_1^{P}(t) \geq \tilde{Q}_1^{P_E}(t)$ and $\tilde{Q}_2^{P}(t) \geq \tilde{Q}_2^{P_E}(t)$
2. Corresponding to every user attached to BS1 under policy P_E, there exists a user attached to BS1 under policy P, that is served at lower rates both when BS2 is idle and active.
3. Corresponding to every user attached to BS2 under policy P_E, there exists a user attached to BS2 under policy P, that is served at lower rates both when BS1 is idle and active.

Now, consider a sequence of user arrivals and departures resulting from a static load allocation policy that associates users in region r_1 with base station 1, and users in region r_2 with base station 2. We construct an alternate sample path based on this sequence of user arrivals. User arrivals in region r_1 are moved to instead arrive in region r_2 while still being served by base station 1, and user arrivals in region r_2 are moved to r_1 and served by base station 2. All other user arrivals are unchanged. Since the probability of user arrivals in region r_1 is equal to the probability of user arrivals in r_2, and there are no correlations between user arrivals, the constructed sequence of user arrivals is also representative of the arrival process.

The user queues associated with the two base stations evolve identically until a user arrives in either region r_1 or r_2. As proved previously, this user is served at a higher rate in the alternate sample path. All other users currently in the queues are served at exactly the same rates as in the original sample path as the queue lengths of the two queues are identical. As a result the user that arrived to one of the regions r_1 or r_2 is served and leaves the system earlier in the alternate sample path. This results in all the other remaining users in the system being served at the same or greater rate. Thus, all users in the alternate sample path perceive delays that are less than or equal to those in the original sample path.

Since both systems are ergodic, the sample mean of the user delays in both sample paths converge eventually to the expected values, and the expected user delay in the alternate sample path has to be lower or equal to that in the original. Note that this alternate sample path corresponds to a policy which associates users in region r_2 with base station 1, and users in r_1 to base station 2.

Optimal File Splitting for Wireless Networks with Concurrent Access

Gerard Hoekstra[1,2], Rob van der Mei[1,3],
Yoni Nazarathy[1,4,5], and Bert Zwart[1,3,4,6]

[1] CWI, Amsterdam, The Netherlands
[2] Thales Nederland B.V., Huizen, The Netherlands
[3] VU University Amsterdam, The Netherlands
[4] Eindhoven University of Technology, EURANDOM, The Netherlands
[5] Eindhoven University of Technology, Department of Mechanical Engineering,
The Netherlands
[6] Georgia Institute of Technology, Atlanta, GA, U.S.A.

Abstract. The fundamental limits on channel capacity form a barrier to the sustained growth on the use of wireless networks. To cope with this, multi-path communication solutions provide a promising means to improve reliability and boost Quality of Service (QoS) in areas that are covered by a multitude of wireless access networks. Today, little is known about how to effectively exploit this potential.

Motivated by this, we consider N parallel communication networks, each of which is modeled as a processor sharing (PS) queue that handles two types of traffic: foreground and background. We consider a foreground traffic stream of files, each of which is split into N fragments according to a fixed splitting rule $(\alpha_1, \ldots, \alpha_N)$, where $\sum \alpha_i = 1$ and $\alpha_i \geq 0$ is the fraction of the file that is directed to network i. Upon completion of transmission of all fragments of a file, it is re-assembled at the receiving end. The background streams use dedicated networks without being split.

We study the sojourn time tail behavior of the foreground traffic. For the case of light foreground traffic and regularly varying foreground file-size distributions, we obtain a reduced-load approximation (RLA) for the sojourn times, similar to that of a single PS-queue. An important implication of the RLA is that the tail-optimal splitting rule is simply to choose α_i proportional to $c_i - \rho_i$, where c_i is the capacity of network i and ρ_i is the load offered to network i by the corresponding background stream. This result provides a theoretical foundation for the effectiveness of such a simple splitting rule. Extensive simulations demonstrate that this simple rule indeed performs well, not only with respect to the tail asymptotics, but also with respect to the mean sojourn times. The simulations further support our conjecture that the same splitting rule is also tail-optimal for non-light foreground traffic. Finally, we observe near-insensitivity of the mean sojourn times with respect to the file-size distribution.

Keywords: Concurrent Access, Processor Sharing Queues, Tail Asymptotics, File Splitting.

R. Núñez-Queija and J. Resing (Eds.): NET-COOP 2009, LNCS 5894, pp. 189–203, 2009.
© Springer-Verlag Berlin Heidelberg 2009

1   Introduction

Many of today's wireless networks have already closely approached the Shannon limit on channel capacity, leaving complex signal processing techniques room for only modest improvements in the data transmission rate [7]. An alternative to increase the overall data rate then becomes one in which multiple, likely different, networks are used concurrently because (1) the spectrum is regulated among various frequency bands and corresponding communication network standards, and (2) the overall spectrum usage remained to be relatively low over a wide range of frequencies [10]. The concurrent use of multiple networks simultaneously has opened up possibilities for increasing bandwidth, improving reliability, and enhancing Quality of Service (QoS) in areas that are covered by multiple wireless access networks. Despite the enormous potential for quality improvement, only little is known about how to fully exploit this potential. This motivates us to take a first step towards gaining fundamental insights regarding the implications of the choice of a splitting rule. In particular, we focus on the impact of static splitting rules on file download times. To this end, we study the flow-level performance of file transfers utilizing multiple networks simultaneously.

We study the splitting problem in a queueing theoretical context. Modeling network performance using processor sharing (PS) based models [4, 22, 24] is applicable to a variety of communication networks, including CDMA 1xEV-DO, WLAN, and UMTS-HSDPA. In fact, PS models can actually model file transfers over WLANs accurately [16], hence taking into account the complex dynamics of the file transfer application and its underlying protocol-stack, including their interactions.

The queueing model we consider is the *concurrent access network* model, see Figure 1. There are N PS queues that serve $N+1$ file streams. Stream 0 is called the foreground stream and streams $1, \ldots, N$ are called the background streams. Files of background stream i are served exclusively at PS queue i. Each file of the foreground stream is fragmented (split) upon arrival according to a fixed, splitting rule $\underline{\alpha} = (\alpha_1, \ldots, \alpha_N)$ where $\sum_{i=1}^{N} \alpha_i = 1$ and $\alpha_i \geq 0$, $i = 1, \ldots, N$. After splitting, the fragments are routed to their corresponding queues. Thus, when a file of size B arrives at stream 0, a fragment of size $\alpha_i B$ is directed to each queue i. Once all fragments complete their service, the fragments are reunited, and this completes the file transfer.

Consider a tagged file of the foreground stream that arrives to a network in steady-state. Denote the sojourn time of its i'th fragment operating under the splitting rule $\underline{\alpha}$ by V_i^{α}. This is the time it takes the fragment to complete service at queue i. Denote $\underline{V}_{\underline{\alpha}} = (V_1^{\alpha}, \ldots, V_N^{\alpha})$. The sojourn time of the file through the network is $M_{\underline{\alpha}} = \max \underline{V}_{\underline{\alpha}}$. Our purpose is to analyze the distribution of $M_{\underline{\alpha}}$ and choose a splitting rule $\underline{\alpha}$ such that $M_{\underline{\alpha}}$ is kept minimal.

Our probabilistic and load assumptions are as follows: Arrivals of files in all streams are according to independent Poisson processes with rates $\lambda_i, i = 0, 1, \ldots, N$. File sizes of stream i constitute an i.i.d. sequence of positive random variables with finite expectation. The $N + 1$ sequences of file sizes are mutually independent. Denote the mean file size of stream i by β_i and $\rho_i = \lambda_i \beta_i$ $i =$

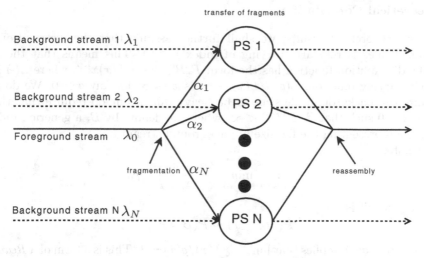

Fig. 1. The concurrent access network

$0, 1, \ldots, N$. We assume that processor sharing queue i operates at rate c_i. For the background streams and queues, denote the corresponding N dimensional vectors $\underline{\rho}$ and $\underline{c}$. We assume that $\rho_0 \mathbf{1} + \underline{\rho} < \underline{c}$. Here $\mathbf{1}$ denotes a vector of 1's. This condition ensures stability irrespective of our choice of splitting proportions.

The Splitting Rule α^*

Our main goal is to provide supporting arguments for using this simple splitting rule:

$$\alpha_i^* := \frac{c_i - \rho_i}{\sum_{j=1}^{N}(c_j - \rho_j)} \tag{1}$$

Note that $c_i - \rho_i$ is the unutilized capacity of queue i due to background traffic and $\sum_{j=1}^{N}(c_j - \rho_j)$ is the total unutilized capacity due to background traffic. Observe that $\underline{\alpha}^*$ does not depend on ρ_0.

To motivate this rule, consider the following heuristic argument: Observe that each queue in isolation is a two class M/G/1 PS queue, allowing us to compute means. It is well known (first shown in [18]) that the mean sojourn time of a job of size B in a processor sharing queue with rate $\tilde{c}$ and load $\tilde{\rho}$ is:

$$\mathbb{E}\left[\tilde{V}|B\right] = \frac{B}{\tilde{c} - \tilde{\rho}}.$$

Assume now for simplicity that $N = 2$ and set $\alpha := \alpha_1$ $(1 - \alpha = \alpha_2)$. Now upon arrival of a foreground job of size B we have

$$\mathbb{E}\left[V_1|B\right] = \frac{\alpha B}{c_1 - \rho_1 - \alpha \rho_0}, \quad \mathbb{E}\left[V_2|B\right] = \frac{(1 - \alpha)B}{c_2 - \rho_2 - (1 - \alpha)\rho_0}.$$

Equating the above quantities and solving for α we obtain α^*.

Theoretical Contribution

For our theoretical results, we shall further assume that the distribution of stream 0 files is regularly varying of index $\nu > 1$. This means that the tail of the distribution function has the form $P(B > x) = L(x)x^{-\nu}$, where $L(\cdot)$ is a slowly varying function: $L(ax)/L(x) \to 1$ as $x \to \infty$ for any $a > 0$. We do not require the background file sizes to be heavy-tailed, but do require that there exist $\epsilon_i > 0$ such that $\mathbb{E}\left[B_i^{1+\epsilon_i}\right] < \infty$, where we denote by B_i a generic random variable representing the file size of background stream i.

Denote,

$$\gamma_m^{\underline{\alpha}} := \min_{i=1,\ldots,N} \left(\frac{c_i - \rho_i}{\alpha_i}\right) - \rho_0. \tag{2}$$

Our key result is:

$$P(M_{\underline{\alpha}} > x) \sim P(B > \gamma_m^{\underline{\alpha}}x). \tag{3}$$

Here $f(x) \sim g(x)$ implies that $\lim_{x\to\infty} f(x)/g(x) = 1$. This is a form of a *Reduced Load Approximation* (RLA) (c.f. [12], [3]) which appears in our network. It is further evident that in this case, the splitting rule which maximizes $\gamma_m^{\underline{\alpha}}$ is $\underline{\alpha}^*$ and thus we have the tail asymptotic optimality:

$$\limsup_{x\to\infty} \frac{P(M^{\underline{\alpha}^*} > x)}{P(M^{\underline{\alpha}} > x)} \leq 1, \ \forall \text{ splitting rules } \underline{\alpha}. \tag{4}$$

This tail asymptotic optimality of the design parameter $\underline{\alpha}^*$ is similar to the tail optimality properties of scheduling disciplines discussed in [5].

In this paper we present a proof of (3) for the case of *light foreground traffic*. In this case we set $\lambda_0 = 0$ and assume that a single foreground job arrives to a steady state system. We further conjecture that (3) is true for the general case. Extensive simulation experiments demonstrate our conjecture to be true.

Related Work

In the context of telecommunication systems the concurrent use of multiple network resources in parallel was already described for a Public Switched Digital Network (PSDN)[9]. Here inverse multiplexing was proposed as a technique to perform the aggregation of multiple independent information channels across a network to create a single higher-rate information channel. Various approaches have appeared to exploit multiple transmission paths in parallel. For example by using multi-element antennas, as adopted by the IEEE802.11n draft [8] standard, at the physical layer or by switching datagrams at the link layer [6, 19], and also by using multiple TCP sessions in parallel to a file-server [23]. In the latter case each available network transports part of the requested data in a separate TCP session. Previous work has indicated that downloading from multiple networks concurrently may not always be beneficial [11], but in general significant performance improvements can be realized [14, 15, 17]. Under these circumstances of using a combination of different network types in particular the transport layer-approaches have shown their applicability [17] as they allow appropriate link layer adaptations for each TCP session.

In [13], the authors investigate the same queueing model in the context of web-server farms. A slight difference is that they do not consider background streams. The major difference is that they analyze the routing policy Join the Shortest Queue (JSQ) while we concentrate on a splitting policy. Note that as opposed to communication networks, splitting in the context of web-server farms is not always possible. Other two related papers are [20] and [21]. In these papers the author analysis a similar network but with FCFS queues and with probabilistic splitting. We further refer the reader to [1], where the authors consider routing policies of the model in a distributed vs. centralized optimization. In general our queueing model falls within the framework of a fork-join queueing network [2]. To the best of our knowledge such a queueing network in which nodes are PS queues have not been investigated.

Organization of the Text

The rest of this paper is organized as follows: In Section 2 we heuristically deduce (3) and (4). In Section 3 we prove (3) for the light foreground traffic case and conjecture it for the general case. In Section 4 we present our simulation results. These results put a strong basis regarding our conjecture. They further show "near insensitivity" with regards to file size distributions and exhibit the fact in the case of light-tailed foreground file sizes our result does not hold. In Section 5 we discuss the relation between minimization of expected sojourn times and minimization of tails.

2   Heuristic Derivation of the Proposed Splitting Rule

Denote by B a random variable distributed as the file size of the foreground traffic files. Denote by $Q_i^{\underline{\alpha}}(t)$ the number of files in queue i at time t, operating under a splitting rule $\underline{\alpha}$. Define,

$$R_i^{\underline{\alpha}}(x) := \int_0^x \frac{1}{1 + Q_i^{\underline{\alpha}}(t)} dt,$$

this is the amount of service that a permanent customer obtains in queue i during the time $[0, x]$ when operating under the splitting rule $\underline{\alpha}$. Further denote by $\underline{R}^{\underline{\alpha}}(x)$ the N dimensional vector of $R_i^{\underline{\alpha}}(x)$. We have the following:

$$P(M_{\underline{\alpha}} > x) = 1 - P(M_{\underline{\alpha}} \le x) = 1 - P(\underline{V}_{\underline{\alpha}} \le x\mathbf{1}) = 1 - P(B\underline{\alpha} \le \underline{R}^{\underline{\alpha}}(x)). \quad (5)$$

The first and second equalities are trivial. The third equality is due to the fact that in a processor sharing queue $P(\tilde{V} > \tilde{x}) = P(\tilde{B} > \tilde{R}(\tilde{x}))$. Observe now that,

$$\lim_{x \to \infty} \frac{1}{x} \underline{R}^{\underline{\alpha}}(x) = \underline{c} - \underline{\rho} - \rho_0 \underline{\alpha} \quad \text{a.s..} \quad (6)$$

As a consequence, since for large x, $\underline{R}^{\alpha}(x) \approx (\underline{c} - \underline{\rho} - \rho_0\underline{\alpha})x$, we can hope to have that for large x:

$$P(B\underline{\alpha} > \underline{R}^{\alpha}(x)) \approx P(B\underline{\alpha} > (\underline{c} - \underline{\rho} - \rho_0\underline{\alpha})x). \tag{7}$$

Here we replaced the N dimensional random process $\underline{R}^{\alpha}(x)$ by its asymptotic value. Heuristically, such an equivalence should hold when $\underline{R}^{\alpha}(x)/x$ converges fast compared to the decay of the tail of B. In the next section we prove this relationship holds in the light foreground traffic case and conjecture it also holds in the general case.

Assuming (7) to be true and continuing heuristically from (5) we have:

$$P(M_{\underline{\alpha}} > x) \approx 1 - P(B\underline{\alpha} \leq (\underline{c} - \underline{\rho} - \rho_0\underline{\alpha})x)$$

$$= 1 - P\left(B \leq \min_{i=1,\ldots,N} \left(\frac{c_i - \rho_i - \rho_0\alpha_i}{\alpha_i}\right) x\right)$$

$$= P(B > \gamma_m^{\alpha} x).$$

Where γ_m^{α} is given by (2). Thus we have heuristically arrived at our reduced load approximation (3).

Observe now that maximizing γ_m^{α} minimizes $P(B > x \gamma_m^{\alpha})$ for any x. As a result, finding the tail optimal $\underline{\alpha}$ means solving:

$$\max_{\underline{\alpha}} \min_{i=1,\ldots,N} \left(\frac{c_i - \rho_i}{\alpha_i}\right) \tag{8}$$

$$\text{s.t. } \sum_{i=0}^{N} \alpha_i = 1$$

$$\underline{\alpha} \geq 0.$$

It is clear that an optimizer of (8) achieves the tail asymptotic optimality (4). We now show that this solution is easily found to be $\underline{\alpha}^*$ as in (1).

Lemma 1. *The unique solution of (8) is given by $\underline{\alpha}^*$.*

Proof. For clarity denote $f_i = c_i - \rho_i$. Denote by $\underline{\alpha}'$ an optimal solution such that (w.l.o.g.):

$$\frac{f_1}{\alpha'_1} \leq \cdots \leq \frac{f_N}{\alpha'_N}.$$

Observe that under $\underline{\alpha}^*$, the objective function is $\sum_{j=1}^{N} f_j$. Thus optimality of $\underline{\alpha}'$ yields:

$$\frac{f_i}{\alpha'_i} \geq \frac{f_1}{\alpha'_1} \geq \sum_{j=1}^{N} f_j,$$

or,

$$f_i \geq \alpha'_i \sum_{j=1}^{N} f_j \quad \forall i.$$

Summing over i we obtain an equality thus equality also holds for each component:

$$f_i = \alpha_i' \sum_{j=1}^{N} f_j \quad \forall i,$$

since the summands are non-negative. This shows that $\underline{\alpha}' = \underline{\alpha}^*$ is the unique optimal solution.

3 The Reduced Load Equivalence

For ease of notation of this section, we fix an arbitrary splitting rule and remove the subscript/superscript $\underline{\alpha}$ from all variables defined previously. Denote,

$$\gamma_i := \frac{c_i - \rho_i - \alpha_i \rho_0}{\alpha_i},$$

and observe that as in (2), $\gamma_m = \min_{i=1,\dots,N} \gamma_i$.

The following lemma states conditions under which the RLA (3) holds for our model. It is a direct application of results from [25] and [12]. See [3] for a survey.

Lemma 2. *Assume that*

$$\max\left(\frac{R_1(x)}{\alpha_1 x}, \dots, \frac{R_N(x)}{\alpha_N x}\right) \to \max(\gamma_1, \dots, \gamma_N) \ a.s., \tag{9}$$

and that there exists a positive finite constant K_m such that

$$P\left(\max\left(\frac{R_1(x)}{\alpha_1}, \dots, \frac{R_N(x)}{\alpha_N}\right) \le \frac{x}{K_m}\right) = o(P(B > \max(\gamma_1, \dots, \gamma_N)x)), \tag{10}$$

then we have the reduced load approximation (3): $P(M > x) \sim P(B > \gamma_m x)$.

Proof. Each of the processor sharing queues is a multi-class queue with two classes: foreground and background. Since background file sizes have a $1 + \epsilon$ finite moment and foreground file sizes have a regularly varying distribution, we apply Theorem 4.2 of [3] (originally from [25]) to obtain:

$$P\left(B > \frac{R_i(x)}{\alpha_i}\right) \sim P(B > \gamma_i x), \quad i = 1, \dots, N. \tag{11}$$

Now using the assumptions (9) and (10) we apply Theorem 1 of [12] to obtain:

$$P\left(B > \max\left(\frac{R_1(x)}{\alpha_1}, \dots, \frac{R_N(x)}{\alpha_N}\right)\right) \sim P(B > \max(\gamma_1, \dots, \gamma_N)x). \tag{12}$$

The rest of the proof is for the case $N = 2$ (the general case is more tedious but not more complicated, it requires using the inclusion exclusion law for the union of N events). First observe:

$$P(M > x) = P(V_1 > x \text{ or } V_2 > x)$$
$$= P(V_1 > x) + P(V_2 > x) - P(V_1 > x, V_2 > x)$$
$$= P(\alpha_1 B > R_1(x)) + P(\alpha_2 B > R_2(x)) - P(\alpha_1 B > R_1(x), \alpha_2 B > R_2(x))$$
$$= P(B > \frac{R_1(x)}{\alpha_1}) + P(B > \frac{R_2(x)}{\alpha_2}) - P(B > \max(\frac{R_1(x)}{\alpha_1}, \frac{R_2(x)}{\alpha_2})).$$

Now assume that $\gamma_1 \leq \gamma_2$ and thus $\gamma_m = \gamma_1$ and $\max(\gamma_1, \gamma_2) = \gamma_2$:

$$\frac{P(M > x)}{P(B > \gamma_m x)} = \frac{P(B > \frac{R_1(x)}{\alpha_1}) + P(B > \frac{R_2(x)}{\alpha_2}) - P(B > \max(\frac{R_1(x)}{\alpha_1}, \frac{R_2(x)}{\alpha_2}))}{P(B > \gamma_1 x)}$$

$$= \frac{P(B > \frac{R_1(x)}{\alpha_1})}{P(B > \gamma_1 x)} + \frac{P(B > \gamma_2 x)}{P(B > \gamma_1 x)} \left(\frac{P(B > \frac{R_2(x)}{\alpha_2})}{P(B > \gamma_2 x)} - \frac{P(B > \max(\frac{R_1(x)}{\alpha_1}, \frac{R_2(x)}{\alpha_2}))}{P(B > \max(\gamma_1, \gamma_2) x)} \right).$$

Now,

$$\frac{P(B > \gamma_2 x)}{P(B > \gamma_1 x)} = \frac{L(\gamma_2 x)}{L(\gamma_1 x)} \left(\frac{\gamma_2}{\gamma_1}\right)^{-\nu} \to \left(\frac{\gamma_2}{\gamma_1}\right)^{-\nu},$$

and from (11) and (12) we have our result. The case of $\gamma_2 > \gamma_1$ is symmetric.

We are now in a position to establish the RLA (3) and the asymptotic optimality of α^*. Our result is for the light foreground traffic case.

Theorem 1. *Consider the concurrent access network in light foreground traffic: there is a single foreground arrival to steady state with $\lambda_0 = 0$. Then the reduced load approximation (3): $P(M_{\underline{\alpha}} > x) \sim P(B > \gamma_{\overline{m}}^{\alpha} x)$ holds.*

Proof. We apply Lemma 2: (9) follows from the SLLN. To see (10) observe that:

$$P(\max(\frac{R_1(x)}{\alpha_1}, \ldots, \frac{R_N(x)}{\alpha_N}) \leq \frac{x}{K_m}) = P(\frac{R_1(x)}{\alpha_1} \leq \frac{x}{K_m}, \ldots, \frac{R_N(x)}{\alpha_N} \leq \frac{x}{K_m})$$
$$= \prod_{i=1}^{N} P(\frac{R_i(x)}{\alpha_i} \leq \frac{x}{K_m})$$

Here we used the fact that under the light foreground traffic assumption all queues are in steady state and there is a single arrival, thus $R_i(\cdot)$ are independent. Now as proved in [12] (Theorem 2), each of the terms can be made $o(P(B > x))$ by choosing K_m appropriately. Thus (10) is achieved.

Using this proof method to repeat the above for the non-light foreground traffic case requires more care in obtaining (9) and (10). We conjecture that these conditions indeed hold and thus:

Conjecture 1. Theorem 1 holds also in the non-light foreground traffic case and thus the splitting rule α^* is in general tail optimal.

In the next section we present simulation results that support the validity of this conjecture.

4 Simulation Results

We now summarize the results of some extensive simulations for evaluating $P(M_\alpha > x)$ on some examples with $N = 2$. For convenience we denote $\alpha := \alpha_1$ ($1 - \alpha = \alpha_2$), similary for α^*. With respect to the tail probabilities, our primary purpose is to assert Conjecture 1 and the behavior of our tail optimality claim (4) by estimating,

$$\alpha^*(x) = \text{argmin}_\alpha P(M_\alpha > x), \quad \text{and} \quad P^*(x) = P(M_{\alpha^*(x)} > x).$$

In this respect, we attempt to observe graphically that $\hat{\alpha}^*(x) \to \alpha^*$ as $x \to \infty$, where we denote estimators by hats. In addition it is fruitful to look at the relative suboptimality for a finite x when using α^* instead of $\alpha^*(x)$. For this purpose we plot:

$$\frac{\hat{P}(M_{\alpha^*} > x) - \hat{P}^*(x)}{\hat{P}^*(x)}. \tag{13}$$

In general, obtaining such results by simulation requires some long runs since we are trying to optimize probabilities of a rare event. In addition, we use the data of the simulation runs to analyze $\mathbb{E}[M_\alpha]$, show that it is nearly insensitive to the file size distributions and compare our splitting rule to the JSQ routing policy.

In all runs we set $\beta_0 = \beta_1 = \beta_2 = 1$ and $c_1 = c_2 = 1$. The types of file size distributions we consider are deterministic, exponential, Erlang 2 (a sum of two i.i.d. exponentials) and Pareto 3 (which is regularly varying with index $\nu = 3$). Here we take the case with support $[0, \infty)$, i.e. $P(B > x) = (1 + x/2)^{-3}$. We further parameterize the runs by the following:

$$\rho = \frac{\lambda_0 + \lambda_1 + \lambda_2}{2}, \quad \kappa = \frac{1 - \lambda_1}{1 - \lambda_2}, \quad \eta = \frac{\lambda_0}{\lambda_1 + \lambda_2}.$$

ρ is the total load on the system, κ is the ratio of free capacity and η is the ratio of foreground to background traffic. These 3 values uniquely define λ_0, λ_1 and λ_2. The table below specifies the parameters of the systems that we have simulated.

System	ρ	κ	η	Distribution 0	Distribution 1	Distribution 2	$(\lambda_0, \lambda_1, \lambda_2)$	α^*
1	0.5	1.5	0.5	Pareto 3	Pareto 3	Pareto 3	$(\frac{1}{3}, \frac{1}{5}, \frac{7}{15})$	0.6
2	0.5	1.5	0.5	Pareto 3	Deterministic	Deterministic	as System 1	-
3	0.5	1.5	0.5	Pareto 3	Exponential	Exponential	as System 1	-
4	0.5	1.5	0.5	Pareto 3	Exponential	Deterministic	as System 1	-
5	0.5	1.5	0.5	Deterministic	Deterministic	Deterministic	as System 1	-
6	0.5	1.5	0.5	Erlang 2	Erlang 2	Erlang 2	as System 1	-
7	0.5	1.5	0.5	Exponential	Pareto 3	Erlang 2	as System 1	-
8	0.5	2.0	0.5	Pareto 3	Pareto 3	Pareto 3	$(\frac{1}{3}, \frac{1}{9}, \frac{5}{9})$	$\frac{2}{3}$
9	0.5	1.0	0.5	Exponential	Exponential	Exponential	$(\frac{1}{3}, \frac{1}{3}, \frac{1}{3})$	0.5

Systems 1 through 7 all have the same rate parameters but vary in the file size distributions. System 8 is an additional example of an unbalanced system having $\kappa = 2.0$ and thus $\alpha^* = 2/3$. System 9 is a balanced system which we have simulated for some additional sanity checking: we expect symmetric behavior of this system.

Simulation runs are composed of 5×10^7 foreground jobs, starting empty. For each system we repeated the simulation for various values of α, using the same seed for all values. We used a fine grid of steps of 0.005 for α within the range of $[\alpha^* - 0.10, \alpha^* + 0.10]$. Outside of this range but within the range $[\alpha^* - 0.25, \alpha^* + 0.25]$ we used a grid of steps of 0.02. In the remaining region we used a grid of 0.05. In addition we ran each system using the Join the Shortest Queue (non-splitting) policy.

Per system we repeated over the above specified range of α using 50 different seeds. Note that keeping the same seed while changing α is useful for optimizing the behavior of the queue given a single sample path of primitive file sizes over α. The total number of runs that we performed is about 30,000 and the total number of foreground jobs that have passed through the simulated system is of the order of 1.5×10^{12}. The simulations use a short and efficient C program which we have coded.

4.1 Tail Behavior

Figure 2 is a representative view of our results. It is a plot of some of the data collected in the simulation runs of System 4. We first estimate the tail

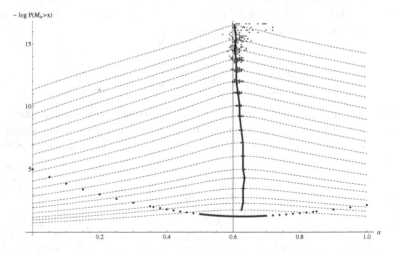

Fig. 2. An illustration of our data analysis approach: System 4 as an example. Dashed curves are plots of estimates of $-\log P(M_\alpha > x)$ for $x = 1, 2, 3, 5, 8, 11, 17, 25, 35, 48, 64, 85, 115, 160, 210, 270, 350, 500$. These curves are maximized by the thick trajectory of $\alpha^*(x)$ which converges to the vertical line at $\alpha^* = 0.6$. Clouds of optimizers over the 50 repetitions are plotted in order to present the dispersion in the argmax estimates. The convex dotted curve is the estimate of $\mathbb{E}[M_\alpha]$ drawn on the same scale.

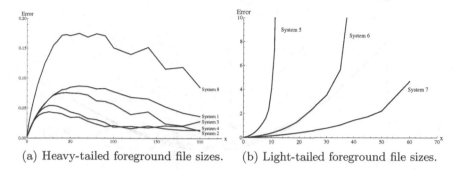

(a) Heavy-tailed foreground file sizes.   (b) Light-tailed foreground file sizes.

Fig. 3. Graphs of (13), the relative distance from optimality for finite x: (a) Heavy-tailed foreground file sizes. (b) Light tailed foreground file sizes.

probabilities $P(M_\alpha > x)$ for increasing values of x. These are plotted on a $-\log$ scale (dashed lines). We then optimize these over α for increasing values of x. This gives us the trajectory of $\hat{\alpha}^*(x)$ (thick curve). Obviously, as x grows the accuracy of this optimization is decreased due to the rarity of the tail event. We pictorially depict this in the figure by plotting the clouds of the 50 $(\text{argmax}_\alpha, \text{max}_\alpha)$ pairs which result for increasing x's, one pair per seed. The thin vertical line in the figure is at $\alpha^* = 0.6$ and indeed, in agreement with the main conjecture and claim of this paper, it appears as the limiting value of $\alpha^*(x)$. We further plot the estimate $\mathbb{E}\,[M_\alpha]$ with a dot for every α in the grid. We comment on the mean in the next subsection.

Note that while Figure 2 shows that the argmax appears to converge rather slowly in x, it is more important to observe that the relative error (13) is always kept low. This can be observed in Figure 3a where we plot (13) for the systems in which the foreground files have a heavy-tailed regularly varying service distribution. The same quantity for systems with light-tailed foreground files is plotted in Figure 3b. Here it appears the relative error explodes. Thus suggesting that α^* is not tail optimal in the light-tailed foreground file size case. Note that the fact that tail optimality of policies/rules is sometimes dependent on the tails of the primitive distributions also appears in other similar works. See for example [5] and [21].

4.2   Mean Behavior

In Figure 4 we plot the estimated values of $\mathbb{E}\,[M_\alpha]$ for systems $1-9$ for a range of α values. We also mark the values of α^* for the various systems by vertical dashed lines and on these lines we dot the mean sojourn times that are obtained for the systems using the JSQ routing policy. We note that at α^*, the width of 99% confidence intervals for the mean (using 50 observations) are in the order of 10^{-4}.

Some comments are due: First observe that in all these examples the following applies:

$$\mathbb{E}\,[M_{\alpha^*}] < \mathbb{E}\,[M_{\text{JSQ}}].$$

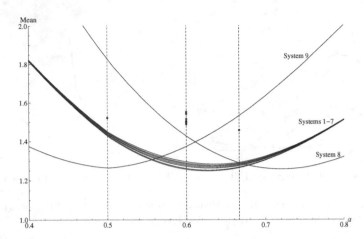

Fig. 4. Mean sojourn time curves. Vertical lines are at $\alpha^* = 0.5, 0.6, 2/3$. Dots on the vertical lines are mean sojourn times using JSQ for the corresponding systems.

Secondly, observe that $\min_\alpha \mathbb{E}\,[M_\alpha] \approx \mathbb{E}\,[M_{\alpha^*}]$. This is a key result: The simple splitting rule that we propose (which is tail optimal) is nearly optimal with respect to the mean. We further comment on this in the next section.

A third observation that appears from Systems $1-7$ is that the mean sojourn times (and mean queue sizes) are quite insensitive to the file size distribution. This property of JSQ was first observed and heavily investigated in [13] (for a system without background streams). Obviously using our file splitting rule and taking $\alpha = 0$ or 1 yields two multi-class PS queues which are known to be exactly insensitive (one of the two queues is single class). When $\alpha \neq 0, 1$ this is no longer the case, yet the figure show that even when using $\alpha = \alpha^*$, the queues are "nearly insensitive". It is important to note that in [13] the authors show that not all routing policies have this "near insensitivity" property (even though a single PS queue is insensitive). Note that the "magnitude" of the sensitivity of our splitting rule is similar to that of JSQ: The maximum difference in mean sojourn times due to the file size distribution is of the order of 4%.

5   Tail Behavior vs. Mean Behavior

Following Theorem 1 and Conjecture 1, we know that α^* is a tail optimal splitting rule. In addition, as observed in Figure 4 it nearly optimizes the mean. We now present two possible reasons for this "*buy one, get an approximate one for free*" relation between the optimization of the sojourn time tail and optimization of the mean sojourn time. Explanation 1 below is specific to our model and uses the asymptotic properties of the processes $R_i(x)$. Explanation 2 that follows presents a simple general result regarding performance analysis of tails and means.

Explanation 1. Fix an arbitrary splitting rule α. Denote $R(x) := \min_{i=1,\dots,N} \frac{R_i(x)}{\alpha_i}$. Observe that $\frac{R(x)}{x} \to \gamma_m$ and $\frac{R^{-1}(x)}{x} \to \frac{1}{\gamma_m}$, where the convergences are a.s.

We have that $P(M > x) = P(B > R(x))$ and thus defining $M(b)$ as the sojourn time of a foreground file of size b, we have that $M(b) = R^{-1}(b)$. Define $\mu(b) := \mathbb{E}[M(b)]$. Since the underlying queue is regenerative, the almost sure convergence implies, $\frac{\mu(b)}{b} \to \frac{1}{\gamma_m}$ as $b \to \infty$. As a result, for large b:

$$\mu(b) \approx \frac{b}{\gamma_m}. \tag{14}$$

Thus selecting α such that γ_m is maximal minimizes $\mu(b)$ when b is large. It thus also approximately minimizes the unconditional sojourn time $\mathbb{E}[M] = \mathbb{E}_B[\mu(B)]$ where B is distributed as a foreground file size.

Further observe that the relation (14) is similar to the distinctive feature of a standard processor sharing queue where the approximate equality is exact. This property also sheds light on the near insensitivity of our system since for large b it behaves similarly to a processor sharing queue.

A further observation is that the splitting rule α^* ensures $\mathbb{E}[V_i]$ equal. We know that $\mathbb{E}[M] \geq \mathbb{E}[V_i]$ and also for a job of size b, we have $\mathbb{E}[M(b)] \geq \mathbb{E}[V_i(b)]$. The auxiliary results we get for the reduced load equivalence suggest that, especially for large jobs, $\mathbb{E}[M(b)]$ and $\mathbb{E}[V_i(b)]$ are not too far apart.

Explanation 2 Consider an arbitrary stochastic model parameterized by α. Assume that the choice of α induces a non-negative distribution $1 - \overline{F}_\alpha(x)$ with mean μ_α. For simplicity assume that α is scalar and that $1 - \overline{F}_\alpha(x)$ is absolutely continuous. In the case of our model (for $N = 2$), $\alpha = \alpha_1$ and the distribution is that of the sojourn time.

Lemma 3. *Assume that $\overline{F}_\alpha(x)$ is unimodal in α and that $\overline{F}_\alpha(x)$ and μ_α are differentiable in α, then there exists an $x > 0$ such that*

$$argmin_\alpha \mu_\alpha = argmin_\alpha \overline{F}_\alpha(x)$$

The above result may be observed in Figure 2 where the trajectory of $\alpha^*(x)$, appears to cross the dotted $\mathbb{E}[M_\alpha]$ curve at its minimum. While typically finding the x at which these two curves cross, is difficult and not of practical importance, systems in which $\alpha^*(x)$ does not vary greatly in x will nearly optimize the mean when optimizing the tail. This appears to be the case in our system. Since $\alpha^*(x)$ trajectories do not vary greatly in x.

Proof. Denote $\tilde{\alpha}$ a minimizer of μ_α. Denote $\mu'(\alpha) = \frac{d}{d\alpha}\mu_\alpha$. Then we have $\mu'(\tilde{\alpha}) = 0$. We also know that $\mu_\alpha = \int_0^\infty \overline{F}_\alpha(u)du$. Denote $\overline{F}'(\alpha, u) = \frac{d}{d\alpha}\overline{F}_\alpha(u)$ Combining the above we have,

$$0 = \int_0^\infty \overline{F}'(\tilde{\alpha}, u)du,$$

Thus $\overline{F}'(\tilde{\alpha}, u)$ is either constantly 0 or has to be both negative and positive and thus there must be a $\tilde{u}$ for which it equals 0. Thus since $\overline{F}_\alpha(x)$ is unimodal in α then for $x = \tilde{u}$ it is optimized by $\tilde{\alpha}$.

Acknowledgments

We would like to thank Yoav Kerner for useful discussions. The work reported in this paper was supported, in part, by the Netherlands Organization for Scientific Research (NWO) under the Casimir project: Analysis of Distribution Strategies for Concurrent Access in Wireless Communication Networks. Bert Zwart's research is partly supported by NSF grants 0727400 and 0805979, an IBM faculty award, and a VIDI grant from NWO.

References

[1] Altman, E., Ayesta, U., Prabhu, B.: Load balancing in processor sharing systems. In: Proceedings of the Second International Workshop on Game Theory in Communication Networks 2008, GameComm 2008, Athens Greece, October 20. HAL - CCSD (2008)

[2] Baccelli, F., Massey, W.A., Towsley, D.: Acyclic fork-join queuing networks. Journal of the ACM 36(3), 615–642 (1989)

[3] Borst, S., Núnez-Queija, R., Zwart, B.: Sojourn time asymptotics in processor-sharing queues. Queueing Systems: Theory and Applications 53(1-2), 31–51 (2006)

[4] Borst, S.C., Boxma, O.J., Hegde, N.: Sojourn times in finite-capacity processor-sharing queues. In: Proceedings NGI 2005 Conference (2005)

[5] Boxma, O., Zwart, B.: Tails in scheduling. SIGMETRICS Performance Evaluation Review 34(4), 13–20 (2007)

[6] Chandra, R., Bahl, P., Bahl, P.: Multinet: Connecting to multiple IEEE 802.11 networks using a single wireless card. In: Proceedings of IEEE INFOCOM (2004)

[7] Cox, D.: Fundamental limitations on the data rate in wireless systems. IEEE Communications Magazine 46(12), 16–17 (2008)

[8] IEEE Unapproved Draft Std P802.11n D3.00. Part 11: Wireless LAN Medium Access Control (MAC) and Physical Layer (PHY), amendment 4: Enhancements for higher throughput (September 2007)

[9] Duncanson, J.: Inverse multiplexing. IEEE Communications Magazine 32(4), 34–41 (1994)

[10] Federal Communications Commission Spectrum Policy Task Force. Report of the spectrum efficiency working group. Technical report, FCC-Federal Communications Commission (November 2002)

[11] Gkantsidis, C., Ammar, M., Zegura, E.: On the effect of large-scale deployment of parallel downloading. In: WIAPP 2003: Proceedings of the The Third IEEE Workshop on Internet Applications, Washington, DC, USA, p. 79. IEEE Computer Society, Los Alamitos (2003)

[12] Guillemin, F., Robert, P., Zwart, A.P.: Tail asymptotics for processor sharing queues. Advances in Applied Probability 36, 525–543 (2004)

[13] Gupta, V., Harchol Balter, M., Sigman, K., Whitt, W.: Analysis of join-the-shortest-queue routing for web server farms. Performance Evaluation 64(9-12), 1062–1081 (2007)

[14] Hasegawa, Y., Yamaguchi, I., Hama, T., Shimonishi, H., Murase, T.: Deployable multipath communication scheme with sufficient performance data distribution method. Computer Communications 30(17), 3285–3292 (2007)

[15] Hoekstra, G.J., Panken, F.J.M.: Increasing throughput of data applications on heterogeneous wireless access networks. In: Proceedings 12th IEEE Symposium on Communication and Vehicular Technology in the Benelux (2005)

[16] Hoekstra, G.J., van der Mei, R.D.: On the processor sharing of file transfers in wireless lans. In: Proceedings of the 69th IEEE Vehicular Technology Conference, VTC Spring 2009, Barcelona, Spain, April 26-29. IEEE, Los Alamitos (2009)

[17] Hsieh, H.Y., Sivakumar, R.: A transport layer approach for achieving aggregate bandwidths on multi-homed mobile hosts. In: MobiCom 2002: Proceedings of the 8th annual international conference on Mobile computing and networking, pp. 83–94. ACM, New York (2002)

[18] Kleinrock, L.: Time-shared systems: a theoretical treatment. Journal of the ACM 14(2), 242–261 (1967)

[19] Koudouris, G.P., Agero, R., Alexandri, E., Choque, J., Dimou, K., Karimi, H.R., Lederer, H., Sachs, J., Sigle, R.: Generic link layer functionality for multi-radio access networks. In: Proceedings 14th IST Mobile and Wireless Communications Summit (2005)

[20] Lelarge, M.: Packet reordering in networks with heavy-tailed delays. Mathematical Methods of Operations Research 67(2), 341–371 (2008)

[21] Lelarge, M.: Tail asymptotics for discrete event systems. Discrete Event Dynamic Systems 18(4), 563–584 (2008)

[22] Litjens, R., Roijers, F., Van den Berg, J.L., Boucherie, R.J., Fleuren, M.J.: Performance analysis of wireless LANs: An integrated packet/flow level approach. In: Proceedings of the 18th International Teletraffic Congress - ITC18, Berlin, Germany, pp. 931–940 (2003)

[23] Rodriguez, P., Kirpal, A., Biersack, E.: Parallel-access for mirror sites in the internet. In: INFOCOM, pp. 864–873 (2000)

[24] Wu, Y., Williamson, C., Luo, J.: On processor sharing and its applications to cellular data network provisioning. Performance Evaluation 64(9-12), 892–908 (2007)

[25] Zwart, A.P.: Sojourn times in a multiclass processor sharing queue. In: Key, P., Smith, D. (eds.) Proceedings of the 16th International Teletraffic Congress - ITC16, Edinburgh, UK, pp. 335–344. North-Holland, Amsterdam (1999)

Control of Multipath TCP and Optimization of Multipath Routing in the Internet*

Damon Wischik, Mark Handley, and Costin Raiciu

UCL
Computer Science department, Gower Street, London WC1E 6BT, UK
Tel.: +44 20 76790442
d.wischik@cs.ucl.ac.uk

Abstract. There are moves in the Internet architecture community to add multipath capabilities to TCP, so that end-systems will be able to shift their traffic away from congested parts of the network. We study two problems relating to the design of multipath TCP. (i) We investigate stochastic packet-level behaviour of some proposed multipath congestion control algorithms, and find that they do not behave how we might expect from fluid modeling: they tend to flap randomly between their available paths. We explain why, and propose a congestion control algorithm that does not flap. (ii) We consider how the path choice offered by the network affects the ability of end-systems to shift their traffic between a pool of resources. We define a 'resource poolability' metric, which measures for each resource how easy it is for traffic to be shifted away from that resource e.g. in the event of a traffic surge or link failure.

Keywords: multipath TCP, congestion control, resource pooling, fluid model, load balancing.

1 Introduction

It has been argued that the natural next step in the evolution of the Internet is to harness the responsiveness of end systems to achieve better network-wide traffic management [1]. If end systems can spread their load across multiple paths in the right way, with the right reaction to the right congestion signals from the network, then traffic will quickly and automatically move away from congested or failed links in favour of uncongested links. This will relieve stress on the Internet's routing system (BGP), which is overwhelmed [2].

End-systems already do shape traffic to some extent: TCP backs off in response to congestion; peer-to-peer systems choose peers that give good throughput; content distribution networks route traffic to well-chosen server farms. These disparate mechanisms can pull in different directions, and they can conflict with the traffic management algorithms used by network operators [3]. There is now

---

* This work arises from participation in the EU-funded Trilogy project, and particular thanks are due to Rolf Winter, Marcel Bagnulo and Pascal Merindol. Damon Wischik is supported by a university research fellowship from the Royal Society.

R. Núñez-Queija and J. Resing (Eds.): NET-COOP 2009, LNCS 5894, pp. 204–218, 2009.

an opportunity to do things right: The Internet Engineering Task Force has recently begun to consider the practical design of a multipath version of TCP [4], and if the longevity of Jacobson's TCP is any indication then we will be living with the consequences of their decisions for several decades. This is a perfect opportunity for mathematical modeling to assist in the design process.

The fundamental challenge of relying on end-systems to manage network-wide traffic is this: how can the system as a whole achieve a desirable outcome, when the end-systems only have local knowledge? The key mathematical insight was provided by Kelly et al. [5], who showed that congestion control at end-systems can be thought of as a distributed control system for solving a network-wide optimization problem. They also realized that routing can be seen as an extension of congestion control—choosing route r_1 rather than r_2 is an extreme case of increasing traffic on the first route and reducing it on the second, and it should presumably be done in response to signals from the network about congestion levels along the two paths. There has since been a great deal of theoretical work on congestion control, some of it on multipath. There are six parts to the multipath-modeling research agenda:

(i) How does a fluid model arise from stochastic packet-level behaviour of a multipath congestion control algorithm?
(ii) Is the fluid model stable? [6, 7, 8]
(iii) What is the flow-level behaviour, assuming that congestion control works properly? [9, 10]
(iv) How should a flow learn which of many possible available paths it should use? What are the consequences for flow-level behaviour, both for multipath TCP[1] and for overlay networks such as peer-to-peer applications? [11, 13]
(v) What sort of path choice does the network need to offer?
(vi) What signals should the network use to affect the behaviour of multipath traffic? What will be the impact of end-system multipath on the peering and pricing contracts between network operators? [3]

This paper fills in some gaps in items (i) & (v). Section 2 is concerned with item (i). It turns out that the stochastic packet-level behaviour is quite surprising, and one needs to think carefully about what fluid models actually represent in order to understand the problem. This is important to get right, if one is to implement a reliable robust congestion control algorithm. We believe we have an algorithm that performs reliably enough to be deployed today, and we have a Linux implementation.

---

[1] Key et al. [11] propose a simple and appealing answer: 'if every end-system is given a choice of two paths, then flow-level behaviour is near optimal'. The theory behind this answer assumes that paths are chosen independently from a large collection of equivalent links. However the Internet's topology is likely to impose correlations between the choices, and this means that two paths might not be sufficient [12], unless the paths are well chosen—hence the need for (v).

Section 3 is concerned with item (v). There are several technologies with which path choice might be offered: end-systems could set a few path selector bits in each packet header and the network could route according to what those bits say; or path choice could be achieved via multiple IP addresses at multi-homed end-systems; or it could be completely managed by overlay networks. It is vital to be able to judge the benefit of each of these mechanisms, so that Internet architects can decide if it is worth making wide-ranging changes e.g. to the Internet's routing system (BGP) or to the interpretation of the IPv4 'type of service' bits.

Terminology. We shall use the word flow to refer to a source of traffic. Each flow can send its traffic over one or more paths. The traffic it sends on a single path is called a subflow.

2   Designing a Multipath Congestion Control Algorithm

There have been four proposals for multipath congestion control algorithms: an original proof of concept by Kelly et al. [5], a translation of techniques from optimization and control theory by Wang et al. [6], and algorithms derived from fluid models by Kelly and Voice [8] and Han et al. [7]. In the latter three pieces of work, it was assumed that fluid models are an appropriate description of the system, and the work was to analyse the stability of the fluid models.

We simulated the algorithms suggested by these fluid models, and found surprising behaviour: even when the stability analysis says the system should be stable, the algorithms behaved erratically, flipping from sending almost all traffic on one path to sending almost all traffic on a different path, and the flips were non-periodic. In this section we describe this behaviour, and explain why it arises and how the fluid models should be interpreted. We will be concerned with the behaviour of an individual flow, not with aggregates.

Another issue is that the proposed fluid models are for an Internet in which a user's traffic rates are determined by the congestion he/she sees, whereas in the current Internet it is his/her window size that is determined by congestion, and traffic rates are determined by window size and round trip time. We describe how to adapt the multipath congestion control algorithm so that it plays nicely with today's protocols (or indeed with any other benchmark for fairness that we might set).

Notation. Suppose a flow can send its traffic over several paths, indexed by r. Suppose that the congestion control algorithm is window-based, like TCP, i.e. it maintains a window size w_r on each path and attempts to keep w_r packets in flight on path r. Congestion is controlled by adjusting the w_r. Let $w = \sum_r w_r$. The throughput i.e. traffic rate it gets on path r is $x_r = w_r/\mathsf{RTT}_r$, where RTT_r is the round trip time on that path. Assume that RTT_r does not vary with congestion; this is reasonable when the routers along the path all have small buffers, and a matter for further study when they do not. Let p_r be the packet drop probability (or the packet marking probability, if Explicit Congestion Notification is enabled).

2.1   Flappiness and Resource Pooling

Consider a very simple system consisting of a single flow with two paths, each path with constant packet drop probability p_r. Assume that both paths have equal round trip time, so that we might as well replace rates by window sizes in the fluid models. Also, assume that the drop probabilities are small so that $1 - p_r \approx 1$. A fluid model from [8, equation (21)[2]] is[3]

$$\frac{d}{dt} w_r(t) = \frac{w_r(t)}{\mathsf{RTT}_r} \Big[a - bw(t)p_r \Big]. \tag{1}$$

This corresponds to the congestion control algorithm that increases w_r by a whenever it receives an acknowledgement on path r, and decreases it by $bw(t)$ when it detects a drop. We will refer to this as Algorithm (1). A simulation is shown in the left column of Figure 1. The horizontal axis shows w_1 and the vertical axis shows w_2, and we plot lines to show the evolution of (w_1, w_2) between drops.

- If $p_1 > p_2$ then the fixed point of (1) is $\hat{w}_1 = 0$ and $\hat{w}_2 = a/(bp_2)$, and the simulation confirms that the algorithm uses path 2 almost exclusively.
- If $p_1 = p_2$ then any solution $(\hat{w}_1, \hat{w}_2)$ with $\hat{w} = \hat{w}_1 + \hat{w}_2 = a/(bp)$ is a fixed point of (1). The simulation shows however that the system flaps between $w_1 \approx 0$ and $w_2 \approx 0$. If we plot $w_1(t)$ as a function of t, we observe that the flaps occur at random (non-periodic) times. Note that multipath congestion control will tend to equalize congestion throughout the network, so the $p_1 = p_2$ case is generic.

We also simulated another algorithm, Algorithm (2), adapted from [7, equation (14)]:

$$\frac{d}{dt} w_r(t) = \frac{w_r(t)}{\mathsf{RTT}_r} \Big[a \frac{w_r(t)}{w(t)} - bw_r(t)p_r \Big]. \tag{2}$$

This algorithm has the same fixed point as (1) but it has gentler increases and decreases. We thought it might be less flappy but Figure 1 shows otherwise.

What causes flappiness? To understand how flappiness arises, consider a somewhat contrived scenario in which both paths use a single bottleneck link, and packet drops occur whenever $w_1 + w_2 = 100$, and the flow is using Algorithm (1) with $a = 1$ and $b = 1/4$. Starting from $w_1 = w_2 = 1$, both windows increase until $w_1 = w_2 = 50$. Suppose that path 1 experiences a drop and w_1 decreases. The two window sizes will then grow until $(w_1, w_2) = (33.3, 66.7)$. Just one more drop on path 1 is enough to push w_1 down to 8.3 packets. At this point it will take six consecutive drops on path 2 for the two windows to equalize again.

---

[2] The control-theoretic analyses in [7, 8] uses $x_r(t - \mathsf{RTT}_r)$ rather than $x_r(t)$, to reflect the fact that acknowledgements received at time t are for packets sent at time $t - \mathsf{RTT}_r$; but they also show that removing the lag to give (1) should only improve the stability of the dynamical system.

[3] It is understood in this and in all other fluid model equations that if $w_r = 0$ then we take the positive part of the right hand side.

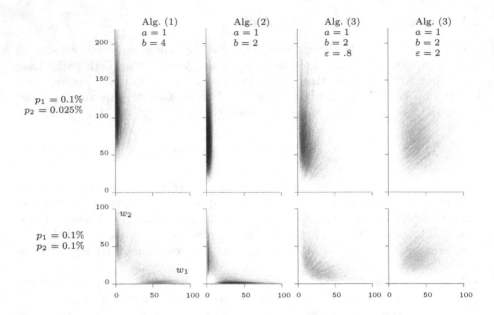

Fig. 1. Window size dynamics for a two-path flow. The axes are w_1 and w_2, and the plots show the increase phases of the process $(w_1(t), w_2(t))$.

There seem to be two drivers of flappiness. (i) Both algorithms move traffic off congested paths and onto uncongested paths. Even when two paths have the same drop probability, chance fluctuations will mean that from time to time one path suffers a few extra drops, so it will look momentarily more congested, so the flow will flip to the other path. To overcome this, it will be necessary either to accept less perfect resource pooling, or to use smoothed estimates of loss which will result in a more sluggish response. (ii) The second driver of flappiness in Algorithm (1) is the problem of capture: if flow 1 experiences a couple of drops, flow 2 needs to experience many more drops to bring the traffic rates back into balance.

We have simulated networks where the drop probabilities are not fixed but instead depend on the offered traffic, and still find flappiness.

Interpretation of fluid models. The issue with the fluid model is that it only holds in the limit as the number of flows tends to infinity, and in this limit $w_r(t)$ represents the average window size among a large ensemble of equivalent flows at time t. This was argued heuristically in [14], and proved rigorously for a simplified model in [15]. In a large ensemble of multipath flows, any linear combination $(\lambda, 1 - \lambda)\hat{w}$ may appear as the average, if each individual flow flaps randomly between $(w_1, w_2) = (0, \hat{w})$ and $(w_1, w_2) = (\hat{w}, 0)$. We suspect that λ performs a symmetric random walk in $[0, 1]$, since by symmetry it is just as likely for a flow to flip from path 1 to path 2 as *vice versa*.

We note as an aside that the illustrations in this paper come from a semi-fluid simulator along the lines of [16], which we validated using a packet-level implementation. Our simulator solves a differential equation for the increase phase, e.g. $\dot{w}_r(t) = (w_r(t)/\mathsf{RTT}_r)(aw_r(t)/w(t))$ for algorithm (2), and applies packet drops randomly according to an inhomogeneous Poisson process.

2.2   Alleviating Flappiness

Consider Algorithm (3), the congestion controller corresponding to

$$\frac{d}{dt}w_r(t) = \frac{w_r(t)}{\mathsf{RTT}_r}\left[\frac{a}{w(t)}\left(\frac{aw_r(t)}{w(t)}\right)^{1-\varepsilon} - bp_r w_r(t)\right].\tag{3}$$

At $\varepsilon = 0$ this is flappy, and if there are several paths with joint lowest drop probability then the fixed point is not unique. It is much like Algorithm (2), except for the $1/w(t)$ in the increase term which we put in so as to better reflect TCP's increase rule. At $\varepsilon = 2$ the subflows are uncoupled, and Figure 1 shows that this is completely unflappy and completely useless at shifting traffic away from the more congested path. At $\varepsilon = 0.8$ there is a reasonable compromise between flappiness and load-shifting.

For any $\varepsilon > 0$ it is easy to solve for the fixed point of (3) and to see it is unique[4]. The fixed point solves $w_r = (a^{2-\varepsilon}/bp_r\hat{w}^{2-\varepsilon})^{1/\varepsilon}$. Note that the total window size $\hat{w}$ is divided between paths in proportion to $1/p_r^{1/\varepsilon}$, so the smaller ε the greater the aversion to congestion. We can also use the equation $\hat{w} = \sum_r \hat{w}_r$ to solve for $\hat{w}$. It turns out that if there are several paths through a single bottleneck link, then $\hat{w}$ depends on the number of paths that the flow is using; this is clearly undesirable on grounds of fairness, and it was not the case for (1) or (2). In the next section we give a general-purpose method for removing unfairness.

2.3   Compensating for Round Trip Time

Here is a simple way to design a multipath congestion control algorithm so that it fits in gracefully with other traffic, in particular with TCP and its dependence on round trip time. We set ourselves two goals. To state them, we first define $\hat{x}_r^{\mathsf{TCP}} = \sqrt{2/p_r}/\mathsf{RTT}_r$ to be the throughput that a single-path TCP flow would get if it experienced packet drop probability p_r and had round trip time RTT_r. Let $\hat{w}_r^{\mathsf{TCP}} = \sqrt{2/p_r}$ be the corresponding window size. Our goals are (i) A multipath flow should not get more than $\hat{x}_r^{\mathsf{TCP}}$ on any single path, though it may get less. This means that other flows cannot suffer, and may benefit, if I deploy multipath TCP. (ii) A multipath flow should get total throughput $\max_r \hat{x}_r^{\mathsf{TCP}}$. This means that the more paths I have access to the more I benefit. These goals explicitly use TCP as a reference, but the argument applies straightforwardly to any other reference throughput formula $\hat{x}_r^{\mathsf{ref}}(p_r, \mathsf{RTT}_r)$.

---

[4] There was also a $\varepsilon > 0$ parameter introduced in [7, equation (1)] to guarantee uniqueness of the fixed point; we however intend that ε should be a design parameter, say $\varepsilon \approx 0.8$, rather than a negligible term for making the maths tractable.

Our goals can be achieved using a congestion controller corresponding to the fluid model

$$\frac{d}{dt}w_r(t) = x_r(t)\left[\frac{a}{w(t)}\left(\frac{aw_r(t)}{w(t)}\right)^{1-\varepsilon} \wedge \frac{1}{w_r(t)} - p_r\frac{w_r(t)}{2}\right] \qquad (4)$$

where $x \wedge y = \min(x, y)$. The $\wedge$ ensures that a window does not increase any faster than TCP would, and the decreases are the same as TCP, so goal (i) is satisfied by a coupling argument. To satisfy goal (ii), we want to choose a so that the equilibrium window sizes satisfy

$$\sum_r \frac{\hat{w}_r}{\mathsf{RTT}_r} = \max_r \frac{\hat{w}_r^{\mathsf{TCP}}}{\mathsf{RTT}_r}. \qquad (5)$$

Figure 2 illustrates the constraints. The axes show $\hat{w}_1$ and $\hat{w}_2$ for a two-path flow with $p_1 = 0.025\%$, $p_2 = 0.1\%$, and $\mathsf{RTT}_1 = 2.5\mathsf{RTT}_2$. Goal (i) says that $(\hat{w}_1, \hat{w}_2)$ should lie below and to the left of the dashed lines. Goal (ii) says that it should lie on the sloping line. Since $p_1 < p_2$ we would ideally put as much traffic as possible on path 1, i.e. choose the black dot in the leftmost plot. In the middle plot, the bold line shows the fixed points $(\hat{w}_1, \hat{w}_2)$ that we can get by tuning a (with $\varepsilon = 0.8$); we propose to choose a to just meet goal (ii), i.e. to choose the black dot. To calculate a, first write out the fixed point equation for (4),

$$\frac{a}{\hat{w}}\left(\frac{a\hat{w}_r}{\hat{w}}\right)^{1-\varepsilon} \wedge \frac{1}{\hat{w}_r} = p_r\frac{\hat{w}_r}{2},$$

then rewrite it in terms of $\hat{w}_r^{\mathsf{TCP}} = \sqrt{2/p_r}$ to get

$$\hat{w}_r^{\mathsf{TCP}} = \hat{w}_r \vee \hat{w}_r^{\varepsilon/2}(\hat{w}/a)^{1-\varepsilon/2}$$

where $x \vee y = \max(x, y)$. Substituting into (5),

$$\sum_r \frac{\hat{w}_r}{\mathsf{RTT}_r} = \max_r\left\{\frac{\hat{w}_r}{\mathsf{RTT}_r} \vee \frac{\hat{w}_r^{\varepsilon/2}(\hat{w}/a)^{1-\varepsilon/2}}{\mathsf{RTT}_r}\right\}.$$

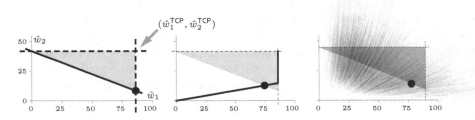

Fig. 2. The two design goals place constraints on what the equilibrium window sizes should be, and a can be chosen to meet them

Equality cannot occur when the right hand side is equal to $\hat{w}_s/\mathsf{RTT}_s$ for some s, since that would require all the other $\hat{w}_r$ to be equal to 0, hence

$$\sum_r \frac{\hat{w}_r}{\mathsf{RTT}_r} = \max_r \frac{\hat{w}_r^{\varepsilon/2}(\hat{w}/a)^{1-\varepsilon/2}}{\mathsf{RTT}_r}.$$

Solving for a gives

$$a = \hat{w}\left(\frac{\max_r \hat{w}_r^{\varepsilon/2}/\mathsf{RTT}_r}{\sum_r \hat{w}_r/\mathsf{RTT}_r}\right)^{1/(1-\varepsilon/2)}.$$

From instant to instant the algorithm may not actually know the fixed point window sizes, so it cannot compute a exactly. We propose using the current window sizes $w_r(t)$ to estimate the fixed point window sizes $\hat{w}_r$, yielding an estimated value for a. Maybe it might be useful to smooth this estimate, but in our simulations it was not necessary. The rightmost plot in Figure 2 shows a simulation trace.

3   Resource Poolability

In a multipath network, congestion at one resource can be alleviated by shifting traffic onto other resources. The extent to which this is possible depends on (i) how much of a flow's traffic is shifted between its paths in response to congestion, and (ii) which paths it has available. This section is concerned with the second point. we will explain what a resource pool is, and we will define a metric that measures the poolability of a resource.

Notation. Suppose the network comprises an interconnection of a set of flows S with a set of resources J. Each flow $s \in S$ identifies a unique source-destination pair. Associated with each flow is a collection of paths, each path being a set of resources. If path r belongs to flow s then we write $r \in s$. If a path r uses a resource j we write $j \in r$. (If two flows share a route, we deem there to be two paths that happen to use exactly the same resources.)

It is helpful to introduce matrices to succinctly express the relationships between flows, paths and resources. Let $A_{jr} = 1$ if $j \in r$ i.e. if path r uses resource j, and let $A_{jr} = 0$ otherwise. Let $H_{sr} = 1$ if $r \in s$ i.e. if path r serves flow s, and $H_{sr} = 0$ otherwise. The two 0–1 matrices A and H express all the details of the topology and multipath routing that we are concerned with.

Each path r has associated with it a traffic rate $x_r \geq 0$. The total traffic rate for flow s is $y_s = \sum_{r \in s} x_r$, and the total traffic at resource j is $z_j = \sum_{r:j \in r} x_r$. In matrix notation, $z = Ax$ and $y = Hx$. Also define the traffic intensity at j to be $\rho_j = z_j/C_j$.

3.1   Five Optimization Problems

In the classic multicommodity flow problem, we imagine that there is a fixed demand $y \geq 0$, and that each resource j has a fixed capacity C_j, and we seek an allocation x such that $Hx = y$ and $Ax \leq C$. The optimization problem

FEAS(y, C) :

minimize δ over $\delta \in \mathbb{R}, x \geq 0$

such that $Ax \leq C + \delta, \ Hx = y,$

indicates whether this is possible: there exists such an allocation when FEAS$(y, C) \leq 0$. The dual problem is important—

POOL(y, C) :

maximize $\sum_s y_s q_s - \sum_j C_j p_j$ over $p \geq 0, q$

such that $\sum_j p_j = 1$ and $q_s \leq \min_{r \in s} \sum_{j \in r} p_j$ for all s.

For the case of end-system congestion control, Kelly et al. [5] supposed that end-systems choose their traffic rates in response to congestion signals from the network. Let $p_j(z_j/C_j)$ be the drop probability (or marking probability, or price signal) at resource j when the load is z_j, and define $L_j(\rho) = \int p_j(\rho) \, d\rho$. Assume that $L_j(\cdot)$ is strictly convex. Suppose each flow s has a utility function $U_s(y_s)$ associated with its total traffic rate y_s, and consider the problem

SYSTEM(C) :

maximize $\sum_s U_s(y_s) - \sum_j C_j L_j(z_j/C_j)$ over $y \geq 0, x \geq 0, z \geq 0$

such that $Ax = z, \ Hx = y.$

In the case of single-path traffic (when H is the identity matrix), the equilibrium throughput of TCP is in fact the solution to this optimization problem with $U_s(y_s) = -1/(\mathsf{RTT}_s^2 y_s)$ where RTT_s is the round trip time for that flow. SYSTEM(C) is a natural generalization to multipath; [6, 7, 8] define multipath congestion control algorithms and show they have equilibrium throughputs which solve SYSTEM(C) or closely related problems. We can rewrite SYSTEM(C) as $\max_y \{ \sum_s U_s(y_s) - \mathrm{MINL}(y, C) \}$ where the latter optimization is

MINL(y, C) :

minimize $\sum_j C_j L_j(z_j/C_j)$ over $x \geq 0, z \geq 0$

such that $Hx = y, \ Ax = z.$

The dual to MINL(y, C) is

OPTP(y, C) :

maximize $\sum_s y_s q_s - \sum_j C_j L_j^*(p_j)$ over $p \geq 0, q \geq 0$

such that $\qquad q_s \leq \min_{r \in s} \sum_{j \in r} p_j.$

Here $L_j^*(p)$ is the Fenchel-Legendre transform $L^*(p) = \sup_{\rho \geq 0} p\rho - L(\rho)$.

3.2   Resource Pooling in the Multicommodity Flow Problem

Here are some examples that give intuition about POOL. Consider the middle scenario in Figure 3. From explicit calculation, a flow y is feasible if and only if $y_I + y_{II} \leq C_1 + C_2$ and $y_I + y_{III} \leq C_1 + C_3$; it is like a single-path system with two 'resource pools' $\hat{C}_1 = C_1 + C_2$ and $\hat{C}_2 = C_1 + C_3$ where y_{II} uses $\hat{C}_1$, y_{III} uses $\hat{C}_2$ and y_I uses both. The two constraints reflect the two extreme feasible solutions $p = (1/2, 1/2, 0)$ and $p = (0, 1/2, 1/2)$ of POOL. Or consider the rightmost scenario in Figure 3. Here the single feasibility constraint is $2y_I + y_{II} \leq 2C_1 + C_2 + C_3$; it is like a single-resource system where y_I uses the resource twice and y_{II} only once. The constraint reflects the single extreme feasible solution $p = (1/2, 1/4, 1/4)$ to POOL. [17] calls these 'generalized cut constraints', and gives several illuminating examples.

We tried running multipath congestion control on these three scenarios (and thereby solved SYSTEM and OPTP). In the rightmost scenario for example we found that flow II balances its traffic so that $p_2 = p_3$ i.e. so that congestion is balanced on those two resources, and flow I also balances its traffic so that $p_1 = p_2 + p_3$, resulting in $p_1 = 2p_2 = 2p_3$. This solution to OPTP somehow corresponds to the POOL solution $p = (1/2, 1/4, 1/4)$—which suggests that OPTP also tells us about resource pools. This is discussed further in Section 3.3.

POOL can also tell us about the effect of adding or removing capacity. Consider the leftmost scenario in Figure 3, and suppose $y = (6, 5, 5)$ and $C = (8, 2, 4, 3)$. This is not feasible, as exemplified by the dual variables $p = (0, 1/3, 1/3, 1/3)$ and $q = (0, 1/3, 1/3)$: we could add $\delta = q^\mathsf{T} y - p^\mathsf{T} C = 1/3$ unit of capacity to each link to make it feasible. Alternatively, $d\delta/dC_j = p_j$, which means we could make y feasible by adding $\delta/p_4 = 1$ unit of capacity to link 4, for example. The corresponding analysis of OPTP is the basis for Section 3.4.

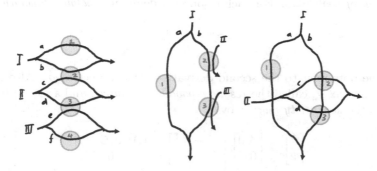

Fig. 3. Three scenarios for examining multipath flow problems. Flows are labelled I, II, III, paths are labelled $a, b, \ldots$ and resources are labelled $1, 2, 3, 4$.

3.3 Finding Resource Pools

Given the similarity between $\mathrm{POOL}(y, C)$ and $\mathrm{OPTP}(y, C)$, we conjecture that the extreme optimal solutions to $\mathrm{OPTP}(y, C)$ tell us about which of the resource pools are tight, in the same way as do the extreme optimal solutions to $\mathrm{POOL}(y, C)$. In particular, based on simulation experiments, we conjecture the following:

The extreme optimal solutions to $\mathrm{OPTP}(y, C)$ *may be found as follows. Find the solution to* $\mathrm{SYSTEM}(C)$, *for example by simulating the fluid model for a multipath congestion control algorithm of the sort described by [8]. Denote the optimal flows and drop probabilities by* $\hat{y}$ *and* $\hat{p}$. *All extreme optimal solutions* p *to* $\mathrm{OPTP}(\hat{y}, C)$ *have the form* $p_j = \hat{p}_j 1_{j \in P}$ *for some set* $P \subseteq J$. *Call these sets* P *the resource pools.*

If this conjecture is correct, then one might employ heuristic techniques to discover the resource pools. One might then display them as a visualization aid, to assist a network operator in choosing alternative paths. For example, if some resource pool is a bottleneck then there is no point providing alternative paths that go through the same bottleneck. A well-connected network operator is likely to be able to find good alternative paths, but a poorly-connected operator is not. This is how network operators can provide value to their customers, even in a world of dumb pipes, intelligent end-systems and network neutrality.

3.4 Resource Poolability Matrix

In a multipath congestion control problem, what is the effect on $\mathrm{OPTP}(y, C)$ when we change the capacity of one of the resources? What is the effect on the drop probabilities? Intuitively, we might expect that if a resource's capacity is reduced then the drop probabilities of all the other resources in the same resource pool will increase, and other resources will not be affected. We might also expect that if a resource is in a large pool then drop probabilities are not much affected if the resource fails, but if it is in a small pool then failure has a much bigger impact.

Definition of poolability. For each resource j define its *poolable capacity* $\tilde{C}_j$ by

$$\tilde{C}_j = \frac{C_j}{\ddot{L}_j(\rho_j)}$$

where the dots refer to the second derivative with respect to ρ_j. Also define a $|J| \times |J|$ matrix Ψ, called the *resource poolability matrix*, and a $|S| \times |J|$ matrix Φ, called the *sensitivity matrix*, by

$$\begin{bmatrix} \Psi \\ \Phi \end{bmatrix} = \begin{bmatrix} \bar{A} & 0 \\ 0 & I \end{bmatrix} \begin{bmatrix} M & -\bar{H}^{\mathsf{T}} \\ \bar{H} & 0 \end{bmatrix}^{-1} \begin{bmatrix} \bar{A}^T & \mathrm{d}(\tilde{C}^{-1}) \\ 0 \end{bmatrix}$$

Here $\bar{A}$ denotes the adjacency matrix A restricted to those paths with non-zero traffic, $\bar{H}$ denotes H restricted similarly, $M = \bar{A}^{\mathsf{T}} \mathrm{d}(\tilde{C}^{-1}) \bar{A}$, and $\mathrm{d}(\tilde{C}^{-1})$ denotes the diagonal matrix with diagonal entry j given by $1/\tilde{C}_j$. If the inverse of the middle matrix does not exist, then use the Moore-Penrose pseudoinverse. It is shown in Section 3.5 that $dz_i/dC_j = \rho_j \Psi_{ij}$.

The resource poolability matrix lets us read off a variety of interesting quantities. For example, if the capacity of link j changes from C_j to $(1 - \delta)C_j$, then how much does the traffic intensity at that link change? It changes by roughly

$$-\delta C_j \frac{d\rho_j}{dC_j} = -\delta C_j \Big(\frac{1}{C_j} \frac{dz_j}{dC_j} - \frac{z_j}{C_j^2} \Big) = \delta \rho_j (1 - \Psi_{jj}).$$

What is the impact on drop probability at that link? It changes by roughly

$$-\delta C_j \frac{d}{dC_j} \dot{L}_j(\rho_j) = \frac{\delta C_j}{\tilde{C}_j} \rho_j (1 - \Psi_{jj}).$$

From these two equations, we see that $\Psi_{jj} = 1$ means perfect resource pooling—if link j looses capacity then its traffic can be routed elsewhere and drop probability at j does not increase. If $\Psi_{jj} = 0$ then there is no resource pooling, and the answers are exactly what they would be for an isolated resource.

If the capacity of link j changes from C_j to $(1 - \delta)C_j$, the total traffic at some other link i changes by roughly

$$-\delta C_j \frac{dz_i}{dC_j} = -\delta C_j \rho_j \Psi_{ij}.$$

Observe that $\delta C_j \rho_j$ is roughly the amount of traffic that has to move away from link j, hence $-\Psi_{ij}$ tells us what share link i takes of the knock-on traffic.

Examples of resource poolability. The resource poolability matrices for the three examples in Figure 3, assuming that all the shown routes are in use, are as follows. For the leftmost network Ψ is

$$\frac{1}{\sum_j \tilde{C}_j} \begin{bmatrix} \tilde{C}_2 + \tilde{C}_3 + \tilde{C}_4 & -\tilde{C}_1 & -\tilde{C}_1 & -\tilde{C}_1 \\ -\tilde{C}_2 & \tilde{C}_1 + \tilde{C}_3 + \tilde{C}_4 & -\tilde{C}_2 & -\tilde{C}_2 \\ -\tilde{C}_3 & -\tilde{C}_3 & \tilde{C}_1 + \tilde{C}_2 + \tilde{C}_4 & -\tilde{C}_3 \\ -\tilde{C}_4 & -\tilde{C}_4 & -\tilde{C}_4 & \tilde{C}_1 + \tilde{C}_2 + \tilde{C}_3 \end{bmatrix}$$

and for the middle and rightmost networks respectively Ψ is

$$\frac{1}{\sum_j \tilde{C}_j^{-1}} \begin{bmatrix} \tilde{C}_1^{-1} & -\tilde{C}_2^{-1} & -\tilde{C}_3^{-1} \\ -\tilde{C}_1^{-1} & \tilde{C}_2^{-1} & -\tilde{C}_3^{-1} \\ -\tilde{C}_1^{-1} & -\tilde{C}_2^{-1} & \tilde{C}_3^{-1} \end{bmatrix}, \quad \frac{1}{4\tilde{C}_1 + \tilde{C}_2 + \tilde{C}_3} \begin{bmatrix} \tilde{C}_2 + \tilde{C}_3 & -2\tilde{C}_1 & -2\tilde{C}_1 \\ -2\tilde{C}_2 & 4\tilde{C}_1 + \tilde{C}_3 & -\tilde{C}_2 \\ -2\tilde{C}_3 & -\tilde{C}_3 & 4\tilde{C}_1 + \tilde{C}_2 \end{bmatrix}$$

There seems to be some sort of algebra here, akin to the algebra of electrical circuits in series and parallel, but we have not uncovered it.

3.5   Derivation of Resource Poolability

First write down the Lagrangian for $\mathrm{MINL}(y, C)$ or equivalently $\mathrm{OPTP}(y, C)$:

$$\mathcal{L}(x, z; p, q) = \sum_j C_j L_j(z_j/C_j) - \sum_j p_j \Big(z_j - \sum_r A_{jr} x_r \Big) + \sum_s q_s \Big(y_s - \sum_r H_{sr} x_r \Big).$$

The complementary slackness conditions are

$$p_j = \dot{L}_j(\rho_j) \text{ for all } j, \text{ where } \rho_j = z_j/C_j$$

$$q_s = \sum_j A_{jr} p_j \text{ for all paths } r \text{ in use by } s$$

$$z_j = \sum_r A_{jr} x_r \text{ for all } j$$

$$y_s = \sum_r H_{sr} x_r \text{ for all } s. \tag{6}$$

The dot in $\dot{L}_j(\rho_j)$ refers to the derivative with respect to ρ_j. Substituting for p_j and z_j, the first three become

$$q_s = \sum_j A_{jr} \dot{L}_j \left(C_j^{-1} \sum_v A_{jv} x_v \right). \tag{7}$$

Now consider changing the capacity of resource C_i while leaving the other resources C and the total flow rates y unchanged. Differentiating (6) & (7) with respect to C_i we obtain

$$q_s' = \sum_j A_{jr} \ddot{L}_j(\rho_j) \left\{ \frac{1}{C_j} \sum_v A_{jv} x_v' - \frac{\rho_j}{C_j} 1_{i=j} \right\} \tag{8}$$

$$0 = \sum_r H_{sr} x_r'. \tag{9}$$

Here the primes q_s' and x_r' refer to derivatives with respect to C_i, the dots $\ddot{L}_j(\rho_j)$ refer as before to a double derivative with respect to ρ_j, and $1_{\{\cdot\}}$ is the indicator function, $1_{\text{true}} = 1$ and $1_{\text{false}} = 0$. Assume for now that all derivatives exist. Rearranging (8),

$$\rho_i A_{ir} \frac{\ddot{L}_i(\rho_i)}{C_i} = \sum_v x_v' \left(\sum_j A_{jr} A_{jv} \frac{\ddot{L}_j(\rho_j)}{C_j} \right) - \sum_s q_s' H_{sr}. \tag{10}$$

In matrix terms we can write (9) & (10) as

$$H x' = 0 \quad \text{and} \quad \left[M x' - H^{\mathsf{T}} q' \right]_r = \rho_i A_{ir}/\tilde{C}_i \text{ for each } r \text{ in use} \tag{11}$$

where $\tilde{C}_j = C_j/\ddot{L}_j(\rho_j)$ and $M = A^{\mathsf{T}} \mathrm{d}(\tilde{C}^{-1}) A$ and $\mathrm{d}(\tilde{C}^{-1})$ denotes the diagonal matrix with diagonal entry j given by $1/\tilde{C}_j$. These equations are easier to deal with if we expand our focus and work simultaneously with derivatives with respect to each of the link capacities. It will also be convenient to rescale by ρ_i^{-1}. Accordingly, define the matrix $\tilde{x}'$ by $\tilde{x}_{ri}' = \rho_i^{-1} \mathrm{d} x_r/\mathrm{d} C_i$, and the matrix $\tilde{q}'$ by $\tilde{q}_{si}' = \rho_i^{-1} \mathrm{d} q_s/\mathrm{d} C_i$. With these definitions (11) becomes

$$\begin{bmatrix} M & -H^{\mathsf{T}} \\ H & 0 \end{bmatrix} \begin{bmatrix} \tilde{x}' \\ \tilde{q}' \end{bmatrix} = \begin{bmatrix} A^{\mathsf{T}} \mathrm{d}(\tilde{C}^{-1}) \\ 0 \end{bmatrix} \tag{12}$$

We want to know how drop probability is affected by a change in capacity, and this is straightforward to calculate from dz_j/dC_i, which it is convenient to rescale: let $\tilde{z}'_{ji} = \rho_i^{-1} dz_j/dC_i$. If we knew $\tilde{x}'$ we could simply compute $\tilde{z}' = A\tilde{x}'$, which is what we named as the poolability matrix Ψ. We named $\tilde{q}'$ as the sensitivity matrix Φ.

Existence and uniqueness. Now we must answer the questions: are $\tilde{x}'$, $\tilde{q}'$ and $\tilde{z}'$ uniquely determined? Do they even exist?

First, note that the original optimization problem $\mathrm{MINL}(y, C)$ always has a unique solution for z, because we assumed that L is strictly convex. It may be that $\tilde{z}'$ does not exist, in corner cases, e.g. when a path swaps in or out of use as capacities change. But if we are in a part of the capacity space where marginal changes in C do not alter the set of paths in use, $\tilde{z}'$ exists and is unique.

Second, observe that x may not be unique, for example when two flows have exactly the same choice of resources to use. However, if $\tilde{z}'$ exists then there must be some solution for $\tilde{x}'$ even if it is not unique. Therefore we might as well take the pseudo-inverse of the matrix in (12), since any solution for $\tilde{x}'$ is as good as any other for the purpose of computing $\tilde{z}'$.

Third, z determines p which determines q, so $\tilde{q}'$ is unique when it exists.

Final thoughts. Our analysis of resource poolability asks what happens when the network changes, assuming the total demand y does not change. This leads to clean maths. It also reflects a division of responsibilities—it is the role of the network to provide good paths, and the role of end-systems to decide how much traffic to send, and it is reasonable for the network to assume that end-systems will use low-congestion paths when they are available. We conjecture that our technique may be extended to other forms of load balancing that can be described by means of an optimization problem; congestion controllers such as (3) fall into this category.

References

[1] Wischik, D., Handley, M., Braun, M.B.: The resource pooling principle. ACM/SIGCOMM CCR 38(5) (2008)

[2] Handley, M.: Why the Internet only just works. BT Technology Journal 24(3) (2006)

[3] Acemoglu, D., Johari, R., Ozdaglar, A.: Partially optimal routing. IEEE Journal of Selected Areas in Communications (2007)

[4] Ford, A., Raiciu, C., Handley, M., Barre, S.: TCP Extensions for Multipath Operation with Multiple Addresses. Internet draft, IETF (2009), http://tools.ietf.org/html/draft-ford-mptcp-multiaddressed-01

[5] Kelly, F.P., Maulloo, A.K., Tan, D.K.H.: Rate control in communication networks: shadow prices, proportional fairness and stability. Journal of the Operational Research Society 49 (1998)

[6] Wang, W.H., Palaniswami, M., Low, S.H.: Optimal flow control and routing in multi-path networks. Performance Evaluation 52(2-3) (2003)

[7] Han, H., Shakkottai, S., Hollot, C.V., Srikant, R., Towsley, D.: Multi-path TCP: a joint congestion control and routing scheme to exploit path diversity in the Internet. IEEE/ACM Transactions on Networking 14(6) (2006)

[8] Kelly, F.P., Voice, T.: Stability of end-to-end algorithms for joint routing and rate control. ACM/SIGCOMM CCR 35(2) (2005)

[9] Key, P., Massoulié, L., Towsley, D.: Combining multipath routing and congestion control for robustness. In: Proceedings of IEEE CISS (2006); Expands on 2005 technical reports Microsoft TR-2005-111 and UMass CMPSCI 05-55

[10] Kang, W.N., Kelly, F.P., Lee, N.H., Williams, R.J.: State space collapse and diffusion approximation for a network operating under a fair bandwidth sharing policy. Annals of Applied Probability (2009)

[11] Key, P., Massoulié, L., Towsley, D.: Path selection and multipath congestion control. In: Proceedings of IEEE INFOCOM (2007); Also appeared in proceedings of IEEE ICASSP 2007

[12] Godfrey, P.B.: Balls and bins with structure: balanced allocations on hypergraphs. In: Proceedings of ACM/SIAM SODA (2008)

[13] Wang, B., Wei, W., Kurose, J., Towsley, D., Pattipati, K.R., Guo, Z., Peng, Z.: Application-layer multipath data transfer via TCP: schemes and performance tradeoffs. Performance Evaluation 64(9-12) (2007); Expands on 2005 technical report UMass CMPSCI 05-45

[14] Raina, G., Towsley, D., Wischik, D.: Part II: Control theory for buffer sizing. ACM/SIGCOMM CCR 35(3) (2005); Summarizes [18]

[15] McDonald, D.R., Reynier, J.: Mean field convergence of a model of multiple TCP connections through a buffer implementing RED. Annals of Applied Probability 16(2) (2006)

[16] Misra, V., Gong, W.B., Towsley, D.: Fluid-based analysis of a network of AQM routers supporting TCP flows with an application to RED. ACM/SIGCOMM CCR 30(4) (2000)

[17] Laws, C.N.: Resource pooling in queueing networks with dynamic routing. Advances in Applied Probability 24(3) (1992)

[18] Raina, G., Wischik, D.: Buffer sizes for large multiplexers: TCP queueing theory and instability analysis. In: Proceedings of EuroNGI conference on Next Generation Internet (2005)

Alpha-Fair Resource Allocation under Incomplete Information and Presence of a Jammer*

Eitan Altman[1], Konstantin Avrachenkov[1], and Andrey Garnaev[2]

[1] INRIA Sophia Antipolis, France
{altman,k.avrachenkov}@sophia.inria.fr
[2] St. Petersburg State University, Russia
agarnaev@rambler.ru

Abstract. In the present work we deal with the concept of alpha-fair resource allocation in the situation where the decision maker (in our case, the base station) does not have complete information about the environment. Namely, we develop a concept of α-fairness under uncertainty to allocate power resource in the presence of a jammer under two types of uncertainty: (a) the decision maker does not have complete knowledge about the parameters of the environment, but knows only their distribution, (b) the jammer can come into the environment with some probability bringing extra background noise. The goal of the decision maker is to maximize the α-fairness utility function with respect to the SNIR (signal to noise-plus-interference ratio). Here we consider a concept of the expected α-fairness utility function (short-term fairness) as well as fairness of expectation (long-term fairness). In the scenario with the unknown parameters of the environment the most adequate approach is a zero-sum game since it can also be viewed as a minimax problem for the decision maker playing against the nature where the decision maker has to apply the best allocation under the worst circumstances. In the scenario with the uncertainty about jamming being in the system the Nash equilibrium concept is employed since the agents have non-zero sum payoffs: the decision maker would like to maximize either the expected fairness or the fairness of expectation while the jammer would like to minimize the fairness if he comes in on the scene. For all the plots the equilibrium strategies in closed form are found. We have shown that for all the scenarios the equilibrium has to be constructed into two steps. In the first step the equilibrium jamming strategy has to be constructed based on a solution of the corresponding modification of the water-filling equation. In the second step the decision maker equilibrium strategy has to be constructed equalizing the induced by jammer background noise.

Keywords: Wireless networks, Power Control, Incomplete Information, Nash Equilibrium, Saddle Point.

---

* The work was supported by EGIDE ECO-NET grant no.18933SL "Game Theory for Wireless Networks" and RFBR Grant no.09-01-00334-a.

R. Núñez-Queija and J. Resing (Eds.): NET-COOP 2009, LNCS 5894, pp. 219–233, 2009.

1   Introduction

Fairness concepts have been playing a central role in networking. In the ATM standards [9], the maxmin fairness and its weighted versions appear as the way to allocate throughput to connections using the ABR (Available Bit Rate) best effort service. The proportional fairness has been introduced in [5,6]. Later it was implemented in wireless communications (e.g. in the Qualcomm High Data Rate (HDR) scheduler) as a way to allocate throughputs (through time slots); it has also been shown to correspond to the way that some versions of the TCP Internet Protocol share bottleneck capacities [8]. A unifying mathematical formulation to fair throughput assignment (which we call the "α-fairness") has been proposed in [7].

In the present work we deal with the concept of alpha-fair resource allocation in the situation where the decision maker (in our case, a base station) does not have complete information about environment. Namely, we develop a concept of α-fairness under uncertainty to allocate power resource in the presence of a jammer under two types of uncertainty: (a) the decision maker does not have complete knowledge about the parameters of the environment but knows only their distribution, (b) the jammer can come into the environment with some probability bringing extra background noise. These scenarios have not been considered previously in the literature (see e.g., [1,2,3,4] and references therein). The goal of the decision maker is to maximize the α-fairness utility function with respect to the SNIR (signal to noise-plus-interference ratio). Here we consider a concept of the expected fairness as well as fairness of expectation. The expected fairness concept is appropriate for the case of slow fading when the decision maker dynamics is faster than the evolution of the environment. Whereas the fairness of expectation concept is more appropriate for the case of fast fading when the state of the environment changes quicker than the dynamics of the control system. We can also say that the expected fairness can be used as a short-term fairness concept while the fairness of expectation can be applicable for long-term fairness.

In the scenario with the unknown parameters of the environment the most adequate approach is a zero-sum game since it can also be viewed as a minimax problem for the decision maker playing against the nature where the decision maker has to apply the best allocation under the worst circumstances. In the scenario with the uncertainty about jamming being in the system the Nash equilibrium concept is employed since the agents have non-opposite goals: the decision maker would like to maximize either the expected fairness or the fairness of expectation while the jammer would like to minimize the fairness if he comes in on the scene. For all the plots the equilibrium solutions are found in closed form.

2   Dependent Fading Channel Gains: Expected Fairness

In this section we consider the following power resource allocation problem. There is a single decision maker (say, the base station) that decides how to allocate the power between n different users. The base station transmits to the mobiles simultaneously using independent channels, e.g. different directional antennas or frequency bands (e.g. as in OFDM, where one should assign different power levels for different sub-carriers [10]).

The strategy of the decision maker is $P = (P_1, \ldots, P_n)$ such that $P_i \geq 0$ for $i \in [1, n]$ and $\sum_{i=1}^{n} P_i = \bar{P}$, where $\bar{P}$ is the total power which the decision maker has to distribute among all the users and P_i corresponds to a power level assigned to the i-th user.

In the environment a jammer could be present bringing extra background noise of the total power $\bar{J}$ to the natural one distributing it among users. So, the pure strategy of the jammer is $J = (J_1, \ldots, J_n)$ where $J_i \geq 0$ for $i \in [1, n]$ and $\sum_{i=1}^{n} J_i = \bar{J}$.

The decision maker does not know the fading channels gains of users with certainty. Namely, the fading channel gains can be random, i.e. with probability p^k, $k \in [1, K]$ they are g_i^k (for the user) and h_i^k (for the jammer), respectively, $i \in [1, n]$. The uncontrolled noise for user i is N_i^{0k} also with probability p^k, $k \in [1, K]$. Thus, in this section we assume that the fading channel gains are dependent. The users know with certainty that a jammer is present in the system. As a payoff we consider α-fairness ($\alpha > 0$) utility function of the expected SNIRs:

$$v(P, J) = \frac{1}{1 - \alpha} \sum_{k=1}^{K} p^k \sum_{i=1}^{n} \left(\frac{g_i^k P_i}{N_i^{0k} + h_i^k J_i} \right)^{1-\alpha} \quad \text{for } \alpha \neq 1 \tag{1}$$

and

$$v(P, J) = \sum_{k=1}^{K} p^k \sum_{i=1}^{n} \ln \left(\frac{g_i^k P_i}{N_i^{0k} + h_i^k J_i} \right) \quad \text{for } \alpha = 1, \tag{2}$$

We assume that all the fading channel gains g_i^k, h_i^k and the power level of the uncontrolled noise N_i^{0k} for $i \in [1, n]$, the probabilities p^k which the system is in as well as the total power resource $\bar{P}$ of the decision maker and the total noise $\bar{J}$ induced by the jammer are fixed and known to both agents.

In this setting the jammer more naturally has to be interpreted as a natural background noise which is present in the system. The total power of the jammer is known to the decision maker but the decision maker does not know its distribution among the users. The decision maker wants to distribute resources among the users in the worst situation, so it faces a maxmin problem. Thus, here we deal with a zero-sum game, and the payoff to the jammer is $-v(P, J)$. We will look for the saddle point and the value of the game, that is, we want to find the strategies $(P^*, J^*) \in A \times B$ such that

$$v(P, J^*) \leq v(P^*, J^*) \leq v(P^*, J) \quad \text{for any } (P, J) \in A \times B,$$

where A and B are the sets of all the strategies of the decision maker and jammer, respectively and $v = v(P^*, J^*)$ is the value of the game and (P^*, J^*) is the saddle point.

Before starting studying our problem introduce the following notation. Denote by $\mathcal{P}$ the decision maker strategy assigning to allocate resources uniformly among all the users, namely, $\mathcal{P}=(\bar{P}/n,\ldots,\bar{P}/n)$.

The next Lemma based on the Kuhn-Tucker Theorem describes the structure of the saddle point.

Lemma 1. *Let* $\alpha \in (0,1]$ *then* (P,J) *is a saddle point if and only if there are* ω *and* ν *(Lagrange multipliers) such that*
(a) for $0 < \alpha < 1$

$$\frac{1}{P_i^\alpha} \sum_{k=1}^{K} p^k \left(\frac{g_i^k}{N_i^{0k} + h_i^k J_i} \right)^{1-\alpha} \begin{cases} = \omega, & P_i > 0, \\ \leq \omega, & P_i = 0, \end{cases} \tag{3}$$

$$P_i^{1-\alpha} \sum_{k=1}^{K} p^k \frac{h_i^k}{N_i^{0k} + h_i^k J_i} \left(\frac{g_i^k}{N_i^{0k} + h_i^k J_i} \right)^{1-\alpha} \begin{cases} = \nu, & J_i > 0, \\ \leq \nu, & J_i = 0, \end{cases} \tag{4}$$

(b) for $\alpha = 1$

$$\frac{1}{P_i} \begin{cases} = \omega, & P_i > 0, \\ \leq \omega, & P_i = 0, \end{cases} \tag{5}$$

$$\sum_{k=1}^{K} p^k \frac{h_i^k}{N_i^{0k} + h_i^k J_i} \begin{cases} = \nu, & J_i > 0, \\ \leq \nu, & J_i = 0. \end{cases} \tag{6}$$

First we will study the case with $0 < \alpha < 1$. From (3) it follows that necessarily $P_i > 0$ for all i. Then

$$P_i = \frac{1}{\omega^{1/\alpha}} \left(\sum_{k=1}^{K} p^k \left(\frac{g_i^k}{N_i^{0k} + h_i^k J_i} \right)^{1-\alpha} \right)^{1/\alpha} \quad \text{for } i \in [1,n].$$

Thus, by (4),

$$\left(\sum_{k=1}^{K} p^k \left(\frac{g_i^k}{N_i^{0k} + h_i^k J_i} \right)^{1-\alpha} \right)^{(1-\alpha)/\alpha} \sum_{k=1}^{K} \frac{p^k h_i^k}{N_i^{0k} + h_i^k J_i} \left(\frac{g_i^k}{N_i^{0k} + h_i^k J_i} \right)^{1-\alpha}$$

$$\begin{cases} = \nu \omega^{(1-\alpha)/\alpha}, & J_i > 0, \\ \leq \nu \omega^{(1-\alpha)/\alpha}, & J_i = 0. \end{cases} \tag{7}$$

Let

$$R_i(x) := \left(\sum_{k=1}^{K} p^k \left(\frac{g_i^k}{N_i^{0k} + h_i^k x} \right)^{1-\alpha} \right)^{(1-\alpha)/\alpha} \sum_{k=1}^{K} p^k \frac{h_i^k}{N_i^{0k} + h_i^k x} \left(\frac{g_i^k}{N_i^{0k} + h_i^k x} \right)^{1-\alpha}.$$

It is clear that $R_i(x)$ is a continuous and decreasing function on $x \in [0,\infty)$ such that $R_i(x) \to 0$ for $x \to \infty$. Then we can define $J_i(\tau)$ as follows

$$J_i(\tau) = \begin{cases} \text{the unique root of } R_i(x) = \tau, & \text{if } R_i(0) > \tau, \\ 0, & \text{if } R_i(0) \leq \tau. \end{cases} \tag{8}$$

It is clear that $J_i(x)$ is continuous for $x \in [0, \infty)$ and decreasing while it is positive. Also, $J_i(\tau) \to \infty$ for $\tau \to 0$, and $J_i(x) = 0$ for $\tau \geq J_i(0)$. Thus, there is the unique $x = \tau^*$ such that

$$\sum_{i=1}^{n} J_i(x) = \bar{J}. \tag{9}$$

Thus, we have proved the following result supplying the saddle point strategies:

Theorem 1. *Let $0 < \alpha < 1$ then the saddle point of jammer is given by (8) where $\tau = \tau^*$ is the unique root of (9). The saddle point strategy of the decision maker is given as follows*

$$P_i = \frac{\left(\sum_{k=1}^{K} p^k \left(\dfrac{g_i^k}{N_i^{0k} + h_i^k J_i(\tau_*)}\right)^{1-\alpha}\right)^{1/\alpha}}{\sum_{r=1}^{n} \left(\sum_{k=1}^{K} p^k \left(\dfrac{g_r^k}{N_r^{0k} + h_r^k J_r(\tau_*)}\right)^{1-\alpha}\right)^{1/\alpha}} \bar{P} \quad for \ i \in [1, n].$$

It is interesting about these strategies that in the optimal behavior the jammer can harm only the best sub-carriers while the decision maker uses all of them.

Similarly we can study the case where $\alpha = 1$, namely, we show in the following theorem that the saddle point jammer strategy has a water-filling structure while the saddle point decision maker strategy has to be the uniform one.

Theorem 2. *Let $\alpha = 1$ then the saddle point jammer strategy is given as follows*

$$J_i(\nu) = \begin{cases} \text{the unique root of } F_i(x) = \nu, & \text{if } F_i(0) > \nu, \\ 0, & \text{if } F_i(0) \leq \nu, \end{cases}$$

where

$$F_i(x) := \sum_{k=1}^{K} p^k \frac{g_i^k}{N_i^{0k} + h_i^k x}$$

and $\nu = \nu^*$ is the unique root of $\sum_{i=1}^{n} J_i(\nu) = \bar{J}$. The saddle point decision maker strategy is the uniform one $\mathcal{P}$.

3 Independent Fading Channel Gains: Expected Fairness

In this section we assume that the fading channel gains are independent. Namely, with probability p^k, $k \in [1, K]$ the fading channel gain of the jammer on the channel of user i is h_i^k and the uncontrolled noise for user i is N_i^{0k}. With probability q^l, $l \in [1, L]$ the fading channel gain of user i is g_i^l. As a payoff we consider the expected α-fairness ($\alpha \geq 0$) utility function of the SNIRs

$$v(P, J) = \frac{1}{1-\alpha} \sum_{k=1}^{K} \sum_{l=1}^{L} p^k q^l \sum_{i=1}^{n} \left(\frac{g_i^l P_i}{N_i^{0k} + h_i^k J_i}\right)^{1-\alpha} \quad for \ \alpha \neq 1 \tag{10}$$

and

$$v(P, J) = \sum_{k=1}^{K} \sum_{l=1}^{L} p^k q^l \sum_{i=1}^{n} \ln \left(\frac{g_i^l P_i}{N_i^{0k} + h_i^k J_i} \right) \quad \text{for } \alpha = 1. \tag{11}$$

It is clear that (10) is equivalent to

$$v(P, J) = \frac{1}{1 - \alpha} \sum_{k=1}^{K} p^k \sum_{i=1}^{n} \bar{g}_i \left(\frac{P_i}{N_i^{0k} + h_i^k J_i} \right)^{1-\alpha} \quad \text{for } \alpha \neq 1, \tag{12}$$

where

$$\bar{g}_i = \sum_{l=1}^{L} q^l (g_i^l)^{1-\alpha}.$$

Then from Theorem 3 the following result supplying the optimal strategies follows:

Theorem 3. *(a) Let $0 < \alpha < 1$ then the saddle point jammer strategy is given as follows*

$$J_i = J_i(\tau^*) \text{ for } i \in [1, n],$$

where τ^* is the unique root of $\sum_{i=1}^{n} J_i(\tau) = \bar{J}$ and

$$J_i(\tau) = \begin{cases} \text{the unique root of } R_i(x) = \tau, & \text{if } R_i(0) > \tau, \\ 0, & \text{if } R_i(0) \leq \tau, \end{cases}$$

where

$$R_i(x) := \bar{g}_i^{1/\alpha - 1} \left(\sum_{k=1}^{K} \frac{p^k}{(N_i^{0k} + h_i^k x)^{1-\alpha}} \right)^{(1-\alpha)/\alpha} \sum_{k=1}^{K} p^k \frac{h_i^k}{(N_i^{0k} + h_i^k x)^{2-\alpha}}.$$

The saddle point decision maker strategy is given as follows

$$P_i = \frac{\left(\sum\limits_{k=1}^{K} p^k \dfrac{\bar{g}_i}{(N_i^{0k} + h_i^k J_i)^{1-\alpha}} \right)^{1/\alpha}}{\sum\limits_{r=1}^{n} \left(\sum\limits_{k=1}^{K} p^k \dfrac{\bar{g}_r}{(N_r^{0k} + h_r^k J_r)^{1-\alpha}} \right)^{1/\alpha}} \bar{P} \text{ for } i \in [1, n].$$

(b) Let $\alpha = 1$ then the saddle point jammer strategy is given as follows

$$J_i(\nu) = \begin{cases} \text{the unique root of } F_i(x) = \nu, & \text{if } F_i(0) > \nu, \\ 0, & \text{if } F_i(0) \leq \nu, \end{cases}$$

where

$$F_i(x) := \sum_{k=1}^{K} p^k \frac{\bar{g}_i}{N_i^{0k} + h_i^k x}$$

and $\nu = \nu^*$ is the unique root of $\sum_{i=1}^{n} J_i(\nu) = \bar{J}$. The saddle point decision maker strategy is the uniform one in $[1, n]$, namely, it is given as follows $P_i = \bar{P}/n$ for $i \in [1, n]$.

4 Dependent Fading Channel Gains: Fairness of Expectation

In this section as a payoff to the decision maker we consider α-fairness ($\alpha > 0$) utility function of the expected SNIRs:

$$v(P, J) = \frac{1}{1-\alpha} \sum_{i=1}^{n} \left(\sum_{k=1}^{K} p^k \frac{g_i^k P_i}{N_i^{0k} + h_i^k J_i} \right)^{1-\alpha} \quad \text{for } \alpha \neq 1 \tag{13}$$

and

$$v(P, J) = \sum_{i=1}^{n} \ln \left(\sum_{k=1}^{K} p^k \frac{g_i^k P_i}{N_i^{0k} + h_i^k J_i} \right) \quad \text{for } \alpha = 1, \tag{14}$$

where $\alpha \geq 0$. The next Lemma based on the Kuhn-Tucker Theorem describes the structure of the saddle point.

Lemma 2. *Let $\alpha \in (0, 1]$ then (P, J) is a saddle point if and only if there are ω and ν (Lagrange multipliers) such that*
(a) for $0 < \alpha < 1$

$$\frac{1}{P_i^{\alpha}} \left(\sum_{k=1}^{K} \frac{p^k g_i^k}{N_i^{0k} + h_i^k J_i} \right)^{1-\alpha} \begin{cases} = \omega, & P_i > 0, \\ \leq \omega, & P_i = 0, \end{cases} \tag{15}$$

$$P_i^{1-\alpha} \frac{\displaystyle\sum_{k=1}^{K} \frac{p^k h_i^k g_i^k}{(N_i^{0k} + h_i^k J_i)^2}}{\left(\displaystyle\sum_{k-1}^{K} \frac{p^k g_i^k}{N_i^{0k} + h_i^k J_i} \right)^{\alpha}} \begin{cases} = \nu, & J_i > 0, \\ \leq \nu, & J_i = 0, \end{cases} \tag{16}$$

(b) for $\alpha = 1$

$$\frac{1}{P_i} \begin{cases} = \omega, & P_i > 0, \\ \leq \omega, & P_i = 0, \end{cases} \tag{17}$$

$$\sum_{k=1}^{K} p^k \frac{h_i^k g_i^k}{N_i^{0k} + h_i^k J_i} \begin{cases} = \nu, & J_i > 0, \\ \leq \nu, & J_i = 0. \end{cases} \tag{18}$$

The lemma implies the following result supplying the saddle point.

Theorem 4. *Let $0 < \alpha \leq 1$ then the saddle point decision maker strategy is given as follows*

$$P_i = \frac{\left(\displaystyle\sum_{k=1}^{K} \frac{p^k g_i^k}{N_i^{0k} + h_i^k J_i(\tau_*)} \right)^{(1-\alpha)/\alpha}}{\displaystyle\sum_{r=1}^{n} \left(\displaystyle\sum_{k=1}^{K} \frac{p^k g_r^k}{N_i^{0k} + h_r^k J_r(\tau_*)} \right)^{(1-\alpha)/\alpha}} \bar{P} \quad \text{for } i \in [1, n].$$

The saddle point jammer strategy is given by

$$J_i(\tau) = \begin{cases} \text{the root of } R_i(x) = \tau, & \text{if } R_i(0) > \tau, \\ 0, & \text{if } R_i(0) \leq \tau. \end{cases} \qquad (19)$$

where

$$R_i(x) := \left(\sum_{k=1}^{K} \frac{p^k g_i^k}{N_i^{0k} + h_i^k x} \right)^{1/\alpha - 2} \sum_{k=1}^{K} \frac{p^k h_i^k g_i^k}{(N_i^{0k} + h_i^k x)^2}.$$

and $\tau = \tau^*$ is the root of the equation $\sum_{i=1}^{n} J_i(x) = \bar{J}$. In particular if $\alpha \leq 1/2$ this saddle point is unique and if $\alpha = 1$ then the saddle point decision maker strategy is the uniform one $\mathcal{P}$.

5   Independent Fading Channel Gains: Fairness of Expectation

In this section we assume that the fading channel gains are independent. Namely, with probability p^k, $k \in [1, K]$ the fading channel gain of the jammer on the channel of user i is h_i^k and the uncontrolled noise for user i is N_i^{0k}. With probability q^l, $l \in [1, L]$ the fading channel gain of user i is g_i^l. As a payoff we consider the expected α-fairness ($\alpha \geq 0$) utility function of the SNIRs

$$v(P, J) = \frac{1}{1 - \alpha} \sum_{i=1}^{n} \left(\sum_{k=1}^{K} \sum_{l=1}^{L} p^k q^l \frac{g_i^l P_i}{N_i^{0k} + h_i^k J_i} \right)^{1 - \alpha} \quad \text{for } \alpha \neq 1 \qquad (20)$$

and

$$v(P, J) = \sum_{i=1}^{n} \ln \left(\sum_{k=1}^{K} \sum_{l=1}^{L} p^k q^l \frac{g_i^l P_i}{N_i^{0k} + h_i^k J_i} \right) \quad \text{for } \alpha = 1. \qquad (21)$$

It is clear these payoffs are equivalent to the following ones:

$$v(P, J) = \frac{1}{1 - \alpha} \sum_{i=1}^{n} \left(\sum_{k=1}^{K} p^k \frac{P_i \bar{g}_i}{N_i^{0k} + h_i^k J_i} \right)^{1 - \alpha} \quad \text{for } \alpha \neq 1,$$

and

$$v(P, J) = \sum_{i=1}^{n} \ln \left(\sum_{k=1}^{K} p^k \frac{\bar{g}^l P_i}{N_i^{0k} + h_i^k J_i} \right) \quad \text{for } \alpha = 1.$$

where

$$\bar{g}_i = \sum_{l=1}^{L} q^l g_i^l.$$

The next theorem supplies the saddle point strategies.

Theorem 5. *Let* $0 < \alpha \le 1$ *then the saddle point decision maker strategy is given as follows*

$$P_i = \frac{\left(\sum_{k=1}^{K} \dfrac{p^k \bar{g}_i}{N_i^{0k} + h_i^k J_i(\tau_*)}\right)^{(1-\alpha)/\alpha}}{\sum_{r=1}^{n} \left(\sum_{k=1}^{K} \dfrac{p^k \bar{g}_r}{N_i^{0k} + h_r^k J_r(\tau_*)}\right)^{(1-\alpha)/\alpha}} \bar{P} \; for \; i \in [1, n].$$

The saddle point jammer strategy is given by

$$J_i(\tau) = \begin{cases} the \; root \; of \; R_i(x) = \tau, & if \; R_i(0) > \tau, \\ 0, & if \; R_i(0) \le \tau. \end{cases} \tag{22}$$

where

$$R_i(x) := \left(\sum_{k=1}^{K} \frac{p^k \bar{g}_i}{N_i^{0k} + h_i^k x}\right)^{1/\alpha - 2} \sum_{k=1}^{K} \frac{p^k h_i^k \bar{g}_i}{(N_i^{0k} + h_i^k x)^2}.$$

and $\tau = \tau^*$ *is the root of the equation* $\sum_{i=1}^{n} J_i(x) = \bar{J}$. *In particular, if* $\alpha \le 1/2$ *this saddle point is the unique one and if* $\alpha = 1$ *then the saddle point decision maker strategy is the uniform one* $\mathcal{P}$.

6 The Decision Maker Does Not Know If the Jammer Is Present: Expected Fairness

In this section we consider the power resource allocation problem where in the environment a jammer could either be present, bringing extra background noise to the natural one, or be absent. The decision maker has no exact knowledge about either presence or absence of the jammer. Namely, it knows that in the environment only a natural background noise could be with probability γ meanwhile with probability $1 - \gamma$ a jammer could come into the action distributing an extra noise of the total power $\bar{J}$ among users. The decision maker payoff is given as follows:

for $\alpha \ne 1$:

$$v_P(P, J) = \frac{1}{1-\alpha} \sum_{i=1}^{n} \left(\gamma \left(\frac{g_i P_i}{N_i^0}\right)^{1-\alpha} + (1-\gamma) \left(\frac{g_i P_i}{N_i^0 + h_i J_i}\right)^{1-\alpha} \right), \tag{23}$$

for $\alpha = 1$:

$$v_P(P, J) = \sum_{i=1}^{n} \left(\gamma \ln \left(\frac{g_i P_i}{N_i^0}\right) + (1-\gamma) \ln \left(\frac{g_i P_i}{N_i^0 + h_i J_i}\right) \right). \tag{24}$$

As a cost function to the jammer we consider α-fairness ($\alpha > 0$) utility function of the SNIRs . Thus, his payoff is equal to his cost function taken with minus sign and it is given as follows:

$$v_J(P,J) = -\frac{1}{1-\alpha}\sum_{i=1}^{n}\left(\frac{g_iP_i}{N_i^0 + h_iJ_i}\right)^{1-\alpha} \quad \text{for } \alpha \neq 1 \qquad (25)$$

and

$$v_J(P,J) = -\sum_{i=1}^{n}\ln\left(\frac{g_iP_i}{N_i^0 + h_iJ_i}\right) \quad \text{for } \alpha = 1. \qquad (26)$$

We assume that all the fading channel gains g_i, h_i and the power level of the uncontrolled noise N_i^0 for $i \in [1,n]$, the probabilities γ which the system is in as well as the total power resource $\bar{P}$ of the decision maker as well as the total noise $\bar{J}$ induced by the jammer are fixed and known to both players.

We shall look for a Nash equilibrium (NE), that is, we want to find $(P^*, J^*) \in A \times B$ such that

$$v_P(P, J^*) \leq v_P(P^*, J^*), \quad v_J(P^*, J) \leq v_J(P^*, J^*) \text{ for any } (P,J) \in A \times B,$$

where A and B are the sets of all the strategies of the decision maker and the jammer, respectively. In particular, we shall show that the NE exists and is unique and we shall provide closed form analytic expressions for its calculation.

It is interesting that this non-zero-sum game is a particular case of the zero-sum game from Section 4. Namely, for this situation we have two states, so $K = 2$ with the same user fading channel gains $g_i^1 = g_i^2 = g_i$. The probability that the environment is in the first state is $p^1 = \gamma$ and the probability that the environment is in the second state is $p^2 = 1 - \gamma$. The jammer fading channel gains for the first state equals to zero, namely, $h_i^1 = 0$, while the jammer fading channel gains for the second state is positive $h_i^2 = h_i$. Then the jammer payoff (25) turns into

$$v_J(P,J) = -\frac{1}{1-\alpha}\sum_{i=1}^{n}\left(\gamma\left(\frac{g_iP_i}{N_i^0}\right)^{1-\alpha} + (1-\gamma)\left(\frac{g_iP_i}{N_i^0 + h_iJ_i}\right)^{1-\alpha}\right). \qquad (27)$$

It is clear that the first part of (27) does not depend on J, thus it is equivalent to (25).

The following result providing the equilibrium in the closed form holds.

Theorem 6. *The game has the unique equilibrium* (P, J).

(a) *If* $0 < \alpha < 1$ *then the equilibrium decision maker strategy is given as follows:*

$$P_i = \frac{\left(\gamma\left(\frac{g_i}{N_i^0}\right)^{1-\alpha} + (1-\gamma)\left(\frac{g_i}{N_i^0 + h_iJ_i}\right)^{1-\alpha}\right)^{1/\alpha}}{\sum_{m=1}^{n}\left(\gamma\left(\frac{g_m}{N_m^0}\right)^{1-\alpha} + (1-\gamma)\left(\frac{g_m}{N_m^0 + h_mJ_m}\right)^{1-\alpha}\right)^{1/\alpha}}\bar{P}, \; i \in [1,n], \quad (28)$$

The equilibrium jammer strategy is $J_i = J_i(\tau)$ *where*

$$J_i(\tau) = \begin{cases} \text{the unique root } x \text{ of the equation } R_i(x) = \tau, & D_i > \tau, \\ 0, & D_i \leq \tau. \end{cases} \qquad (29)$$

where

$$R_i(x) = \left(\gamma \left(\frac{g_i}{N_i^0} \right)^{1-\alpha} + (1-\gamma) \left(\frac{g_i}{N_i^0 + h_i x} \right)^{1-\alpha} \right)^{(1-\alpha)/\alpha} \frac{h_i g_i^{1-\alpha}}{(N_i^0 + h_i x)^{2-\alpha}},$$

$$D_i := R_i(0) = \frac{g_i^{(1-\alpha)/\alpha}}{(N_i^0)^{1/\alpha}} h_i \tag{30}$$

and $\tau = \tau^*$ is the unique root of the equation $\sum_{i=1}^n J_i(\tau) = \bar{J}$.

(b) If $\alpha = 1$ then the equilibrium decision maker strategy is the uniform one $\mathcal{P}$. The equilibrium jammer strategy is $J_i = [1/\nu - N_i^0/h_i]_+$ where $\nu = \nu^*$ is the unique root of the following water-filling equation: $\sum_{i=1}^n [1/\nu - N_i^0/h_i]_+ = \bar{J}$.

7 The Decision Maker Does Not Know If the Jammer Is Present: Fairness of Expectation

In this section we consider a modification of the problem where the decision maker payoff is the fairness of expectation. So, the decision maker payoff is given as follows:

$$v_P(P, J) = \frac{1}{1-\alpha} \sum_{i=1}^n \left(\gamma \frac{g_i P_i}{N_i^0} + (1-\gamma) \frac{g_i P_i}{N_i^0 + h_i J_i} \right)^{1-\alpha} \quad \text{for } \alpha \neq 1 \tag{31}$$

and

$$v_P(P, J) = \sum_{i=1}^n \ln \left(\gamma \frac{g_i P_i}{N_i^0} + (1-\gamma) \frac{g_i P_i}{N_i^0 + h_i J_i} \right) \quad \text{for } \alpha = 1. \tag{32}$$

The jammer still wants to minimize fairness of the resource allocation. The following result shows that the game has the unique equilibrium and it also supplies the equilibrium in the closed form.

Theorem 7. *The game has the unique equilibrium (P, J).*

(a) If $0 < \alpha < 1$ then the equilibrium decision maker strategy is given as follows:

$$P_i = \frac{\left(\gamma \frac{g_i}{N_i^0} + (1-\gamma) \frac{g_i}{N_i^0 + h_i J_i} \right)^{(1-\alpha)/\alpha}}{\sum_{m=1}^n \left(\gamma \frac{g_m}{N_m^0} + (1-\gamma) \frac{g_m}{N_i^0 + h_m J_m} \right)^{(1-\alpha)/\alpha}} \bar{P} \quad \text{for } i \in [1, n], \tag{33}$$

The equilibrium jammer strategy is $J_i = J_i(\tau)$ where

$$J_i(\tau) = \begin{cases} \text{the unique root } x \text{ of the equation } R_i(x) = \tau, & D_i > \tau, \\ 0, & D_i \leq \tau. \end{cases} \tag{34}$$

where

$$R_i(x) = \left(\gamma \frac{g_i}{N_i^0} + (1-\gamma)\frac{g_i}{N_i^0 + h_i x}\right)^{(1-\alpha)^2/\alpha} \frac{h_i g_i^{1-\alpha}}{(N_i^0 + h_i x)^{2-\alpha}}, \qquad (35)$$

and D_i is given by (30) (so, it is the same as for the expected fairness model) and $\tau = \tau^*$ is the unique root of the equation $\sum_{i=1}^n J_i(\tau) = \bar{J}$.

(b) If $\alpha = 1$ then the equilibrium decision maker strategy is the uniform one $\mathcal{P}$. The equilibrium jammer strategy is $J_i = J_i(\nu)$ where

$$J_i(\nu) = \begin{cases} \text{the unique root } x \text{ of the equation } R_i^1(x) = \tau, & D_i^1 > \nu, \\ 0, & D_i^1 \le \nu, \end{cases} \qquad (36)$$

where

$$R_i^1(x) = \frac{(1-\gamma)h_i N_i^0}{(N_i^0 + h_i x)(N_i^0 + \gamma h_i x)}, \qquad D_i^1 := R_i^1(0) = \frac{(1-\gamma)h_i}{N_i^0}$$

and $\nu = \nu^*$ is the unique root of the equation: $\sum_{i=1}^n J_i(\nu) = \bar{J}$.

8   Numerical Examples for the Game Plots

Here we apply the developed closed form solution to compare the saddle point strategies of the decision maker for the expected fairness game with dependent and independent plots and also their Jain's fairness indexes of P. Let there be five users, so $n = 5$ and the system can be in two states ($K = 2$). Let the total power be $\bar{P} = 3$, the background noise is permanent and $N_i^{0k} = 1$ for all k and i. The optimal payoffs v_D, v_I and the Jain's fairness indexes $\mathcal{J}_D, \mathcal{J}_I$ for dependent and independents plots are given in Table 1 as functions on $\alpha = 0.1(0.2)0.9$ and $p^1 = 0.0(0.1)1.0$. We assume that $g = ((5,1),(4,2),(3,3),(2,4),(1,5))$ and $h = ((1,1),(1,1),(1,1),(1,1),(1,1))$ and for the independent plot we assume that $K = L\ q^i = p^i$, $i \in [1, K]$. We consider three cases of jamming power: (a) a small total jamming power $\bar{J} = 0.1$ (Table 1), (b) a comparable total jamming power $\bar{J} = 1$ with the base station power (Table 2) and (c) an overwhelming jamming power over the base station one $\bar{J} = 30$ (Table 3).

It is interesting that the value of the game for dependent plot is less than or equal to the value of the game for independent plot while the Jain's fairness indexes have the opposite relations. The difference between the values of the game for two plots is decreasing in α. The small total jamming power (Table 1) produces unnoticeable effect for big α compared to the optimization plot but decreasing α has impact on the value of the game as well as on the Jain's index of fairness. For overwhelming jamming power over the base station one the players tend to equalizing behavior but to switch to the equalizing behavior the independent plot requests larger jamming power threshold compared to the independent plots (Table 3). Equalizing behavior becomes earlier for large α then for small one (Table 2 and 3). Also, an increase in the total jamming power causes an increase of the Jain's fairness index.

Table 1. The case $\bar{J} = 0.1$

J/v	α	p^1 0.0	p^1 0.1	p^1 0.2	p^1 0.3	p^1 0.4	p^1 0.5	p^1 0.6	p^1 0.7	p^1 0.8	p^1 0.9	p^1 1.0
J_D	0.1	0.33	0.37	0.44	0.56	0.79	1.00	0.79	0.56	0.44	0.37	0.33
J_D	0.3	0.61	0.69	0.78	0.88	0.96	1.00	0.96	0.88	0.78	0.69	0.61
J_D	0.5	0.84	0.88	0.93	0.97	0.99	1.00	0.99	0.97	0.93	0.88	0.84
J_D	0.7	0.96	0.97	0.98	0.99	1.00	1.00	1.00	0.99	0.98	0.97	0.96
J_D	0.9	1.00	1.00	1.00	1.00	1.00	1.00	1.00	1.00	1.00	1.00	1.00
v_D	0.1	12.02	11.21	10.46	9.80	9.32	9.16	9.32	9.80	10.46	11.21	12.02
v_D	0.3	11.42	11.05	11.03	10.52	10.39	10.35	10.39	10.52	10.74	11.05	11.42
v_D	0.5	13.21	13.08	12.98	12.91	12.87	12.86	12.87	12.91	12.98	13.08	13.21
v_D	0.7	19.30	19.26	19.24	19.22	19.21	19.21	19.21	19.22	19.24	19.26	19.30
v_D	0.9	52.27	52.27	52.27	52.26	52.26	52.26	52.26	52.26	52.27	52.27	52.27
J_I	0.1	0.27	0.30	0.35	0.45	0.70	0.99	0.70	0.45	0.35	0.30	0.27
J_I	0.3	0.60	0.68	0.77	0.87	0.96	1.00	0.96	0.87	0.77	0.68	0.60
J_I	0.5	0.83	0.88	0.93	0.97	0.99	1.00	0.99	0.97	0.93	0.88	0.83
J_I	0.7	0.96	0.97	0.98	0.99	1.00	1.00	1.00	0.99	0.98	0.97	0.96
J_I	0.9	1.00	1.00	1.00	1.00	1.00	1.00	1.00	1.00	1.00	1.00	1.00
v_I	0.1	12.30	11.47	10.66	9.94	9.38	9.16	9.38	9.94	10.66	11.47	12.30
v_I	0.3	11.44	11.06	10.75	10.53	10.39	10.36	10.39	10.53	10.75	11.06	11.44
v_I	0.5	13.21	13.08	12.98	12.91	12.87	12.86	12.87	12.91	12.98	13.08	13.21
v_I	0.7	19.30	19.26	19.24	19.22	19.21	19.21	19.21	19.22	19.24	19.26	19.30
v_I	0.9	52.27	52.27	52.28	52.26	52.26	52.26	52.26	52.26	52.27	52.27	52.27

Table 2. The case $\bar{J} = 1$

J/v	α	p^1 0.0	p^1 0.1	p^1 0.2	p^1 0.3	p^1 0.4	p^1 0.5	p^1 0.6	p^1 0.7	p^1 0.8	p^1 0.9	p^1 1.0
J_D	0.1	0.59	0.62	0.72	0.86	0.99	1.00	0.99	0.86	0.72	0.62	0.59
J_D	0.3	0.75	0.82	0.90	0.96	0.99	1.00	0.99	0.96	0.90	0.82	0.75
J_D	0.5	0.89	0.93	0.96	0.99	1.00	1.00	1.00	0.99	0.96	0.93	0.89
J_D	0.7	0.97	0.98	0.99	1.00	1.00	1.00	1.08	1.00	0.99	0.98	0.97
J_D	0.9	1.00	1.00	1.00	1.00	1.00	1.00	1.00	1.00	1.00	1.00	1.00
v_D	0.1	8.95	8.55	8.20	7.98	7.91	7.91	7.91	7.98	8.20	8.55	8.95
v_D	0.3	9.62	9.43	9.31	9.25	9.24	9.24	9.24	9.25	9.31	9.43	9.62
v_D	0.5	11.95	11.90	11.87	11.85	11.85	11.85	11.85	11.85	11.87	11.90	11.95
v_D	0.7	18.31	18.30	18.30	18.30	18.30	18.30	18.30	18.30	18.30	18.30	18.31
v_D	0.9	51.42	51.42	51.42	51.42	51.42	51.42	51.42	51.42	51.42	51.42	51.42
J_I	0.1	0.27	0.30	0.35	0.45	0.70	0.99	0.70	0.45	0.35	0.30	0.27
J_I	0.3	0.64	0.72	0.80	0.89	0.97	1.00	0.97	0.89	0.80	0.72	0.64
J_I	0.5	0.87	0.92	0.95	0.98	0.99	1.00	0.99	0.98	0.95	0.92	0.87
J_I	0.7	0.97	0.98	0.99	0.99	1.00	1.00	1.00	0.99	0.99	0.98	0.97
J_I	0.9	1.00	1.00	1.00	1.00	1.00	1.00	1.00	1.00	1.00	1.00	1.00
v_I	0.1	10.41	9.78	9.16	8.57	8.11	7.92	8.11	8.57	9.16	9.78	10.41
v_I	0.3	9.83	9.61	9.46	9.34	9.27	9.24	9.27	9.34	9.46	9.61	9.83
v_I	0.5	11.99	11.92	11.89	11.87	11.86	11.86	11.86	11.87	11.89	11.92	11.99
v_I	0.7	18.31	18.30	18.30	18.30	18.30	18.30	18.30	18.30	18.30	18.30	18.31
v_I	0.9	51.42	51.42	51.42	51.42	51.42	51.42	51.42	51.42	51.42	51.42	51.42

Table 3. The case $\bar{J} = 30$

$\mathcal{J}/v$	α	p^1 0.0	p^1 0.1	p^1 0.2	p^1 0.3	p^1 0.4	p^1 0.5	p^1 0.6	p^1 0.7	p^1 0.8	p^1 0.9	p^1 1.0
$\mathcal{J}_D$	0.1	0.84	0.89	0.94	0.97	0.99	1.00	0.99	0.97	0.94	0.89	0.84
$\mathcal{J}_D$	0.3	0.89	0.93	0.96	0.98	0.99	1.00	0.99	0.98	0.96	0.93	0.89
$\mathcal{J}_D$	0.5	0.94	0.96	0.98	0.99	1.00	1.00	1.00	0.99	0.98	0.96	0.94
$\mathcal{J}_D$	0.7	0.97	0.98	0.99	1.00	1.00	1.00	1.00	1.00	0.99	0.98	0.97
$\mathcal{J}_D$	0.9	1.00	1.00	1.00	1.00	1.00	1.00	1.00	1.00	1.00	1.00	1.00
v_D	0.1	1.62	1.62	1.62	1.62	1.62	1.62	1.62	1.62	1.62	1.62	1.62
v_D	0.3	2.69	2.69	2.69	2.69	2.69	2.69	2.69	2.69	2.69	2.69	2.69
v_D	0.5	4.91	4.91	4.91	4.91	4.91	4.91	4.91	4.91	4.91	4.91	4.91
v_D	0.7	10.78	10.78	10.78	10.78	10.78	10.78	10.78	10.78	10.78	10.78	10.78
v_D	0.9	43.11	43.12	43.11	43.11	43.11	43.11	43.11	43.11	43.11	43.11	43.11
$\mathcal{J}_I$	0.1	0.27	0.30	0.35	0.45	0.70	0.99	0.70	0.45	0.35	0.30	0.27
$\mathcal{J}_I$	0.3	0.64	0.72	0.80	0.89	0.97	1.00	0.97	0.89	0.80	0.72	0.64
$\mathcal{J}_I$	0.5	0.88	0.92	0.95	0.98	0.99	1.00	0.99	0.98	0.95	0.92	0.88
$\mathcal{J}_I$	0.7	0.97	0.98	0.99	0.99	1.00	1.00	1.00	0.99	0.99	0.98	0.97
$\mathcal{J}_I$	0.9	1.00	1.00	1.00	1.00	1.00	1.00	1.00	1.00	1.00	1.00	1.00
v_I	0.1	2.10	1.96	1.83	1.82	1.62	1.58	1.62	1.71	1.83	1.96	2.10
v_I	0.3	2.85	2.80	2.75	2.72	2.70	2.69	2.70	2.72	2.75	2.80	2.85
v_I	0.5	4.95	4.93	4.92	4.92	4.91	4.91	4.91	4.92	4.92	4.93	4.95
v_I	0.7	10.79	10.78	10.78	10.78	10.78	10.78	10.78	10.78	10.78	10.78	10.79
v_I	0.9	43.11	43.11	43.11	43.11	43.11	43.11	43.11	43.11	43.11	43.11	43.11

9 Conclusions

In the present work we have dealt with the concept of alpha-fair resource allocation in the situation where the decision maker does not have complete information about the environment. Namely, we develop a concept of α-fairness under uncertainty to allocate power resource in the presence of a jammer under two scenarios: (a) the decision maker does not have complete knowledge about the parameters of the environment but only knows their distribution, (b) the jammer can come into the environment with some probability bringing extra background noise. The goal of the decision maker is to maximize the α-fairness utility function with respect to the SNIR. We have considered short-term fairness (the expected fairness) as well as long-term fairness (the fairness of expectation). We have modeled these plots using game-theoretical approaches since the jammer can be considered as an active agent acting against the decision maker. For all the plots the equilibrium strategies are found in closed form. We have shown that for all the scenarios the equilibrium has to be constructed in two steps. In the first step the equilibrium jamming strategy has to be constructed based on a solution of the corresponding modification of the water-filling equation. In the second step the decision maker equilibrium strategy has to be constructed equalizing the induced by jammer background noise.

References

1. Altman, E., Avrachenkov, K., Garnaev, A.: A jamming game in wireless networks with transmission cost. In: Chahed, T., Tuffin, B. (eds.) NET-COOP 2007. LNCS, vol. 4465, pp. 1–12. Springer, Heidelberg (2007)
2. Altman, E., Avrachenkov, K., Garnaev, A.: Fair resource allocation in wireless networks in the presence of a jammer. In: Proc. of Value Tools 2008 (2008)
3. Amariucai, G.T., Wei, S.: Jamming in Fixed-Rate Wireless Systems with Power Constraints - Part I: Fast Fading Channels. arXiv:0808.3431v1 [cs.IT] (2008)
4. Amariucai, G.T., Wei, S., Kannan, R.: Jamming in Fixed-Rate Wireless Systems with Power Constraints - Part II: Parallel Slow Fading Channels. arXiv:0808.3418v1 [cs.IT] (2008)
5. Kelly, F.P.: Charging and rate control for elastic traffic. European Trans. on Telecom. 8, 33–37 (1998)
6. Kelly, F.P., Maulloo, A., Tan, D.: Rate control for communication networks: shadow prices, proportional fairness and stability. Journal of the Operational Research Society 49, 237–252 (1998)
7. Mo, J., Walrand, J.: Fair end-to-end window-based congestion control. IEEE/ACM Trans. on Networking 8, 556–567 (2000)
8. Low, S.H., Peterson, L., Wang, L.: Understanding TCP vegas: A duality model. In: Proc. SIGMETRICS/Performance 2001, pp. 226–235 (2001)
9. Traffic management specification, The ATM forum Technical Committee, version 4.0 (April 1996)
10. Tse, D., Viswanath, P.: Fundamentals of Wireless Communication. Cambridge University Press, Cambridge (2005)

Tariffs, Mechanisms and Equilibria at a Single Internet Link

Costas Courcoubetis and Antonis Dimakis

Department of Informatics
Athens University of Economics and Business
Patission 76, Athens 10434, Greece
{courcou,dimakis}@aueb.gr

Abstract. We analyze the interplay between the demand for downloads, choice of congestion control mechanism, and tariff structure at a single link, when users have preferences in terms of average download delay and they are charged according to the number of ECN marked packets they receive. Our model involves a timescale separation approach, where in the fast timescales active flows compete for instantaneous bandwidth share by optimally tuning congestion control parameters in a noncooperative fashion. This is modeled by letting flows choose utility functions within the network utility maximization framework laid down by Kelly [1]. On a slower timescale, users selfishly change their otherwise unrestricted demand for downloads based on the average experienced download delay and charges incurred. We study the equilibrium of this loop of interactions from the point of view of social welfare.

For homogeneous users we find that optimal equilibria are induced when they choose among linear utility functions, while this is not the case for logarithmic, i.e., proportionally fair congestion controllers. We next consider two types of users, web-browsing and bittorrent, where the latter are much less sensitive to download delay than the former. If bittorrent users respond to congestion according to proportionally fair utility functions the charge induced by ECN marked packets does not provide the correct signal for service differentiation and the resulting equilibrium is suboptimal. On the other hand, if flows are charged for the volume of bits they transfer as well, then social welfare maximum is attained for some price per bit. This reveals a new role for bit volume pricing: to provide bittorrent users the correct incentives for choosing congestion controllers that effectively give priority to web-browsing users.

Keywords: pricing, congestion control, congestion marks, noncooperative equilibrium.

1   Introduction

In analyzing the performance of congestion control mechanisms through either simulation or theory, one assumes a given level of demand. But if we are asked to answer questions such as

R. Núñez-Queija and J. Resing (Eds.): NET-COOP 2009, LNCS 5894, pp. 234–248, 2009.
© Springer-Verlag Berlin Heidelberg 2009

- What is the impact of different tariffs on user-perceived performance and Internet service provider (ISP) profits?
- Given a specific tariff, what congestion control algorithm should a user use in order to improve performance and charges his traffic incurs?
- Is it beneficial for an ISP to buy more link capacity from a wholesale provider?
- What is the outcome of competition between ISPs?

then we need to precisely determine the equilibrium level of demand that results from the complex interactions between ISPs, users and congestion control algorithms.

Indeed, a user may improve his download delays by using a more aggressive congestion control algorithm but will be charged more by a tariff scheme that penalizes congestion. Hence this user must optimally balance his preference for short download delays with the level of charges he incurs. If he discovers that despite the optimal choice of congestion control he pays more than he ought to for the download delay he experiences, he might lower his frequency with which he is initiating downloads. On a much slower timescale, the ISP may notice a drop in demand and may need to lower its price in order to maintain its previous level of profits. In turn, the user will observe the price drop and will again reconsider his choice of congestion control aggressiveness and so on.

Hopefully, given enough time this loop of interactions will converge to some noncooperative equilibrium level of demand as a result of the tariff structure employed by the ISP, and the choice of congestion control algorithms users are optimizing their aggressiveness over.

In search for a tractable model for exploring equilibria of this sort, we isolate three timescales and consider the relevant stakeholders and their actions involved in each of these timescales.

- ISP chooses prices (of marks/bits or something else), expands capacity [slow timecale]
- Users decide whether to download or not, what congestion control parameters to use. [medium timescale]
- Congestion control reacts on instantaneous congestion. [fast timescale]

There are decisions taking place on even slower timescales, e.g., users change congestion control algorithms, switch between providers, operating systems vendors publish their congestion control software, but we have decided to omit those in order to make the analysis tractable. In fact, in this paper we consider the case of a single bottleneck link with fixed capacity.

Our main goal is to understand the incentive properties of pricing when this is based on primal congestion control algorithms, i.e., based on volume of ECN marked packets (congestion marks) [3], versus pricing based on data volume or on combinations of both. Our basic modelling assumption that is used to carry out the above analysis is that network users are separated into two different classes: the 'web-browsing' users class, where latency in downloading files is important, and the p2p users, the 'bittorrent users', for which downloading delay is orders of magnitude less important. Using this separation assumption we look at the sequence of systems when delay importance on bittorrent users becomes negligible and study the efficiency properties of the equilibria as this limit is reached. A main result of this analysis is that if bittorrent users choose among α-fair utility functions with $\alpha > 0$ [2], such as logarithmic, the charge induced by congestion marks alone does not provide the correct signal for service differentiation and the resulting equilibrium is suboptimal. This results from our assumption that the demand for downloads is potentially unrestricted, and sensitive to the download delay. Under this assumption, as we will see later, it is possible that an increasingly high number of bittorrent users joins as their delay sensitivity decreases. Thus bittorrent flows accummulate a non-negligible number of congestion marks. In contrast, consider what happens when demand for bittorrent downloads is fixed. Bittorrent users will not be willing to incur any congestion marks as they become less sensitive to delay.

Now if flows are charged for the volume of bits they transfer as well, then social welfare maximum is attained for some price per bit. This reveals a new role for bit volume pricing: to provide bittorrent users the correct incentives for choosing congestion controllers that effectively give priority to web-browsing users.

We must finally comment that our results are asymptotic results when Internet users can be abstracted into two classes regarding their delay sensitivity. Probably our results may not hold when we add another user type whose delay sensitivity goes also to zero but at a slower rate than the bittorrent type. However, it is under the two type model where the properties we bring out become most apparent.

The paper is organized as follows. In Section 2 we relate our work to previous work done in the area. In Section 3 we introduce the model and notation to be used throughout the paper, and define the concept of equilibrium. The main results concerning social welfare of equilibria under a single and multiple user types are contained in Sections 4 and 5 respectively. Finally, we summarize in Section 6.

2   Related Work

In an important paper Naor [4] has posed the question of noncooperative equilibrium arrival rate in a FCFS queue, and considered the case where an arriving customer knows the queue length and is allowed to balk. He showed that the equilibrium is inefficient in terms of social welfare if no pricing is imposed, and this is fixed when an appropriate toll is imposed on non balking customers. The same model under the assumption that customers do not observe the queue length is considered in [5] and similar tolls to [4] were proposed. Such tolls that internalize externalities were well known to economists and queueing theorists [6,7]. In Section 5 the bit volume charge will have a similar internalizing role, in the case of two extreme user types.

Another way to internalize externalities without the imposition of tolls is by changing the service discipline. In an intriguing result, [8] has shown that the

LCFS service discipline provides the correct incentives for customers to optimally balk. Another important result by [9] has shown that if customers bid for their priority so that the higher bidder gets full priority, then the resulting equilibrium is efficient. Such a combination of bids and service discipline, as we will see, corresponds in our framework to a particular choice of congestion control parameters by the users. One can view the results of this paper as an extension of the demand models of [4,5,9,10,11], where users are allowed to bid for instantaneous service in a very general way.

Kelly and Gibbens in [3] view the choice of congestion controller by the end-to-end users as a game between them, where users have preferences in terms of instantaneous bandwidth. Additionally, they propose flows to be charged proportionally to the amount of ECN marked packets they generate. In contrast to [4,5,9,10,11], the flow arrival rate is fixed, i.e., balking is not allowed, but flows affect the service discipline by tuning the parameters of congestion control algorithms. The ECN mark charge offers a way to provide service differentiation since at times of high congestion, bandwidth is allocated to the flows that value it most. Interestingly, when balking is allowed a mark charge may not be sufficient to achieve the maximum social welfare (see Section 5). Inefficiency of Nash equilibria resulting from the noncooperative choice of congestion control parameters, is observed in [12,13] when users have preferences on instantaneous bandwidth. In contrast to the models of [12,13], here inefficiency can arise even when all users are of the same type.

References [14,15] consider whether class differentiated pricing at a queueing system offering two classes of priority, gives the correct incentives for customers to select the appropriate class. It is found that this is possible under identical service requirements by all customers. Although we seek for similarly defined efficient equilibria as in [14,15], here prices are not set by a central planner but they result from user choices. Thus, potentially there is an infinite number of service classes.

3   Model

Consider a single link of capacity C bits/s shared by n flow types. We assume that there is an arbitrarily high number of flows where each decides whether to join the system or balk in a random (e.g., after a coin toss) and independent manner. We further assume that flows possess no information about the actual state of the system, e.g., the number of active downloads. The only information available to them is the number of flow types along with their defining parameters. That is, we consider a nonobservable model according to the terminology in [11]. Thus after each flow has made its decision, the resulting arrival process of type-i flows forms a Poisson process with rate λ_i flows/s. Each nonbalking type-i flow terminates once the download of an exponentially distributed file size of mean $1/\mu_i$ bits completes. We use θ_i to denote the demand λ_i/μ_i (in bit/s) of type i-flows.

A nonbalking flow, at the instant of its arrival, also decides which congestion control mechanism to use throughout its duration. Since we are interested in the (fast timescale) equilibrium service rates, congestion control mechanisms are modeled by nondecreasing concave functions and the use of the convex optimization framework of Kelly [1] to determine the equilibrium allocations which we assume are reached instantaneously. We allow a randomized choice of congestion control mechanisms, so the choice is over the set $\mathcal{P}(\mathcal{U})$ of distributions on $\mathcal{U}$, a subset of concave, nondecreasing, continuously differentiable utility functions. We will frequently consider $\mathcal{U} = \mathcal{U}_\alpha$, the set of α-fair utilities $\{u : u(x) = -wx^{1-\alpha}/(1 - \alpha), \forall x > 0$, and some $w \geq 0\}$ with $\alpha \geq 0, a \neq 1$ [2]. The case $\alpha = 1$ corresponds to instantaneous bandwidth allocations that are (weighted) propoportionally fair [1], and can be defined by $\mathcal{U}_1 = \{u : u(x) = w \log x, \forall x > 0$, and some $w \geq 0\}$; here, the gain parameter w is interpreted as the willingness to pay per unit of time [1]. Since for fixed α, the elements of $\mathcal{U}_\alpha$ are indexed by the gain parameter $w \geq 0$, we can take $\mathcal{P}(\mathcal{U}_\alpha)$ to be the set of probability distributions on $\mathbb{R}_+$. We also introduce the relation $>$ on $\mathcal{P}(\mathcal{U})$, defined by

$$\pi_1 > \pi_2 \Leftrightarrow (\pi_1 \times \pi_2)(\{(u_1, u_2) \in \mathcal{U} \times \mathcal{U} | u_1'(x) > u_2'(y) \text{ for all } x, y > 0\}) = 1 .$$

This is defined to signify that the flows of some type take full priority over flows of another type. Moreover, $\mathcal{P}(\mathcal{U})$ is equipped with the Prohorov metric, i.e., $\pi_n \rightarrow \pi$ means weak convergence of probability distributions.

If at any instant t, a flows are active with utilities $u_1, \ldots, u_a$, then the instantaneous bandwidth share $x_j(t)$ (in bit/s) of flow $j = 1, \ldots, a$ is determined by the optimum solution of

$$\max_{x_1, \ldots, x_a \geq 0} \sum_{j=1}^{a} u_j(x_j) \text{ over } \sum_{j}^{a} x_j \leq C ,$$

and the instantaneous charge rate is $\lambda(t)x_j(t)$ per second, where $\lambda(t)$ is the Lagrange multiplier of the capacity constraint. In [3] it is demonstrated how the rate of congestion marks conveys the value of the Lagrange multiplier $\lambda(t)$, so, as in [3], in the sequel we identify congestion mark pricing with the imposition of a charge $\lambda(t)$ on each unit of allocated bandwidth. Thus, during the lifetime of a flow an average charge per bit equal to

$$m_i(\theta, \pi) = E^0 \left(\int_0^T \lambda(t)x_j(t)dt \right) \mu_i ,$$

is incurred, if flow j is of type-i and T its download delay. Here, E^0 is expectation under the Palm distribution P^0 on arrivals of type-i flows, i.e., P^0 characterizes statistically what is seen by a typical arriving type-i flow.

Let $d_i(\pi'; \theta, \pi)$ be the average download delay of a type-i flow divided by the average file size, i.e., $1/\mu_i$, when this flow chooses congestion control mechanism according to $\pi' \in \mathcal{P}(\mathcal{U})$ and all other flows (including those of the same type) choose according to $\pi = (\pi_1, \ldots, \pi_n)$. ($m_i(\pi'; \theta, \pi)$ is defined similarly.) Thus $d_i(\pi_i; \theta, \pi)$ is the average delay per bit of a typical type-i flow, which we denote simply by $d_i(\theta, \pi)$. For α-fair utility functions we conveniently write $d_i(w; \theta, \pi)$

for $d_i(\delta_w; \theta, \pi)$ where $\delta_w \in \mathcal{P}(\mathcal{U}_\alpha)$ assigns unit probability to the utility function in $\mathcal{U}_\alpha$ with parameter w. (The value of α will be clear from the context.) Each type-i download brings a reward $r_i - c_i d_i(\theta, \pi)$ per bit, where r_i represents a delay independent reward, and c_i is the cost of each second of delay per bit. Consequently, the net value per bit of a type-i flow is

$$r_i - c_i d_i(\theta, \pi) - m_i(\theta, \pi) \tag{1}$$

Since the maximum potential demand for each flow type is arbitrarily high, if (1) is positive more type-i flows will join and ultimately drive (1) to zero after delay increases sufficiently. This gives rise to the following definition.

Definition 1. *For each i let $\mathcal{A}_i$ be a subset of $\mathcal{P}(\mathcal{U})$, where $\mathcal{U}$ is the set of nondecreasing, concave, continuously differentiable functions on $\mathbb{R}_+$. The vector (θ, π) is an* equilibrium *if the following hold for all i:*

1. $r_i - c_i d_i(\theta, \pi) - m_i(\theta, \pi) \leq 0$. If the inequality is strict then $\theta_i = 0$.
2. π_i maximizes $r_i - c_i d_i(\pi'; \theta, \pi) - m_i(\pi'; \theta, \pi)$ over $\pi' \in \mathcal{A}_i$.

In our model θ_i is the result of a Wardrop type of equilibrium that is induced by (1), hence it is outside the control of the individual user; the choice of π_i is strategic. We have not developed a theory for existence and uniqueness of equilibria in general. In what follows we deal with specific $\mathcal{U}$ where explicit calculation of equilibria is possible.

To any vector (θ, π) irrespective of it being an equilibrium or not, we associate a level of social welfare equal to

$$\mathcal{W}(\theta, \pi) = \sum_{i=1}^{n} \theta_i (r_i - c_i d_i(\theta, \pi)) . \tag{2}$$

A vector (θ, π) is called *efficient* if it maximizes (2) over $\theta \geq 0, \sum_{i=1}^{n} \theta_i \leq C, \pi_i \in \mathcal{A}_i$.

In the following section we consider the simplest case of a system consisting of a single user type. We consider this simpler case first in order to highlight some key efficiency results.

4   Single User Type

Here we consider the case $n = 1$. The number of active flows behaves as an M/M/1 queue, so $d_1(\theta, \pi) = 1/(C - \theta_1)$ for any $\mathcal{U}$ and $\pi \in \mathcal{P}(\mathcal{U})$. Thus the optimal demand θ_1^* maximizes $\theta_1(r_1 - c_1/(C - \theta_1))$, which gives

$$\theta_1^* = \max\left(C - \sqrt{\frac{c_1 C}{r_1}}, 0\right) . \tag{3}$$

Contrary to the case where the demand for downloads is fixed [1,3,13,12], not all congestion controllers possess efficient equilibria when users selfishly optimize demand.

Proposition 1.   *1. If $\mathcal{A}_1 = \mathcal{P}(\mathcal{U}_0)$ there exists a unique efficient equilibrium.*
2. If $\mathcal{A}_1 = \mathcal{P}(\mathcal{U}_1)$ the only symmetric pure equilibrium is inefficient.

Proof. Part 1 is shown in [9]. The intuition of why this should hold is the following. An arriving flow that picks a parameter value p will take preemptive priority over all active flows with lower parameter values. Moreover, if the instantaneous bandwidth at any time during the lifetime of the flow is nonzero, then the shadow price will be exactly p. Thus, the equilibrium choice of parameter is such that it does not pick any particular value with a positive probability, i.e., does not have atoms, since an infinitesimally small parameter increase results into taking priority over a positive number of flows, with positive probability. Hence, any parameter p within some range will result into identical net values per bit (1). Since this is true for the smallest p within this range, i.e., for the smallest priority, it is optimal for an arriving flow to join if and only if it is optimal to join under the LCFS policy. But under such a policy a nonbalking flow does not pose any delay penalties to subsequently arriving flows, and thus will join if it is socially optimal to do so [8].

For the second part, let $f(w)$ be the average delay per bit of a flow with willingness to pay w when all other flows have a unit willingness to pay. By [10],

$$f(w) = \frac{1 + w - w\theta/C}{1 + w - \theta/C} \frac{1}{1 - \theta/C} \frac{1}{C} . \tag{4}$$

If w^* is the equilibrium willingness to pay then the maximum net value per bit $r_1 - c_1 f(w/w^*) - wf(w/w^*)$ must be achieved at $w = w^*$, so

$$\frac{d}{dw}(c_1^* f(w/w^*) + wf(w/w^*))\Big|_{w=w^*} = 0 \implies w^* = -\frac{c_1 f'(1)}{f'(1) + f(1)} = \frac{c_1\theta_1}{2(C + \theta_1)} .$$

Such payment will induce a demand θ_1 with

$$r_1 - \frac{c_1}{C - \theta_1} = \frac{c_1\theta_1\mu_1}{2(C + \theta_1)(C - \theta_1)} ,$$

which clearly is not the optimal demand (3).

We conjecture that a similar inefficiency outcome as for $\mathcal{U}_1$ holds for any $\mathcal{U}_\alpha$ with $\alpha > 0$. Congestion control mechanisms that correspond to the set $\mathcal{U}_0$ of linear utility functions have been proposed in [1,3,16,17].

5   Two Extreme User Types

Here we consider the efficiency of equilibria for two flow types, where one of them is nearly insensitive to download delay. To do this, we consider a sequence of systems as the coefficient c_2 of type-2 converges to zero and determine the limit (θ^0, π^0) of equilibria $(\theta^{c_2}, \pi^{c_2})$ of the c_2-systems. Thus (θ^0, π^0) provides an asymptotically exact approximation for $c_2 > 0$, and it is easier to determine than $(\theta^{c_2}, \pi^{c_2})$ directly. We believe that the case $n = 2, c_2 = 0$ provides valuable intuition for more general systems because the key properties become most apparent.

We first determine the limit of the efficient allocation vectors as $c_2 \downarrow 0$. As expected, it is optimal for the delay sensitive type to take full preemptive priority at the limit. (To emphasize the dependence on c_2 we write $\mathcal{W}(\theta, \pi, c_2)$ for the social welfare when the linear coefficient of type-2 users is c_2.)

Proposition 2. *Let $\mathcal{U}$ be as in Definition 1. Then,*

$$\max_{\theta \geq 0, \theta_1 + \theta_2 \leq C, \pi \in \mathcal{P}(\mathcal{U}) \times \mathcal{P}(\mathcal{U})} \mathcal{W}(\theta, \pi, c_2) \to \mathcal{W}^*, \quad as \ c_2 \downarrow 0, \tag{5}$$

where

$$\mathcal{W}^* = \max_{\theta \geq 0, \theta_1 + \theta_2 \leq C, \pi \in \mathcal{P}(\mathcal{U}) \times \mathcal{P}(\mathcal{U})} [\theta_1(r_1 - c_1 d_1(\theta, \pi)) + r_2\theta_2]$$

$$= \max_{0 \leq \theta_1 \leq C} \left[\theta_1 \left(r_1 - \frac{c_1}{C - \theta_1} \right) + r_2(C - \theta_1) \right] . \tag{6}$$

Moreover, if maximizing vectors $(\theta^{c_2}, \pi^{c_2})$ of $\mathcal{W}(\cdot, \cdot, c_2)$ have a limit (θ^0, π^0) it must satisfy $\theta^0 = \theta^*$. Also, $\theta_1^0 > 0 \implies \pi_1^0 > \pi_2^0$, where θ^* is the optimizing demand in (6).

Proof. For small but fixed $\epsilon > 0$,

$$\max_{\theta_1 + \theta_2 \leq C - \epsilon, \pi} \mathcal{W}(\theta, \pi, c_2) \to \max_{\theta_1 + \theta_2 \leq C - \epsilon, \pi} \mathcal{W}(\theta, \pi, 0)$$

as $c_2 \downarrow 0$. Moreover, the right hand side converges to $\mathcal{W}^*$ as $\epsilon \downarrow 0$. Now, since

$$\max_{\theta_1 + \theta_2 \leq C - \epsilon, \pi} \mathcal{W}(\theta, \pi, c_2) \leq \max_{\theta_1 + \theta_2 \leq C, \pi} \mathcal{W}(\theta, \pi, c_2) \leq \mathcal{W}^*,$$

we conclude that (5) is true.

Now any limit demand θ^0 equals θ^* because (6) possesses a unique solution. If $\theta_1^0 > 0$ but $\pi_1^0 > \pi_2^0$ does not hold then $d_1(\theta^{c_2}, \pi^{c_2}) \to +\infty$ since $\theta_1^0 + \theta_2^0 = C$. But this contradicts the fact that $\mathcal{W}(\theta^{c_2}, \pi^{c_2}, c_2) \geq 0$, hence $\pi_1^0 > \pi_2^0$.

Next, we would like to determine whether the tariff based on congestion marks [3] is adequate to enforce socially optimal equilibria $(\theta^{c_2}, \pi^{c_2})$ as $c_2 \downarrow 0$, i.e., whether $(\theta^0, \pi^0) = \lim_{c_2 \downarrow 0}(\theta^{c_2}, \pi^{c_2}) = (\theta^*, \pi^*)$ holds. As the next proposition shows, (θ^0, π^0) is not efficient when $\mathcal{A}_1 = \mathcal{P}(\mathcal{U}_\alpha)$ for any $\alpha \geq 0$, and $\mathcal{A}_2 = \mathcal{P}(\mathcal{U}_1)$. We conjecture that the same result holds for more general $\mathcal{A}_2$ except the case $\mathcal{A}_2 = \mathcal{P}(\mathcal{U}_0)$. Although we do not fully determine (θ^0, π^0) we find that no limit of the equilibria sequence $(\theta^{c_2}, \pi^{c_2})$ can be efficient. This is surprising since if demand was fixed, i.e., the maximum potential demand of both types is strictly below C, then as c_2 becomes smaller, type-2 flows should be less willing to pay for instantaneous bandwidth because these will be served anyway when no type-1 flows are present, and this extra delay is bounded. Thus, type-2 flows will become second priority at the limit $c_2 \downarrow 0$.

However if demand varies, then in systems with small c_2, one may observe a higher number of type-2 flows on the average, since more flows will join if their payments draw close to zero. Thus at equilibrium, the net value per bit will be close to zero as well. In other words, a tragedy of the commons situation is plausible among type-2 flows. If on the other hand such a situation does not arise and payments from type-2 flows come to the system at a positive rate, then type-2 flows will take up some of the bandwidth during times when type-1 flows are present. As $c_2 \downarrow 0$ this amount of bandwidth becomes non-negligible and the system does not behave as a priority system as it is supposed to in order to be efficient.

Proposition 3 (Inefficiency of tariff based on congestion marks alone).
Let $\mathcal{A}_1 = \mathcal{P}(\mathcal{U}_\alpha), \alpha \geq 0$ and $\mathcal{A}_2 = \mathcal{P}(\mathcal{U}_1)$. If $(\theta^{c_2}, \pi^{c_2})$ is equilibrium for each $c_2 > 0$ then

$$\limsup_{c_2 \downarrow 0} \mathcal{W}(\theta^{c_2}, \pi^{c_2}, c_2) < \mathcal{W}^* ,$$

where $\mathcal{W}^*$ is as in Proposition 2.

Proof. We follow the discussion prior to the statement of this proposition, and first show that type-2 flows achieve a decreased level of welfare if their rate of payments is not r_2. Since $0 \leq m_2(\theta^{c_2}, \pi^{c_2}) \leq r_2$ we can take a subsequence of $(\theta^{c_2}, \pi^{c_2})$, which by abuse of notation we denote again by $(\theta^{c_2}, \pi^{c_2})$, such that $\lim_{c_2 \downarrow 0} m_2(\theta^{c_2}, \pi^{c_2}) = \delta$, and $(\theta^{c_2}, \pi^{c_2}) \to (\theta^0, \pi^0)$.

As in the proof of Proposition 2 one can show that $\lim_{c_2 \downarrow 0} \mathcal{W}(\theta^{c_2}, \pi^{c_2}, c_2) = \mathcal{W}^*$ implies $\lim_{c_2 \downarrow 0} \theta^{c_2} = \theta^*$. Moreover by Definition 1, $r_2 - c_2 d_2(\theta^{c_2}, \pi^{c_2}) \leq m_2(\theta^{c_2}, \pi^{c_2})$ for each c_2, so if $\delta < r_2$ we have that

$$\lim_{c_2 \downarrow 0} \mathcal{W}(\theta^{c_2}, \pi^{c_2}, c_2) \leq \theta_1^*(r_1 - c_1 d_1(\theta^*, \pi^*)) + \delta\theta_2^* < \mathcal{W}^* .$$

i.e., on this subsequence the system is inefficient.

Now consider the case where the payment rate is exactly r_2, i.e.,

$$\delta = \lim_{c_2 \downarrow 0} m_2(\theta^{c_2}, \pi^{c_2}) = \lim_{c_2 \downarrow 0} \frac{E_{c_2}\left(\sum_{i=1}^{n_2(0)} w_i\right)}{\theta_2^{c_2}} = r_2 ,$$

where $n(t) = (n_1(t), n_2(t))$ is the vector of active type-1 and type-2 flows at time t, and w_i is the congestion control parameter chosen by the i-th active type-2 flow.

We will show that type-1 flows see strictly larger average delays than what they would observe at a priority system. Since a typical type-1 flow sees time averages upon arrival, we have

$$\liminf_{c_2 \downarrow 0} P_{c_2}^0 \left(\sum_{i=1}^{n_2(0-)} w_i > \frac{r_2 \theta_2^*}{2} \right) > 0 ,$$

where $P_{c_2}^0$ is the Palm probability on arrivals of type-1 flows and the dependence on c_2 is shown explicitly. Now, define the following events:

$$F_1 = \left\{ \sum_{i=1}^{n_2(0-)} w_i > \frac{r_2 \theta_2^*}{2} \right\} , \quad F_2 = \{n_1(0-) = 0\} ,$$

$$F_3 = \{\text{no type-1 flows arrive during } (0,1]\} ,$$

$$F_4 = \{\text{no flows depart from the system during } (0,1]\} .$$

Now we can assume that $\lim_{c_2} P_{c_2}^0(F_2) > 0$ holds, otherwise the limit is not efficient and we are done. Moreover, $\lim_{c_2} P_{c_2}^0(F_3) = e^{-\theta_1^* \mu_1 - \theta_2^* \mu_2}$ and

$$\liminf_{c_2 \downarrow 0} P_{c_2}^0(F_4 | F_1, F_2, F_3) \geq e^{-(\mu_1 + \mu_2)C} .$$

Thus,

$$\liminf_{c_2 \downarrow 0} P_{c_2}^0(F_1 \cap F_2 \cap F_3 \cap F_4) > 0 . \tag{7}$$

Let $x_1(t)$ be the instantaneous bandwidth at time $t \geq 0$, allocated to the type-1 flow arriving at time 0. On $\omega \in F_1 \cap F_2 \cap F_3 \cap F_4$ we have $x_1(t) = x_1(0), n(t) = n(0)$ for all $t \in (0,1]$ and $x_1(0)$ is given by the optimum x_1 in

$$\max_{x_1, x_2 \geq 0} u(x_1) + \sum_{i=1}^{n_2(0)} w_i \log x_2 , \text{ over } x_1 + x_2 \leq C ,$$

which is less than the optimum x_1' in

$$\max_{x_1', x_2 \geq 0} u(x_1') + \frac{r_2 \theta_2^*}{2} \log x_2 , \text{ over } x_1' + x_2 \leq C . \tag{8}$$

Now lets compare the rate allocated to the type-1 flow that arrived at time 0 when type-2 flows give up priority. On the same probability space, consider a second system with the same type-1 flow arrival instances, same file sizes, and the same choice of utility functions but where type-1 takes full preemptive priority. If we denote by $\hat{n}(t) = (\hat{n}_1(t), \hat{n}_2(t))$ the vector of active flows at time t, and by $\hat{x}_1(t)$ the instantaneous bandwidth allocated to the type-1 flow that arrives at time 0, then it is evident that $n_1(t) \geq \hat{n}_1(t), x_1(t) \leq \hat{x}_1(t)$ at any t. Furthermore at any time instant, any type-1 flow that is present at the priority system is also present at the system without full priority. Now, on $\omega \in F_1 \cap F_2 \cap F_3 \cap F_4$ we have $\hat{x}_1(t) = C$ for all $t \in (0,1]$. Moreover, we need consider only $u \in \mathcal{U}_\alpha$ with (uniformly in c_2) bounded gain parameters, since the charge per bit never exceeds r_1. So for any utility function u in (8), $\hat{x}_1(t) - x_1(t) > \phi$ for some $\phi > 0$ not dependent on c_2. Thus for such ω, the delay of arriving type-1 flows is greater than that achieved by full priority, by more than ϕ/C. As $c_2 \downarrow 0$, a non-negliglible proportion of type-1 flows encounters a delay difference of ϕ/C, by (7). For the rest of type-1 flows we know that their delay is at least as large as the one under full priority in the coupled system. Therefore, the average delay of a typical type-1 flow as $c_2 \downarrow 0$ is strictly greater than what the optimal allocation (6) would result in.

The inefficiency could be eliminated if prioritization and payments are linked differently than by the congestion mark tariff. Indeed, in Proposition 4 we show that when $\mathcal{A}_1 = \mathcal{P}(\mathcal{U}_0)$, $\mathcal{A}_2 = \mathcal{P}(\mathcal{U}_1)$ and a charge is imposed on the volume of downloaded bits as well as on the volume of congestion marks, the system is efficient in the limit as $c_2 \downarrow 0$. The intuition of why this is true is the following. Suppose a charge v^{c_2} is imposed on every bit carried by the link. Then, the net value per bit of type-i becomes,

$$r_i - c_i d_i(\theta, \pi) - v^{c_2} - m_i(\theta, \pi), i = 1, 2,$$

under any demand/parameter vector (θ, π). Also redefine the definition of equilibrium such that part 1 in Definition 1 becomes "$r_i - c_i d_i(\theta, \pi) - v^{c_2} - m_i(\theta, \pi) \leq 0$. If the inequality is strict then $\theta_i = 0$.". Now, if $v^{c_2} \approx r_2$ then type-2 flows have a very small margin for extracting value out of their bits. Thus, the charges incurred by congestion marks should be kept small, and so type-2 flows have the incentive of choosing low priority. On the other hand, since they pay a nonzero price v for each bit, a tragedy of the commons situation does not arise.

We also observe that Proposition 4 may not hold for other $\mathcal{A}_1$ beyond $\mathcal{P}(\mathcal{U}_0)$. This is because, by Proposition 2, efficiency implies that the system asymptotically behaves as a priority system, so the equilibrium demand reached by type-1 flows should be the same as in the single type case (see Section 4) for a delay independent reward equal to $r_1 - v^{c_2} \approx r_1 - r_2$ instead of r_1. But as Proposition 1 shows, a choice of $\mathcal{A}_1 = \mathcal{P}(\mathcal{U}_1)$ would not generate the maximum welfare for type-1 flows; one should have $\mathcal{P}(\mathcal{U}_0)$ instead.

Proposition 4 (Efficiency of two part tariff). *Let $\mathcal{A}_1 = \mathcal{P}(\mathcal{U}_0)$ and $\mathcal{A}_2 = \mathcal{P}(\mathcal{U}_1)$. For each $c_2 > 0$ let $(\theta^{c_2}, \pi^{c_2})$ be an equilibrium under bit price v^{c_2} with $v^{c_2} \to r_2$, and $(\theta^{c_2}, \pi^{c_2}) \to (\theta^0, \pi^0)$. The following hold:*

1. *If $r_1 > r_2$ then $\pi_1^0 > \pi_2^0$, $\pi_2^0(\{0\}) = 1$.*
2. *$\mathcal{W}(\theta^{c_2}, \pi^{c_2}, c_2) \to \mathcal{W}^*$ as $c_2 \to 0$, where $\mathcal{W}^*$ is as in Proposition 2.*

Proof. Since $(\theta^{c_2}, \pi^{c_2})$ is an equilibrium for each c_2, we have $0 \leq m_2(\theta^{c_2}, \pi^{c_2}) = r_2 - v^{c_2} - c_2 d_2(\theta^{c_2}, \pi^{c_2}) \leq r_2 - v^{c_2}$. But $v^{c_2} \uparrow r_2$, so $E_{c_2}^0(wT)\mu_2 = m_2(\theta^{c_2}, \pi^{c_2}) \to 0$, where w, T is the willingness to pay and download delay of an arriving type-2 flow at time 0. Since $T \geq Z/C$ where Z is the random file size, we have $E_{c_2}^0(w)/(\mu_2 C) = E_{c_2}^0(wZ)/C \leq E_{c_2}^0(wT) \to 0$. Thus, $\pi_2^{c_2} \to \pi_2^0$ where $\pi_2^0(\{0\}) = 1$, i.e., as type-2 users become less sensitive to delay they tend to be less aggressive. We now show that this is not the case for any significant proportion of type-1 users by arriving at a contradiction. If $\pi_1^0(\{0\}) > 0$ then for any $\gamma > 0$ there exists a sequence $p^{c_2} \downarrow 0$ with

$$r_1 - c_1 d_1(p^{c_2}; \pi^{c_2}, \theta^{c_2}) - v^{c_2} - p^{c_2} = r_1 - c_1 d_1(\pi^{c_2}, \theta^{c_2}) - v^{c_2} - m_1(\theta^{c_2}, \pi^{c_2}) = 0,$$
$$\text{and } \pi_1^{c_2}((p^{c_2}, +\infty)) \geq 1 - \gamma.$$

We show that a type-1 user is better off by choosing a constant parameter $\epsilon > 0$ for all c_2 small enough. By Lemma 1 and the fact $d_1(p^{c_2}; \theta^{c_2}, \pi^{c_2}) \geq d_1(0; ((1 - \gamma)\theta_1^{c_2}, \theta_2^{c_2}), \pi^0)$, we have

$$\limsup_{c_2 \downarrow 0} \left[c_1 d_1(\epsilon; \theta^{c_2}, \pi^{c_2}) + \epsilon - c_1 d_1(p^{c_2}, \theta^{c_2}, \pi^{c_2}) - p^{c_2} \right]$$

$$\leq \frac{c_1 C}{\left(C - \theta_1^0 \pi_1^0((\epsilon, +\infty))\right)^2} + \epsilon - \frac{c_1 C}{\left(C - \theta_1^0(1 - \gamma)\right)^2} . \qquad (9)$$

But $\pi_1^0((\epsilon, +\infty)) \leq 1 - \pi_1^0(\{0\}) < 1$, so the right hand side of (9) is less than or equal to

$$\frac{c_1 C}{\left(C - \theta_1^0(1 - \pi_1^0(\{0\}))\right)^2} + \epsilon - \frac{c_1 C}{\left(C - \theta_1^0(1 - \gamma)\right)^2} ,$$

which is strictly negative for sufficiently small $\epsilon > 0$ and some $\gamma > 0$. Hence for such ϵ, γ

$$r_1 - c_1 d_1(\theta^{c_2}, \pi^{c_2}) - v^{c_2} - m_1(\theta^{c_2}, \pi^{c_2})$$
$$< r_1 - c_1 d_1(\epsilon; \theta^{c_2}, \pi^{c_2}) - v^{c_2} - m_1(\epsilon; \theta^{c_2}, \pi^{c_2}) = 0 ,$$

for sufficiently small c_2, which contradicts the fact that $(\theta^{c_2}, \pi^{c_2})$ is an equilibrium for all c_2.

We now proceed to prove part 2. If $r_1 < r_2$ then for all values of c_2 for which $r_1 < v^{c_2} < r_2$, the equilibrium allocation $\theta^{c_2} = (0, C)$ is efficient. So assume $r_1 > r_2$ in what follows. If $0 < r_1 - r_2 < c_1/C$ then again $\theta^{c_2} = (0, C)$ is efficient since type-1 flows will never find it beneficial to join as it is optimal to balk even at an empty system, so we are left with $r_1 - r_2 > c_1/C$. By part 1 and Lemma 2, (θ_1^0, π_1^0) is characterized as the equilibrium that results when type-2 flows are absent, and the delay independent reward in (1) for type-1 users is $r_1 - r_2$ (instead of r_1 originally). Since $\mathcal{A}_1 = \mathcal{P}(\mathcal{U}_0)$, by Proposition 1 we have that θ_1^0 maximizes

$$\theta_1 \left(r_1 - r_2 - \frac{c_1 \mu_1}{C - \theta_1} \right) = \mathcal{W}(\theta_1, C - \theta_1, 0) - r_2 C ,$$

with respect to θ_1, hence $\theta_1^0 = \theta_1^*$.

The next lemma shows that if the average rate of payments by type-2 flows is negligible and they tend to choose less aggressive parameters, then they do not interfere with type-1 flows in the limit.

Lemma 1. *Under the assumptions of Proposition 4, for every $p > 0$*

$$d_1(p; \theta^{c_2}, \pi^{c_2}) \to d_1(p; \theta^0, \pi^0) = \frac{C}{\left(C - \theta_1^0 \pi_1^0((p, +\infty))\right)^2} , \quad as \ c_2 \downarrow 0 .$$

Proof. For fixed c_2 we calculate the instantaneous bandwidth $x_i(t)$ allocated to all type-i flows at time t when $n_i(t)$ type-i flows are present, for $i = 1, 2$. Furthermore, let $p_1, \ldots, p_{n_1(t)}$ and $w_1, \ldots, w_{n_2(t)}$ be the congestion control parameters chosen by the active type-1 and type-2 flows respectively. $x_1(t), x_2(t)$ are given by the optimal solution of the optimization problem

$$\max_{x_1, x_2 \geq 0} \left(\max_{i=1,\ldots,n_1(t)} p_i x_1 + \sum_{j=1}^{n_2(t)} w_j \log x_2 \right) , \quad where \ x_1 + x_2 \leq C .$$

For fixed but arbitrary $\delta > 0$, $x_1(t)$ dominates $\hat{x}_1(t)$ the optimum x_1 in

$$\max_{x_1, x_2 \geq 0} \left(\max_{i=1,\dots,n_1(t)} I(t)p_i x_1 + \delta \log x_2 \right) , \quad \text{where } x_1 + x_2 \leq C .$$

where $I(t) = 1$ if $\sum_{j=1}^{n_2(t)} w_j \leq \delta$ and zero otherwise.

Now,

$$P_{c_2}(I(t) = 1) = 1 - P_{c_2} \left(\sum_{j=1}^{n_2(t)} w_j > \delta \right)$$

$$\geq 1 - \frac{E_{c_2}\left(\sum_{j=1}^{n_2(t)} w_j \right)}{\delta} = 1 - \frac{m_2(\theta^{c_2}, \pi^{c_2})}{\delta} \to 1 ,$$

as $c_2 \downarrow 0$. Thus, most of the time the departure rate is no less than $\mu_1 \hat{x}_1(t)$, which for small δ is arbitrarily close to C when $n_1(t) > 0$. Hence, as $c_2 \downarrow 0$ the distribution of $n_1(t)$ at stationarity converges to that of a birth-death process with birth rate $\theta_1^0 \mu_1$ and death rate C, and an arriving type-1 flow with parameter p will see an M/M/1 queue with arrival rate $\mu_1 \theta_1^0 \pi_1^0((p, +\infty))$ and departure rate $\mu_1 C$. That is, it will have the least priority in this queue, and so

$$d_1(p; \theta^0, \pi^0) = \frac{C}{\left(C - \theta_1^0 \int_p^\infty d\pi_1^0 \right)^2} ,$$

using standard results for the M/M/1 queue.

The next lemma shows that the limit (θ^0, π^0) of equilibria as $c_2 \downarrow 0$, is itself an equilibrium of a system where type-2 flows are completely insensitive to delay. This permits a narrowing down of the possible limits by analyzing a simpler system.

Lemma 2. *Under the assumptions of Proposition 4, (θ^0, π^0) satisfies,*

1. $r_1 - r_2 - c_1 d_1(\theta^0, \pi^0) - m_1(\theta^0, \pi^0) = 0$.
2. π_1^0 *maximizes* $r_1 - r_2 - c_1 d_1(\pi_1'; \theta^0, \pi^0) - m_1(\pi_1'; \theta^0, \pi^0)$ *over* $\pi_1' \in \mathcal{A}_1$.

Proof. By Lemma 1 and since $\pi^0(\{0\}) = 0$, we have

$$d_1(\theta^{c_2}, \pi^{c_2}) = \int_0^\infty d_1(p; \theta^{c_2}, \pi^{c_2}) d\pi_1^{c_2}(p) \to \int_0^\infty d_1(p; \theta^0, \pi^0) d\pi_1^0(p) = d_1(\theta^0, \pi^0),$$

as $c_2 \downarrow 0$. Moreover,

$$0 = r_1 - c_1 d_1(\theta^{c_2}, \pi^{c_2}) - v^{c_2} - m_1(\theta^{c_2}, \pi^{c_2}) ,$$

for all c_2, and $m_1(\theta^{c_2}, \pi^{c_2}) = \int p \, d\pi_1^{c_2}$. Thus,

$$0 = r_1 - c_1 d_1(\theta^0, \pi^0) - m_1(\theta^0, \pi^0) .$$

We now show part 2. We have,

$$r_1 - c_1 d_1(\pi'_1; \theta^{c_2}, \pi^{c_2}) - v^{c_2} - m_1(\pi'_1; \theta^{c_2}, \pi^{c_2})$$
$$\leq r_1 - c_1 d_1(\theta^{c_2}, \pi^{c_2}) - v^{c_2} - m_1(\theta^{c_2}, \pi^{c_2})$$
$$\leq r_1 - c_1 d_1(\theta^{c_2}, \pi^0) - v^{c_2} - \int_0^\infty p \, d\pi_1^{c_2}(p) \, .$$

Taking $c_2 \downarrow 0$ and using Lemma 1 yields
$$r_1 - c_1 d_1(\pi'_1; \theta^0, \pi^0) - r_2 - m_1(\pi'_1; \theta^0, \pi^0) \leq r_1 - c_1 d_1(\theta^0, \pi^0) - r_2 - m_1(\theta^0, \pi^0) \, .$$

6   Discussion

In the simple model of this paper we find that congestion control mechanisms coming from linear utilities have better properties than those based on logarithmic ($\alpha = 1$). The linear utility functions $\mathcal{U}_0$ correspond to the FileTransfer algorithm in [3] and are used in [16,17] along with slow timescale mechanisms that vary the slope of the linear utility according to user preferences over average rates rather than instantaneous one. But in practice, users decide whether their flows join or balk on the basis of some knowledge of the state, e.g., congestion level. Models allowing this type of information are surveyed in [11] and may prove helpful in the context of this paper.

Notice that logarithmic utility functions produce inefficient outcomes when users have linear valuations in average download delay. But this does not immediately imply the inadequacy of similarly behaving algorithms such as TCP. Since users might value higher moments of delay as well, e.g., variance, it will be interesting to account for these as well.

The existence and uniqueness of equilibria when utility functions vary over larger sets is an open problem, even in the single type case. For linear and logarithmic utility functions existence is shown by explicitly computing the effect of different parameters on net value per bit. For general utility functions we expect that more general methods such as fixed point theorems will prove fruitful.

Finally, in this paper we have not determined the welfare loss of inefficient outcomes. It is an open problem whether similar statements as in [12] regarding the price of anarchy, hold in the present model.

Acknowledgements. The authors would like to thank Bob Briscoe and Damon Wischik for useful discussions and suggestions on the subject of this paper, as well as the anonymous reviewers for their helpful comments. This research was supported by Trilogy (http://www.trilogy-project.org), a research project (ICT-216372) partially funded by the European Community under its Seventh Framework Programme.

References

1. Kelly, F.P.: Charging and Rate Control for Elastic Traffic. European Transactions on Telecommunications 8, 33–37 (1997)
2. Mo, J., Walrand, J.: Fair End-to-End Window-Based Congestion Control. IEEE/ACM Transactions on Networking 8, 556–567 (2000)

3. Gibbens, R., Kelly, F.P.: Resource Pricing and the Evolution of Congestion Control. Automatica 35, 1969–1985 (1999)
4. Naor, P.: The Regulation of Queue Size by Levying Tolls. Econometrica 37, 17–24 (1969)
5. Edelson, M., Hildebrand, K.: Congestion Tolls for Poisson Queueing Processes. Econometrica 43, 81–92 (1975)
6. MacKie-Mason, J., Varian, H.: Pricing Congestible Network Resources. IEEE Journal on Selected Areas in Communications 13, 1141–1149 (1995)
7. Gallager, R.: A Minimum Delay Routing Algorithm Using Distributed Computation. IEEE Transactions on Communications 25, 73–85 (1977)
8. Hassin, R.: On the Optimality of First Come Last Served Queues. Econometrica 53, 201–202 (1985)
9. Hassin, R.: Decentralized Regulation of a Queue. Management Science 41, 163–173 (1995)
10. Haviv, M., Van der Wal, J.: Equilibrium Strategies for Processor Sharing and Random Queues with Relative Priorities. Probability in the Engineering and Informational Sciences 11, 403–412 (1997)
11. Hassin, R., Haviv, M.: To Queue or not to Queue: Equilibrium Behavior in Queueing Systems. Kluwer Academic Publishers, Dordrecht (2005)
12. Johari, R., Tsitsiklis, J.: Efficiency Loss in a Network Resource Allocation Game. Mathematics of Operations Research 29, 407–435 (2004)
13. Hajek, B., Gopalakrishnan, G.: Do Greedy Autonomous Systems Make for a Sensible Internet? In: Conference on Stochastic Networks, Stanford University (2002)
14. Mendelson, H., Whang, S.: Optimal Incentive-Compatible Priority Pricing for the M/M/1 Queue. Operations Research 38, 870–883 (1990)
15. Mandjes, M.: Pricing Strategies Under Heterogeneous Service Requirements. In: IEEE INFOCOM 2003, pp. 1210–1220. IEEE Press, San Francisco (2003)
16. Key, P., Massoulié, L., Vojnovic, M.: Farsighted Users Harness Network Time-Diversity. In: IEEE INFOCOM 2005, pp. 2382–2394. IEEE Press, Miami (2005)
17. Courcoubetis, C., Dimakis, A.: Congestion Control and Pricing of Volume Intensive Applications. In: Proceedings of the 21st International Teletraffic Congress (2009), http://nes.aueb.gr/research/volume.pdf

Understanding and Preventing Tacit Collusion among Telecommunication Operators

Patrick Maillé[1], Maurizio Naldi[2], and Bruno Tuffin[3]

[1] Institut Telecom, Telecom Bretagne
2 rue de la Châtaigneraie CS 17607
35576 Cesson Sévigné Cedex, France
patrick.maille@telecom-bretagne.eu
[2] Università di Roma Tor Vergata
Dip. di Informatica Sistemi Produzione
Via del Politecnico 1
00133 Roma, Italy
naldi@disp.uniroma2.it
[3] INRIA Rennes - Bretagne Atlantique
Campus universitaire de Beaulieu
35042 Rennes Cedex, France
btuffin@irisa.fr

Abstract. Modeling the competition among telecommunication operators (or providers) as a repeated game may explain why tacit collusion to maintain high charging prices can be observed. Such outcomes clearly do not benefit the users, nor do they provide operators with incentives to improve the network quality of service to outperform their competitors. We propose a simple regulation based on price stability over time, to modify the game played by operators in a way that could prevent collusion.

Keywords: Competition, Game theory, Repeated games.

1 Introduction

Competition in the telecom sector has been hard since liberalization, being characterized by a number of subsequent market twists (booms and downturns), resulting e.g. in a flurry of new operators followed by market concentration periods [1]. Due to the asymmetry existing between the incumbent operator and the new entrants, these have been forced to move boldly to gain market shares. Though competitors could use several leverages, telecom providers have typically acted on prices, sometimes engaging in a price war, where a price reduction by a provider is immediately followed by similar price reductions by its competitors, spurring a downward spiral [2]. Price wars are generally considered to be quite harmful for providers in the long term, since they cut the revenues of all the competitors despite the demand increase [3]. Instead, customers largely benefit from the general reduction of prices, as long as the benefit of expense reduction is not

R. Núñez-Queija and J. Resing (Eds.): NET-COOP 2009, LNCS 5894, pp. 249–263, 2009.

accompanied by worsening quality of service [4]. However, Chamberlin showed that, in a scenario with a limited number of competitors, oligopolistic coordination is likely to occur, resulting in the joint maximization of profits rather than a price war [5,6]. Cases of collusion (explicit or tacit) have been reported in the literature, both in the long distance market [7] and in the mobile sector [8] [9].

In this paper we analyse the game resulting from the competition between providers and the strategies leading to price war or collusion. Though the analysis of competition is generally dealt with in a static setting, a customer is continually confronted with the task of choosing the best provider, even on a call by call basis. Hence we consider here the competition between providers as a repeated game, where providers may continually update their prices to regain lost customers. The time aspect makes competition on prices different from a one-shot game. We show that a solution strategy in the repeated game leads to tacit collusion, hence to the prices resulting from the joint maximization of profits. We then propose imposing price stability as a regulation tool to prevent joint profit maximization from being a Nash equilibrium of the game and we also show that it can be effective to deter providers from tacit collusion.

The paper is organized as follows. Section 2 presents the demand model and the competition game that is repeatedly played between two providers, highlighting two possible outcomes of that game (the noncooperative and the cooperative ones). In Section 3, we recall the main results on repeated game theory and show how a repeated game model is well-suited to our problem, thereby leading to collusion among providers as an equilibrium. Section 4 proposes a regulatory measure based on price stability, and Section 5 investigates its effect when both providers are identical (symmetric game). Some asymmetric examples are studied in Section 6 to illustrate some particularities of the game and the proposed regulation. Conclusions and directions for future work are given in Section 7.

2   Demand Model and Competition Game among Providers

In this paper we focus on the case of two providers. We introduce in this section the dependence of provider demands with the prices they set, and present the game played between the competing providers seeking to maximize their profit.

Assumption 1. *Following [10], we consider the following demand model where demand at each provider depends on all providers' prices. Demand D_i at provider $i \in \{1, 2\}$ is given by*

$$D_1 = D_{0,1} - b_1 p_1 + \beta_1 p_2 \tag{1}$$
$$D_2 = D_{0,2} - b_2 p_2 + \beta_2 p_1 \tag{2}$$

where $D_{0,i}$ is the demand level if prices were set to zero, $b_i > 0$ represents the negative effect of provider i's price on his demand, and $\beta_i > 0$ the positive effect of the concurrent's price.

Remark that the expressions in (1)-(2) can give negative demands for some values of the parameters. However for the cases we will consider (namely, non-cooperative and cooperative situations among providers), the demand for each provider will be nonnegative.

It is also assumed that a uniform price increase by any firm cannot produce a total demand increase, implying $b_1 \geq \beta_2$ and $b_2 \geq \beta_1$. Moreover, we expect the direct effect of price b_i on demand D_i to be strictly larger than the indirect effect of the competitor's price β_i. We summarize those conditions below

$$\forall i \neq j, \quad \begin{cases} b_i > \beta_i \\ b_i \geq \beta_j. \end{cases} \tag{3}$$

The utilities of the providers are given by their revenues, i.e. the products $price \times demand$:

$$U_1(p_1, p_2) = p_1 D_1 = p_1(D_{0,1} - b_1 p_1 + \beta_1 p_2) \tag{4}$$
$$U_2(p_1, p_2) = p_2 D_2 = p_2(D_{0,2} - b_2 p_2 + \beta_2 p_1). \tag{5}$$

Investigating the best response of provider 1, we can see that $\partial U_1/\partial p_1 = D_{0,1} - 2b_1 p_1 + \beta_1 p_2$, and a maximum is obtained at $p_1 = (D_{0,1} + \beta_1 p_2)/(2b_1) > 0$. Similarly, the best response for provider 2 in function of provider 1's price p_1 is $p_2 = (D_{0,2} + \beta_2 p_1)/(2b_2) > 0$. A Nash equilibrium (if any) is therefore a point satisfying those two equations. The system has a unique solution

$$(p_1^N, p_2^N) = \left(\frac{2b_2 D_{0,1} + \beta_1 D_{0,2}}{4b_1 b_2 - \beta_1 \beta_2}, \frac{2b_1 D_{0,2} + \beta_2 D_{0,1}}{4b_1 b_2 - \beta_1 \beta_2} \right). \tag{6}$$

Remark that those prices are positive since $4b_1 b_2 > \beta_1 \beta_2$ from (3).

The corresponding utility values at the Nash equilibrium are denoted by U_1^N and U_2^N, and given by

$$U_1^N = b_1 \left(\frac{2b_2 D_{0,1} + \beta_1 D_{0,2}}{4b_1 b_2 - \beta_1 \beta_2} \right)^2$$
$$U_2^N = b_2 \left(\frac{2b_1 D_{0,2} + \beta_2 D_{0,1}}{4b_1 b_2 - \beta_1 \beta_2} \right)^2.$$

If we are now interested in the cooperative case where both providers try to maximize the sum of their utilities. $U(p_1, p_2) = U_1(p_1, p_2) + U_2(p_1, p_2) = p_1(D_{0,1} - b_1 p_1 + \beta_1 p_2) + p_2(D_{0,2} - b_2 p_2 + \beta_2 p_1)$, the maximum is obtained when $\partial U/\partial p_1 = \partial U/\partial p_2 = 0$, i.e., $D_{0,1} - 2b_1 p_1 + \beta_1 p_2 + p_2 \beta_2 = 0$ and $p_1 \beta_1 + D_{0,2} - 2b_2 p_2 + \beta_2 p_1 = 0$. It yields

$$p_1^* = \frac{2b_2 D_{0,1} + (\beta_1 + \beta_2) D_{0,2}}{4b_1 b_2 - (\beta_1 + \beta_2)^2}$$
$$p_2^* = \frac{2b_1 D_{0,2} + (\beta_1 + \beta_2) D_{0,1}}{4b_1 b_2 - (\beta_1 + \beta_2)^2}.$$

We can verify that under (3), those prices are positive, as well as the corresponding revenue for each provider.

Remark 1. Notice that competition actually leads to a price reduction with respect to the cooperative setting. The ratio indeed gives

$$\frac{p_1^N}{p_1^*} = \frac{4b_1b_2 - (\beta_1 + \beta_2)^2}{4b_1b_2 - \beta_1\beta_2} \frac{2b_2D_{0,1} + \beta_1D_{0,2}}{2b_2D_{0,1} + (\beta_1 + \beta_2)D_{0,2}},$$

which is in the interval $(0, 1)$ since both terms in the product are.
Similarly, we can also show that $p_2^N < p_2^*$, therefore from the user point of view the noncooperative situation is preferable.

3   Competition as a Repeated Game

One of the aims of opening the telecommunication market and allowing several providers was to induce competition that would be beneficial for the end users. Indeed, with the possibility of losing customers, providers are incentivized to improve their quality of service, and minimize their costs so as to propose attractive prices to users, in order to retain them or attract new customers. That pricing aspect is illustrated in the previous section: if the two providers play noncooperatively (i.e. under competition), then the prices set are lower than if providers are actually owned by the same entity and maximize the sum of their revenues. Here, competition intends to make providers play a so-called "prisoner's dilemma" game [11], with a unique Nash equilibrium that does not optimize the sum of their revenues: providers have interest in cooperating so as to maximize that sum [5], but then the temptation to cheat (i.e., decrease one's price to attract more customers) is very strong.

The providers being trapped in lowering prices results in benefits to users, and in that sense is a socially desirable outcome. A possible way to quantify the performance of an outcome is the total amount of demand that is served, that is the number of users that find the price of the service low enough and subscribe. In that sense, the Nash outcome of the pricing game outperforms the joint-maximization one: from (1)-(2) the sum of the demands $D_1 + D_2$ is

$$D_1 + D_2 = D_{0,1} + D_{0,2} - (b_1 - \beta_2)p_1 - (b_2 - \beta_1)p_2,$$

which is nonincreasing in both prices from (3). Since we saw in Remark 1 that $p_i^N < p_i^*$ for each provider i, then total demand with Nash prices is larger than with joint revenue maximization prices.

However, the pricing game described in the previous section does not take into account the *time* aspect: the game among providers is not played only once, but over several time periods (days, months or years). In general, user demand does not immediately adapt to prices, because switching providers may take time. However, users may choose their provider only for a specific service session (say, to connect to a WiFi hotspot). In that case, it is reasonable to assume that there is no delay in user reaction to provider price changes. In this paper, we consider that framework, and therefore assume that at each time period the same game is repeated. In such a case, joint-maximization, that we interpret as collusion among providers, may indeed occur despite the incentives to behave non-cooperatively in the one-shot game. Fisher [12] summarizes that issue:

The study of any real oligopoly has largely become the study of how the joint-optimization solution is or is not achieved and the reasons why.[...] Tacit collusion is only made possible by the fact that the game, or games like it, will be played again.

A provider strategy in the repeated game is now a function that at each time period, associates an action (or a distribution over the possible actions) to the one-shot game strategies that have been played so far[1]. That set of previously played strategies is called the *history* of the game. Morerover, at each time period the players could make their action choice also dependent on some public signal, i.e. they can play *correlated* strategies [14]. We will not explicitly use such correlated strategies, so we do not enter the details here.

Provider i's utility for the repeated game is now defined as the sum of the utilities that he obtained at each time period, where a per-period discount factor $\delta \leq 1$ is used to compare gains obtained at different times. Consequently, if we denote by s_t the set of strategies for the one-shot game that are played at time t, the normalized[2] expected utility of provider i is

$$V_i = (1 - \delta) \sum_{t=0}^{+\infty} \delta^t U_i(s_t). \tag{7}$$

The discount factor represents the "patience" of the players: the smaller it is, the more players value present gains against future ones. That factor δ can have different interpretations:

- it can represent the price in the current period of a monetary unit in the next period: if a per-period interest rate $r > 0$ is applied, then this gives $\delta = \frac{1}{1+r}$.
- Independently of interest rates, the factor δ can also stand for the probability of the game continuing at next period. Indeed, especially in telecommunication networks, the rapid evolution of technologies and services may lead to some services being abandoned by customers, consequently ending the competition game among providers.
- The most realistic interpretation is to consider that δ represents both of those aspects, and could for example be expressed as

$$\delta = \frac{1}{1+r} \mathbb{P}(\text{game continues at next period}).$$

3.1 General Results on Repeated Games

In this subsection, we recall the main existing results on repeated games that are related to our problem. We particularly focus on different versions of the

---

[1] Remark that in general, mixed strategies are not directly observable, since only actions are observed. Nevertheless the general results given in the next section also hold when only actions are observed [13].

[2] We add the multiplicative constant $(1-\delta)$, so that the sum in (7) gives the weighted mean of the player utilities over time periods, with weight δ^t for period t.

so-called *Folk Theorem*, that investigates the possible outcomes of a repeated game. Consider a game with N players, that is repeated over time periods. For the simple game, the set of actions of each player i is A_i, and we represent the actions of all players as a vector $a := (a_1, ..., a_N) \in \prod_{i=1}^N A_i$ where $a_i \in A_i$ is the action of player i.

We denote by $U_i^{\min}$ the *minimax* utility of player i, i.e. the minimal utility that he can ensure when the other players try to minimize i's utility:

$$U_i^{\min} := \min_{a_{-i} \in A_{-i}} \max_{a_i \in A_i} U_i(a_i, a_{-i}),$$

where a_{-i} (resp. A_{-i}) stands for the actions (resp. set of possible actions) of players different from i, and we write the overall action vector as $a = (a_i, a_{-i})$. Consequently, $U_i^{\min}$ is the worst utility that i can ensure if he knows the actions of his opponents. It can also be interpreted as the worst utility that the other players can impose on player i, and the corresponding strategies that they play to do so are called the *minimax* strategies against player i.

We also denote by $\mathbf{U}$ the set of "reachable" utility vectors of the simple game, i.e.

$$\mathbf{U} := \{(U_1(a), \ldots, U_N(a)) : a \in \prod_{i=1}^N A_i\}$$

The basic version of the Folk Theorem is as follows.

Theorem 1 (The Folk Theorem). *For any $(v_1, ..., v_N)$ in the convex hull of $\mathbf{U}$, such that $v_i > U_i^{\min}$, if δ is sufficiently close to 1 then there exists a Nash equilibrium of the infinitely repeated game where, for all i, $V_i = v_i$.*

The proof is simple: the utility vector $(v_1, ..., v_N)$ is reachable via a (correlated) strategy vector $(s_1, ..., s_N)$ (see for example [15] for a proof). The Nash strategies consist in each player i playing s_i while everybody does, and if a player j deviates then all other players should minimize his utility forever, playing the minimax strategy against j.

However, in repeated games the notion of Nash equilibrium might not be strong enough: for example the previously described Nash strategies impose each player to sanction the first deviator forever, although this might be costly to them. Therefore, there might be no incentive to sanction the deviators. As a result, for a potential deviator the threat of being sanctioned might not be credible, and the deviator can reasonably expect that he will not be sanctioned.

For that reason, we use the stronger equilibrium concept of *perfect* (or subgame perfect) Nash equilibrium. A perfect Nash equilibrium strategy should be a Nash strategy for any subgame of the game, i.e. in any situation that can be attained. Therefore, if there exists a perfect Nash equilibrium implying sanctions, then it includes incentives for the sanctioning players to actually perform the sanctions.

Below we give three versions of the Folk Theorem involving perfect equilibria, with different hypotheses.

Theorem 2 (Aumann-Shapley [16]/Rubinstein [17]). *If $\delta = 1$ then the Folk Theorem holds with perfect equilibrium.*

Theorem 3 (Friedman [18]). *For all $v = (v_1, ..., v_N)$ in the convex hull of U, if $v_i > U_i(a^N)$ where a^N is a Nash equilibrium of the simple game, then if δ is sufficiently close to 1, there exists a perfect Nash equilibrium of the infinitely repeated game where, for all i, $V_i = v_i$.*

Theorem 4 (Fudenberg and Maskin [13]). *With two players, the Folk Theorem holds with perfect equilibrium. Moreover, for more than three players, if the convex hull V^* of the reachable utility vectors dominating the minimax utilities is of dimensionality N, then for any $(v_1, ..., v_N) \in V^*$, if δ is sufficiently close to 1 then there exists a perfect equilibrium of the infinitely repeated game in which player i's average payoff is v_i.*

The proofs for those results are built the same way: the perfect equilibrium strategy consists of playing at each period the same strategy that gives utility vector v until someone deviates, and following a sanction procedure against the first deviator. The constraint of the equilibrium being perfect makes the sanction procedure more complex than for the classical version of the Folk Theorem. We do not enter the details of those strategies in this paper.

3.2 Implications for Our Problem

If we consider that the only pure strategies available to the providers are the Nash and joint-maximization prices exhibited in Section 2, then the one-shot game is a somehow classical prisoner's dilemma game, where the minimax sanctioning strategies are actually the Nash strategies of the one-shot game. Since it is not likely that absolutely no discounting occurs, Theorem 2 does not apply. However, it is actually realistic that the per-period discount rate be very close to 1, because interest rates are low and/or periods are short. Therefore Folk Theorem versions in Theorems 3 and 4 apply to our model.

In particular, we focus on the particular outcome of the repeated game corresponding to tacit collusion between providers, i.e. the joint-maximization prices. Both Theorems 3 and 4 imply that if the parameter δ is sufficiently close to 1, then providers playing joint-maximization prices at each period is a subgame-perfect Nash outcome of the repeated game. This is undesirable from the point of view of users, since it means competition does not play its role in terms of price reduction.

If δ is large enough, it is very likely that the joint-maximization outcome is the Nash equilibrium that occurs among the infinity of possible perfect Nash equilibria. In the rest of the paper, we therefore look for ways to prevent such tacit collusion between the providers, by using regulatory tools.

4 Imposing Price Stability to Prevent Collusions

We propose here to build a regulation tool that would prevent joint-maximizing prices from being a perfect Nash equilibrium of the game played between providers.

To do so, the regulation that is applied needs to modify the game perceived by providers, so that the hypotheses of Theorems 3 and 4 do not hold anymore. Both theorem assumptions (as well as the classical Folk Theorem) involve a δ that is sufficiently close to 1, so those theorems do not apply anymore if we manage to reduce the value of δ. The value of δ is not chosen by the regulator, but is a fixed value perceived by providers, that cannot be affected by regulator's decision. However, the regulatory measure that we propose has an effect that is equivalent to reducing the value of δ when $\delta < 1$.

We suggest that the regulator imposes some stability in the provider price decisions. More precisely, providers should be allowed to modify their price every k periods instead of every period, where k is the stability constraint over time, fixed by the regulator. This can be written formally as follows: for each provider i and each $m \in \mathbb{N}$ we impose price stability for a duration of k periods, i.e.

$$a_{km+\ell} = a_{km} \quad \forall m \in \mathbb{N}, i = 1, ..., N, \ell < k. \tag{8}$$

Now rewrite the objective function (overall utility) of each player i:

$$V_i = (1 - \delta) \sum_{t=0}^{\infty} \delta^t U_i(a_t)$$

$$= (1 - \delta) \sum_{m=0}^{\infty} \delta^{km} \sum_{\ell=0}^{k-1} \delta^\ell U_i(a_{km+\ell})$$

$$= (1 - \delta) \sum_{\ell=0}^{k-1} \delta^\ell \sum_{m=0}^{\infty} \delta^{km} U_i(a_{km})$$

$$= (1 - \delta^k) \sum_{m=0}^{\infty} (\delta^k)^m U_i(a_{km}),$$

where the third line comes from (8). We find the same expression as in (7), but with δ^k instead of δ as the discount factor.

As a result, the price stability measure has the same effect on providers as a change of δ into δ^k, since the repeated game strategies only affect the actions at time periods $(km)_{m \in \mathbb{N}}$. Therefore, if $\delta < 1$, then the provider's "new perceived value" of the discount factor can be made as close to 0 as needed, through an appropriate choice of k. Notice however that introducing too much rigidity will be badly perceived by providers[3], so k should be chosen just large enough to prevent tacit collusion, as we will see next.

In what follows, we will keep the same notation for δ to designate the perceived discount factor, but we now consider the value of δ as a strategic variable for the regulator (who can reduce the original value of δ to δ^k).

---

[3] On the contrary, end users may prefer such price stability to fast time-varying tariffs.

5   Study of the Symmetric Competition Game

We study here our regulatory proposition, in the case when the game is perfectly symmetric. Moreover, we impose a condition on the relative values of the direct and indirect price influence factors, i.e. respectively, the b_i and β_i in (1) and (2).

Assumption 2. *We consider the linear demand model described in (1)-(2), and assume that both providers are identical:*

$$D_{0,1} = D_{0,2}, \qquad b_1 = b_2, \qquad \beta_1 = \beta_2.$$

Let us denote by D_0, b and β those common values for $D_{0,i}$, b_i and β_i, respectively.

Moreover, assume that the influence factor β of one provider's price over the demand of his opponent is sufficiently low with respect to the direct influence over his own demand, more precisely

$$\beta < \frac{2}{3}b. \tag{9}$$

In that case, the game that is repeated has symmetric Nash prices

$$p_1^N = p_2^N = \frac{D_0}{2b - \beta} := p^N,$$

leading to provider revenues

$$U_1^N = U_2^N = b\left(\frac{D_0}{2b - \beta}\right)^2 := U^N.$$

On the other hand, joint-maximizing prices are

$$p_1^* = p_2^* = \frac{D_0}{2b - 2\beta} := p^*,$$

and the corresponding provider revenues are

$$U_1^* = U_2^* = \frac{D_0^2}{4(b - \beta)}.$$

We have $p^* > p^N$ as proved before in the general case.

We now assume that providers only have the choice between playing price p^N or p^*. In cases when one provider plays p^N and the other p^*, the one playing the Nash price gets revenue

$$U_1(p^N, p^*) = U_2(p^*, p^N) = D_0^2 \frac{2b^2 + \beta^2 - 2b\beta}{(2b - 2\beta)(2b - \beta)^2},$$

while the opponent gets revenue

$$U_2(p^N, p^*) = U_1(p^*, p^N) = D_0^2 \frac{2b^2 - 3b\beta}{(2b - \beta)(2b - 2\beta)^2}.$$

	p^N	p^*
p^N	$(0,0)$	$\left(\frac{\beta^2}{2b(b-\beta)}, -\frac{\beta^2}{(2b-2\beta)^2}\right)$
p^*	$\left(-\frac{\beta^2}{(2b-2\beta)^2}, \frac{\beta^2}{2b(b-\beta)}\right)$	$\left(\frac{\beta^2}{4b(b-\beta)}, \frac{\beta^2}{4b(b-\beta)}\right)$

Fig. 1. The one-shot competition game among symmetric providers (under Assumption 2), with relative utilities $X = (U - U^N)/U^N$. Lines and columns represent the strategic choices of provider 1 and 2, while the values in the table are of the form (X_1, X_2).

We normalize the revenues at those outcomes through the linear transformation $X = (U - U^N)/U^N$. The results therefore give relative revenue values with respect to the Nash equilibrium utilities of the one-shot game. They are summarized in Figure 1.

Interestingly, the relative (with respect to the one-shot game Nash equilibrium) provider utilities depend only on the price sensitivities b and β, regardless of the value of D_0. Therefore, to study the game and set an appropriate value for the price stability duration, the regulator only needs to evaluate those sensitivities, and the per-period discount factor δ.

Moreover, notice that $\frac{\beta^2}{(2b-2\beta)^2} > \frac{\beta^2}{4b(b-\beta)}$ whenever $\beta < b$, so that we can write

$$\frac{\beta^2}{(2b-2\beta)^2} = (1+\alpha)\frac{\beta^2}{4b(b-\beta)}$$

with $\alpha > 0$.

We simplify again the writing of game without changing the relative preference of providers, by dividing all utilities by the constant factor $\frac{\beta^2}{4b(b-\beta)}$. That normalization of utilities yields the game depicted in Figure 2.

We can then apply Theorem 3 to the one-shot game depicted in Figure 2. If δ is large enough, joint-maximization can be attained by the following perfect Nash strategy for each provider.

	p^N	p^*
p^N	$(0,0)$	$(2, -1-\alpha)$
p^*	$(-1-\alpha, 2)$	$(1,1)$

Fig. 2. Simplified writing of the one-shot competition game among symmetric providers (under Assumption 2)

- Play p^* while both do,
- If one provider deviates, then play p^N forever.

This is a Nash equilibrium if the sanction in future periods for being in the situation (p^N, p^N) instead of (p^*, p^*) exceeds the immediate gain for deviating. The sanction in future periods equals $(1 - 0) \times \sum_{m=1}^{\infty} \delta^m = \delta/(1 - \delta))$, while the immediate gain for a deviator is $2 - 1 = 1$, therefore if $\delta/(1 - \delta) > 1$, or equivalently $\delta > 1/2$, then the strategy described before is a perfect Nash strategy.

On the contrary, if $\delta < 1/2$ then no outcome other than (p^N, p^N) can be sustained as a perfect Nash equilibrium of the repeated game. Indeed, any point (U_1, U_2) in the convex hull of $\mathbf{U}$ defined in Subsection 3.1 is such that $U_1 + U_2 \leq 2$, therefore necessarily at least one of the two providers expects an average weighted revenue less than 1 at a perfect Nash equilibrium. Consequently for that provider, switching from p^N to p^* represents an immediate gain larger than 1, and a total future sanction lower than $\delta/(1 - \delta) < 1$, which implies that he will always prefer playing p^N. Anticipating that, the competitor will also play p^N.

Recall that δ is actually close to 1 in real situations, but we can artificially reduce it through the price stability regulation policy explained before. For the game we are studying, if we choose a "price stability period" k such that $\delta^k < 1/2$ then no collusion should occur. We therefore have a threshold on the stability period k to prevent collision from occurring as a (perfect) Nash equilibrium of the repeated game.

Proposition 1. *Consider a repeated competition game between two identical providers. Under Assumptions 1 and 2, then the high-prices situation (p^*, p^*) can be attained as a Nash equilibrium of the regulated repeated game between providers if and only if the price stability duration k is such that $\delta^k \geq 1/2$.*

On the contrary, if $\delta^k < 1/2$, then the only Nash equilibrium of the regulated repeated game is for each provider to play p^N at each period.

If we consider a quite stable technology, i.e. we neglect the probability that the technology be abandoned at the next time period, then the value of δ should be determined by the interest rate r, that we can take close to 5% per year to fix ideas. This would give a per year discount factor of $\delta = \frac{1}{1+r} = 0.95$. With such a value, remark that the price stability period imposed by the regulator should be of the order of $k = 15$ years so that the "regulated" discount factor δ^k become lower than $1/2$. Such a rigidity imposed by the regulator is much too strong to be acceptable[4], implying that for a perfectly symmetric game between providers, the regulation method we are suggesting cannot be applied to prevent collusion. However, we will see next in Subsection 6.2 that regulating through the imposition of a reasonable price stability can be efficient to elicit providers to actually play the competition game instead of colluding.

---

[4] We assume that a reasonable price stability period should be less than one year, or two at most.

6   Some Numerical Examples

In this section, we point out two specific examples where the game is not symmetric, that highlight different phenomena.

6.1   Joint-Maximization Is Not Always Beneficial to Both Providers

Consider the situation where $(D_{0,1}, D_{0,2}) = (1, 2)$, that can be interpreted as provider 2 being able to reach more customers (e.g. through a more extended coverage region). Then it can also seem realistic to consider that the price effects modeled by b_i and β_i, $i = 1, 2$, are also proportional to the covered population since only it can be affected by price changes. We take here the case where $b_i = 2\beta_i = \alpha D_{0,i}$ with a strictly positive constant α. Remark that α has no influence over normalized utilities, since it just depends on the price unit chosen; likewise, the influence on absolute utilities (revenues) is only through a multiplicative constant and does not affect the analysis of the game.

We give in Figure 3 the absolute utility values for the one-shot game with $\alpha = 1$. Interestingly, while the price profile (p_1^*, p_2^*) maximizes the sum of the

	p_2^N	p_2^*
p_1^N	$(0.44, 0.88)$	$(0.54, 0.72)$
p_1^*	$(0.14, 1.25)$	$(0.38, 1.25)$

Fig. 3. Provider utilities when $(D_{0,1}, D_{0,2}) = (3, 4)$ and $b_i = 2\beta_i = D_{0,i}$, $i = 1, 2$

provider revenues, we remark that provider 1 would prefer the profile (p_1^N, p_2^N) in terms of its own revenue. Therefore the collaborative price profile (p_1^*, p_2^*) is not sustainable as a Nash equilibrium of the repeated game. Possibly other kinds of collusions could occur, but they would imply some cycles in price strategies (e.g. provider 1 agrees to play p_1^*, in the exchange for provider 2 to tolerate a period where (p_1^N, p_2^*) later on), or mixed pricing strategies. Both possibilities are not realistic outcomes for a telecommunication market, where frequent price changes are badly perceived by customers. Therefore in such situations, the most likely outcome is that providers play at each time period the Nash equilibrium prices of the one-shot game, i.e. no collusion occurs.

6.2   A Limited Regulation Period May Be Sufficient to Prevent Collusions

Consider the same situation as in the previous subsection, but where the asymmetry between providers is less marked. We assume that $(D_{0,1}, D_{0,2}) = (3, 4)$, and still consider that $b_i = 2\beta_i = \alpha D_{0,i}$ with $\alpha > 0$.

The absolute (for the case $\alpha = 1$) and normalized provider utilities for the four outcomes of the one-shot game are given in Figure 4 and 5, respectively.

	p_2^N	p_2^*
p_1^N	$(1.33, 1.78)$	$(1.63, 1.42)$
p_1^*	$(0.86, 2.30)$	$(1.34, 2.18)$

Fig. 4. Provider utilities when $(D_{0,1}, D_{0,2}) = (3, 4)$ and $b_i = 2\beta_i = D_{0,i}$, $i = 1, 2$

	p_2^N	p_2^*
p_1^N	$(0, 0)$	$(64.45, -0.87)$
p_1^*	$(-101.76, 1.29)$	$(1, 1)$

Fig. 5. Normalized utilities when $(D_{0,1}, D_{0,2}) = (3, 4)$ and $b_i = 2\beta_i = \alpha D_{0,i}$, $i = 1, 2$

We remark in Figure 4 that the gain of collusion is quite low for provider 1 (less than 1% utility improvement) with respect to the noncooperative outcome (p_1^N, p_2^N), while it represents a revenue increase of more than 20% for provider 2. On the other hand, the incentive to cheat is strong for provider 1. Consequently, the collusion outcome (p_1^*, p_2^*) can only be sustained if the immediate gain to provider of playing p_1^N instead of p_1^* is lower than the loss in the remaining time periods. From Figure 5, this means that collusion can occur only if $(64.45 - 1) \leq \frac{\delta^k}{1-\delta^k}$, or equivalently $\delta^k \geq \frac{63.45}{64.45} = 0.9845$ if providers are allowed to change prices every k time periods. Remark that provider 2 is much more incentivized to keep on collaborating with his competitor, since the gain from collusion is large, and the temptation to cheat is quite low.

We assume that the game can be played on a monthly basis. Under that assumption, the probability that the technology be abandoned the period after is very low in general, while the interest rate can be reasonably taken of the order of 0.5% per month. Therefore, a monthly discount factor of $\delta = \frac{1}{1+0.005} = 0.995$ is reasonable. From the reasoning above, such a discount factor is sufficiently high to sustain collusion. But we also remark that the regulatory method based on price stability manages to prevent collusion as soon as prices have to be fixed for 4 months.

Therefore in that situation, the regulation method we are considering in this paper can be effective against provider collusion, with a limited flexibility restriction imposed on providers.

7   Conclusions

We have proposed to model competition between telecommunication service providers as a repeated noncooperative game, in order to understand some tacit collusion phenomena that have been recently observed in practice. We have remarked that the time aspects allows providers to build credible threats to each other so as to maintain high prices, even if each provider could improve its short-term revenue by a price decrease.

A simple regulation tool imposing some price stability could make the sanction threat between providers less efficient, and could thereby in some cases prevent high price situations to occur as a Nash equilibrium of the repeated game.

However, for some other cases (like when the game is perfectly symmetric), only a prohibitively long price stability period could be efficient against collusion. Some other regulation mechanisms need thus be found to make competition benefit to users in those cases.

Acknowledgments

The authors would like to acknowledge the support of Euro-NF Network of Excellence through the specific research project PRECO, and the French research agency through the CAPTURES project.

References

1. Cheng, J.Z., Tsyu, J.Z., Yu, H.C.D.: Boom and gloom in the global telecommunications industry. Technology in Society 25(1), 65–81 (2003)
2. Bergen, M.E., Rao, A.R., Davis, S.: How to fight a price war. Harvard Business Review 78(2), 107–116 (2000)
3. Brandenburger, A.M., Nalebuff, B.J.: Co-Opetition: A Revolution Mindset That Combines Competition and Cooperation: The Game Theory Strategy That's Changing the Game of Business, 1st edn. Doubleday Business (1997)
4. Currier, K.M.: A practical approach to quality-adjusted price cap regulation. Telecommunications Policy 31(8-9), 493–501 (2007)
5. Chamberlin, E.H.: A Theory of Monopolistic Competition. Cambridge, Massachusets (1933)
6. Fellner, W.: Competition among the Few: Oligopoly and Similar Market Structures. Alfred A. Knopf, New York (1949)
7. MacAvoy, P.W.: Tacit Collusion Under Regulation in the Pricing of Interstate Long-Distance Telephone Services. Journal of Economics & Management Strategy 4(2), 147–185 (1995)
8. Massey, P., McDowell, M.: Joint Dominance and Tacit Collusion: An Analysis of the Irish Vodafone/O2 Case and the Implications for Competition and Regulatory Policy. Working Paper WP08/05, UCD Centre for Economics Research, University College Dublin (2008)
9. Grzybowski, L., Karamti, C.: Competition in Mobile Telephony in France and Germany. Working Paper Series Working Paper 07-24, NET Institute (2007)
10. Allon, G., Federgruen, A.: Service competition with general queueing facilities. Operations Research 56(4), 827–849 (2008)
11. Fudenberg, D., Tirole, J.: Game Theory. MIT Press, Cambridge (1991)
12. Fisher, F.M.: Games economists play: A noncooperative view. The RAND Journal of Economics 20(1), 113–124 (1989)
13. Fudenberg, D., Maskin, E.: The folk theorem in repeated games with discounting or with incomplete information. Econometrica 54(3), 533–554 (1986)

14. Aumann, R.: Subjectivity and correlation in randomized strategies. Journal of Mathematical Economics 1(1), 67–96 (1974)
15. Osborne, M.J., Rubinstein, A.: A Course in Game Theory. MIT Press, Cambridge (1994)
16. Aumann, R., Shapley, L.: Long term competition: A game theoretic analysis. Mimeo, Hebrew University (1976)
17. Rubinstein, A.: Equilibrium in supergames with the overtaking criterion. Journal of Economic Theory 21, 1–9 (1979)
18. Friedman, J.: A noncooperative equilibrium for supergames. Review of Economic Studies 38, 1–12 (1971)

Competition and Cooperation between Nodes in Delay Tolerant Networks with Two Hop Routing

Eitan Altman

INRIA B.P.93, 2004 Route des Lucioles, 06902 Sophia-Antipolis Cedex, France

Abstract. This paper revisits the two-hop forwarding policy in delay tolerant networks (DTNs) and provides a rich study of their performance and optimization which includes (i) Derivation of closed form expressions for the main performance measures such as success delivery probability of a packet (or a message) within a given deadline. (ii) A study of competitive and cooperative operations of DTNs and derivation of the structure of optimal and of equilibrium policies. (iii) A study of the case in which the entity that is forwarded is a chunk rather than a whole message. For a message to be received successfully, all chunks of which it is composed have to arrive at the destination within the deadline. (iv) A study of the benefits of adding redundant chunks. (v) The convergence to the mean field limit.

1 Introduction

Through mobility of devices that serve as relays, Delay Tolerant Networks (DTNs) allow non connected nodes to communicate with each other. Such networks have been developed in recent years and adapted both to human mobility where the contact process is between pedestrians [5], as well as to vehicle mobility [7].

The source does not know which of the nodes that it meets will reach the destination within a requested time, so it has to send many copies in order to maximize the successful delivery probability. How should it use its limited energy resources for efficient transmission? Assume that the first relay node to transfer the copy of the packet to the destination will receive a reward, or that some reward is divided among the nodes that participated in forwarding the packet. With what probability should a mobile participate in the forwarding, what is the optimal population size of mobiles when taking into account energy and/or other costs that increase as the number of nodes increase? If it is costly to be activated, how should one control the activation periods?

We propose in this paper some answers to these questions using simple probabilistic arguments. We identify structural properties of both static and dynamic optimal policies, covering both cooperative and non cooperative scenarios.

This paper pursues the research initiated in [2] where the authors already studied the optimal static and dynamic control problems using a fluid model that represents the mean field limit as the number of mobiles becomes very large. That work has been extended in [3] to model the separable nature of a packet, which is composed of K blocks called chunks. Only once all chunks

R. Núñez-Queija and J. Resing (Eds.): NET-COOP 2009, LNCS 5894, pp. 264–278, 2009.
© Springer-Verlag Berlin Heidelberg 2009

corresponding to a packet are received, the packet is considered to be available at the destination. The authors of [3] also study adding H redundant chunks such that the packet can be reconstructed at the destination once it receives any K out of the $K + H$ chunks.

In this paper we revisit the work of [2,3] with the following differences. (i) In [3] it is assumed that memory is limited so that a mobile can only carry one chunk. In this paper we restrict to systems that do not have such constraints. (ii) Both problems [2,3] were modeled using a mean field limit. We consider here the exact models and show that the mean field limit serves as a bound for the performance of the original system. The bound becomes tight as the number of mobiles increases.

In [4], a related optimal dynamic control problem was solved in a discrete time setting. The optimality of a threshold type policy, already established in [2] for the fluid limit framework, was shown to hold in [4] for some discrete control problem. A game problem between two groups of DTN networks was further studied in [4]. We complement these in the current work by focusing on other types of game theoretical problems: those concerning competition between individual mobiles. We obtain the structure of equilibrium policies and compare them to the cooperative case.

2   Model

Consider n mobiles, and moreover, a single static source and destination. The source has a packet generated at time 0 that it wishes to send to the destination. Assume that any two mobiles meet each other according to a Poisson process with parameter λ. Whenever the mobile meets the source, the source may forward a packet to it. We consider the two hop routing scheme [1] in which a mobile that receives a copy of the packet from the source can only forward it if it meets the destination. It cannot copy it into the memory of another mobile.

Consider an active mobile with non-controlled transmission rate. Let T_1 be the first time it meets the source and let $T_1 + T_2$ be the first time after T_1 that it meets the destination. Denote

$$q_\rho = \exp(-\lambda\rho), \qquad Q_\rho = Q_\rho(\lambda) = (1 + \lambda\rho)\exp(-\lambda\rho)$$

Consider the event that the mobile relays a packet from the source to the destination within time ρ, i.e. $T_1 + T_2 \leq \rho$. $T_1 + T_2$ is an Erlang(2) random variable and therefore the probability of the above event is $1 - Q_\rho$. Note that $Q_\rho - q_\rho$ is the probability that $T_1 < \rho$ but that $T_1 + T_2 > \rho$.

Control problems. We consider central control, in which the source decides whether to transmit a packet when it is in contact with a mobile, and distributed control, in which the mobiles are those who take decisions, concerning both the transmission of packets to the destination as well as of receiving packets from the source.

As energy is limited or costly, we either limit the number of active mobiles, or we control dynamically the transmission rate. The first case corresponds to a *static optimization problem*; the decision variable u^i then stands for the probability of participation. The dynamic control problem in which one controls dynamically the transmission rates. An individual dynamic control u^i of mobile i then stands for a piecewise continuous function u_t^i taking values in $[0, 1]$.

We shall consider two control frameworks: a centralized control at the source, and a decentralized control at the mobiles. When dynamic control is applied at the source it will affect transmissions from the source to the mobiles. When mobiles control the transmission then both transmission from the source to the mobiles as well as those from the mobile to the destination are controlled[1].

Interpretation of a dynamic control policy. If a mobile meets the source at time t then it receives a packet with probability u_t^i. Moreover, in the case of decentralized control at the mobiles, if at time t, a mobile has a packet and it meets the destination then it delivers the packet with probability u_t^i.

Define $\zeta_t(j)$ to be the indicator that the jth mobile among the n receives the packet during $[0, t]$. $\{\zeta_t(j)\}_j$ are i.i.d. with the expectation and the Laplace Stieltjes Transform (LST) given by:

$$w_t^j := E[\zeta_t(j)] = 1 - \exp\left(-\lambda \int_0^t u_s^j ds\right)$$

$$E\left[\exp\left(-s\zeta_t(j)\right)\right] = w_t^j \exp(-s) + (1 - w_t^j) = 1 - (1 - \exp(-s))w_t^j$$

$$= 1 - (1 - \exp(-s))(1 - \exp(-\int_0^t u_s^j ds) = g\left(\int_0^t u_s^j ds\right)$$

where $g(Z) = \exp(-s) + (1 - \exp(-s))\exp(-sZ)$.

The probability that the destination does not receive a packet from mobile j by time τ is given by $E\left[\exp\left(-\lambda \int_0^\tau \zeta_t(j)dt\right)\right]$ in the case of control at the source, and by $E\left[\exp\left(-\lambda \int_0^\tau \zeta_t(j)u_t^j dt\right)\right]$ for the case of decentralized control by the mobiles.

Dynamic control at the source: A state representation. Let X_t be the number of mobiles with a copy of the packet at time t. We call X_t the state. The intensity of the process that counts the number of contacts between nodes with copies of the packet and the destination at time t is λX_t. Thus the number of contacts during the interval $[0, \tau]$ between the destination and mobiles that have copies of the packets is a Poisson random variable with intensity $\lambda \int_0^\tau X_s ds$. Consider the dynamic control policy u assumed to be common to all mobiles. Then $X_t = \sum_{j=1}^n \zeta_t(j)$ where $\{\zeta_t(j)\}_j$ are i.i.d. The LST of X_t satisfies

$$X_t^*(\lambda) := E\left[e^{-\lambda X_t}\right] = E\left[e^{-\lambda\left(\sum_{i=1}^n \zeta_t(i)\right)}\right] = \left(E\left[e^{-\lambda \zeta_t(1)}\right]\right)^n \tag{1}$$

---

[1] Receiving packets also requires energy. This is in particular the case if a mobile that does not have the packet has to send periodically a beacon to signal its presence so that the source would know when it is in transmission range.

Conditioned on X_t for $t \in [0, \tau]$, the number of packets that arrive at the destination has a Poisson distribution with parameter $\lambda \int_0^\tau X_t dt$. Define $F_D(\tau)$ as the probability that the destination receives the packet by time τ. Then

$$F_D(\tau) = 1 - E\left[\exp\left(-\lambda \int_0^\tau X_t dt\right)\right].$$

3   The Static DTN Game

It is assumed that the packet has to arrive at the destination τ units of time after it was created, otherwise it brings no utility to the destination. Let u^i be the probability that mobile i participates. $\{u^i, i = 1, ..., n\}$ is a symmetric equilibrium if u^i have the same value for all i and if no mobile can benefit from a unilateral deviation to some $v \neq u$.

Let $p(v, u)$ be the probability that the tagged mobile is the first to deliver the packet to the destination when it plays v and all others play u. A mobile other than the tagged one delivers a packet to the destination during the interval $[0, \tau]$ with probability $\beta := u(1 - Q_\tau)$. The probability that exactly $k - 1$ mobiles other than the tagged one deliver a packet to the destination within the time interval is therefore: $\sum_{k=1}^n \binom{n-1}{k-1} \beta^{k-1}(1 - \beta)^{n-k}$. Hence the probability of the tagged mobile to receive the unit award, if it decides to participate, is

$$P(u) = (1 - Q_\tau) \sum_{k=1}^n \binom{n-1}{k-1} \frac{\beta^{k-1}(1 - \beta)^{n-k}}{k}$$
$$= \frac{(1 - Q_\tau)(1 - (1 - \beta)^n)}{\beta n} = \frac{(1 - (1 - (1 - Q_\tau)u)^n)}{un}. \tag{2}$$

We shall sometime write $P_{n,\tau}(u)$ in order to make explicit the dependence on n and τ.

The utility and equilibrium. A mobile that participates receives a unit of reward if it is the first to deliver a copy of the packet to the destination. It further pays some energy cost $g\tau$ where $g > 0$ is some constant. $\mathcal{W}(1, u) = P(u) - g\tau$ is thus the (expected) utility for a tagged mobile of participating when each of the other mobiles participates with probability u. We assume that the utility $\mathcal{W}(0, u)$ for not participating is zero for all u. The utility for a mobile that participates with probability v when each other participates with probability u is $\mathcal{W}(v, u) = v\mathcal{W}(1, u)$. The following indifference property easily follows:

Lemma 1. *If there exists a policy u such that $\mathcal{W}(1, u) = 0$ then u is a symmetric equilibrium.*

$P(u)$ is a continuous convex decreasing function, $\lim_{u \to 0} P(u) = 1 - Q_\tau$ and $P(1) = (1 - Q_\tau^n)/n$. Thus the utility for choosing to participate $\mathcal{W}(1, u) = P(u) - g\tau$ is a continuous convex decreasing function, $\lim_{u \to 0} \mathcal{W}(1, u) = 1 - Q_\tau - g(\tau)$ and $\mathcal{W}(1, 1) = (1 - Q_\tau^n)/n - g\tau$. The utility for not participating is assumed to be zero. Thus we have

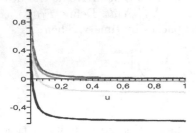

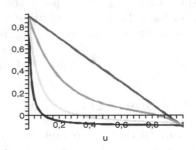

Fig. 1. The utility of participating as a function of u, for various values of the duration τ

Fig. 2. The utility of participating as a function of u, for various values of the number n of users

Lemma 2. *If* $(1 - Q_\tau^n)/n < g\tau$ *then there exists a unique symmetric equilibrium* u *which is the unique solution of* $\mathcal{W}(1, u) = \mathcal{W}(0, u) = 0$.

Numerical Examples. Figure 1 presents the utility for choosing to participate as a function of the strategy u of all other players for various values of the maximum duration τ: $\tau = 1, 5, 20, 60$. $\lambda = 10$ is taken to be a constant. The other parameters are $n = 100, g = 0.01$. We obtain four curves (one for each τ). We see that indeed for each value of τ there is a unique value of u for which $\mathcal{W}(1, u) = 0$, and this is the equilibrium. Here the curve that is the highest corresponds to $\tau = 1$, and the larger τ is, the lower the corresponding curve is. This then implies that the equilibrium value of u increases with τ.

In Figure 2 we repeat the same but with a fixed value $\tau = 10$ and varying values of n: $n = 3, 10, 30$ and 100. Again, the larger n is, the larger is also the curve. The equilibrium is thus increasing in n.

4   The Static Control Problem

We shall consider both the optimal symmetric control policy as well as the general non-symmetric one. We recall that we consider this as a problem in which the source controls the activation. A general activation policy is one that activates mobile i with probability u^i. A symmetric policy is one for which u^i are the same for all i. We consider here the utility

$$\mathcal{W}(u) = P_s(u) - g\tau \sum_{k=1}^{n} u^k$$

where
$$P_s(u) = 1 - \prod_{k=1}^{n}(u^k Q_\tau + (1 - u^k)) = 1 - \prod_{k=1}^{n}(1 - (1 - Q_\tau)u^k)$$

is the probability of successful transmission by time τ. The term $g\tau \sum_{k=1}^{n} u^k$ corresponds to a cost per expected energy.

Let U_d be the set of policies for which each u^k is either 0 or 1. We next show that the global utility for a general policy is minimized by a symmetric policy and maximized by a policy in U_d.

Lemma 3. *(i) There exists an optimal policy among U_d.*
(ii) A necessary condition for a policy u to be globally optimal is the following:

$$\boxed{\begin{array}{c} \textit{Except for at most one mobile, the probability} \\ \textit{of activating each mobile } i \textit{ is either } u^i = 0 \textit{ or } u^i = 1. \end{array}} \quad (3)$$

(iii) Any non-symmetric policy u performs strictly better than the symmetric policy v that has the same sum $\sum_{k=1}^{n} u^k = \sum_{k=1}^{n} v^k$.

Proof.(i) Let u be a policy for which for some k, $0 < u^k < 1$. We show that there exists a policy $v \in U_d$ that performs at least as well. Since the utility is linear in each u^k, we can change u^k to either 0 or to 1 without decreasing the utility. Repeating this procedure for all the remaining j's that are not extreme points, we obtain a policy in U_d that performs at least as well as u. This implies (i).

Choose an arbitrary $u = (u^1, ..., u^n)$. Consider now the problem of finding $v \in \mathcal{W}(u)$ under the constraint $\sum_{i=1}^{n} v^k = \sum_{i=1}^{n} u^k$. With this constraint, the policy maximizes this objective if and only if it minimizes the function $f(u)$ defined as

$$f(u) := \sum_{k=1}^{n} \psi(u^k) \quad \text{where } \psi(u) = \log(1 - (1 - Q_\tau)u).$$

ψ is a concave function of its argument, which implies that f is a Schur concave function, see Appendix. For any policy u which does not satisfy (3), we can construct a policy u' which satisfies (3) and $\sum_{k=1}^{n} u'^k = \sum_{k=1}^{n} u^k$. Then u' strictly majorizes u and therefore u strictly outperforms u'. In the same way one shows that any policy performs strictly better than the symmetric policy that has the same sum of components. ◇

In Figure 3 we compare the best solution among the symmetric policies and the global optimal solution.

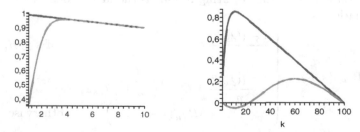

Fig. 3. Control case: Utility as a function of k

The left subfigure is obtained with the same parameters as used for the equilibrium in Figure 1: $g = 1, n = 100, \lambda = 10, \tau = 1$. The vertical axis corresponds to the utility, and the horizontal axis corresponds to the integer k. There are two curves. The top one is the utility under the non-symmetric policies, and the bottom is the one corresponding to symmetric ones. In the top figure, the integer k has the meaning that exactly k mobiles are activated. In the bottom curve, each mobile participates with probability u. u is defined by the ratio $u = k/n$. k varies between 1 to 10.

The right subfigure repeats the same experiment but with $\lambda = 1$ and with $n = 100$. In both subfigures we see that there is indeed a difference between the global optimal solution and the one obtained with the best symmetric policy. The latter is indeed seen to provide a smaller optimum.

Remark 1. The fact that an optimal policy exists among U_d means that there is an optimal number of mobiles that should participate. It can also be viewed as an optimal coalition size. We plan to study in the future the question of optimal coalition size in the case that there is competition between a given number N of coalitions.

5   The Dynamic DTN Game

In the last section we assumed a static game: a mobile took one decision, at time 0, on whether to participate or not. We now consider a dynamic game in which a mobile can switch on or off at any time. A pure policy u^i for a mobile i consists of the choice of time periods during which it is activated. $u_t^i = 1$ if the mobile is activated at time t and is zero if it is not. We may allow u_t^i to take also values in the interior of the unit interval. u_t^i is then interpreted as a mixed strategy: the mobile is activated at time t with probability u_t^i. The energy cost for the mobile is given by $g \int_0^\tau u_t^i dt$.

We introduce next threshold policies. A time threshold policy R is a policy that keeps a mobile active till time R and then deactivates it. We shall identify threshold equilibria for our problem. More precisely, assume that all mobiles use threshold policies with a common threshold R. We shall consider deviation of a single mobile to another threshold policy s and look for R such that $s = R$ is an optimal response of the deviating mobile.

The probability that the deviating mobile is the first to deliver the packet to the destination is

$$
P_{succ}(s, R) = \begin{cases} \dfrac{1 - (Q_s)^n}{n} & \text{if } s \leq R, \\[2ex] \dfrac{1 - (Q_R)^n}{n} + Q_R^{n-1}\Big(q_R(1 - Q_{s-R}) \\[1ex] \quad + \lambda R q_R(1 - q_{s-R})\Big) & \text{otherwise} \end{cases}
$$

The first term corresponds to the event that the first successful delivery occurs before time R, and the second term is related to its occurrence between time R

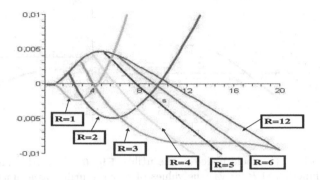

Fig. 4. Equilibria in threshold policies: The utility $\mathcal{W}(s, R)$ (vertical axis) for a mobile that uses a threshold policy s (horizontal axis) while all the other use a threshold policy with R. Each curve corresponds to another value of R.

and s. More precisely, the second term corresponds to the event that no one of the other $n-1$ mobiles met the source till time R, where as the tagged mobile either (i) did not meet the source before time R and then, during time interval $(R, s]$ met the source and then the destination, or (ii) it met the source at least once before R but did not meet the destination before R, and then it met the destination during $(R, s]$.

The utility for a player who uses a threshold s while all others use a threshold R is given by $\mathcal{W}(s, R) = P_{succ}(s, R) - gs$.

Figure 4 shows the utility $\mathcal{W}(s, R)$ for s varying between 0 and 20 and for $R = 1, 2, 3, 4, 5, 6, 12$. The horizontal axis corresponds to s and the vertical axis - to the utility. The remaining parameters are $g = .001, \lambda = .049, n = 95$. We observe the following.

• There are many equilibria. For R between 3 and 5, the best response is $s = R$ and hence any value of R in the interval [3,5] is a symmetric threshold equilibrium (for any horizon τ that is greater than R).

• $1 \le R < 3$ are also equilibria but only for some value of τ. For example, for $R = 2$, $s = 2$ is the best response as long as we restrict s to be smaller than 10.5; thus if $\tau \le 10.5$ then all R's between 2 and 5 are symmetric threshold equilibria. If we restrict to $\tau \le 4$ then the values of R in the whole range [1,5] provide symmetric equilibria.

An alternative way to see the multiple equilibria phenomenon is by plotting $\mathcal{W}(s, R)$ as a function of R for various values of s. We do so in Figure 5. This time we take $s = 1, 2, 3, 4, 5, 6, 12$. The intersection of the curves corresponding to the different values of s with the vertical axis are increasing with s. We indeed see that the best response to $R = 3$ is $s = 3$ but at the same time, $s = 4$ is the best response to $R = 4$. (To get the best response for $R = 3$, we take a vertical line that intersects the horizontal axis at $R = 3$. We see that the curve that corresponds to $s = 3$ achieves the largest utility.)

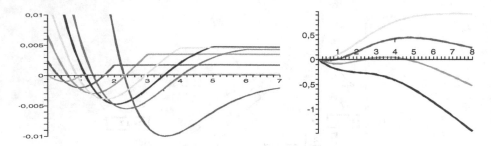

Fig. 5. Equilibria in threshold policies: The utility **Fig. 6.** The dynamic control $\mathcal{W}(s, R)$ as a function of R for various values of s case: utility as a function of R

6 The Dynamic Control Problem

We consider the optimization problem restricted to symmetric policies, i.e. where all mobiles use threshold policies and the threshold value R is the same for all mobiles. Using the theory of Markov Decision Processes it can be shown that there is no loss of optimality in doing so.

The global utility is then $\mathcal{W}(R) = 1 - (Q_R)^n - ngR$. We have

$$\frac{\partial \mathcal{W}(R)}{\partial R} = \frac{(Q_R)^n n \lambda^2 R}{1 + \lambda R} - ng, \qquad \frac{\partial^2 \mathcal{W}(R)}{\partial R^2} = \frac{n(Q_R)^n \lambda^2 (n\lambda^2 R^2 - 1)}{(1 + \lambda R)^2}$$

From the first derivative we see that $\mathcal{W}(R)$ is monotone. For all R sufficiently large, it is negative if $g < 1$ and is positive if $g > 1$. From the second derivative we see that $\mathcal{W}(R)$ is convex for $R < 1/(\lambda\sqrt{n})$ and is concave for $R > 1/(\lambda\sqrt{n})$.

An example is given in Figure 6. The experiment was done with $n = 95$. Each curve corresponds to another value of the parameter g: $g = 0.0001$ (top curve), $g = 0.0033$ (next to top), $g = 0.001$ and $g = 0.002$. We see that there may be one or two optimal values to the threshold R: it is either an extreme point ($R = 0$ or $R = \infty$) or it is an interior point.

Theorem 1. *There exists a unique optimal threshold policy. A policy is optimal only if (except for a set of Lebesgue measure zero) it agrees with this policy at all t.*

Proof. With X^* defined in (1), we have

$$1 - F_D(n) = E\left[\exp\left(-\lambda \int_0^\tau X_t dt\right)\right] = \exp \int_0^\tau \log(X_t^*(\lambda)) dt$$

where the last equality follows from the Lévy Khinchine formula. Hence

$$P(no\ success) = \exp\left(\int_0^\tau \log E\left[\exp\left(-\lambda X_t\right)\right] dt\right)$$

$$= \exp\left(n \int_0^\tau \log \gamma \left(\int_0^t u_s ds\right) dt\right)$$

$$\text{where} \quad \gamma(Z) := e^{-\lambda} + (1 - e^{-\lambda}) \exp(-\lambda Z) \tag{4}$$

Assume that u is not a threshold policy. Let v be the threshold policy that transmits till time $s^* := \int_0^\tau u_t dt$ and then stops transmitting. Then for every t,

$$\int_0^t u_s ds \le \int_0^t v_s ds$$

This implies that the first integral $\int_0^\tau$ is smaller under u and hence also the success probability.   ◇

A similar characterization of the optimal policy has been derived in [4] for the case of discrete time.

7   Transmitting Chunks

We assume below that a message is composed of K chunks. Consider some mobile that wishes to get the message within some time τ. We wish to compute the success probability (given by the probability to receive all K chunks within time τ). Assume that there are initially z_i nodes that have a copy of chunk i. It is assumed that the source can send at most one chunk when meeting another node. The dissemination of each chunk i follows the same dynamics as the one described in Section 2. Thus the probability of successful delivery is given by

$$F_D = \prod_{j=1}^{K} \left(1 - E\left[\exp\left(-\lambda \int_0^\tau X_t^j dt \right) \right] \right) \quad \text{so that}$$

$$\log F_D = \sum_{j=1}^{K} \log \mathbf{z}(u^j) \quad \text{where } \mathbf{z}(u^j) = 1 - \exp\left(n \int_0^\tau \log \gamma \left(\int_0^t u_s^j ds \right) dt \right) \tag{5}$$

and where $\gamma(Z)$ is given in (4). The above derivation follows the same steps as in Theorem 1.

We shall study below "constant" transmission policies which are special case of dynamic policies, as well as general dynamic policies. With a constant transmission policy u^i, mobile i is active. It receives a chunk from the source after an exponentially distributed time with parameter $u^i \lambda$. Once it has a chunk, it forwards it to the destination after an exponentially distributed time with parameter λ.

7.1   Optimal Transmission Policies

Consider now the following problems:

- (P1) Find a constant policy u^i that maximize $F_D - g\tau \sum_{i=1}^{K} u^i$,

- (P2) Find a dynamic policy $\mathbf{u}$ that maximizes $F_D - g \int_0^\tau \sum_{i=1}^{K} u_s^i ds$.

Lemma 4. *(i) Let u^i be constant in time. Then $\mathbf{z}(u^i)$ is concave in u^i.*
(ii) Let u^i be a threshold policy with threshold parameter σ. Then $\mathbf{z}(u^i)$ is concave in σ.

Proof. We recall that a convex increasing function of a convex function is convex, and that a concave increasing function of a concave function is concave. We prove (ii). (i) is obtained in the same way. Let u^i be a threshold policy with parameter s. We have

$$Z_t := \int_0^t u_r^i dr = \min(s, t)$$

and thus

$$V(t) := \log(\gamma(Z_t)) = \max[\log(\gamma(t)), \log(\gamma(s))]$$

Since $\log(\gamma(Z_t))$ is concave decreasing in Z_t, it is concave decreasing in s. Now

$$w(s) := \int_0^\tau V(t)dt = \int_0^\tau \max[\log(\gamma(t)), \log(\gamma(s))]dt$$

is concave decreasing in s since it is the integral (over t) of concave decreasing functions in s. Thus $nw(s)$ is concave decreasing in s. Since $1 - \exp$ is concave decreasing, then $1 - \exp(nw(s))$ is concave increasing. Since $\log$ is concave increasing, we obtain the concavity of $\mathbf{z}$.   ◇

Theorem 2. *Assume that the system is initially empty. Then*
(i) the policy that achieves the maximum in P1 is one whose components u^i are all equal.
(ii) Each component u^i of the policy u that achieves the maximum in P2 is a threshold policy, and the thresholds s are the same for all i.

Proof. Let u^i be given static policies. We have by Jensen's inequality

$$\frac{\log F_D(u)}{K} = \frac{\sum_{j=1}^K \log \mathbf{z}(\tau u^j)}{K} \le \log \mathbf{z}\left(\frac{\sum_{j=1}^K \tau u^j}{K}\right)$$

with equality holding above only when u^i is the same for all i. This establishes (i). (ii) The fact that one may restrict to threshold policies for each i follows by applying the proof of Theorem 1 to each u^i. So now let $s(i)$ be the threshold used by policy u^i. Then we have again by Jensen's inequality

$$\frac{\log F_D(u)}{K} = \frac{\sum_{j=1}^K \log \mathbf{z}(s(j))}{K} \le \log \mathbf{z}\left(\frac{\sum_{j=1}^K s(j)}{K}\right).$$

with equality holding above only when $s(j)$ is the same for all j.   ◇

7.2 Adding Redundant Chunks

We add H redundant chunks and code them in a way to ensure that the reception of any K chunks out of the $K + H$ ones is sufficient for the destination to be able to reconstruct the whole message.

Let $S_{n,p}$ be a binomially distributed r.v. with parameters n and p, i.e.

$$P(S_{n,p} = m) = B(p, n, m) := \binom{n}{m} p^m (1 - p)^{n-m}$$

The probability of a successful delivery of the message by time τ is thus

$$P_s(\tau, K, H) = \sum_{j=K}^{K+H} B(\mathbf{z}(Z_j), K + H, j), \quad \text{where} \quad Z_i := \int_0^t u_s^i ds.$$

Theorem 3. *Assume that the system is initially empty and assume that information is coded in a way that from any K different chunks out of $K + H$ different chunks, the destination can reconstruct the whole original message (that was composed by K initial chunks), Then*
(i) the policy that achieves the maximum in P1 is one whose components u^i are all equal.
(ii) each component u^i of the policy u that achieves the maximum in P2 is a threshold policy, and the thresholds s are the same for all i.

Proof. Let $A(K, H)$ be the set of subsets $h \subset \{1, ..., K + H\}$ that contain at least K elements. For example, $\{1, 2, ..., K\} \in A(K, H)$. Fix p_i such that $\sum_{i=1}^{K+H} p_i = u$. Then the probability of successful delivery by time τ is given by

$$P_s(\tau, K, H) = \sum_{h \in A(H,K)} \prod_{i \in h} \mathbf{z}(Z_i)$$

For any i and j in $\{1, ..., K + H\}$ we can write

$$P_s(\tau, K, H) = \mathbf{z}(Z_i)\mathbf{z}(Z_j)\phi_1 + (\mathbf{z}(Z_i) + \mathbf{z}(Z_j))\phi_2 + \phi_3$$

where ϕ_1, ϕ_2 and ϕ_3 are nonnegative functions of $\{Z(p_m), m \neq i, m \neq j\}$. For example,

$$\phi_1 = \sum_{h \in A_{\{i,j\}}(H,K)} \prod_{\substack{m \in h \\ m \neq i, m \neq j}} \mathbf{z}(Z_m)$$

where $A_v(K, H)$ is the set of subsets $h \subset \{1, ..., K + H\}$ that contain at least K elements and such that $v \subset h$.

Now consider maximizing $F_D(\tau, K, H)$ over Z_i and Z_j.

Assume that $Z_i' \neq Z_j'$. Since $\mathbf{z}(\cdot)$ is strictly concave, it follows by Jensen's inequality that $\mathbf{z}(Z_i') + \mathbf{z}(Z_j')$ can be strictly improved by replacing Z_i' and Z_j' by $Z_i = Z_j = (Z_i' + Z_j')/2$. This is also the unique maximum of the product $\mathbf{z}(Z_i)\mathbf{z}(Z_j)$ (using again Jensen's inequality applied to $\log \mathbf{z}$) and hence of

$F_D(\tau, K, H)$. This holds for any i and j and for any $p' \leq p$, hence it implies the Theorem.   ◇

The optimality of a symmetric choice of the transmission probabilities of chunks has a direct implication on the monotonicity of the performance with respect to the number H of redundant chunks.

Fix any τ, K and H. Let p^* be the optimal probability of sending a chunk of type i for these given τ, K and H. (As we saw, this does not depend on i). The success probability under p^* is the same as when increasing the redundancy to $H+1$ and using the vector $(p^*, ..., p^*, 0)$. Thus the utility when using p^* for a given τ, K and H is the same as when we increase the redundancy to $H+1$ and use the vector $(p^*, ..., p^*, 0)$. By definition, the latter is smaller than the optimal utility for the problem with $\tau, K, H+1$. We thus conclude that the utility is increasing in the amount of redundancy of chunks.

8   Asymptotic Approximations

8.1   The Message Model

We study the model of dynamic transmission control (by the source) of Section 2; we shall consider the limit of the model (appropriately scaled) as the population size grows to infinity.

Denote $\overline{\lambda} = n\lambda$ (n is the population size). Then for any population size n, w_t is the solution of the linear differential equation:

$$\dot{w}_t = u_t \overline{\lambda}(1 - w_t) \qquad \text{or equivalently,} \qquad \frac{dE[X_t]}{dt} = u_t \lambda(n - E[X_t]).$$

Bound. Dente $\xi_t(n) := X_t(n)/n$ where we add explicitly n in the notation in order to stress the dependence of X_t on n. By Jensen's inequality we have

$$F_D(\tau, n) = 1 - E\left[\exp\left(-\overline{\lambda}\int_0^\tau \xi_t(n)dt\right)\right] \leq 1 - \exp\left(-\overline{\lambda}\int_0^\tau w_t dt\right).$$

Tightness. We show that the bound is tight as n grows. Consider a sequence of systems where the nth DTN has n mobiles and where the contact process in the nth system is given by $\lambda(n) = \overline{\lambda}/n$.

Note that $w_t = E[\xi_t(n)]$ does not depend on n. We shall establish that

$$\lim_{n\to\infty} F_D(\tau, n) = 1 - \lim_{n\to\infty} E\left[\exp\left(-\overline{\lambda}\int_0^\tau \xi_t(n)dt\right)\right] = 1 - \exp\left(-\overline{\lambda}\int_0^\tau w_t dt\right).$$

By the Strong Law of Large Numbers we have P-a.s.

$$\lim_{n\to\infty} \xi_t(n) = \lim_{n\to\infty} \frac{\sum_{i=1}^n \zeta_t(i)}{n} = w_t.$$

It then follows from the bounded convergence theorem that $\lim_{n\to\infty}\int_0^\tau \xi_t(n)dt = \int_0^\tau w_t dt$. Using again the bounded convergence Theorem we see that the corresponding LST converge to the LST of the limit, i.e.

$$\lim_{n \to \infty} E \left[\exp \left(-\overline{\lambda} \int_0^\tau \xi_t(n) dt \right) \right] = \exp \left(-\overline{\lambda} \int_0^\tau w_t dt \right)$$

which establishes the tightness of the bound.

8.2   The Chunk Model

We extend the above model to the case of transmission of chunks which we introduced in Section 7. If we denote by $\zeta_t^j(i)$ the indicator that the jth mobile among the n receives chunk j during [0,t], then $X_t^j = \sum_{i=1}^n \zeta_t^j(i)$. We next define

$$\xi_t^j(n) := \frac{X_t^j(n)}{n}, \qquad w_t^j = E[\zeta_t^j(i)] = 1 - \exp \left(-\lambda \int_0^\tau u_s^j ds \right)$$

As a direct extension of the case of message transfers, we have the following bound due to Jensen's inequality:

$$F_D = \prod_{j=1}^K \left(1 - E \left[\exp \left(-\lambda \int_0^\tau X_t^j dt \right) \right] \right) \le \prod_{j=1}^K \left(1 - \left[\exp \left(-\lambda \int_0^\tau w_t^j dt \right) \right] \right)$$

Here again we can show as for the message-based model that the above bound becomes tight as the number of players n increases.

9   Concluding Comments

This paper is part of our intensive ongoing research on performance issues and optimal control of Delay Tolerant Networks (DTNs). Most of the existing analysis of DTNs uses the mean field asymptotics to obtain explicit expressions and to solve optimal control issues, or it uses Markov chain techniques which often do not allow to obtain exact close form formulas for the steady state probabilities. In obtaining these close form expressions we are able to carry the investigation of DTNs on and solve various optimal control problems as well as non-cooperative games.

Acknowledgements

This work has been partially supported by the European Commission within the framework of the BIONETS project, IST-FET-SAC-FP6-027748, www.bionets.eu. It was also supported in part by the Arc Popeye collaborative project of INRIA.

References

1. Al-Hanbali, A., Nain, P., Altman, E.: Performance of Ad Hoc Networks with Two-Hop Relay Routing and Limited Packet Lifetime. In: First International Conference on Performance Evaluation Methodologies and Tools (Valuetools), Pisa (2006)

2. Altman, E., Basar, T., De Pellegrini, F.: Optimal monotone forwarding policies in delay tolerant mobile Ad-Hoc networks. In: Inter-Perf 2008: Workshop on Interdisciplinary Systems Approach in Performance Evaluation and Design of Computer & Communication Systems, Athens, Greece (October 2008)
3. Altman, E., De Pellegrini, F.: Forward Correction and Fountain codes in Delay Tolerant Networks. In: IEEE Infocom, Rio de Janeiro, Brazil, April 19-25 (2009)
4. Altman, E., Neglia, G., De Pellegrini, F., Miorandi, D.: Decentralized Stochastic Control of Delay Tolerant Networks. In: IEEE Infocom, Rio de Janeiro, Brazil, April 19-25 (2009)
5. Erramilli, V., Chaintreau, A., Crovella, M., Diot, C.: Diversity of forwarding paths in pocket switched networks. In: Proceedings of the 7th ACM SIGCOMM conference on Internet measurement, San Diego, California, USA, pp. 161–174 (2007)
6. Marshall, A.W., Olkin, I.: Inequalities: Theory of Majorization and its Applications. Mathematics in Science and Engineering, vol. 143. Academic Press, London (1979)
7. Luo, P., Huang, H., Shu, W., Li, M., Wu, M.-Y.: Performance Evaluation of Vehicular DTN Routing under Realistic Mobility Models. In: Wireless Communications and Networking Conference, WCNC 2008, March 31 - April 3, pp. 2206–2211 (2008)

Appendix: Majorization and Schur Concavity

Definition 1. *(Majorization and Schur-Concave Function [6])*
Consider two n-dimensional vectors $d(1), d(2)$. $d(2)$ majorizes $d(1)$, which we denote by $d(1) \prec d(2)$, if $\sum_{i=1}^{n} d_{[i]}(1) = \sum_{i=1}^{n} d_{[i]}(2)$ and

$$\sum_{i=1}^{k} d_{[i]}(1) \leq \sum_{i=1}^{k} d_{[i]}(2), \quad k = 1, ..., n-1, \quad and$$

where $d_{[i]}(m)$ is a permutation of $d_i(m)$ satisfying $d_{[1]}(m) \geq d_{[2]}(m) \geq ... \geq d_{[n]}(m)$, $m = 1, 2$.
A function $f : R^n \to R$ is Schur concave if $d(1) \prec d(2)$ implies $f(d(1)) \geq f(d(2))$. It is strictly Schur concave if strict inequality holds whenever $d(1)$ is not a permutation of $d(2)$.

Lemma 5. *[6, Chapter 3] Assume that a function $g : R^n \to R$ can be written as the sum $g(d) = \sum_{i=1}^{n} \psi(d_i)$ where ψ is a concave (resp. strictly concave) function from R to R. Then g is Schur (resp. strictly) concave.*

Author Index